American Characters

YALE UNIVERSITY PRESS

NEW HAVEN & LONDON

R. W. B. LEWIS & NANCY LEWIS

American Characters

Selections from the National Portrait Gallery, Accompanied by Literary Portraits

Endpapers: Patent Office Building, Sachse Edward & Co.,
lithograph, c. 1855. National Portrait Gallery, Smithsonian Institution.
Title page illustrations (l. to r.): *John Caldwell Calhoun* by George Peter
Alexander Healy (p. 52), *Thomas Alva Edison* by Abraham Archibald
Anderson (p. 185), *Cole Porter* by Soss Melik (p. 356), *Lillian Hellman*
by Irving Penn (p. 317), *Peter Perkins Pitchlynn [Ha-Tchoc-Tuck-Nee]* by
George Catlin (p. 124). Page x: The Great Hall, National Portrait
Gallery. National Portrait Gallery, Smithsonian Institution.

Other photography credits and copyright information appear
on page 412.

Designed by Nancy Ovedovitz and set in Adobe Garamond type
by B. Williams & Associates. Printed in Italy by
Conti Tipocolor.

Library of Congress Cataloging-in-Publication Data
Lewis, R. W. B. (Richard Warrington Baldwin)
American characters : selections from the National Portrait Gallery,
accompanied by literary portraits / R.W.B. Lewis and Nancy Lewis.
    p.   cm.   Includes index.
ISBN 0-300-07895-1 (cloth)   0-300-07945-1 (pbk.)
    1. United States—Biography.   2. United States—Biography—
Portraits.   3. Portraits, American.   I. Lewis, Nancy.   II. National
Portrait Gallery (Smithsonian Institution)   III. Title.
    CT215.L49   1999   920.073–dc21   98-53021

A catalogue record for this book is available from the British Library.

The paper in this book meets the guidelines for permanence and
durability of the Committee on Production Guidelines for Book
Longevity of the Council on Library Resources.
            10   9   8   7   6   5   4   3   2   1

For Daniel Avery
our associate editor during the first years of this
endeavor. Our loving thanks to him for the great
range of his contributions, and for the imagination
and energy he brought to the work. What a joy to
have him in the family!

and for Brian Drutman
for his cunning and knowledgeable pursuit
of crucially needed portrait images in far-off places,
and for his friendship of more than three decades,
our most affectionate gratitude.

Contents

Cast of Characters

Director's Foreword

The National Portrait Gallery is a deceptive place. A very new museum, in one of Washington's oldest buildings, it occupies part of the handsome Greek Revival building started in 1836 to house the Patent Office of the United States. The Patent Office was built on a site designated by Pierre l'Enfant as a nondenominational church for national purposes, which "will be likewise a proper shelter for such monuments as were voted by the late Continental Congress, for those heroes who fell in the cause of liberty, and for such others as may hereafter be decreed by the voice of a grateful Nation." While the Patent Office never served as a national church, it did serve as a gallery for patent models and also as a national musuem, displaying portraits of George Washington and other leaders, along with artifacts relating to them and to the early history of the United States. In the 1950s the vacated building was given to the Smithsonian Institution to use for a National Portrait Gallery—an idea that had been debated and deferred since it was proposed by Charles Willson Peale in 1782. In 1962 it was established by act of Congress, and in 1968 it opened to the public.

When the Gallery opened, the secretary of the Smithsonian Institution then, S. Dillon Ripley, wrote that American portraiture had "already reached the zenith in price and the nadir in supply," making the new enterprise an "act of bravery indeed." He and the staff of the fledgling Gallery believed that they would have to do their work through the display of borrowed portraits to supplement the few examples they had been able to gather. Everything else worth having, they feared, was already firmly in place in some other institution. Nonetheless, a mechanism for acquiring portraits was put in place, and a board of commissioners of the National Portrait Gallery was charged, among other duties, with approving all portraits that enter the permanent collection.

Secretary Ripley need not have worried. The commissioners have done their work brilliantly, as is seen in the examples in this book—a fragment of the more than seventeen thousand portraits that are in the Gallery's permanent collections, along with other portraits retained for study or research.

Selecting portraits for the Gallery might seem a simple matter, and it would be if the only subjects considered were people entitled to recognition in a national pantheon by virtue of their high office or internationally recognized accomplishments. In fact, it is not at all simple to decide who should be admitted. When there have been great divisions of opinion in our land, as there were about slavery in the years preceding the Civil War, people of considerable reputation could be found on both sides of the argument, and no one then or now regards all the parties as equally admirable. Yet if we are to recall the leaders of political and social thought in that period we must include John C. Calhoun as well as

Daniel Webster, Abraham Lincoln as well as Jefferson Davis, Robert E. Lee as well as Ulysses S. Grant. Ours is a nation that has embraced people of diverse wisdom, and we try to suggest this complex texture in the halls of the National Portrait Gallery.

The debates in the commission meetings, then, are often heartfelt and fascinating. The staff and director of the Gallery find these meetings the most challenging and important work we do, for the growth and refinement of our collection are at the center of everything else. Most of our special exhibitions illuminate objects in our collections. Our publications on these collections are intended as enduring documents in support of further scholarship and interpretation. And our galleries of notable Americans are continuously being enriched and expanded as new portraits are acquired.

Our commissioners have served us in many ways. All of them share insights from their field of expertise. Some have contributed portraits. Some have supported a research project or the purchase of objects. But until now, no commissioner has compiled a book on the collections of the National Portrait Gallery, and few of those who have served are as brilliantly qualified to do this as is R. W. B. Lewis.

From the beginning, the Gallery has placed brief biographical texts next to the portraits, to explain the distinction of the subject and provide a context for the understanding of his or her achievement. We spend a great deal of time on these wall labels. Concise writing is the hardest kind of writing, especially when it must be as nuanced yet accurate as these labels must be. The Lewises have demonstrated their aptitude for this lapidary style in the biographical notes at the end of each of their texts. Since this is their book, not an "official" publication of the Gallery, it is instructive for me to see how they judge their subjects, and it is refreshing to note how their interpretations occasionally differ from the Gallery staff's collective view. But the uniqueness of this book lies in the juxtaposition of the portrait with the cunningly chosen literary passages facing each image.

These "literary portraits," as the Lewises have called them, give this book its special dimension. As Professor Lewis observes in his Preface, I encouraged him in this undertaking, believing the result would be revealing and delightful. I could not have imagined how well it would turn out, and I am astonished at how elegantly the texts and pictures play together. The Gallery fundamentally is a center of visual biography. Professor Lewis and Nancy Lewis have distinguished themselves as biographers in the traditional meaning of the word. But here they have caught the spirit of what the Gallery is about, and their book magnificently instructs us about the resonance of the word and the image working together. I am grateful that R. W. B. and Nancy Lewis have given us the gift of their insight and learning, and communicated so abundantly their enthusiasm for the work we do in this unique gallery of American characters.

ALAN FERN
Director
National Portrait Gallery

Preface

This enterprise began some years ago in several light-hearted exchanges between Alan Fern, the director of the National Portrait Gallery in Washington, and me as a board member of that entity. The board meets twice a year to consider proposed acquisitions and to discuss questions of policy. I was appointed, in 1986, to help advise on candidates from literature and general cultural history; other members during this time have included a distinguished historian of American art, a former senator and expert on political affairs, a person well versed in legal and economic matters, a U.S. congressman, a science specialist. After a while, as though to earn my keep, I took to providing an occasional literary response to particular acquisitions.

In the fall of 1989, for example, we happily purchased the striking portrait of William Faulkner by the eminent photographer Henri Cartier-Bresson. The picture (it can be found later in the book) shows Faulkner standing in his garden, with two small dogs nearby. After perusing it, as we sat around the long table, I scribbled a few words and passed the sheet to Director Fern. They were a slightly revised version of the opening of Faulkner's novella *The Bear:* "There was a man and a dog too this time. Two dogs." A few days later, Alan, one of the most cultivated individuals you could ever hope to meet, found his Faulkner text and copied and sent me the corrected reading: "There was a man and a dog too this time. Two beasts, counting Old Ben the bear, and two men, counting Boon Hogganbeck," and so on.

At another meeting, we voted to buy the 1889 poster based on Rosa Bonheur's delightful portrait of William F. Cody, Buffalo Bill, astride his white horse, outside the artist's chateau near Fontainbleu. This time I passed along the e. e. cummings poetic epitaph of 1917 or thereabouts, which might have been written with the Bonheur picture in mind:

> Buffalo Bill's
> defunct
>   who used to
>   ride a watersmooth-silver
>   stallion
> and break onetwothreefourfive pigeons just like that
>   Jesus
>
> he was a handsome man
>   and what i want to know is
> how do you like your blueeyed boy
> Mister Death

After a few more such offerings, Alan Fern raised the idea of my putting together an entire volume of portraits, each one matched—this would be the new feature—by a literary image, a verbal portrait, so to say. The proposal was attractive; but it soon became clear that the work involved—at least 150 pairs of visual and verbal portraits, from earliest times to the present, with some kind of biographical information in each case—was more than any one person could possibly attempt. As it happened, Nancy Lewis and I had only recently completed and published an edited collection of the letters of Edith Wharton, and had had lots of practice at working together; so we became co-editors of the big venture to which we gave the name *American Characters*. Overall, I should say, the work has been pretty well divided fifty-fifty, with each of us supplying such expertise, preferences, prejudices, individual style, and pace of work as each possesses.

The National Portrait Gallery was brought into being in 1962 by an act of Congress, as part of the vast complex called the Smithsonian Institution, and placed in the old Patent Office building (at F Street and Eighth), a structure begun in 1836 and one of the handsomest and most elegantly proportioned architectural works of its epoch. The act declared it the Gallery's mission to record the "men and women who have made a significant contribution to the history, development, and culture of the United States," and to honor the artists "who created such portraiture."

Our own revised phrasing refers to men and women who have "*made a difference*" in our history. The revision can remind the reader that not all the figures who appear here are saints or heroes. The requirement is that each made a difference; Senator Joseph McCarthy made a difference; so did the outlaw Jesse James (who was of course a hero to many). As to this, in the introductory essay to the catalogue of the Gallery's inaugural exhibition in 1968 (the show was called *This New Man*), the director, Charles Nagel, made the same point, and expressed the hope that the Gallery might someday possess a portrait of John Wilkes Booth. It now does so, an 1865 lithograph, in the Gallery's listing of which Booth is identified as "Actor, Assassin."

Nagel also emphasized the fact that the Gallery is first of all a "history museum" rather than a "gallery of art"; that the sitter, the historical person, is of primary importance when it comes to selection and purchase. Obviously, as Nagel says, the Gallery would always seek the finest portrait available of any subject chosen; and for sheer aesthetic enjoyment, in the pages following, we would draw the reader's attention to J. S. Duplessis's Benjamin Franklin, Gilbert Stuart's Washington, Francis Alexander's Daniel Webster, Edouard Manet's Edgar Allan Poe, Alexander Gardner's Lincoln, E. S. Curtis's Chief Joseph of the Nez Perce, Augustus Saint-Gaudens's bas-relief of William Dean Howells and his daughter, Edgar Degas's Mary Cassatt, Jo Davidson's bust of Clarence Darrow, Rhoda Sherbell's statue of Casey Stengel, Robert Capa's Ernest Hemingway, George Tames's Harry Truman, David Lee Iwerks's Louis Armstrong, and Augustus John's Tallulah Bankhead.

That listing is intended to suggest the range and variety of the book's presentations: statesman and poet, Indian chief and defense lawyer, artist and baseball manager, trumpeter and novelist. The gathering in turn reflects the range and variety of the Gallery, both as to sitters and to modes of portraiture—painting, assortments of drawing (including caricature), prints, posters, many genres of photography (from earliest daguerreotype days to Steichen, Stieglitz, and Capa), modes of sculpture. We have hoped to provide a matching variety in the verbal portraits, which come from memoirs, letters, poems, newspaper reports, biographical passages, self-assessments, and more. Some of the literary sources will be seen to recur, most notably Robert Penn Warren and Robert Lowell: imaginative writers given by temperament and legacy (the South, New England) to probing the far corners of our history and to contriving poetic shapes for their findings.

Some further points may be made about our selections. The individual, needless to say, must have his or her picture in the Gallery to start with; which explains why a number of important Americans do not show up here—Herman Melville, Emily Dickinson, Henry Adams, Huey Long, Ty Cobb, John Ford, in a quick sampling. And by our own decision, the candidate must be dead at least *fifteen years* by 1998. The Gallery's criterion in this respect is that any person must be dead ten years before a portrait can be displayed (except with living presidents). It seemed to us that the decision process would be a trifle easier with the longer interval.

Even so, questions may well arise about the presence or absence of this or that individual, the relative attention given to this or that segment of American life. Almost every friend we have consulted and every member of our family has expressed astonishment that so-and-so is or is not in the book. We can say only that we thought and studied and investigated long and hard; and we have from the start kept a growing list of other possible candidates. One factor might be mentioned: in order to include the many different categories of characters, we have had perforce to limit the number of sitters who could appear in any one of them. So, in a manner of speaking, if we had decided to bring Aaron Burr into the "Early Republic" section (an inviting notion, in fact), we would have had to eliminate, say, Louis Armstrong from the "Artists of Entertainment" section (an unthinkable proposition). But as the reader will notice, a great many figures over the centuries whose pictures are not on display here are named, and sometimes described a little, in the appropriate places. And meanwhile, the Gallery, under the astute leadership of Alan Fern, is always on the alert for ways to enlarge its holdings in some areas and perhaps even open up new fields of cultural contribution.

R. W. B. LEWIS

The reader's attention is drawn to the Commentary at the back of the book, where further discussion of individual entries can be found, along with annotation.

Acknowledgments

We want, first of all, to express our deepest gratitude to those writers who have added a dimension of vision and vitality to this book by composing new verbal portraits for it. It is an illustrious list, and a source of enduring pride: Harold Bloom on Joseph Smith; Edward Hoagland on John Muir; Russell Baker on H. L. Mencken; Irene Worth on Ruth Draper; John Updike on Ernest Hemingway; John Guare on Eugene O'Neill; John Hollander on Wallace Stevens; Robert B. Parker on Dashiell Hammett.

American Characters was put together in constant happy association with the National Portrait Gallery and its staff. The Gallery's director, Alan Fern, is the instigator of the book, and he has been its wise overseer, helping solve problems large and small, pointing us in the right directions. The deputy director, Carolyn Carr, has given special help in matters of art history and format (her own 1987 volume *Then and Now,* on American portraits of the past century, has been a kind of model for us). Carole Kurfehs, special assistant to the director, has been simply indispensable from the start: arranging, planning, passing messages and requests back and forth, and all with thoughtful efficiency.

We can only name the other staff members who have supplied superb service over the years (some are mentioned later in the text): Ellen G. Miles, chief curator of painting and sculpture, and Brandon Fortune, assistant curator; Mary Panzer, curator of photographs, and Ann Shumard, assistant curator; Wendy Wick Reaves, curator of prints and drawings, and Ann Wagner, curatorial assistant; Fred Voss, senior historian; Cecilia Chin, librarian, and her staff. Our dealings with these individuals—on our many wonderfully profitable visits to the Gallery, and on the phone and by mail—are among our most cherished memories.

Jodi Fain, manager of rights and reproductions, has earned our particular thanks by her heroic work in providing prints and transparencies of 160 portraits, no few at very short notice.

On the local scene, Barbara Lassonde has served invaluably as our chief research assistant for the past several years; our gratitude is immense, as is the pleasure we have taken in our meetings and planning sessions. More recently, Lisa Haarlander has stepped in to offer the same assistance at key moments.

Michael Anderson, of the *New York Times Book Review,* has deployed his journalistic resources to give us several varieties of crucially needed help, and always with remarkable speed and accuracy (and high good humor).

Elizabeth Dillon, of the Yale English department, very kindly wrote an insightful overview of women's emergence in literature and social activism in the later nineteenth century—to serve as the verbal portrait accompanying the group portrait "Eminent Women."

The Woodbridge Library has been invaluable in many ways. Our thanks go to reference librarians Mary Kelley, Rick Frisone, and Karen Andrews, and to other members of the staff, especially Ann Tiesler, Sandy Alpert, and Barbara Wolfer.

A great many individuals have been helpful with regard to particular entries or historical eras. We list them here in the chronological order of their expertise, and with apologies for any names we may have neglected: Barbara Oberg and Claude Lopez (Benjamin Franklin); the late Lillian Miller (Charles Willson Peale and family); Letty McPhedran (donor of the four-volume *National Portrait Gallery* of 1856); Matthew Munich (rare documents at Brown University); Jules Prown (figures and trends in American art history through the nineteenth century); Alan Trachtenberg (history of American photography); Sue Berger (research and copy for mid-book sections); Glen Wallach (women activists, nineteenth century and later); Sidney Hyman (the American presidency, from Lincoln to Truman); Howard Lamar and Jay Gitlin (American Indian history); Patricia Willis (turn-of-the-century documentation); Robert Westbrook (John Dewey); Daniel Aaron (a range of advice and help, most recently regarding Sacco and Vanzetti); Nicholas Fox Weber and Katharine Weber (twentieth-century art history, and the career of George Gershwin); Phil and Sharon McBlain (Harlem Renaissance and black writing generally); Edward T. Cone (Charles Ives); Paul Garon (on the trail of W. C. Handy); Sister Maureen Delaney (a quote for W. C. Handy); Ralph Fredericks (ardent supporter of Tallulah Bankhead's candidacy).

We completed work on this book at the National Humanities Center in Research Triangle Park, North Carolina, the world's best workplace, and we record our special thanks to Robert Connor and Kent Mullikin, director and deputy director.

Finally, we record the pleasure and honor it has been to work in close harmony with Yale University Press, with its far-seeing director, John Ryden; with Judy Metro, our highly skilled editor; Heidi Downey, meticulous copy editor; Mary Mayer, production controller; and Nancy Ovedovitz, designer. These good neighbors knew no fences.

R. W. B. LEWIS
NANCY LEWIS

American Characters

Puritans and Colonials

ASSEMBLED HERE ARE SEVEN FIGURES FROM THE AMERICAN SEVENTEENTH and eighteenth centuries, seven characters who "made a difference" of some sort in American life and history. The earliest, the Indian princess whose public name was Pocahontas, was born, probably, in 1595; the latest to depart the scene, the artist Charles Willson Peale, died in 1827. Two Puritan stalwarts, Cotton Mather and Jonathan Edwards—their surviving works date from the 1690s to the 1750s—make their appearance. Benjamin Franklin, the most distinguished American colonial figure in matters of diplomacy and perhaps of science—and the most productively busy American who ever lived—is here. There is one Revolutionary War general, he of radically divided fame, Benedict Arnold: the first of our historically important nonheroes, or lost leaders. George Washington finds his place in the next section, along with Thomas Jefferson and John Adams, cofounders of the republic.

Representing the first real flowering of the fine arts in the New World is Charles Willson Peale. And in the world of letters there is the young woman (she died at age thirty-one in 1784) who was both a slave and a poet, Phillis Wheatley.

The image of Pocahontas (by a Dutch artist visiting in England) predates portraiture in America by almost half a century. The first surviving portrait we have—in fact the first painting of any kind that we know about—is dated 1664. The information is provided by Jules David Prown in his masterly overview *American Painting: From Its Beginnings to the Armory Show* (1969). Prown points out that there were other kinds of pictorial art— French, English, Spanish—from the time of the first continental explorations; and that the Indian residents were practicing their manifold arts long before the first explorers arrived. But for better or worse, anything that could be called New World art—with continuing and developing subjects, methods, and conventions—originated in the colonial output of the 1660s and 1670s. For the colonials, those recognizable early Americans, had other, more practical things to do—art could wait its turn; and the Puritans congenitally feared and distrusted image, graven or otherwise. When art did begin to be practiced, tentatively, portraiture was by all odds its dominant mode. It would remain so for almost a hundred years.

The line of development in colonial art is faintly discernible even in the few portraits displayed in this section. The Bostonian Joseph Badger (1708–66), who did the original for the engraving of Jonathan Edwards, is a typical pioneer in the medium: unskilled and conservative but sometimes straightforward and pleasing. There is a direct line from Peter Pelham (painter and engraver of the Cotton Mather portrait) to John Singleton Copley to Charles Willson Peale (whose self-portrait is here on view)—and with Copley and Peale we reach the zenith of painting and portraiture in the colonial age. Pelham (1697–1751) married the widowed mother of John Singleton Copley and was a crucial influence on the boy. Copley in turn gave inspirational advice to Charles Willson Peale when the young Philadelphian came up to Boston to ask his help. Peale then went to London to work in the studio of Benjamin West, an ex-Philadelphian and the other name in the tiny gallery of truly gifted eighteenth-century American artists.

Of the verbal portraits, some are contemporary with the figure addressed and others come from later perspectives, a mixture that will be repeated in sections following. As to contemporaries: we have an eyewitness account of Pocahontas doing cartwheels at age twelve; two contrasting reminiscences of Benjamin Franklin in Paris; and from Charles Willson Peale, two self-analyses at different moments in his life. Nathaniel Hawthorne, the first of our great writers to exercise a genuinely potent sense of the past, the American past, and ambivalent as always about his Puritan predecessors, has predictably differing things to say about Cotton Mather: a man in whom (as his spokesman, Grandfather, says in a passage not included in our entry) "there was so much good, and yet so many failings and frailties." Robert Lowell, the most readily identifiable descendant of Hawthorne in our time (he has written with agile perceptivity about Hawthorne in both poetry and prose), can be heard adapting Jonathan Edwards's troubled New England voice to his own.

Hart Crane knew the description of twelve-year-old Pocahontas doing cartwheels and used it as the epigraph to "Powhatan's Daughter," Part II of his modernist epic *The Bridge.* But Crane was bent on mythologizing Pocahontas for poetic purposes; he is chief among the poets Philip Young describes as having "beatified" the Indian girl. Here Crane transforms the real-life playful child into a divine female inhabiting the natural spring landscape.

At another extreme, Alice Walker is looking across two centuries at the figure of Phillis Wheatley, in what might be called a demythologizing expedition. She is trying to rescue Wheatley from the decorous, Africa-scorning individual her owners made her into (in Walkers's understanding) in order to find some manner of continuity and kinship between the black slave poet of the 1770s and black American women writers in the 1970s.

Phillis Wheatley was a phenomenon of cultural history. She was one of the first two (some say three) women in America to publish poetry. Even more, she was the first slave woman to do so: she was brought to America from West Africa at the age of eight, and four or five years later (under the devoted tutelage of her mistress' daughter Mary Wheatley) she was reading the Bible, English and Latin literature, and works of history and religion—and writing poetry. But the *portrait* of Phillis Wheatley by Scipio Moorhead is hardly less exceptional. A portrait by a slave painter, especially one as skillful and sensitive as this one, was virtually unheard of. Beyond that, the presentation of the sitter was unprecedented. Portraits of Indians or of blacks in the colonial period (things changed toward 1800) were unusual enough; Indians, when portrayed, were normally seen negotiating humbly with white authorities, and blacks appeared as attentive servants or military cupbearers, rather like Kipling's Gunga Din. (See the illuminating essay by Ellen G. Miles in *American Colonial Portraits: 1700–1776,* 1987.) But the 1773 portrait by Moorhead shows Wheatley alone at her desk, pen in hand and a book at her elbow, face raised in meditation or imaginative flight; a compacted and realized self.

The case of Benjamin Franklin is exceptional in a different way. The problem here is finding a verbal description of Franklin that does justice to the subject, that is balanced and acute, and that (if possible) has something of the liveliness and play of the man. For the discoverable and disconcerting fact is that Franklin from the outset was the target of resentment, derision, and often venom. This was true in his lifetime—not least amid the political and economic intrigues of colonial Pennsylvania, and increasing, if anything, when he was the American envoy in Europe. The hostile tone and manner continued, with shifts in stress, throughout the late nineteenth century and into our contemporary era. The story of Franklin's adversaries is large and complex, and Robert Middlekauff has devoted an entire book to it: *Benjamin Franklin and His Enemies* (1996), itself an outsize example of the kind of verbal portrait—balanced, witty, and full of insight—that one looks for elsewhere, mostly in vain.

Middlekauff summarizes the enmity aroused by Franklin in the colonial and early republic days: "To his enemies he was a threatening man—to some a democrat and an egalitarian in an aristocratic age, to others an advocate of change when stability was needed, and finally a libertine given to a dissolute life when self-control and severe morality were required." John Adams, in his several animadversions on Franklin (one of which is offered in this section), represents some of the above fears and complaints—his rancor against Franklin was the talk of colonial circles; though Adams's attitudes, as Middlekauff emphasizes, underwent sea changes, and Adams in his own being was a person of great human and political stature.

The list of Franklin downgraders in later epochs is a distinguished one. The narrator of Melville's *Israel Potter* (1855) describes Franklin, whom Israel meets in Paris, with a certain seeming respect, but he concludes that "Franklin was everything but a poet." Robert Lowell comes to much the same opinion (see *Uncollected Prose,* 1987). He calls Franklin "a *real* inventor, one of genius," but says that his writings "sought only ease and clarity and shunned soaring"; Lowell himself (the thought-sequence is not entirely coherent) would prefer "Walt Whitman or the tough moderation of Horace's epistles."

Mark Twain in the nineteenth century and D. H. Lawrence in *Studies in Classic American Literature* (1923) excoriated Franklin as the author of *Poor Richard's Almanack* and the alleged proponent of the virtuous, frugal, hard-working, unadventurous life. Mark Twain did this with some of his most unhinging humor, remarking, for example, that many a boy had been "hounded to death and robbed of his natural rest, because Franklin said once in one of his inspired flights of malignity—'Early to bed and early to rise / Makes a man healthy and wealthy and wise.'" Lawrence, on the contrary, wrote humorlessly, out of his hatred for Franklin's anti-British stances and his own distaste for everything culturally American, and ended with a petulant and ill-grounded piece. John Keats, meanwhile, had referred to Franklin as a "philosophical Quaker full of mean and thrifty maxims," and as clear evidence that the human intellect would never be fostered in the United States as it had been in England. William Carlos Williams, often so beguiling, indulged in tedious, long-winded irony at Franklin's expense (*In the American Grain,* 1925).

Meanwhile, of course, Franklin in his later years was the toast of colonial America and the most popular American in Europe. By the second half of the twentieth century Franklin's stature in his native country had grown to nearly Mount Rushmore magnitude. The extraordinary diversity of Franklin's reputation, of the public and the literary images of him, would argue for a measure of caution in offering any portrait, verbal *or* visual, as the final one.

Puritans and Colonials

Pocahontas C. 1595–1617 Indian Princess

Pocahontas, a well featured but wanton young girle, Powhatan's daughter, sometymes resorting to our Fort, of the age then of 11 or 12 yeares, [would] gett the boyes forth with her into the markett place and make them wheele, falling on their hands turning their heeles upwardes, whome she would follow, and wheele so her self naked as she was all the fort over.

> WILLIAM STRACHEY, *Historie of Travell into Virginia Britania* (c. 1615)

She is an American legend, a woman whose actual story has blended with imaginary elements in time become traditional. . . . She is one of our few, true native myths, for with our poets she has successfully attained the status of goddess, has been beatified, made holy and offered as a magical and moving explanation of our national origins.

> PHILIP YOUNG, "The Mother of Us All: Pocahontas,"
> in *Three Bags Full: Essays in American Fiction* (1972)

> There was a bed of leaves, and broken play;
> There was a veil upon you, Pocahontas, bride—
> O Princess whose brown lap was virgin May;
> And bridal flanks and eyes hid tawny pride.
>> HART CRANE, "The Dance,"
>> in "Powhatan's Daughter," *The Bridge* (1930)

Secret clan name: Matoaka; public name: Pocahontas ("Playful"). Daughter of Powhatan, powerful chief of the Confederacy, the Algonkian-speaking tribes of Tidewater, Virginia. She may or may not have saved Captain John Smith of the Jamestown colony from death. In 1613, Pocahontas was tricked into captivity by the English. She was well treated and was converted to Christianity, taking the name Rebecca. In 1614 she married Captain John Rolfe; in 1616 they went to England with their son Thomas. She was much fêted in London. In 1617, preparing to return to Jamestown, she was stricken with smallpox and died.

MATOAKA ALS REBECCA FILIA POTENTISS PRINC POWHATANI IMP VIRGINIÆ

Ætatis suæ 21. A. 1616.

Matoaks als Rebecka daughter to the mighty Prince
Powhatan Emperour of Attanoughskomouck als virginia
converted and baptized in the Christian faith, and
wife to the wor:ᵗ M.ʳ Joh Rolff.

Si: Paß: sculp: Compton Holland excud:

Unidentified artist, engraving, based on the 1616 engraving
by Simon van de Passe (1595–1647)

Cotton Mather 1663–1728 Minister and Writer

In Grandfather's Chair, Hawthorne's fictive grandfather tells his grandchildren how his oakwood chair was brought to the New World and handed down over the generations. By 1700 it belonged to a Boston schoolmaster, Ezekiel Cheever.

When Master Cheever died [Grandfather continues], he bequeathed the chair to the most learned man that was educated at his school, or that had ever been born in America. This was the renowned Cotton Mather, minister of the North Church in Boston.

"And author of the Magnalia, Grandfather, which we sometimes see you reading," said Laurence.

"Yes, Laurence," replied Grandfather. "The Magnalia is a strange, pedantic history, in which true events and real personages move before the reader with the dreamy aspect which they wore in Mather's mind." . . .

"Was not the witchcraft delusion partly caused by Cotton Mather?" inquired Laurence.

"He was the chief agent of the mischief," answered Grandfather, "but we will not suppose that he acted otherwise than conscientiously. He believed that there were evil spirits all about the world."

In 1721, when Boston was being visited by a smallpox epidemic, Mather hit upon an inoculation against the disease. Physicians and citizens alike responded to his claim for it in a fury of disbelief.

The people's wrath grew so hot at Cotton Mather's attempt to guard them from the smallpox that he could not walk the streets in peace. Wherever the venerable form of the old minister, meagre and haggard with fasts and vigils, was seen approaching, hisses were heard, and shouts of derision, and scornful and bitter laughter. The women snatched away their children from his path, lest he should do them a mischief. Still, however, bending his head meekly, and perhaps stretching out his hands to bless those who reviled him, he pursued his way.

NATHANIEL HAWTHORNE, *Grandfather's Chair* (1841)

Cotton Mather was the son of Increase Mather, eminent Puritan minister and president of Harvard, 1685–1706; and the grandson both of Richard Mather, a founder of New England Congregationalism, and of John Cotton, the religious leader of the first American generation. Cotton was admitted to Harvard at age twelve. Later he became his father's co-minister at the North Church in Boston, where he remained until his death.

Among Mather's many and prodigiously learned writings are works of history, biography, and theology. In *The Wonders of the Invisible World* (1693) he offered narratives of the recent witchcraft trials in Salem. He has long been held responsible for that terrible interlude. But in his best work, *Magnalia Christi Americana* (*The Annals of Christ in America*, 1702), he voiced strong opposition to the conduct of the trials. His interest in science and medicine deepened steadily.

Portrait by Peter Pelham (1697–1751), mezzotint, 1728,
from his own painting

Jonathan Edwards 1703–1758 Theologian

. . . I love you faded,
old, exiled and afraid
to leave your last flock, a dozen
Houssatonic Indian children;

afraid to leave
all your writing, writing, writing,
denying the Freedom of the Will.
You were afraid to be president
of Princeton, and wrote:
"My defects are well known;
I have a constitution
peculiarly unhappy;

flaccid solids,
vapid, sizzy, scarse fluids,
causing a childish weakness,
a low tide of spirits,

I am contemptible,
stiff and dull.

Why should I leave behind
my delight and entertainments,
these studies
that have swallowed up my mind?"

ROBERT LOWELL, "Jonathan Edwards in Western Massachusetts," in
For the Union Dead (1964). The quotation is from Edwards's letter
of October 19, 1757, seeking to decline the invitation to become
president of the College of New Jersey (later Princeton).
"Sizzy" or "sizy": thick and glutinous.

Born in Connecticut; graduated from Yale, 1720. Married Sarah Pierpont, 1727. Associated with the Presbyterian pastorate in Northampton, Massachusetts, until 1750, when he was dismissed because of doctrinal disputes. He became a missionary to the Housatonic Indians and a pastor in Stockbridge, Massachusetts. In his last months he served as president of the College of New Jersey. Edwards's great achievement—in such treatises as *Divine and Supernatural Light* (1734), *Freedom of Will* (1754), and *The Great Christian Doctrine of Original Sin Defended* (1758)—was to reaffirm radical Protestant doctrine by drawing on the new psychology of Locke and the new physics of Newton. His most memorable performance was his terror-inspiring sermon "Sinners in the Hands of an Angry God," delivered at Enfield, Massachusetts, in 1741.

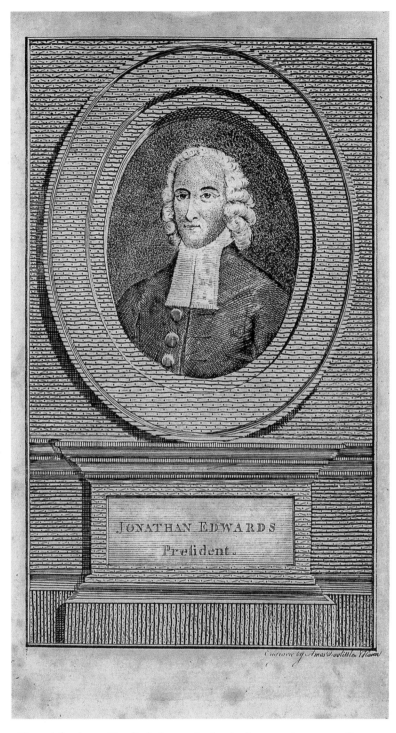

JONATHAN EDWARDS
President.

Portrait by Amos Doolittle (1754–1832), stipple engraving, 1793, after a
painting by Joseph Badger (1708–66)

Portrait by Joseph Siffrede Duplessis (1725–1802), oil on canvas, probably 1785,
painted in Paris

Benjamin Franklin 1706–1796
Author, Scientist, Statesman

His name was familiar to government and people, to kings, courtiers, nobility, clergy and philosophers, as well as plebeians, to such a degree that there was scarcely a peasant or a citizen, a valet de chambre, coachman or footman, a lady's chambermaid or scullion in the kitchen who was not familiar with it and who did not consider him a friend to human kind. . . . When they spoke of him they seemed to think he was to restore the Golden Age. . . . His plans and his example would abolish monarchy, aristocracy and hierarchy throughout the world.

JOHN ADAMS, on Franklin in Paris, in *Works,* vol. 1

Franklin's most original trait, the one that would have made him unique no matter in what country he lived, was his art of living in the best fashion for himself and for others, making the most effective use of all the tools nature has placed at the disposal of man. . . . He would eat, sleep, work whenever he saw fit, according to his needs, so that there was never a more leisurely man, though he certainly handled a tremendous amount of business. No matter when one asked for him, he was always available. His house in Passy, where he had chosen to live because he loved the country and fresh air, was always open for all visitors; he always had an hour for you.

PIERRE-GEORGES CABANIS, physician and close friend of Franklin in Paris,
in Claude-Anne Lopez, *Mon Cher Papa* (2nd ed., 1990)

Born in Boston, the son of a soapmaker. During his adolescence he was apprenticed as a printer to his brother William. In 1723 he went to Philadelphia to try his fortune, eventually taking over the *Pennsylvania Gazette* and making it the most successful paper in the colonies. From 1733 to 1758 he brought out *Poor Richard's Almanack,* with its aphorisms about the good and successful life. At the same time he did much for his adopted city; he oversaw the paving, cleaning, and lighting of the streets, founded the American Philosophical Society and what became the University of Pennsylvania. He invented the efficient "Franklin stove" and bifocal glasses. He gave up the newspaper in 1748 and turned to science; in a legendary experiment he proved that lightning and electricity are identical. His public service began in 1757, when he was sent to England, in effect as the minister of the thirteen colonies in their dealings with the mother country. He began gradually, then strongly, to favor independence; in 1775 he was back in America in time to consult with Jefferson over the framing of the Declaration of Independence. From 1776 to 1785 he was in France as minister plenipotentiary to King Louis XVI; the Paris years were the busiest and happiest, socially and diplomatically, of his life, climaxing (with the help of John Adams and John Jay) in the Treaty of Paris (1783), which brought the Revolution to an end. In his last years he played a major role in the Constitutional Convention, worked on his *Autobiography* (first American edition, 1818), and wrote a powerful antislavery statement.

Benedict Arnold 1741–1801 Revolutionary General

He was . . . a mass of outward contradictions. Arnold had astonishing physical valor but no moral courage, a rigid code of "honor" without a shred of inner integrity, and superior intelligence with no understanding. To fill in the gaps, to become the ideal hero he wished to be, Arnold became a master of self-delusion.

CLARE BRANDT, *The Man in the Mirror: A Life of Benedict Arnold* (1994)

Summer 1780: Arnold has informed the British that he is coming over to their side, and is poised at his American headquarters near West Point awaiting the crucial moment.
After all the months of uncertainty and disappointment, Arnold's way was clear. He had not felt so sure of himself since the afternoon nearly three years before when he had ridden alone into battle on Bemis's Heights in defiance of Horatio Gates's orders. Now he rode alone again, in defiance of the United States of America and all who served her.

The money, it appeared, was secondary. What counted most was to start over again, clean. The American Patriot-Hero was dead; long live the British Patriot-Hero; to this concept he was totally committed. . . .

What was extraordinary was his absolute conviction that purity would spring from treachery; that his past, his own, old self would be consumed by the same flames that destroyed the United States of America, and that out of the ashes would arise the ideal Arnold, the hero, the man he saw reflected in his wife's eyes.

CLARE BRANDT, *Man in the Mirror*

Born in Norwich, Connecticut, of a locally prominent family. The repressive home atmosphere led Arnold to run away twice during adolescence and join a colonial militia. In 1767, after a few years working in New York, he married Margaret Manseld of New Haven; she bore him three sons in five years, and died in 1775. In the Revolutionary War, Arnold performed a series of brilliant and daring military exploits, among them the capture of Fort Ticonderoga and the defeat of General Burgoyne at Bemis's Heights, New York. But he felt that his achievements were insufficiently recognized by Congress, and he was subjected to endless attacks by enemies and rivals. In 1779, Arnold began his act of betrayal by sending coded information to the enemy; in October 1780 he fled his West Point command and joined the British. His remaining years were spent in England, engaged in desultory commercial ventures. He was as unpopular in England as in America. Arnold fathered four sons and a daughter by his second wife.

Le Général ARNOLD

déserté de l'Armée des États-Unis

le 3. Octobre 1780.

Portrait by Benoit Louis Prevost (1735–1804), engraving, 1780, done in Paris
from a drawing made from the life in Philadelphia
by Pierre Eugene Du Simitiere (c. 1736–84)

Self-portrait, oil on canvas, c. 1791

Charles Willson Peale 1741–1827 Artist

My reputation is greatly increased by a Number of new Yorkers haveing been here, who have given me the character of being the best painter of America—that I paint more certain and handsomer likenesses than Copley. What more could I wish? I am glad I can please. But, Sir, how far short of that excellence of some painters, innately below that perfection that even portrait Painting may be carried to. My enthusiastic mind forms some Idea of it, but I have not the execution, have not the abilitys, nor am I a Master of Drawing. What little I do is by mear imitation of what is before me. Perhaps I have a good eye, that is all, and not half the application that I now think is necessary. A good painter of either portrait or History must be well acquainted with the Greesian and Roman Statues, to be able to draw them at pleasure by memory, and account for every beauty, must know the original cause of beauty in all he sees. These are some of the requisites of a good painter.

CHARLES WILLSON PEALE to John Beale Bordley, former student
of Peale's father and longtime friend, November 1771

The fact is that I have a choleric disposition and therefore am obligated to keep a bridle constantly tight-reined to stay my tongue and hands from mauling everyone that approaches me. My temper being very irritable gives me a wonderful deal of trouble to keep my resentment from teasing those I have to deal with, who would retort back on me. Therefore, knowing this, self-love induces me to trial of the exercise of patience, with some endeavors to please others in order that I may be favored with some indulgences. If we do not exercise gentleness and do some kind actions to others, can we expect any favor or even civility from the world? Our best interest is by every means in our power to please and serve our fellow creatures, to obtain a like return, and even to carry the Christian into action by doing good to those who despitefully treat you.

CHARLES WILLSON PEALE to Angelica Kauffmann Robinson,
his daughter, 1813

Born in Maryland, the son of a schoolmaster. He was trained as a saddler but then turned to painting. In Boston he was given crucial advice from John Singleton Copley; in the late 1760s, in London, he studied in Benjamin West's studio. Back in Maryland he developed into the finest portraitist in the middle colonies; among his sitters were Washington (several images), John Adams, Jefferson, Franklin, Joel Barlow, and Zebulon Pike. Peale's portrait of the English statesman William Pitt—as an ancient Roman champion of freedom—expressed his own political dedication and made him famous. His long career was marked by extraordinary versatility. In 1775 he moved to Philadelphia, where he opened the first American museum of natural history. He fathered seventeen children, naming many of them after his own primary interests: artists—Rembrandt, Rubens, Raphaelle, Titian (all of these sons became reputable artists themselves), Angelica Kauffmann; and scientists—Linnaeus and Franklin.

Phillis Wheatley 1753–1784 Poet, Slave

What then are we to make of Phillis Wheatley, a slave, who owned not even herself? This sickly, frail black girl who required a servant of her own at times—her health was so precarious—and who, had she been white, would have been easily considered the intellectual superior of all the women and most of the men in the society of her day. . . .

Captured at seven, a slave of wealthy, doting whites who instilled in her the "savagery" of the Africa they "rescued" her from . . . one wonders if she was even able to remember her homeland as she had known it, or as it really was. . . .

So torn by "contrary instincts" was black, kidnapped, enslaved Phillis that her description of "the Goddess"—as she poetically called the Liberty she did not have—is ironically, cruelly humorous. And, in fact, has held Phillis up to ridicule for more than a century. It is usually read prior to hanging Phillis's memory as that of a fool. She wrote:

> The Goddess comes, she moves divinely fair.
> Olive and laurel binds her *golden* hair.
> Wherever shines this native of the skies,
> Unnumber'd charmes and recent graces rise. [emphasis added]

It is obvious that Phillis, the slave, combed the "Goddess's" hair every morning; prior, perhaps, to bringing in the milk, or fixing her mistress's lunch. She took her imagery from the one thing she saw elevated above all others.

With the benefit of hindsight we ask "How could she?"

But at last, Phillis, we understand. No more snickering when your stiff struggling, ambivalent lines are forced on us. We know now that you were not an idiot or a traitor; only a sickly little black girl, snatched from your home and country and made a slave; a woman who still struggled to sing the song that was your gift, although in a land of barbarians who praised you for your bewildered tongue.

ALICE WALKER, *In Search of Our Mothers' Gardens* (1984)

Born in Africa, purchased and made a slave by a Boston merchant, John Wheatley. The Wheatleys recognized Phillis's remarkable precocity, and in effect set her free. She learned to read and write English in less than two years, and she began to write poetry (influenced above all by Pope) at age thirteen. Her first published poem—on the death of the famous divine George Whitfield—appeared in 1770. Her local fame spread. In 1773, the Wheatleys sent her to England, where she was the guest of the cultivated Countess of Huntingdon, who arranged for the publication of Wheatley's *Poems on Various Subjects, Religious and Moral* (the book was dedicated to the countess). In England she was everywhere received with cordiality and admiration. Back in America, after the death of her patrons, Phillis married John Peters, a "complaisant and agreeable" free black shopkeeper who made a poor husband. None of the three children Phillis bore him survived; her own health gave way in the fall of 1784, and she died in December. The first American edition of her poems was published in 1786; but her reputation really dates from an 1834 edition with a memoir by a Wheatley kinswoman.

Engraving, 1773, after a portrait by Scipio Moorhead

The Early Republic:
Citizens and Interpreters

THE LONG PERIOD REFLECTED IN THIS SECTION—FROM THE 1790S TO THE 1850s—was a time of beginnings: the first American president and the first nationally celebrated political leaders; the first American businessman and millionaire; the first enduring presences in literature (art, and especially portraiture, had been flourishing for decades before 1790); the first woman reformer and advocate of women's rights. It was a time of nation-building that evolved into a period of intensifying national division.

It was also, as a consequence, a time of national stock-taking. One observer in 1835 thought it might happily be called an "age of commemoration." The same writer went on to speak of a "disposition" evident across the land to collect and set down everything that would illustrate the "men and women and events" involved in the making of the country's remarkable history.

The comment came from a review of volume 1 of a four-volume compilation called *National Portrait Gallery,* the editors of which, James Longacre and James Herring, acknowledged that similar previous attempts had failed commercially. But they voiced their belief that "with the advancement of art, a more auspicious age has dawned, and the American people now display a becoming solicitude for the preservation of the relics of their own glory."

The *Gallery* was the most sizable in the series of works that, in their way, are the diverse and honorable predecessors of the present enterprise. Its 144 entries are grouped in clusters, a practice we are following. In volume 1 we find a number of public figures: George Washington, Chief Justice John Marshall, Andrew Jackson, Senators Clay and Webster (Calhoun will follow). They are succeeded by a perhaps surprising number of artists and writers, among them Gilbert Stuart, Washington Irving, and James Fenimore Cooper. The likenesses are caught by an array of the finest portraitists in what was, till then, the greatest age of American portraiture: Copley, Charles Willson Peale, Stuart, Asher Durand, and John Vanderlyn, among others. It was a monumental event, but it was not a financial success. For all the editors' trust in the new solicitude for art and history in America, there was in the busy country at large little interest in these matters. (An exhibition based on this product was held at the actual National Portrait Gallery in Washington in 1969, not long after its inauguration.)

The same ambivalence toward cultural activity in America was noted and analyzed astutely as early as 1815, in the editorial introduction to *Delaplaine's Repository of the Lives and*

Portraits of Distinguished Characters. The work presented eighteen portraits and biographies, of Columbus and Vespucci, and then of sixteen Americans: Washington, Franklin, Hamilton, Jefferson, John Jay, and others, with engraved portraits based on paintings by Copley, Stuart, Benjamin West, John Trumbull, and the like.

In his prefatory essay, Joseph Delaplaine, a Philadelphia publisher with a shrewd eye for the interworkings of culture and the marketplace, put the general case forthrightly. "The universally acknowledged influence of the arts," he said, would "seem to warrant the most sanguine hope" for the work being put forward; but the truth was, "there are not wanting those who lie in wait for the purpose of systematically opposing the advancement of the ornamental arts." "The sordid," he went on, "call the ornamental arts frivolous because they bring no usance [money]; and mischievous, as the indulgence in them tends to diminish the accumulation of avarice." Even in our own day the identification of financial greed as the enemy of cultural advancement has never been put more elegantly. *Delaplaine's Repository* did not earn back its costs.

Despite these examples, yet another venture to enshrine the country's leading characters, by portrait and in word, got under way in 1849–50. This was the *Gallery of Illustrious Americans,* a collaboration of Mathew Brady, who supplied the pictures, Francis d'Avignon, who did the engravings, and C. Edward Lester, who provided the written material. We can come back to the *Gallery* a little later.

A number of the artists whose work we draw on here made their appearances in those nineteenth-century collections. Gilbert Stuart was responsible for our portrait of George Washington; and Stuart is also present in his own person, in a portrait inspired by his young protégé Anson Dickinson. John Wesley Jarvis is the source for John Jacob Astor, and the Andrew Jackson portrait is based on a painting by Thomas Sully. Further along, John Neagle gives us Henry Clay, G. P. A. Healy portrays John C. Calhoun, and Francis Alexander contributes the image of a fiery young Daniel Webster. These artists were working in what has been called the Grand Manner: a phrase associated initially with later eighteenth-century English painting and with the elevated and sometimes statuesque and classically conceived portraits of Sir Joshua Reynolds. In this country the Grand Manner usually refers to carefully posed portraits of the wealthy and well born, though occasionally, as here, to politicians as well.

Other items in the section come from kinfolk and associates. John James Audubon is portrayed by his son John Woodhouse Audubon, in the frontiersman garb the father liked to assume. Washington Irving was rendered by his talented English friend Charles Robert Leslie; and James Fenimore Cooper sat for the French woman Amélie Kautz, who gave his children language lessons in Paris every day.

In the history of American portraiture in these years, a landmark of sorts was the group of silhouettes—our John Quincy Adams entry is among them—created by William Henry Brown and published in 1845. The silhouettes were cut from life and lithographed, with the figure placed in a characteristic surrounding: here, Adams posed in his Washington home, looking out at the national scene. The attraction of the silhouette was its nearly lifelike exactness; but with the advent of the daguerreotype, the silhouette lost its appeal, and by 1860 had disappeared.

The daguerreotype was invented in France, primarily by Jacques Daguerre in the late 1830s. News of it reached the United States in the spring of 1839, and the response was rapid and animated. In an 1840 article Edgar Allan Poe declared that "the Daguerreotype plate is infinitely (we use the term advisedly), is *infinitely* more accurate in its representation than any painting by human hands." Painters were predictably more skeptical. Thomas Cole, for one, held that the art of painting was a "creative as well as an imitative art," that the daguerreotype was purely imitative, and that painting need have no fear of being "superseded by any mechanical contrivance."

Cole became personally acquainted with the daguerreotype in 1845, when (as can be seen here) he sat for the young New York practitioner Mathew Brady. Scarcely twenty-three at the time, Brady had come down to New York from the Lake George region in 1839, and by 1844 he had established his Daguerre Miniature Gallery at Broadway and Fulton Street. No one was more seized than Mathew Brady by the history-recording spirit of the age. In an interview late in life he told a reporter that "from the first, I regarded myself as under obligation to my country to preserve the faces of its historic men and mothers"; and in 1850, as noted, he collaborated with d'Avignon and Lester to produce *The Gallery of Illustrious Americans*.

Lester's introduction announced that the first half of the century had "drifted by" and that the "dim form" of the second was approaching (later moments in the volume suggest a muffled awareness of some large crisis impending in the Union). It was now fitting to "celebrate the men who have made [the epoch] illustrious." In the *Gallery* there would be grouped "those American citizens from the Tribune and in the Field, in Letters and the Arts, who have rendered the most signal service to the nation, since the death of the Founder of the Republic"—that is, since the death of George Washington in 1799. Only a dozen entries for the *Gallery* were completed; and the list is notable, if anything, for the figures it did not include: no Jackson, neither Adams, no Stuart or Cole, no Irving or Cooper or Emerson or Hawthorne.

By the mid-1850s, in any event, the daguerreotype was being replaced by the handier photography: a method that could produce paper prints, as many as wanted, from glass plates. Photography was fully established as a major form of portraiture before the 1870s were over, and so it has remained. It must be added, though, that the debate over whether photography can rightly be considered an art has continued to the present. There are still many, apparently, who would agree with Thomas Cole that photography is an imitative rather than a creative art; for example, the Academy of Arts and Letters in New York has yet to elect a photographer to its regular membership.

In our own list of figures who made their mark on the American world between 1790 and 1850, an impressive number come from what the makers of *The Gallery of Illustrious Americans* calls the Tribune: Washington, John Adams, Jefferson, John Quincy Adams, Jackson, the three Senators Clay, Calhoun, and Webster; to these might be added John Marshall, from the Court. But as all the "galleries" from the period testify, the key figures in it are to be located first of all in the domain of statesmanship and politics: the makers and molders of the new nation, and of its characterizing features and tensions. The very numbers of those who should be included, indeed, forbids the appearance of still others who performed "signal service" for the country: Alexander Hamilton, Jefferson's secretary of the treasury and the archetypal Federalist; Aaron Burr, colorful, brilliant, wayward; James Madison, the fourth president of the United States (though he seems a trifle pedestrian in the present context); James Monroe, who enunciated the doctrine named for him in his presidential address in 1823.

Looking more closely at these founders and molders, one is struck by the energy of animosity among them: Jefferson wrangling with John Adams, John Quincy Adams fulminating against Jefferson, Jackson almost incoherent with rage against Clay. And yet the larger image is of a world in which all these occupants of power were in some way intimate with one another. They belonged to the same metaphorical club; the furies have the air of being family fallings-out, and the more intense because of it. Nowhere on the political spectrum was this truer than with the inseparable Clay, Webster, and Calhoun. Calhoun bespoke the fact, and the age, when he said (or was alleged to have said), "I don't like Clay. He is a bad man, an impostor, a creator of wicked schemes. I wouldn't speak to him, but by God! I love him."

In arts and letters we have five individuals—what we have called the "interpreters": Stuart, Audubon, Cole, Irving, and Cooper. Others could certainly have been added: for example, Asher Durand, the first recognizably accomplished landscape painter, an organizer of the American Academy of Design; and William Cullen Bryant, whose youthful poem "Thanatopsis" became a national threnody, and who continued for six decades to be a valued, if monotonous, voice in the evolving culture.

Of the artists, Gilbert Stuart stands at the head of American painters in the Grand Manner; Audubon is sui generis; with Thomas Cole, we see American artistic genius moving significantly from portraiture to landscape. Irving and Cooper between them enact the major development in American fiction in their lifetime: Irving, the quintessential transitional figure, working with British models but finding new themes on the national landscape (he wrote with surprising cogency about the American Indian character); Cooper, discovering the myth inherent in American history and turning it to his fictional ends.

At the same time, John Jacob Astor begins the line of immoderately successful men of business affairs who have been a major feature of the country's social and economic history (see "The Gilded Decades"). Joseph Smith enters as the extraordinarily gifted religious teacher (it was a choice between Smith and the great Mormon organizer Brigham Young, and we opted for the founding figure); and he represents as well the steady westward expansion of America, about which there will be more later. Lucretia Mott introduces another line of crucially important figures: women reformists and speakers for women's rights. Elizabeth Cady Stanton, Lucretia Mott's protégée, will follow, with others.

The verbal portraits again comprise a mix of eyewitness description (that of Jefferson by Pennsylvania Senator William Maclay is particularly arresting) and present-day perspective (Harold Bloom at his most trenchant on Joseph Smith). Whitman and Emerson are two of the literati who have their say in these pages. Melville can be heard in his paean to Andrew Jackson, and Henry James speaks with fond nostalgia about Washington Irving (as a boy of eleven, he had been introduced to Irving). Robert Penn Warren is here as a critic-historian, talking about Cooper. British writers are heard from: Charles Dickens, reporting to a friend in 1842 how much he had enjoyed meeting Henry Clay in Washington; D. H. Lawrence, in the 1920s, ruminating on the inner divisions of James Fenimore Cooper.

The family of Adamses is present here over four generations, with Henry Adams, coming along last, offering some commentaries on his grandfather John Quincy. In fact, in his *Education* (1907), and speaking of a visit to the White House in 1850, Henry Adams articulates with a poetic precision, spiced with irony, that sense of intimacy between the distinguished and powerful that so pervaded the atmosphere of the age.

Adams recalled that the president, Zachary Taylor, was friendly, and that (talking in his third-person style) "the boy felt no sense of strangeness. . . . What strangeness could he feel? The families were intimate, so intimate that their friendliness outlasted generations."

He continued in classic Adamsian style: "As for the White House, all the boy's family had lived there, and, barring the eight years of Andrew Jackson's reign, had been more or less at home there since it was built. The boy half thought he owned it, and took it for granted that he should some day live in it. He felt no sensation whatever before Presidents. A President was a matter of course in every respectable family; he had two in his own."

George Washington 1732–1799 First President of the United States

His mind was great and powerful, without being of the very first order; his penetration strong, though not so acute as that of a Newton, Bacon, or Locke; and as far as he saw, no judgment was ever sounder. It was slow in operation, being little aided by invention or imagination, but sure in conclusion. . . .

His integrity was most pure, his justice the most inflexible I have ever known, no motives of interest or consanguinity, of friendship or hatred, being able to bias his decision. He was, indeed, in every sense of the word, a wise, a good, and a great man. His temper was naturally irritable and high toned; but reflection and resolution had obtained a firm and habitual ascendancy over it. If ever, however, it broke its bonds, he was most tremendous in his wrath.

THOMAS JEFFERSON to Dr. Walter Jones (historical scholar), January 2, 1814

Our mother [Julia Ward Howe] met Lincoln in 1861, and was presented to him by Governor Andrew. After greeting the party, the President "seated himself so near the famous portrait of Washington by Gilbert Stuart as naturally to suggest some comparison between the two figures. On the canvas we saw the calm presence, the serene assurance of the man who had successfully accomplished a great undertaking, a vision of health and of peace. In the chair beside it sat a tall, bony figure, devoid of grace, a countenance almost redeemed from plainness by two kindly blue eyes, but overshadowed by the dark problems of the moment."

LAURA E. RICHARDS AND MAUD HOWE ELLIOTT,
Julia Ward Howe, 1819–1910 (1916)

Born in Westmoreland County, Virginia, the son of a fairly well-to-do planter. He gradually became heir to the family estate at Mount Vernon. In 1759 he married the young widow Martha Dandridge Custis and settled down at Mount Vernon.

In 1774 he was a delegate to the Continental Congress, and a year later he was made commander-in-chief of the Continental Forces, assuming command on July 3, 1775. He succeeded in driving General Howe and his troops out of Boston; and on Christmas night, 1776, he crossed the Delaware River and went on to defeat a British garrison at Trenton: a feat that enormously boosted native morale. A year later he took his forces into winter quarters at Valley Forge, where (in the words of one historian) "his moral fortitude surmounted problems of misery and want seldom equaled in military history." His last military triumph was the defeat and capture of General Cornwall at Yorktown, Pennsylvania, after which Washington tried to retire to Mount Vernon.

He served as president of the Constitutional Convention in 1787 and was the key figure in the passage of the Constitution. In 1789, by unanimous vote he was elected the first president of the United States. He was reelected in 1792 and would have been swept into a third term had he not declined.

Portrait by Gilbert Stuart (1755–1828), oil on canvas, 1796

John Adams 1735–1826 Second President of the United States

He has a sound head on substantial points, and I think he has integrity. I am glad therefore that he is of the commission [for the Peace Treaty] and expect he will be useful in it. His dislike of all parties, and all men, by balancing his prejudices, may give the same fair play to his reason as would a general benevolence of temper.

THOMAS JEFFERSON to James Madison, February 14, 1783

I am persuaded that he means well for his Country, is always an honest Man, often a wise one, but sometimes, and in some things, absolutely out of his senses.

BENJAMIN FRANKLIN to Robert R. Livingston, July 22, 1783

He was not tall, scarcely exceeding middle height, but of a stout, well-knit frame, denoting vigor and a long life, yet as he grew old, inclining more and more to corpulence. His head was large and round, with a wide forehead and expanded brows. His eye was mild and benignant, perhaps even humorous, when he was free from emotion, but when excited, it fully expressed the vehemence of the spirit that stirred within.

CHARLES FRANCIS ADAMS, grandson of John Adams, son of John Quincy Adams, in *Works I: Life*

The Adams family had been living and farming in Massachusetts for a century before John was born in 1735, in what is now Quincy. He graduated from Harvard in 1755 and began to practice law. In 1764 he married Abigail Smith, a charming, sharp-witted young woman from Weymouth; their first born was named John Quincy.

In actions and writings over the next decade, Adams vigorously opposed British colonial practices. He stood out strongly against the Stamp Act (1765) but deplored the riots it caused. He was a member of the Continental Congress, and in Jefferson's words was a "pillar of support" in getting the Declaration of Independence accepted. In the late 1770s and early 1780s he was in France and England on diplomatic missions; in 1783, with Hamilton and Jay, he secured the Treaty of Paris, which ended the Revolution. He was America's first envoy to England, in 1785–88.

In 1789 he was named the country's first vice president. He described the post as "the most insignificant office that ever the invention of man contrived"; but he effectively established its importance. In 1796 he was elected president, in a manner that alienated Jefferson, and during his troubled term managed to resist his party's effort to open a major war with France.

In the many years remaining after his retirement he enjoyed the political achievements of his son John Quincy, even as he did a notable reconciliation with Jefferson (the two of them died on the same day, July 4, 1826).

Begun by Gilbert Stuart in 1798 and completed by Jane Stuart (1812–88),
oil on canvas, after 1828

Portrait by Charles de Saint-Mémin (1770–1852),
engraving, 1805

Thomas Jefferson 1743–1826 Third President
of the United States

Jefferson is a slender man; has rather an air of stiffness in his manner, his clothes seem too small for him; he sits in a lounging manner, on one hip commonly, and with one of his shoulders elevated much above the other; his face has a sunny aspect; his whole figure has a loose, shackling air. He had a rambling vacant look, and nothing of that firm collected, deportment which I expected would dignify the presence of a secretary or minister. I looked for gravity, but a laxity of manner seemed shed about him. He spoke without ceasing. But even his discourse partook of his personal demeanor. It was loose and rambling, and yet he scattered information wherever he went, and some even brilliant sentiments sparkled from him. The information which he gave us respecting foreign ministers, etc., was all high-spiced.

SENATOR WILLIAM MACLAY, *The Journal of William Maclay* (1965), entry for May 24, 1790, after a meeting between senators and Secretary of State Thomas Jefferson

I think this is the most extraordinary collection of human talent, of human knowledge, that has ever been gathered at the White House—with the possible exception of when Thomas Jefferson dined alone.

JOHN F. KENNEDY, address to forty-nine Nobel Prize winners gathered at the White House, April 1962

Born in the frontier territory of what is now Albemarle County, Virginia. The son of Peter Jefferson, a civil engineer of democratic beliefs, and Jane Randolph, of honorable lineage. In 1769 he entered the Virginia House of Burgesses, where he gave strong voice to anti-British sentiments. In 1772 he married Martha (Wayles) Skelton, a widow; she bore him six children, only two of whom, Martha and Mary, reached maturity, and she died in 1782.

In 1776, as a member of the Continental Congress, Jefferson (with others advising) drafted the Declaration of Independence. In 1785 he succeeded Franklin as the American minister to France. It was in France that his still readable book, *Notes on the State of Virginia*, was published, in 1784.

Jefferson served as secretary of state under Washington until, in 1793, an intensifying quarrel with Hamilton—essentially over individual rights (Jefferson) versus a stronger central government (Hamilton)—led to his resignation. He then became vice president under Adams; and in 1800, after some complicated maneuvering, he was named president by the House of Representatives.

His first term featured the Louisiana Purchase, which, for a payment to Napoleon of $15 million in December 1803, brought the huge heartland of the continent into the United States. Jefferson also sponsored Meriwether Lewis and William Clark's expedition to the Pacific coast.

After his retirement from Washington, Jefferson lived almost exclusively at Monticello, the immense family home he had begun to build in about 1770, an estate that grew to nearly ten thousand acres.

During these later years Jefferson gave vent to his extraordinary range of cultural interests and talents, sponsoring scientific expeditions and founding the University of Virginia.

Portrait by Charles de Saint-Mémin (1770–1852),
engraving, 1808

John Marshall 1755–1835 Third Chief Justice of the United States

A lawyer named Gustavus Schmidt was in Richmond during the last half-dozen years Marshall presided as a judge. He left a detailed description of Marshall the man and the jurist. When Marshall entered the courtroom, Schmidt wrote, a few minutes before the court was called to order, his conversation was cheerful and his mind seemed unclouded. He chatted with the lawyers and "no attempt was ever made to claim superiority, either on account of his age or his great acquirements; neither was there any effort to acquire popularity." Instead his conduct "was evidently dictated by a benevolent interest in the ordinary affairs of life, and a relish for social intercourse." These were Marshall's friends, in that courtroom, and he always had enjoyed associating with them, over wine at his popular lawyers' dinners, over a game of billiards, or in just casual talk. He was constitutionally incapable of aloofness.

Schmidt's account of Marshall continued: "The moment, however, he took his seat on the bench his character assumed a striking change. . . . His brow assumed a thoughtfulness and an air of gravity and reflection, which invested his whole appearance with a certain indefinable dignity, which bore, however, not the slightest resemblance to sternness."

LEONARD BAKER, *John Marshall: A Life in Law* (1974)

Born in a log cabin on the Virginia frontier, the oldest of fifteen children. His father, Thomas Marshall, was a planter of humble origin; his mother was related to the Randolphs and hence to Thomas Jefferson.

Marshall was educated largely at home, by a tutor who instructed him in the classics, and by his father, who introduced him to English literature. He entered the bar in Richmond, where his brilliance in argument began to make him famous. In 1783 he married Mary Willis Ambler, the daughter of Virginia's state treasurer; of their ten children, four died at an early age. "Polly" Marshall was a nervous invalid for much of her life, but she shared her husband's love of reading and of good talk, and she was a cherished companion until her death in 1831.

John Marshall was elected to Congress in 1799. President John Adams then made him secretary of state; and just before his retirement in 1801, Adams appointed Marshall to the Supreme Court. Marshall remained there for thirty-four years, and of the 1,100–odd cases argued during his tenure, Marshall wrote the decisions for 519. "If American law were to be represented by a single figure," Justice Oliver Wendell Holmes was to say, "skeptic and worshipper alike would agree without dispute that the figure could be but one alone, and that one John Marshall."

The Supreme Court arrived at something like its full power and dignity in the Marshall years. In particular, the case of *Marbury vs. Madison* (that is, James Madison) established the principle of judicial review by the Court of state and federal legislation; and Marshall's decision in *McCulloch vs. Maryland* (1819) sanctioned the centralizing of power in the federal government as against the states. Views like these enraged the Jeffersonians—among them Madison, Monroe, and, in a more intense and also more confused manner, Andrew Jackson. Marshall died of a liver ailment.

After William Henry Brown, lithographed silhouette, 1845

John Quincy Adams 1767–1848 Sixth President of the United States

Brooks Adams wrote a biographical essay on John Quincy Adams, which he sent to his brother for comment. These passages are from Henry's letters of reply. Brooks's work was never published.

If only dear grandpapa had been favoured by God with a touch of humor in his long career! if he had indulged in a vice! if he had occasionally stopped preaching! but only when he goes for blood and slays some savage rival does he provoke my filial regard.

HENRY ADAMS to Brooks Adams, February 17, 1909

His limitations . . . were astounding. Though he was brought up in Paris, London and Berlin, he seems to have been indifferent to art. I do not remember that he ever mentions interest in architecture, sculpture or painting. His taste in literature was wholly didactic.

Finally, after all is said, our good grandpapa must always be, in a historical point of view, the most important figure of the half-century 1800–50. The historian must roll half-a-dozen of the other figures into one in order to balance his value in the picture. . . . He is the only Foreign Minister we ever produced who was trained and competent to this task, until the time of John Hay. All the others were mere American politicians or lawyers of more or less ability; these two men alone were educated, from youth upwards, and knew the whole field on which they were to act.

HENRY ADAMS to Brooks Adams, February 18, 1909

Born in Braintree (now Quincy), Massachusetts, the eldest son of John and Abigail Adams. Much of his schooling was in France, Holland, and Germany, where his father served in diplomatic posts from 1778 to 1785. In 1794, Adams was appointed minister to the Hague; while on a visit to London he met and soon married Louisa Catherine Johnson, the daughter of the American consul.

In 1809 he was appointed (by Madison) minister to Russia, where he was a pronounced diplomatic and social success. After serving as minister to Great Britain, in 1815–17, Adams became secretary of state to James Monroe; he supported the Missouri Compromise, managed to acquire Florida from the Spanish, and, in effect, drafted the Monroe Doctrine, opposing foreign intervention in any territory of American national interest.

John Quincy Adams was elected president in 1824, defeating Andrew Jackson by a vote in the House (and what Jackson called a "corrupt bargain" with candidate Henry Clay). His administration was crippled by the cacophony of the attacks on it. Adams was defeated for reelection, in 1828, by Jackson.

Adams's greatest period of public service, however, occurred during his years in the House of Representatives, 1831–48. He was a champion of civil rights in America and the most influential House opponent of slavery ("the great and foul stain upon the North American Union"). He vigorously fought the infamous "gag rule," passed in 1836 to prevent antislavery petitions from even being considered, and saw finally to its repeal in 1844. He shepherded through Congress the Smithson bequest that created the Smithsonian Institution in 1846. In February 1848 he suffered a stroke on the floor of the House, and he died two days later.

Andrew Jackson 1767–1845 Seventh President of the United States

Jackson described by an observer on his entry into New Orleans in January 1815:
The chief of the party . . . was a tall, gaunt man, of very erect carriage, with a countenance full of stern decision and fearless energy, but furrowed with care and anxiety. His complexion was sallow and unhealthy; his hair was iron grey, and his body thin and emaciated. . . . But the fierce glare of his bright and hawk-like grey eye, betrayed a soul and a spirit which triumphed over all the infirmities of the body.

QUOTED BY JOHN WILLIAM WARD, *Andrew Jackson: Symbol for an Age* (1955)

If, then, to meanest mariners, and renegades and castaways, I shall hereafter ascribe high qualities, though dark; weave around them tragic graces . . . then against all mortal critics bear me out in this, thou just Spirit of Equality, which has spread one mantle of humanity over all my kind! Bear me out in it, thou great democratic God! . . . Thou who didst pick up Andrew Jackson from the pebbles, who didst hurl him upon a warhorse, who didst thunder him higher than a throne! Thou who, in all Thy mighty earthly marchings, ever cullest Thy selectest champions from the kingly commons, bear me out in it, O God!

HERMAN MELVILLE, *Moby-Dick* (1851)

Born in South Carolina of an immigrant farming family from Ireland. Jackson took part in the Revolution as a teen-ager and suffered a head wound. He practiced law briefly in western North Carolina, and in 1788 he moved to the stockaded village of Nashville. In 1781 he married Rachel Donelson Robards, his landlord's daughter (they had no children). Around the turn of the century he purchased a cotton plantation near Nashville called Hermitage; it was his increasingly luxurious home (one hundred slaves, eventually) between his military and political ventures.

After performing effectively in the Tennessee militia, Jackson became a major-general in the U.S. army. In 1814 he defeated the Creek Indians in the Mississippi Territory (ending a small war); and in 1815 he defeated the British in the battle of New Orleans, putting a final seal on the War of 1812.

Jackson was by now the most widely admired man in the country. In the 1824 presidential election he received a plurality of votes, but he lost out to John Quincy Adams when the vote was given to the House for decision. In 1828, Jackson won over Adams in a relatively close election.

Jackson's two-term presidency was marked, in the historians' phrase, by the "democratization of politics": a vast increase in the number of people actually voting (from 17 percent in 1824 to 76 percent in 1848); the rise of party politics, the political search for popularity rather than for respect.

Another aspect was the Indian Removal Bill, signed by the old Indian fighter Jackson in 1830, which forced eastern tribes (Cherokees, Seminoles, and others) to move west of the Mississippi, trekking miserably along what was labeled the Trail of Tears and leaving millions of acres for white exploiters.

Jackson engaged in a long, confused, and confusing fight with the Second Bank of the United States. He was opposed simultaneously to the abolitionists and the states-righters, believing passionately if unideologically in the Union. He had, indeed, passions rather than ideas.

Portrait by James Barton Longacre (1794–1869), stipple engraving, 1820,
after 1819 painting by Thomas Sully

Portrait by John Wesley Jarvis (1780–1840), oil on canvas, c. 1825

John Jacob Astor 1763–1848 Businessman

Here on the west side, just below Houston Street, I once saw (it must have been about 1832, of a sharp bright January day) a bent, feeble but stout-built very old man, bearded, swathed in rich furs, with a great ermine cap on his head, led and assisted, almost carried, down the steps of his high front stoop (a dozen friends and servants, emulous, carefully holding, guiding him) and then lifted and tucked into a gorgeous sleigh, envelop'd in other furs, for a ride. The sleigh was drawn by as fine a team of horses as I ever saw. . . . I remember the spirited, champing horses, the driver with his whip, and a fellow-driver by his side, for extra prudence. The old man, the subject of so much attention, I can almost see now. It was John Jacob Astor.

WALT WHITMAN, *Specimen Days and Collect* (1882)

A self-invented money machine.

New York Herald, comment after Astor's death, March 19, 1848

An arrant individualist, selfish, narrow-minded, quite blandly anti-social, he went after whatever he sought and took it by fair means or foul—and whoever didn't like it was welcome to a battle. There was something bafflingly attractive about him. He was surely the essence of humanity, contradictory in disposition, a whimsical blend of faults and virtues, capable at the same time of the loftiest affection and the pettiest meanness. In his features you might trace meditation, courage and masterful resolve—and coldness, indifference and acquisitiveness. . . . On the life of America, he had an influence almost incalculable.

ARTHUR D. HOWDEN SMITH, *John Jacob Astor, Landlord of New York* (1929)

Born in Waldorf, Germany, near Heidelberg, the son of a butcher. In 1783 he came to New York City, where his brother Henry was running a meat stall in the Fulton Market. John Jacob hired out to a fur trader, Robert Browne, beating furs for two dollars a week plus board. By 1786 he had set up his own business on Water Street. He made journeys to Albany and north and west of it, collecting furs (mink, otter, lynx, fox, beaver) from the Indians in return for guns, ironware, and liquor, and selling them at large profits in England and Germany.

In the late 1780s Astor married Sarah Todd, the daughter of his boardinghouse keeper. A second son, William Backhouse, increased the family wealth impressively.

Astor was America's first authentic man of business affairs, and he became its first millionaire. Around the turn of the century he began commercial ventures with China, bartering furs for silk, tea, and spices. By 1800 his personal fortune was reckoned at $250,000 (at a time when, it was said, a gentleman could live on $800 a year). In the 1830s he curtailed his China trade while expanding his American investments: railroads, banks, insurance, and, above all, real estate. He came to own a good stretch of what is now midtown Manhattan. In 1836 he saw to the opening of the Astor House, the city's showiest and costliest hotel.

Astor's largest enterprise was his most dramatic failure: an effort to build a great port city on the Oregon coast, to be called Astoria. The first expedition, by sea, in 1811, was wiped out in an Indian encounter; the second, by land, came to an end with the outbreak of the War of 1812.

Gilbert Stuart 1755–1828 Artist

In a conversation and confabulation he was inferior to no man among us. He made it a point to keep those talking who were sitting to him for their portraits, each in his own way, making them feel free and at ease. This called for all his resources of judgment. To military men he spoke of battles by land and sea; with statesmen, on Hume's and Gibbon's histories; with lawyers on jurisprudence, or remarkable criminal trials; with merchants in their way; with the man of leisure in his way; and with the ladies in all ways. When putting the rich farmer on his canvas, he would go along with him from seed time to harvest; he would descant on the nice points of a horse, an ox, a cow, sheep or pig, and surprise him with his just remarks on the process of making cheese and butter, or astonish him with his profound knowledge of manures, or the food of plants. As to national and individual character, few men could say more to the purpose as far as history and acute personal observation would carry him. He had wit at will—always ample, sometimes redundant.

BENJAMIN WATERHOUSE, distinguished physician and lifelong friend

Born on Narragansett Bay in the colony of Rhode Island; Gilbert Sr. had come to America from Scotland to set up a snuff mill. The family moved to Newport in 1761, and by 1774 Gilbert Jr. had set himself up as a portrait painter—that mode, then and ever, being his only artistic interest.

Stuart was in London from 1775 to 1787, a pupil of Benjamin West, and then he became West's assistant. He began to exhibit portraits at the Royal Academy in 1781, and in 1782 he won widespread attention with *The Skater,* a superbly composed painting of a young Scot moving gracefully on a frozen pond, arms folded, black hat jaunty against the wintry sky. Portraits of Reynolds, Copley, and others followed; and at scarcely thirty Stuart was established as one of the premier portraitists of his time.

In 1786, Stuart married Charlotte Coates, a surgeon's daughter who was musically gifted. Always restless and extravagant, Stuart in 1787 fled England for Dublin, with his family, to escape creditors. He remained there, painting energetically, until 1793.

By 1795, Stuart was established in Philadelphia. That year he painted the first of his numerous portraits of George Washington (the "Vaughan" portrait); in 1796, in Stuart's lodgings in Germantown, Philadelphia, Washington sat for the so-called "Athenaeum" portrait (the one presented in this volume), later making many copies that, evoking the price of each, he called his hundred dollar bills.

Stuart also did memorable portraits of John and Abigail Adams, Jefferson, John Jay, James and Dolly Madison, and others. As the "Chronicler of the faces of the founding fathers," writes Jules Prown, "Stuart is perhaps the best known of all American painters." He continued, at the same time, to be moody, self-indulgent, dilatory, quick-tempered, and extraordinarily accomplished.

He lived in Washington (the nation's new capital) in the early 1800s, and he spent the rest of his fairly long life in Boston, shifting from one residence to another.

Unidentified artist, oil on wood panel, after 1823,
after Anson Dickinson (1779–1852)

Unidentified artist, oil on canvas, 1841, after John Woodhouse Audubon (1812–62)

John James Audubon 1785–1851 Artist and Naturalist

Among the great lakes of the North, he sees beyond the reach of his rifle, a strange gigantic bird sweeping over the waters. He hunts for the bird ten years, and finds it again three thousand miles from the spot where he saw it first. Meanwhile, he has been chilled with eternal frosts, and burned with perpetual heat. He has slept nights across the branches of trees, wakened by panther-screams; and many nights he has passed on canebrakes where he did not dare to sleep. . . . On equatorial rivers, alligators stared at him, as he landed; in polar regions, the water turned to ice as it fell from his benumbed limbs when he struck the bank.

Audubon entry in *The Gallery of Illustrious Americans,* by Mathew Brady,
Francis d'Avignon, and C. Edward Lester

Born in Haiti of French and Creole descent. He grew up in France, where he studied, briefly, with the French painter David. After marrying in 1808 and fathering two sons, Audubon taught drawing for a living and tried his hand at portrait painting. But his liveliest interest was in the study and depiction of nature; and in 1820 he began traveling widely (using New Orleans as his base), shooting, mounting, and painting all the birds he came upon. His aim, he would say, was "to copy [nature] in her own way, alive and moving"; and his paintings showed not merely the exteriors of the objects, but their characteristic postures and their settings.

Failing to find a publisher for his work in America, Audubon went to England in 1826, where he stayed for more than a decade. He quickly found backers and subscribers for his *Birds of America,* which began to appear in 1827; it was published in eighty-seven parts over thirteen years, and contained pictures of 1,065 birds, 425 of them in life-size hand-painted aquatints.

Audubon became recognized in both scientific and literary circles as an original genius of extraordinary quality. He cultivated an air of mystery, and enjoyed rumors about his origins—among them, that he was the Lost Dauphin of France. His favorite pose, however, was that of the archetypal American frontiersman. It was in this guise that he liked being painted.

Audubon returned to America in the late 1830s, and in 1841 he purchased a property of thirty-plus acres on the northern edge of New York City, in what is now Washington Heights. Over a series of long forays from this American home, Audubon put together (1845–46) *The Viviparous Quadrupeds of North America,* appearing in thirty parts and containing fifty plates.

Washington Irving 1783–1859 Author

He had dark gray eyes, a handsome straight nose, which might perhaps be called large; a broad, high, full forehead, and a small mouth. I should call him of medium height, about five feet eight and a half to nine inches, and inclined to be a trifle stout. There was no peculiarity about his voice; but it was pleasant and had a good intonation. His smile was exceedingly genial, lighting up his whole face and rendering it very attractive; while, if he were about to say something humorous, it would beam forth from his eyes even before the words were spoken.

> Relative of Washington Irving, quoted in Charles Dudley Warner,
> *Washington Irving* (1881)

There was no railroad . . . till long after Irving's settlement [at Sunnyside]—he survived the railroad but by a few years, and my case is simply that, disengaging his Sunnyside from its beautiful extensions and arriving thus at the sense of his easy elements . . . his "command" of the admirable river and the admirable country, his command of all the mildness of his life, of his pleasant powers and his ample hours, of his friends and his contemporaries and his fame and his honour and his temper and, above all, of his delightful fund of reminiscence and material, I seemed to hear, in the summer sounds . . . the last faint echo of a felicity forever gone.

> HENRY JAMES describing a visit to Irving's home, Sunnyside, in 1905,
> in *The American Scene* (1907)

Born in New York City, the youngest of eleven children, and named for the recent victor at Yorktown. Irving entered a law office at an early age; but instead of practicing law, he took to writing satirical articles on New York society.

In 1807–8, there appeared a series of jokey, unfocused pieces called *Salmagundi*. They were followed in 1809 by *A History of New York . . . by Diedrich Knickerbocker,* an artful and original parody of historical scholarship, delivered by a deadly serious fictitious narrator.

In 1815 he went to England in an effort to save his family's failing business. The business went into bankruptcy, but Irving stayed on in Europe into the early 1830s, writing steadily. In 1819–20 he brought out *The Sketch-Book,* essays and tales written by the pre-pseudonymous Geoffrey Crayon: essays on English subjects and American and Americanized gothic tales—"Rip Van Winkle" and "The Legend of Sleepy Hollow." The latter two items in particular made Irving the most acclaimed living American writer.

Beginning in 1826 and for two decades, Irving performed a series of diplomatic services. Out of these came several large historical studies, among them a life of Christopher Columbus (1828).

But in the mid-1830s, Irving interrupted his European travels to make a long, adventurous trip through his own country—to the western frontier, across the prairies, down the Mississippi. These wanderings led to *A Tour of the Prairies* (1835) and (with the help of John Jacob Astor) *Astoria* (1836).

After 1846, Irving lived in comfortable retirement at Sunnyside, the property on the Hudson River he had purchased some years before.

Portrait by Hatch and Smillie (1831–32), engraving, 1832, after
Charles Robert Leslie (1794–1859), 1825

James Fenimore Cooper 1789–1851 Author

In actuality, Fenimore loved the genteel continent of Europe, and waited gasping for the newspapers to praise his WORK.

In another actuality, he loved the tomahawking continent of America, and imagined himself Natty Bumppo.

His actual desire was to be *Monsieur Fenimore Cooper, le grand écrivain américain.*

His internal wish was to be Natty Bumppo.

Now Natty and Fenimore, arm-in-arm, are an odd couple . . .

But Natty was Fenimore's great wish; his wish-fulfillment.

D. H. LAWRENCE, *Studies in Classic American Literature* (1923)

In a sense, Cooper is the founder of American literature. There had, of course, been writers before him, but he was the first to create a massive body of work—an *oeuvre*—the first to be a professional writer (who would declare that "a good, wholesome, profitable and continued pecuniary support is the applause talent most craved"), the first to regard literature as, in itself, a commentary on, and corrective of, culture, and at the same time the first to create a complex and enduring myth of American life.

ROBERT PENN WARREN, *American Literature, the Makers and the Making* (1973)

Born in New Jersey of English and Quaker stock. His father, William Cooper, was a vigorous character, a shrewd businessman, a congressman, and a judge. In 1790 the elder Cooper moved the family to his recently founded settlement at Cooperstown, on Lake Otsego, west of Albany, New York. James was expelled from Yale University (for a teacher-deriding prank) in 1806, spent half a dozen years at sea, and in 1811 married Susan De Lancey, a young woman of Tory ancestry and a handsome fortune.

Upon a challenge from his wife, Cooper tried his hand at novel writing, and in 1821 he had considerable success with *The Spy*. In 1823 came *The Pioneers*—the first of the six Leatherstocking tales, the saga of Natty Bumppo—covering 1740 to 1800, the early years of the westward movement and the invasion of the American wilderness. There followed two more Leatherstocking stories, *The Last of the Mohicans* (1826) and *The Prairie* (1827), after which Cooper spent six years moving about Europe, enjoying international acclaim. *Notions of the Americans,* a critical but friendly examination of American society from the European perspective, appeared in 1828. Other novels (among them *The Bravo,* set in Venice) and various social tracts were composed during these years.

Back in America and living at Cooperstown, Cooper continued to produce an astonishing number of novels, satires, commentaries. There were also intermittent lawsuits against Whig newspapers for attacks on his books and his character. The final Leatherstocking volumes, *The Pathfinder* and *The Deerslayer*—both dealing with Natty's youth—appeared in 1840 and 1841. The impressive "Littlepage Trilogy," *Satanstone* and two others, came out in the mid-1840s.

Portrait by Amélie Kautz (1796–1860), lithograph, 1827

Attributed to Mathew Brady (1823–96), daguerreotype, c. 1845

Thomas Cole 1801–1848 Artist

I have laboured hard since I have been in Volterra, sallying forth with my sketchbook every morning at five, and, with the exception of an hour at dinner, continuing until evening. I have had many delightful walks, and the more I see, the more I am pleased. A vast horizon is perpetually before you, and the grandest effects of sun, clouds, and storms are ever succeeding each other. Blue shadows are continually moving from mountain to mountain, from plain to precipice, ever and anon wrapping in their gloom distant villages and towers, which a few minutes before were glittering in the sun-light. Then thunder-storms sweep with their tumultuous clouds over the great expanse: as we see them advancing, a power almost supernatural seems to move the soul; it cannot direct their course, but the eye measures their extent, and marks the village that will soon be enveloped in their troubled darkness.

THOMAS COLE, *Journal,* late August 1831

Born in Lancashire, England, the son of a textile manufacturer. The family moved to America in 1816 and settled in Steubenville, Ohio. In the early 1820s, Cole tried his hand at portrait painting. After several moves the family arrived in New York in 1825. Cole now turned to landscape art, and after a trip up the Hudson River in 1825 he produced three landscape sketches that were bought on sight by the influential painters John Trumbull, William Dunlap, and Asher B. Durand. Durand and later William Cullen Bryant (the country's most honored poet at the time) became close friends of Thomas Cole, and they accompanied him on walks and local travels.

Further visits to the Catskill Mountains led to *The Garden of Eden* and *The Expulsion from the Garden of Eden* (1828). These, with six other works, were exhibited at the recently founded National Academy of Design. Cole, as Jules Prown writes, had "quickly established himself as America's leading landscape painter," and soon a "whole throng of artists, popularly known as the Hudson River School, literally followed in [his] footsteps."

Cole spent three years in Europe, 1829–32: England, where he looked closely at the landscape art of Constable and Turner; Paris, where he viewed the landscapes of Claude Lorrain; and Italy, especially Florence (nine months) and Volterra (many days). His imagination was now seized by landscapes imbued with history and displaying ruins.

Back in New York, Cole's career flourished in an endless series of commissions and exhibitions. His grandest achievement, *The Course of Empire,* commissioned by Luman Reed for his New York home, was completed in 1836: a vast work in five stages—"The Savage State," "The Pastoral State," "The Consummation of Empire," "Destruction," and "Desolation."

The years 1836 to 1841 also saw the production of *View from Mount Holyoke,* perhaps Cole's most influential masterpiece; *View of Florence from San Miniato; View of Schoon Mountain;* and *The Van Rensselaer Manor House.* He died after a very short illness, apparently pleurisy.

Henry Clay 1777–1852 Statesman

Not only was Henry Clay of Kentucky a "typical western gambler" who rarely resisted a "long shot," but whenever he gambled he did it with a certain amount of class. A wonderful sense of style always informed Clay's best efforts, especially his most daring. That probably explains why many of his enemies hated him with such fervor. He had a flair for the dramatic, a gift for the outrageous. He did not annoy his political opponents as much as he infuriated them. His thrusts could be deadly, but were always exquisitely executed. And he never failed to comment on the discomfort he had invoked, usually by denying any intentional malice.

ROBERT V. RIMINI, *Henry Clay: Statesman for the Union* (1991)

In the Senate . . . I made the acquaintance of everyone in the first quarter of an hour—among the rest, of Clay, who is one of the most agreeable and fascinating men I ever saw. He is tall and slim, with long, limp gray hair—a good head—refined features—a bright eye—a good voice—and a manner more frank and captivating than I ever saw in any man, at all advanced in life. I was perfectly charmed by him.

CHARLES DICKENS to Albany Fontblanque, Washington, D.C., 12 March 1842

Born in Hanover County, Virginia. Clay's father died when the boy was four; his mother, Elizabeth Hudson, then married Henry Watkins. By 1797 the family was settled in Lexington, Kentucky, where Clay began to practice law. In 1799 he married Lucretia Hart; they had eleven children in twenty-one years.

From 1811 to 1825, Clay was a member of the House of Representatives, serving as speaker five times. He was secretary of state under John Quincy Adams, 1825–29, and senator from 1831 to 1842, and again from 1849–51. His most passionately cherished dream, never fulfilled, was to become president of the United States.

Clay was uniquely inventive and effective as a legislator; his measures added up to an "American system"—support of home manufacture, "internal improvements" (canals, highways, and banks). His Missouri Compromise, 1820–21—whereby Missouri was admitted to the Union as a slave state and Maine as a free state, with slavery prohibited elsewhere—earned him the title of the Great Compromiser. The title was renewed when the aging Clay, with the help of his old rival Daniel Webster, worked out the Compromise of 1850, accepting California as a free state but letting other territories decide for themselves. The bill was vehemently attacked by the New England intellectuals for its inclusion of an inhuman fugitive slave law, but some historians regard it as Clay's finest hour—an act that postponed the national disaster for another decade.

Andrew Jackson for various reasons spoke of Clay as a "profligate demagogue"; others called him the Star of the East and Prince Hal.

Portrait by John Neagle (1796–1865), oil on canvas, 1842

Portrait by George Peter Alexander Healy (1813–94), oil, c. 1845

John Caldwell Calhoun 1782–1850 Statesman

Had I come across his likeness in a copy of Milton's *Paradise Lost,* I should have at once accepted it as a picture of Satan. . . . He was tall and gaunt. His complexion was dark and Indian like, and there seemed to be an inner complexion of dark soul shining out through the skin of his face. His eyes were large, black, piercing, scintillant. His hair was iron gray, and rising nearly straight from the scalp, fell over on all sides, and hung down in thick masses like a lion's mane. His features were strongly marked, and their expression was firm, stern, aggressive, threatening. . . .

At the beginning of the contest [the senatorial debate over the introduction of slavery into the recently acquired New Mexico], my feelings were opposed to Calhoun. . . . But at the close . . . my personal feelings were in his favor, and his physiognomy seemed to have undergone a change. Instead of looking like a devil, he impressed me as a high toned, elegant gentleman, with a brilliant intellect, a sweet disposition, a sound heart, and a conscientious devotion to what he believed to be right. I was vexed and astonished at myself that such a change should have occurred in my feelings towards the Great Nullifier.

OLIVER DWYER, *Great Senators in the United States Forty Years Ago* (1889)

Born in the Abbeville district of South Carolina, a descendant of Scottish-Irish plantation owners. Calhoun graduated from Yale in 1804, and from 1806 to 1811 he practiced law in upcountry South Carolina. In 1811 he married his young cousin Florida Bonneau Calhoun; her small fortune helped make him financially independent. Of their ten children, seven survived him.

With his entrance into the House of Representatives in 1811, Calhoun began a forty-year career of vigorous, conspicuous public service. He was a militant chairman of Foreign Relations during the War of 1812 and secretary of war during James Monroe's two presidential terms, 1817–25. Calhoun served as vice president under John Quincy Adams, 1825–29, and under Jackson, 1829–32—resigning the latter post after a public split with Jackson over the proposed Act of Nullification (Jackson called it treason). He was senator from South Carolina, 1832–43, secretary of state under John Tyler, 1843–45, and senator again from 1845 until his death in 1850.

Although no implacable foe of the Union, Calhoun was the strongest advocate of states' rights in the country's history: sponsoring the act by which South Carolina declared its authority to nullify a federal action that it opposed; and, as the Senate's most powerful advocate of slavery, standing for the principle that the "minority" southern states must be protected against the "tyranny of the majority." He could beguile even his enemies with the brilliance of his oratory; and he died, on March 31, only four weeks after he made a ringing speech denouncing the Compromise of 1850 as inadequate for southern interests.

Daniel Webster 1782–1852 Statesman

His body is compact and of Atlantan massiveness, without being gross; his head is of magnificent proportions, the perfection of vast capaciousness; his glance is a mingling of the sunshine and the lightning of heaven; his features are full of intellectual greatness.

WILLIAM LLOYD GARRISON, quoted by Claude M. Fuess, *Daniel Webster,* vol. 2

The natural grandeur of his face & manners always satisfies; easily great; there is not strut in his voice or behavior as in the others. Yet he is all wasted. . . . Ah if God had given to this Demosthenes a heart to lead England! what a life & death & glory for him. Now he is a fine symbol & mantel ornament; costly enough for those who must keep it; for the great head aches, & the great trunk must be curiously fed & comforted.

RALPH WALDO EMERSON, *Journals,* August 25, 1845

The sea, the rocks, the woods, have no sign that America and the world had lost the complete man. Nature had not in our days, or not since Napoleon, cut out such a masterpiece.

RALPH WALDO EMERSON, *Journals,* October 1852 (on the news of Webster's death)

Born in New Hampshire; his father was a colonial activist who later served in the state legislature. Webster attended Exeter Academy (briefly) and graduated from Dartmouth College in 1801. For the next years, he practiced law in New Hampshire. In 1808 he married Grace Fletcher, a New Hampshire clergyman's daughter.

He was elected to the House of Representatives, from New Hampshire, in 1813, and served two terms. During the period, however, he gave more attention to law, winning several important cases—including the famous "Dartmouth College Case"—before the Supreme Court. In 1816 he transferred to Boston; and in 1827 he was elected senator from Massachusetts, serving until 1841. He earned national fame as an orator, most especially for his 1830 speech replying to Senator Robert Y. Hayne of South Carolina, and the latter's advocacy (in effect) of a state's right to nullify an unacceptable act of Congress. Webster's four-hour oration (a part of it memorized for years by northern schoolchildren) ended with the ringing appeal to "Liberty and Union, now and forever, one and inseparable."

Webster was secretary of state under William Henry Harrison and then John Tyler, 1841–43, resigning when Tyler began supporting states' rights. He returned to the Senate in 1845, and in 1850, in his "7th of March" speech, he supported Henry Clay's compromise bill, including its fugitive slave law. This act brought vehement denunciations from northeastern intellectuals and literary people, John Greenleaf Whittier and Emerson among them. Upon Webster's death, though, there was an extraordinary wave of mourning.

In later political terminology, Webster—a Federalist in his own day—was a liberal in some respects and a staunch conservative in others. He opposed slavery but opposed disunion more strongly. He took it, as he said, as his "especial business" in Congress to "look to the preservation of the great industrial interests of the country."

Portrait by Francis Alexander (1800–80), oil on canvas, 1835

Lucretia Mott 1793–1880 Reformer

I am carrying on a voluminous correspondence and writing and compiling lectures & visiting people across the miles of the endless squares of this city. Lucretia Mott is the best person I see here. I have called at her house, then dined there yesterday & today heard her speak at the Quaker Meeting. She is the handsomest of women and tutelar and beneficent genius of her church here; so lovely, so liberal, so refining. I do not wonder that they are too proud of her and too much in awe of her to spare her, though they suspect her faith.

RALPH WALDO EMERSON to Lydia Emerson, Philadelphia, 25 March 1843

I scarcely know whether to pronounce Mrs. Mott handsome or not. She appears so to me, though I think it probable that she would not, by others, be called more than "quite good-looking." Her features, taken separately, do not posses that symmetry of proportion which is necessary to constitute beauty; yet the contour of her countenance, with its intellectual, sprightly, and agreeable expression, appears to me not only very interesting, but exceedingly lovely. In her person she is under the middle size. She is very active in her movements, and when in health, elastic. Her manners are very easy, and are marked by a dignified simplicity and grace almost peculiar to herself.

ANNA DAVIS HALLOWELL, *James and Lucretia Mott: Life and Letters* (1884), quoting from an unpublished sketch by a close male friend (unidentified) of the Motts'

Lucretia Mott, born in Nantucket to Thomas and Anne Coffin and descendant of two of Nantucket's original settlers, Tristram Coffin and Peter Folger.

The family moved to Philadelphia in 1809. In 1811, Lucretia married fellow Quaker James Mott; they raised five children. In 1821 she became a minister in the Society of Friends and remained a dedicated member of the more liberal branch.

Independent thinker, radical reformer, and advocate of Women's Rights, she was a pioneer in the antislavery movement. In 1840 she and her husband traveled to London to the first Anti-Slavery Convention. The women attending were refused seating as delegates, solely on account of their sex, and this injustice spurred her to work against women's subordinate position. At the convention she met young Elizabeth Cady Stanton; it was the beginning of a lifelong friendship. With a few others they organized the 1848 Woman's Rights Convention in Seneca Falls, New York.

During the rest of her long life she remained active and articulate, remarkable for her self-possession when facing adversaries, and an inspiration to women. "I grew up so thoroughly imbued with women's rights," she said, "that it was the most important question of my life from a very early day."

Portrait by Joseph Kyle (1815–63), oil on canvas, 1842

Joseph Smith 1805–1844 Founder of the Church of Christ of Latter-Day Saints

If one is not a Mormon believer, then Smith's success has to be attributed to his extraordinary human qualities. . . . An autodidact and inspired personality, Smith emanated a human force and spiritual intensity that converted and kept loyal to him such extraordinary persons as Brigham Young and Parley Pratt. The mystery of his charisma was and is an enduring fact. . . . Even his own people, he insisted, did not know him, and it is still difficult to apprehend how so much energy of being inhabited a single personality. . . .

Joseph Smith . . . was at once a characteristic American God-seeker of his age, and a throwback to the Gnostic and Hermetic visionaries. . . . No other religious imagination of the nineteenth century was as comprehensive and daring as Joseph's. Out of Nauvoo came such audacious doctrines as Celestial (plural) Marriage, a new kind of polytheism, and an evolutionary Godhead. . . . Greater worldly expectations than the Mormons as yet have fulfilled also emanated from Nauvoo: a Kingdom of God first in America, and then in all the world, with Joseph Smith divinely crowned as monarch. . . .

Joseph contained multitudes: he was as cannily pragmatic as he was visionary, and was both kind and ruthless. A lover of thought and women, Smith's most unique endowment (among American religious founders) was his exuberant good humor, and highly developed comic sense. Joseph sought for himself, and for his followers, the Blessing in its most archaic Biblical sense: more life into a time without boundaries.

HAROLD BLOOM (July 1996)

Born in Sharon, Vermont, one of nine children; his farming parents moved often, settling finally in Palmyra, New York, in 1816. In the 1820s, Smith underwent several visions, one of which led him in 1827 to discover a set of gold plates hidden in a hillside. The inscribed words enjoined Joseph to restore the true church of Christ in America. The text was published in 1830 as *The Book of Mormon:* a dry 600-page text that gave strong impetus to what became the Church of Jesus Christ of Latter-Day Saints. The church numbered 30,000 by the time of Smith's death.

Smith founded the church in 1830 in Fayette, New York. His book was attacked in the press, and Smith and his followers were whipped, stoned, tarred and feathered, and even kidnapped—because they encouraged the Indians, opposed slavery, and were otherwise an economic menace. The group moved to Kirtland, Ohio, in 1831; to Independence, Missouri, in 1838; and in 1840 to Nauvoo, Illinois (a name coined by Smith). In 1844, Smith endorsed the practice of plural marriages, stating that multiple marital connections could make one divine.

"Genteel" Americans fiercely resented the Mormons' bloc voting, economic autonomy, and plural marriage. After Smith destroyed a printing plant run by dissident Mormons, he was arrested by the Illinois state militia, which murdered him and his brother Hyrum. The majority of Smith's followers were led by Brigham Young to Utah and what is now Salt Lake City, where the church flourished.

Portrait by Adrian Lamb (1901–88), oil on canvas, 1971, after an unidentified artist

American Renaissance: Science and Letters

"AMERICAN RENAISSANCE"—AS A PHRASE DESCRIPTIVE OF WHAT IS SOME-
times called the age of Emerson—was introduced as the title of a classic 1941 study by
F. O. Matthiessen. Matthiessen focused on the years 1850–55, and on the five writers who
helped create the first great epoch in American literary history, each of them producing a
masterpiece during these years: Ralph Waldo Emerson, *Representative Men;* Nathaniel
Hawthorne, *The Scarlet Letter;* Herman Melville, *Moby-Dick;* Henry David Thoreau,
Walden; and Walt Whitman, *Leaves of Grass.*

No one, today, would seriously argue with Matthiessen's choices, though other names
may be heard claiming consideration. Emerson is generally reckoned the single most influential figure in our cultural history, with descendants as various as William James and
Wallace Stevens. Hawthorne virtually begot the American genre of "romance fiction,"
sending currents forward through Henry James and William Faulkner. Melville produced
what may well be the supreme American work of the fictional art. Thoreau is our model
writer on the world of nature, not to mention on "civil disobedience." Whitman is our
greatest poet.

Any current listing of the writers who made up this literary golden day would almost
certainly include Edgar Allan Poe and Emily Dickinson. Poe would always drag with him
controversy, entertaining and provocative, about his merits and stature (Matthiessen
rather disdained him). As to Emily Dickinson, there is not only the fact that she produced
no volume of poems during her lifetime, and no poem at all until May 1861 (that was
the one beginning "I taste a liquor never brewed"); there is also the fact that the National
Portrait Gallery possesses no picture of her, nor of Melville, and is unlikely ever to acquire
one.*

As with the figures in the preceding section, all the literary folk who show up here, wherever they lived (they are mostly New Englanders, with a couple from farther down the
eastern seaboard), somehow belong together; they comment on one another, they visit
and commune. In the verbal portraits, we find Emerson recalling his walks with Thoreau,
Whitman reliving a storm-swept dream about Poe, Melville darkly appraising Hawthorne. Three members of the James family, two of them from the next generation, sup-

---

* Of Melville, there are three traceable portraits, all by unknown artists: one is in the Harvard Portrait
Collection, and two are in the Berkshire Athenaeum Library in Pittsfield, Massachusetts. The only
dependable life portrait of Emily Dickinson is a daguerreotype made in December 1847, while she was
attending Mount Holyoke Seminary; it is now in the Amherst College Library.

ply glimpses of Emerson: as the intellectual, then as the visitor to the family hearth, then as the visionary. The elder James—no picture of him in the Gallery, unhappily—can also be heard, in a letter to Emerson, talking about Hawthorne.

Poe, in the course of his myriad articles, had his say, often brilliantly derogatory, on Washington Irving, James Fenimore Cooper, and Hawthorne, among our subjects, and on Henry Wadsworth Longfellow (with whom he had a long pointless debate), James Russell Lowell, and no end of their contemporaries. Lowell, in turn, talked rhymingly in *A Fable for Critics* (1848) about almost every American writer then in view (see our Authors Group). In a somewhat similar vein, the publisher James T. Fields, in the Hawthorne entry, reminisces about an excursion up Monument Mountain in Massachusetts, in which Hawthorne and Melville, with other literary lights, took a lively and playful part.

Lowell and Fields remind us that the period 1830–60 was teeming with literary and intellectual accomplishment, far beyond that of the half dozen individuals about to be seen. They draw our attention to Longfellow, Whittier (the abolitionist as well as the poet), Richard Henry Dana, Jr. (author of *Two Years Before the Mast* and later a hardy legal opponent of the Fugitive Slave Law), Lowell himself, Oliver Wendell Holmes, Sr. (physician, novelist, and wit), Bronson Alcott (dreamily idealistic educator and Louisa May's father), Theodore Parker (the archetypal religious dissenter), Orestes Brownson (effective advocate of social causes), and a good many more. The first three or four of these could well have made part of this section, numbers permitting; we have smuggled in a few via the Authors Group composite picture.

In his satirical survey, Lowell introduces Margaret Fuller, under the name of Miranda. Margaret Fuller (1810–50), author of the cultural landmark *Woman in the Nineteenth Century,* editor of *The Dial,* gadfly to Emerson, incisive writer and vibrant personality to the moment of her death in a shipwreck off Fire Island, New York—this splendidly imposing woman would unquestionably have been on display here had the Gallery owned a likeness of her.

The *National Portrait Gallery* of 1839, described in the previous introduction, lists two women writers among its characters: Catharine Maria Sedgwick and Lydia Sigourney. Of these, Sigourney (1791–1865) was a Hartford poet of unremittingly melancholy and pious verse; enormously admired in her time, and with an occasional touching stanza, but not a writer of durable quality. There is, in any case, no portrait of her in the contemporary Gallery. The Gallery does have a picture of Catharine Sedgwick, a shapely silhouette of her seated in her Stockbridge, Massachusetts, home before a large window, made in 1842. Sedgwick (1789–1867) was greatly esteemed in the 1830s and 1840s, for her two historically grounded romances, *Hope Leslie* and *The Linwoods,* tales of female heroics that earned her a ranking alongside James Fenimore Cooper. She also inaugurated a significant female tradition that would carry through Charlotte Perkins Gilman to Edith Wharton, by taking up writing to alleviate severe mental depression. Even so, Catharine Sedgwick does not seem to have "made a difference" (to cite our criterion again) sufficient to include her.

One woman writer who decidedly made a difference was Susan Warner, whose novel *The Wide, Wide World* was such a tremendous commercial success that it has been seen as introducing the very phenomenon of the best seller. Susan Warner (1819–85) wrote, moreover, exactly to *make* money for herself and her indigent sister. The lengthy novel itself, set amid the dark world of financial and social power and oppression, can exert a certain appeal of style and attitude, even today. But no portrait of Warner exists in the Gallery.

Matthiessen's title phrase had a largely literary resonance. We have broadened its connotation to take in the historian Francis Parkman, as well as key early representatives in science and in music. Parkman was of course profoundly literary, the most gifted member of the group known as the literary historians. Even more than William Prescott in this group, Parkman was recognized by his literary contemporaries. Henry Adams wrote to Parkman about the latter's *Montcalm and Wolfe* in 1884 that it was a "great work which puts you at the head of our living historians."

From the world of science there is Joseph Henry, the brilliant and tireless explorer of electronics. Henry is also noteworthy as the first director of the Smithsonian Institution, an enterprise begun in 1846 with a sizable fund—donated to the U.S. government some years earlier—from James Smithson, a British subject, whose aim was to create in Washington "an establishment for the increase and diffusion of knowledge among men." Congress, as so often, was slow to move on this cultural initiative, but it was eventually prodded into action by John Quincy Adams. Joseph Henry directed the Institution for thirty years. The present National Portrait Gallery is the most recent addition to the Smithsonian.

Louis Agassiz, our first great naturalist and a striking personality, is on view next, as remembered in a tribute by William James. Had space allowed it would have been fitting to have begun the science category with Benjamin Rush (1745–1813), the first professor of chemistry in America (at the College of Philadelphia), the most prominent physician of his time, a container of epidemics and an early abolitionist. There is a fine portrait of Benjamin Rush, a profile by the French artist Saint-Mémin, dating from 1802.

Music was the slowest of the arts to develop in the new world, as it has been in other locales. Stephen Foster appears as the first composer in the attractive and important genre known as popular music. He could draw upon Italian melody, as in "Beautiful Dreamer," but more often he found inspiration in minstrel songs for his own unprecedentedly successful tunes. The Civil War would produce a rash of new popular songs ("John Brown's Body," "Marching Through Georgia," "Tenting Tonight"), and the genre would reach a variety of peaks in the twentieth-century jazz age. As to "serious music," no composer before Charles Ives (b. 1874) seems truly to belong in this pantheon.

Concerning the actual portraits here: for the image of Emerson, we found ourselves pausing between a lithograph by Southworth and Hawes and a bust by Daniel Chester French. The lithograph shows the human individual, the person evoked by the younger

Henry James, visiting the family in New York and sitting contentedly near the fireplace. The bust gives us rather the Concord seer, the one heralded by William James. We opted for the seer, partly to have a portrait-work by the artist who created the stupendous female figure (*The Republic*) at the 1890 Columbian Exhibition in Chicago and the Lincoln Memorial in Washington.

Walt Whitman poses for us in the engraving used as the frontispiece for the 1855 edition of *Leaves of Grass.* So exact is the delineation that it might have been chosen by Whitman to illustrate a self-descriptive passage in "Song of Myself" ("Looking with side-curved head, curious what will come next" and so on). Stephen Foster's grave physiognomy is shown on a poster listing all his songs, in a lithograph by the firm of Major and Knapp, Broadway, New York City. For Poe, we present his "French face" (to borrow the title of a fine study of 1957 by Patrick Francis Quinn); the face of the American writer so deeply cherished and adapted in France by Baudelaire, Mallarmé, and Valèry; and here etched by Edouard Manet, drawing, with little swirls of his own, on a daugerreotype made in Providence in 1845 and usually referred to as the Sarah Whitman image.

Ralph Waldo Emerson 1803–1882 Philosopher and Poet

Oh you man without a *handle!* Shall one never be able to help himself out of you, according to his needs, and be dependent only upon your fitful tippings up?

HENRY JAMES, SR., to Emerson, October 3, 1843

I "visualize" . . . the winter firelight of our back-parlor at dusk and the great Emerson—I knew he was great, greater than any of our friends—sitting in it between my parents, before the lamps had been lighted, as a visitor consentingly housed only could have done, and affecting me the more as an apparition sinuously and, I held, elegantly slim, benevolently aquiline, and commanding a tone alien, beautifully alien, to any we heard roundabout, that he bent this benignity upon me by an invitation to draw nearer to him, off the hearthrug, and knew myself as never yet, as I was not indeed to know myself again for years, in touch with the wonder of Boston.

HENRY JAMES, *Notes of a Son and Brother* (1914)

Through the individual fact there ever shone for him the effulgence of the Universal Reason. The great Cosmic Intellect terminates and houses itself in mortal men and passing hours. Each of us is an angle of the eternal vision. . . . If the individual opens thus directly into the Absolute, it follows that there is something in each and all of us, even the lowliest, that ought not to consent to borrowing traditions and living at second hand. . . . This faith that in a life at first hand there is something somehow sacred is perhaps the most characteristic note in Emerson's writings.

WILLIAM JAMES, address at the Emerson Centenary in Concord (1903)

Born in Boston, the son of a Unitarian minister, Emerson graduated from Harvard in 1821. He was ordained in the Second Church, Boston, in 1829; but after his first wife, Ellen Tucker, died (of tuberculosis) in 1831, Emerson resigned his ministry.

In 1835, with his second wife, Lydia Jackson, Emerson settled in Concord, where he associated with Thoreau, Hawthorne, Margaret Fuller, and others. His little book *Nature* in 1836 gave his fundamental beliefs (especially the forward-looking life); there followed other culture-changing lectures, like "The American Scholar" and "The Divinity School Address." His first series of *Essays* ("Self-Reliance," and others) appeared in 1841. Through two more decades, Emerson traveled and lectured widely and published voluminously.

Emerson and Lidian (as he called her) had two sons, one of whom died at age six, and two daughters.

Portrait by Daniel Chester French (1850–1931), bronze, after an 1879 original

Portrait by Emmanuel Gottlieb Leutze (1816–68),
oil on canvas, 1862

Nathaniel Hawthorne 1804–1864 Writer

He had the look all the time, to one who didn't know him, of a rogue who suddenly finds himself in a company of detectives.

HENRY JAMES, SR., to Emerson

In certain moods, no man can weigh this world, without throwing in something, somehow like Original Sin, to strike the uneven balance. At all events, perhaps no writer has ever wielded this terrific thought with greater terror than this same harmless Hawthorne. Still more, this black conceit pervades him through and through. You may be witched by his sunlight, transported by the bright gildings in the skies he builds over you, but there is the blackness of darkness beyond.

HERMAN MELVILLE, "Hawthorne and His Mosses" (1850)

One beautiful summer day, twenty years ago (1850), I found Hawthorne in his little red cottage at Lenox, surrounded by his happy young family. . . . Next morning we were all invited by Mr. Dudley Field, then living in Stockbridge, to ascend Monument Mountain. Holmes, Hawthorne, Duyckinck, Herman Melville, Headley, Sedgwick, Matthews, and several ladies were of the party. In the afternoon we made our way, with merry shouts and laughter, through the Ice-Glen. Hawthorne was among the most enterprising of the merry-makers; and being in the dark much of the time, he ventured to call out lustily and pretend that certain destruction was inevitable to all of us.

JAMES T. FIELDS, *Yesterdays with Authors* (1872)

Born in Salem, Massachusetts, of an old Puritan family. After graduating from Bowdoin in 1825, Hawthorne went into seclusion for thirteen years in his mother's Salem home. In 1837 there appeared *Twice-Told Tales,* with stories—like "The Minister's Black Veil"—that expressed the Hawthornian themes of secret guilt and moral pride.

In 1842, Hawthorne married Sophia Peabody of Salem, and then moved into the Old Manse in Concord. *Mosses from an Old Manse* ("Young Goodman Brown," "Rappacini's Daughter") came out in 1846, followed by *The Scarlet Letter* in 1850. That book, an immediate success, was followed by *The House of the Seven Gables* (1851) and *The Blithedale Romance* (1852).

After a year in the Berkshires (where he came to know Herman Melville), Hawthorne served as American consul in Liverpool (1853–57). His last completed work was *The Marble Faun,* in 1860.

Authors Group 1883

Yonder, calm as a cloud, Alcott stalks in a dream,
And fancies himself in thy groves, Academe . . .
When he talks he is grand, but goes out like a taper,
If you shut him up closely with ink, pen and paper. . . .

There is Whittier, whose swelling and vehement heart
Strains the strait-breasted drab of the Quaker apart,
And reveals the live Man, still supreme and erect,
Underneath the bemummying wrappers of sect. . . .

(Longfellow) Does it make a man worse that his character's such
As to make his friends love him (as you think) too much? . . .
You may say that he's smooth and all that till you're hoarse,
But remember that elegance also is force. . . .

There's Holmes, who is matchless among you for wit;
A Leyden-jar always full-charged, from which flit
The electrical tingles of hit after hit. . . .

There is Lowell, who's striving Parnassus to climb
With a whole bale of *isms* tied together with rhyme . . .
The top of the hill he will ne'er come nigh reaching
Till he learns the distinction 'twixt singing and preaching. . . .

JAMES RUSSELL LOWELL, *A Fable of Critics* (1848),
in which, at a gathering of the gods of Olympus,
a critic passes the various American authors in review

Seated, from left: John Greenleaf Whittier (1807–92), poet; Ralph Waldo Emerson (1803–82), philosopher; John Lothrop Motley (1814–77), historian, diplomat; Nathaniel Hawthorne (1804–64), author; Henry Wadsworth Longfellow (1807–82), poet. *Standing, from left:* Oliver Wendell Holmes, Sr. (1809–94), author; Amos Bronson Alcott (1799–1888), author; James Russell Lowell (1819–91), poet, diplomat; Louis Agassiz (1807–73), naturalist.
By Eugene L'Africain (1859–92), collotype, 1883, after photographs by Notman Photographic Company

Portrait by Mathew Brady (1823–96), carte de visite, 1862

Joseph Henry 1797–1878 Scientist

His head and features were of massive mould; though from the perfect proportion of his form, not too conspicuously so. His expansive brow was crowned with an abundant flow of whitened hair; his lower face always freshly shaven, expressed a mingled gentleness and firmness; and his countenance of manly symmetry was in all its varying moods, a pleasant study of the mellowing, moulding impress of long years of generous feeling, and a worthy exponent of the fine and thoughtful spirit within: wearing in repose a certain pensive but benign majesty.

W. B. TAYLOR, in *A Memorial of Joseph Henry* (1880)

His place [at the Smithsonian Institution] required a love of science, along with a talent for organization. . . . The fund which was under his control was scrupulously used. At our annual meetings as regents I cannot fail to recall the blackboard where his list was chalked with all the exactness of an old accountant and explained with all the nervous solicitude of a schoolboy doing his first sum.

S. S. COX, in *A Memorial of Joseph Henry*

In the year 1870, after visiting the Aar Glacier, the scene of Professor Agassiz's well-known labors, he crossed over the mountains to the Rhone Valley, until, at a sudden turn of the road, he came full in the presence of the majestic Glacier of the Rhone. For minutes he stood silent and motionless; then, turning to the daughter who stood by his side, he exclaimed, with tears running down his cheeks: "This is a place to die in. We should go no further."

J. C. WELLING, in *A Memorial of Joseph Henry*

Born in Albany, the son of a day laborer. While teaching (mathematics and natural philosophy) at the Albany Academy, Henry began research into electrical currents and magnetism; and in 1830— perhaps anticipating Michael Faraday—discovered the phenomenon of inductance. His other research helped develop the electrical motor and transformer.

From 1832 to 1846, Henry served as the first professor of natural philosophy at Princeton. In 1846 he was appointed director of the new Smithsonian Institution, remaining there for thirty years. After his death there was a memorial service attended by the president, members of both houses, and the Supreme Court justices.

Portrait by Carleton E. Watkins (1829–1916), photograph, c. 1871

Louis Agassiz 1807–1873 Naturalist

He was a splendid example of the temperament that looks forward and not backward, and never wastes a moment in regrets for the irrevocable. I had the privilege of admission to his society during the Thayer expedition to Brazil (1865). I well remember one night as we all swung in our hammocks in the fairy-like moonlight, on the deck of the steamer that throbbed its way up the Amazon between the forests guarding the stream on either side, how he turned and whispered, "James, are you awake?" and continued, "I cannot sleep; I am too happy. I keep thinking of these glorious plans." The plans contemplated following the Amazon to its headwaters, and penetrating the Andes in Peru. And yet, when he arrived at the Peruvian frontier and learned that that country had broken into revolution, that his letters to officials would be useless, and that that part of the project must be given up, although he was indeed bitterly chagrined and excited for part of an hour, when the hour had passed over it seemed as if he had quite forgotten the disappointment, so enthusiastically was he occupied already with the new scheme submitted by his active mind.

WILLIAM JAMES, "Louis Agassiz" (1896)

The Swiss-born Agassiz was famous for his book *The Fishes of Brazil* before he came to America in 1846. He became professor of natural history at the Lawrence Scientific School at Harvard and helped found the Harvard Museum of Comparative Zoology. Among his many expeditions was the Thayer Expedition to Brazil (1865–66), on which young William James served as an assistant. In early 1872 he was in San Francisco, on one stage of a long trip, and had his picture taken there by the celebrated Carleton Watkins.

Portrait by Benjamin D. Maxham (active 1854–59), daguerreotype, 1856

Henry David Thoreau 1817–1862 Naturalist and Writer

He is a little under size, with a huge Emersonian nose, bluish gray eyes, brown hair, and a ruddy weather-beaten face, which reminds me of some shrewd and honest animal—some retired philosophical woodchuck or magnanimous fox. He dresses very plainly, wears his collar turned over like Mr. Emerson and often an old dress-coat, broad in the skirts, and by no means a fit. He walks about with a brisk, rustic air, and never seems tired.

FRANKLIN B. SANBORN, Diary, May 1855

It was a pleasure and a privilege to walk with him. He knew the country like a fox or a bird, and passed through it as freely by paths of his own. He knew every track in the snow or on the ground, and what creature had taken this path before him. One must submit abjectly to such a guide, and the reward was great. Under his arm he carried an old music-book to press plants; in his pocket, his diary and pencil, a spy-glass for birds, microscope, jack-knife, and twine. He wore a straw hat, stout shoes, strong gray trousers, to brave scrub-oaks and smilax, and to climb a tree for a hawk's or a squirrel's nest.

RALPH WALDO EMERSON, address given
at Thoreau's funeral service, May 9, 1862

I come to my solitary woodland walk as the homesick go home.

HENRY DAVID THOREAU, *Journals,* January 7, 1857

Born in Concord, Massachusetts. After graduating from Harvard in 1837, Thoreau and his brother John ran a private school in Concord. Thoreau then went to live with the Emersons, serving as their handyman.

From July 4, 1845, to early September 1847, Thoreau lived and wrote in a small cabin on nearby Walden Pond. The account of this experience, *Walden*, came out in 1854. During the same years, Thoreau delivered several notable lectures: "Civil Disobedience," "Walking" (perhaps his finest), and "Slavery in Massachusetts."

Among his other writings are *A Week on the Concord and Merrimack Rivers* (1849), and *The Maine Woods* (1864). Thoreau also wrote two million words in his journals over twenty years.

Edgar Allan Poe 1809–1849 Writer

At the age of thirty three (1842), Poe still made a slight figure, about five feet eight inches tall, slender, with black somewhat curly hair, rather fair complexion, gray eyes that he himself described as "restless." Many of those who knew him remarked on the thinness and delicacy of his lips and, particularly, on the extreme breadth of his forehead, so broad that in profile he seemed to be growing bald. The ordeal of witnessing Sissie's [Virginia Clemm's] alternating progress and deterioration apparently intensified his customarily quiet, sad, and unsmiling manner.

KENNETH SILVERMAN, *Edgar A. Poe: Mournful and
Never-ending Remembrance* (1991)

In a dream I once had, I saw a vessel on the sea, at midnight, in a storm. It was no great full-rigg'd ship, nor majestic steamer, steering firmly through the gale, but seem'd one of those superb little schooner yachts I had often seen lying anchor'd, rocking so jauntily, in the waters around New York, or up Long Island sound—now flying uncontroll'd with torn sails and broken spars through the wild sleet and winds and waves of the night. On the deck was a slender, slight, beautiful figure, a dim man, apparently enjoying all the terror, the murk, and the dislocation of which he was the centre and the victim. That figure of my lurid dream might stand for Edgar Poe, his spirit, his fortunes, and his poems—themselves all lurid dreams.

WALT WHITMAN, quoted in the *Washington Star*, November 16, 1875

Born in Boston. Bereft of both parents by the age of two, Poe was taken in by a Richmond merchant, John Allan. He went to school in England, 1815–20, and later spent a year at the University of Virginia.

Poe's life was a series of fits and starts: a spell in Boston, a stint in the U.S. Army, sporadic publications. In 1831 he joined the Baltimore household of his aunt, Maria Clemm, and in 1835 he married her twelve-year-old daughter, Virginia (she died in 1845).

Thereafter, while serving as literary editor of magazines in Philadelphia and New York, Poe produced some of his best-known tales: "The Fall of the House of Usher," "Ligeia," "The Purloined Letter." "The Raven" appeared in the *New York Mirror* in 1845. Poe died of natural causes in Baltimore.

Portrait by Edouard Manet (1832–83), drypoint, 1860, after daguerreotype
by Hartshorn of Masury and Hartshorn

Walt Whitman 1819–1892 Poet

Apart from the pulling and hauling stands what I am.
Stands amused, complacent, compassionate, idle, unitary,
Looks down, is erect, bends an arm on an impalpable certain rest,
Both in and out of the game, and watching and wondering at it.
WALT WHITMAN, "Song of Myself," lines 66–70

I see him . . . in his late thirties. He is a homosexual building contractor and unemployed journalist, living with his mother in Brooklyn. He is six feet tall, weighs a hundred and eighty pounds, and has a mottled-gray beard and a thatch of prematurely whitening hair, which he likes to compare to hay. He has large freckles on his face. His eyes are a semi-transparent, indistinct light blue, and they have sharp, velvety-black pupils—eyes that like to search the faces of young men on Broadway, hoping to meet the shock of love. He walks slowly around Manhattan all day, or he rides the ferry across the East River, and he keeps his hands in his pockets, now and then extracting one hand and raising it high in the air to greet his friends, who are mostly stage drivers and roustabouts.
"Talk of the Town," *The New Yorker,* April 13, 1992

Born on Long Island; lived in Brooklyn, with family, until 1833. For many years Whitman was variously a printer's devil, schoolteacher, carpenter, editor, and newspaper writer; author of conventional poems and stories; an ardent reader, especially of Emerson; in 1848, a resident of New Orleans. The little collection called *Leaves of Grass*, with its epochal preface, appeared in 1855; enlarged editions followed in 1856 and 1860. Whitman's Civil War experiences led to *Memoranda* and the poems in *Drum-Taps.* The vigorous prose essay *Democratic Vistas* came out in 1871. Whitman aged unexpectedly, and in 1873 he suffered a paralytic stroke. He spent his last years in Camden, New Jersey, editing new enlarged editions of *Leaves of Grass*, and being fêted, especially by English literary admirers.

Portrait by Samuel Hollyer (1826–1919), stipple engraving, 1854–55,
after daguerreotype by Gabriel Harrison (1818–1902)

Attributed to Albert Sands Southworth (1811–94) and Josiah Johnson Hawes
(1808–1901) (studio active 1844–61), daguerreotype, c. 1852

Francis Parkman 1823–1893 Historian

He was the Melville of the historians—incomparably the best writer among them; and about his style the only complaint is that it was almost overwhelmingly masculine. Parkman's masculinity of spirit . . . was very likely an overcompensation for his lifelong feebleness of body; for Parkman, as for Brockden Brown, life was a continuous dull ache—but Parkman did not dramatize the ache, he fought it down; and what he dramatized was the zest of the fighting. Parkman was a dramatizer to the core: but not a self-dramatizer. He brought to his subject not only style, but a histrionic sensibility of the first order. When he was barely coming of age, in Rome during his grand tour, he sympathized dramatically, though not doctrinally, with the histrionic sensibility of the priests themselves on Good Friday. "All the priests looked wretched and disconsolate, as if afflicted with some awful disaster. 'He is not up yet,' whispered Manicinelli to me, in explanation of the dismal appearance of things."

R. W. B. LEWIS, *The American Adam* (1955)

[The] sense of amenity in Parkman's way of life [in his later years] was equally expressive for observers of an inner amenity, a serenity and tranquility of spirit, which stand in marked enough contrast to the *Sturm und Drang* of his earlier years. Such impressions, to be sure, emphasize equally . . . a sense of latent force and fire, of animation and incisiveness, behind the quiet unobtrusiveness of manner, as they do the unaffected simplicity and frankness of way for all at all levels of life, and the lack, even physically, of any appearance of invalidism; the firm chin, square-set frame, upright bearing and good color—or, even when he had to resort to crutches, his briskness in managing them.

HOWARD DOUGHTY, *Francis Parkman* (1962)

Born of a well-known Boston family. During his Harvard years, 1840–44, Parkman made his first excursions into the north woods; and in 1846 he made a trip to Wyoming that led to his book *The Oregon Trail,* in 1849.

Despite spells of extreme exhaustion and failing eyesight, Parkman, in the late 1840s, began his long history of the struggle between the French and English for colonial America ("the history of the American forest," in his phrase). Among the eventual titles were *The Conspiracy of Pontiac* (1851), *La Salle and the Discovery of the Great West* (1869), and *Montcalm and Wolfe* (1884).

Parkman's intense interest in horticulture led to *The Book of Roses* in 1866, and to a professorship of horticulture at Harvard in 1871.

Stephen Collins Foster 1826–1864 Songwriter

"Old Folks at Home" . . . is on everybody's tongue, and consequently in everybody's mouth. Pianos and guitars groan with it, night and day; sentimental young ladies sing it; sentimental young gentlemen warble it in midnight serenades; volatile young "bucks" hum it in the midst of their business and pleasures; boatmen roar it out stentorially at all times; all bands play it; amateur flute blowers agonize over it at every spare moment; the street organist grinds it out at every hour; the "singing stars" carol it, on the theatrical boards, and at concerts; the chamber maid sweeps and dusts to the measured cadence of "Old Folks at Home."

> Albany State Register, reprinted October 2, 1852, in *Dwight's Journal of Music;* quoted in John Tasker Howard, *Stephen Foster, America's Troubadour* (1953)

Foster's mind seemed to be full of melodies, and I never saw him sit down to a piano that he did not play or sing something we had never heard before. He was continually evolving new songs and new melodies, some of them strange, yet peculiarly sweet and pathetic. Often when we were spending an evening with friends, he would suddenly dart to the piano, unmindful of all about him and seemingly unconscious of his surroundings, and pick out on the keyboard the notes of some new melody that seemed to be passing through his brain.

> Anonymous writer in *Pittsburgh Press,* July 1895,
> quoted in Howard, *Stephen Foster*

Born in what is now Pittsburgh, Pennsylvania, of Scottish-Irish descent. Foster attended college briefly, but his passion was always for music. His songs began to appear as early as 1842. All told, Foster wrote some two hundred songs over his short career, and he is now recognized as the most talented and ingenious popular songwriter in America before the era of the Tin Pan Alley composers.

His first successes were so-called "negro songs"—or, in his title phrase for his first collection, *Songs of the Sable Harmonist*. These were songs sung in minstrel shows, and expressing a longing for a world of southern kindly slavery that Foster, of course, never knew: "Old Folks at Home," "My Old Kentucky Home," and others. There were also more spirited ditties: "Camptown Races" and "Oh, Susanna," performed with gusto on stage and in family musical gatherings. And there were the more purely romantic ballads, like "Jeanie with the Light Brown Hair" and "Beautiful Dreamer."

Surprisingly little is known about Foster's actual life. He remained in the Pittsburgh area until 1860. In 1850 he married Jane McDowell of a local family. She may be the Jeanie with the light brown hair; but the marriage was not a happy one. They moved to New York in 1864, and in effect Foster disappeared into a mist of alcohol and general dissipation. He died in a shabby hotel at age thirty-seven.

He left behind the title of an unwritten song: "Dear Friends and Gentle Hearts." "My Old Kentucky Home" is the theme song of the Kentucky Derby.

Portrait by Major and Knapp, lithograph, 1888, music sheet
title page for "Old Black Joe"

The Civil War Years

THE CIVIL WAR, IN THE PHRASING OF ROBERT PENN WARREN, IS "OUR ONLY felt history—history lived in the national imagination." To a great extent, it is as a history so diversely lived in the imagination that we offer the portraits, both visual and verbal, in this section.

Sojourner Truth, for example, comes to us verbally as she appeared in the imagination of Harriet Beecher Stowe, who thought her (in a passage not quoted here) like a once-famous statue of a "Negro woman" at a fountain. The visual portrait was made by an unidentified photographer not long after Truth, at a women's rights convention in Akron, Ohio, in 1851, had made an impromptu speech, the choral theme of which was "A'n't I a woman?"

With John Brown we present the earliest known portrait—Brown, as observed and posed by black daguerreotypist Augustus Washington, in Hartford, Connecticut, in about 1847. Washington, the son of a former slave and an Asian woman, had taught school in Brooklyn and had studied at Dartmouth before dedicating himself, in his own words, to elevating the "social and political position of the oppressed and unfortunate people with whom I am identified." It would be seven years before Brown would make his way to embattled Kansas to perform his first act of antislavery violence; but the fiery personality —grim-eyed, intense, swearing allegiance (no doubt to the cause of freedom for the slaves)—is already there in Augustus Washington's imagining.

Frederick Douglass is also caught in a relatively early moment of his career: in late April 1844, just after he had given a speech at Northampton, Massachusetts (and by an artist whose identity is uncertain). Here, at the young age of twenty-six, he fits the verbal portrait of him given by Elizabeth Cady Stanton at his funeral in 1895: "like an African Prince, conscious of his dignity and power, grand in his proportions, majestic in his wrath." When the National Portrait Gallery arranged an exhibition of Frederick Douglass portraiture in 1996, it was entitled "Majestic in His Wrath."

Douglass in turn supplies an especially stirring view of Harriet Tubman. A life of Tubman had recently (1869) been completed by Sarah Hopkins Bradford, and Douglass had been asked for a word of support. "I need such words from you," Douglass wrote Tubman from Rochester, "far more than you can need them from me." He went on to contrast their two modes of antislavery activity: "Most that I have done and suffered in the service of our cause has been done in public. . . . You, on the other hand, have labored in a private way. I have wrought in the day—you in the night."

The image of Harriet Beecher Stowe, made in London in May 1853, represents a British imagining of the author of *Uncle Tom's Cabin,* which, in a pirated edition, was selling in the hundreds of thousands in England. Stowe was pleased by the likeness, made of her by George Richmond, a portraitist of some note; Richmond, in her view, was a truly clairvoyant artist. It was almost a decade later, in November 1863, that Harriet Beecher Stowe went to Washington to call on President Lincoln. There, in the president's study (according to the family story), the six-foot-four Lincoln looked down at his diminutive guest and commented, "So this is the little woman who made this big war!"

The war had indeed become bigger and more horrendous by the month. In September there had taken place the battle of Antietam, where more than 22,000 men—northerners and southerners—were killed, wounded, or missing; and this not long after the battle of Shiloh, in southern Tennessee, where more than 20,000 were lost. Lincoln issued his Proclamation on September 22. The war was taking the form of history, of a colossal and tragic kind.

Among the political and military figures who pass before us here, no few of the portraits were made by Mathew Brady and his staff. These include images of Jefferson Davis, U. S. Grant, W. T. Sherman and his generals, Robert E. Lee, and Brady himself. The picture of Brady was a carte de visite made in Brady's New York studio in 1861. Whether Brady actually wrote the not easily decipherable words below the portrait, he would certainly have approved of them: "M. B. Brady, Civil War photographer, Artist." He had already taken on his role as the photographer-historian of the Civil War (primarily, of course, from a northern perspective); and he had always described himself as an artist. Mathew Brady had no doubt that the camera could be creative as well as imitative.

The portrait of Jefferson Davis comes from the period before the war: a mezzotint by William Sartain dating from about 1860; but it is based on a photograph by Mathew Brady, one of the full-scale productions known as "imperials," taken in 1856, when Davis was serving as secretary of war in the cabinet of Franklin Pierce.

Brady came into his own with the outbreak of war in April 1861, when Confederate guns opened fire on the Union garrison at Fort Sumter, in the harbor of Charleston, South Carolina. Through some extraordinary intuition of the gigantic process at work, Brady, who spoke of the camera as the "eye of history," applied himself to compiling a visual record of American history in the making. His cameras were everywhere—in the camps, on the battlefields, on fields strewn with the dead, alongside the big guns. It was the first major instance of what has become a characterizing American venture, something enacted not many years back by the television cameras profitably recording the Persian Gulf War as it took place, for the consumption of TV viewers back home.

By 1853, Brady had opened a second New York studio at Broadway and Tenth Street and had started as well a studio closer to the seats of power in Washington. The latter was eventually run by Alexander Gardner, Scottish-born and gifted with a photographic eye for the human suffering amid the confusions of history. Gardner is the source for our portrait of Abraham Lincoln.

As it happens, our first military figure is the southern general Thomas Jonathan Jackson, etched in August 1862 (soon after the gory second battle of Bull Run, which cost the two sides twenty-five thousand men) by the fiercely pro-southern artist Adalbert John Volck, whose many sketches and lampoons recorded the war as it lived in the southern imagination.

Brady's portrait of Ulysses S. Grant was taken on June 20, 1864, outside the general's tent at his headquarters in City Point, Virginia. After more than a month of heavy fighting and frightful casualties in the wilderness and at Spottsylvania and Cold Harbor in central Virginia—Grant lost about forty-five thousand men in all—he moved his army down to an area below Petersburg and set up his new command post on the James River. Here he dug in for what turned out to be a ten-month siege, with daily shelling of the nearby city. Brady's Grant has a certain authoritative look to him, but Brady could be skilled in the imaginative enhancement of his subject. Another observer of Grant in this same place and time, Charles Francis Adams, wrote that "Grant is certainly a very extraordinary man," but that "he does not look it, and might well pass . . . for a dumpy and slouchy little subaltern, very fond of smoking."

William Tecumseh Sherman and his generals sat for a group portrait in Brady's Washington studio in the spring of 1865. The war had come to an end on April 26 in Durham, North Carolina, when—two and a half weeks after Lee surrendered to Grant at the Appomattox Court House near Richmond—southern general Joseph Johnson surrendered his entire force to General Sherman. It was the final moment in Sherman's long campaign, which began in May 1864, continued through the seizure of Atlanta in September, and then the ruthless "march to the sea," from Atlanta to Savannah, the modern world's first example of total warfare.

Along with Sherman, in Brady's tableau, there appear Generals Howard, Logan, Hazen, Slocum, Mowery, and Jefferson C. Davis (no relation to the Confederate statesman). The name F. B. Blair may also be noted at the bottom right. Blair was supposed to take part but could not be located. In some later reproductions of *Sherman and His Generals,* Blair's figure was added, seated comfortably and gazing across (seemingly) at Sherman.

At about the same time, Brady went down to Richmond to photograph Robert E. Lee at his home on Franklin Street. Brady would recall that some people thought that "after [Lee's] defeat, it would be preposterous to ask him to sit"; but Brady, history-conscious as ever, thought it exactly the right moment for the "historical picture." So we have Robert E. Lee, transformed into the complete civilian, on the front porch of his old home.

Of Abraham Lincoln, the National Portrait Gallery possesses some sixty portraits in many modes—as against fifty of George Washington, for example, and thirty-odd of Andrew Jackson. It seems an appropriate ratio, since, all things considered, Lincoln is the greatest figure in American history. The well-known portrait of Lincoln by G. P. A. Healy—the president seated and leaning forward, chin in hand—dominates the second floor corridor of the Gallery. Mathew Brady achieved one of his finest efforts in the picture he took of Lincoln in New York on February 27, 1860, just before Lincoln delivered his Cooper Union address: an appealing portrait of the fifty-four-year-old—tall, erect, decently dressed, beardless. Lincoln would say that the Cooper Union talk combined with Brady's picture were what got him into the White House.

Alexander Gardner's picture of Lincoln gives us the most hauntingly human portrait of the man, and probably the last ever made. It was taken in February 1865, just before the second inaugural. The plate cracked while being developed—hence the line across the head. Gardner assumed there would be ample time for more photographs. But on April 14, Good Friday, in his presidential box at Ford's Theatre, watching the British comedy *Our American Cousin,* Lincoln was assassinated by John Wilkes Booth.

The dramatically posed picture of Booth (a lithograph by J. H. Bufford and Company of Boston, from a photograph by Charles DeForest Fredricks) is an image of John Wilkes Booth the actor and member of a famous theatrical family. But it or something very like it was used in the broadside put out over the name of Edwin M. Stanton, secretary of war, in huge print announcing a reward of $50,000 for the apprehension of "The Murderer of our late beloved President."

Unidentified photographer, photograph, albumen silver print, c. 1851. On the back:
"Entered according to act of Congress in the year 1864, by Sojourner Truth."

Sojourner Truth c. 1797–1883 Evangelist and Abolitionist

On one occasion, when our house was filled with company . . . notice was brought up to me that Sojourner Truth was below and requested an interview. Knowing nothing of her but her singular name, I went down, prepared to make this interview short. . . .

I do not recollect ever to have been conversant with anyone who had more of that silent and subtle power which we call personal presence than this woman. In the modern spiritualistic phraseology, she would be described as having a strong sphere. Her tall form, as she rose up before me, is still vivid to my mind. She was dressed in some stout, grayish stuff, neat and clean, though dusty from travel. On her head she wore a bright Madras handkerchief, arranged as a turban, after the manner of her race. She seemed perfectly self-possessed and at her ease,—in fact, there was almost an unconscious superiority, not unmixed with a solemn twinkle of humor, in the odd, composed manner in which she looked down on me. Her whole air had at times a gloomy sort of drollery which impressed one strangely.

HARRIET BEECHER STOWE, "Sojourner Truth, The Libyan Sybil" (1863),
in *The Writings of Harriet Beecher Stowe,* vol. 4 (1896)

Born the slave of a Dutch-speaking farmer in Hurley, Ulster County, New York, she was religious from an early age. Sold the fourth and final time to John Dumont of New Paltz, New York, in 1810, she escaped in 1826. For about fourteen years after 1829 she was an evangelist in New York City, associating with various religious sects. In 1843 she left the city, taking the name Sojourner Truth, and wandered New England until she encountered abolitionists William Lloyd Garrison and Frederick Douglass and was converted to the cause. In 1850 she was introduced to the women's rights movement, with Lucretia Mott, Elizabeth Cady Stanton, and others. Settling in Battle Creek, Michigan, in the mid-1850s, she spent the Civil War years as a nurse and aide to free slave refugees in Washington. She died at her home in Battle Creek.

Portrait by Augustus Washington, daguerreotype, c. 1847

John Brown 1800–1859 Abolitionist

The man had some kind of constant obsessive interest for me. On the one hand, he's so heroic; on the other, he's so vile, pathologically vile. Some fifteen years ago, when Edmund Wilson was working on *Patriotic Gore,* we'd meet at parties, and he would say, "Red, let's go and sit in the corner and talk about the Civil War," and we always did. And the subject of Brown once or twice came up, and he once said, "But he's trivial, he's merely a homicidal maniac—forget him!" Now this is *half* of Brown. In a strange way the homicidal maniac lives in terms of grand gestures and heroic stances, and is a carrier of high values, but *is* a homicidal maniac! . . . Brown lives in the dramatic stance of his life, rather than in the psychological content of it; he lives in noble stances and noble utterances, and at the psychological and often the *factual* level of conduct was—it's incredible—brutal.

ROBERT PENN WARREN, interview with Marshall Walker, 1974,
in *Robert Penn Warren Talking,* edited by Floyd C. Watkins and John T. Hiers (1980).
(Warren's first book was *John Brown: The Making of a Martyr,* 1929)

Born in Torrington, Connecticut. Brown's early life was marked with business failures and frequent moves. After spending time in Richmond, Pennsylvania (where he ran a tannery and an Underground Railroad station), Springfield, Massachusetts, and several Ohio towns, he settled in North Elba, New York, a community of free blacks. In the mid-1850s he followed five of his sons to Kansas, where he organized, among other things, the murder of five pro-slavery settlers near Pottawatomie Creek. After returning to Massachusetts, Brown began planning to establish a free state in the mountains of the South from which he could attack slave owners and liberate slaves. Apparently to this end he captured the arsenal at Harper's Ferry, Virginia, in October 1859. But instead of fleeing to the mountains, he lingered and was overcome by troops led by Robert E. Lee. Tried and found guilty of murder, treason, and conspiring with slaves to rebel, he was hanged in Charlestown in what is now West Virginia.

Harriet Beecher Stowe 1811–1896 Author

I am a little bit of a woman—somewhat more than 40—about as thin and dry as a pinch of snuff never very much to look at in my best days—& looking like a used-up article now. I was married when I was 25 years old to a man rich in Greek & Hebrew, Latin & Arabic, & alas! rich in nothing else. . . .

During these long years of struggling with poverty & sickness & a hot debilitating climate, my children grew up around me. The nursery & the kitchen were my principal fields of labor.

. . . I used to say to my faithful friend & factotum Anna, who shared all my joys and sorrows, "Now if you'll keep the babies, & attend to all the things in the house for one day, I'll write a piece, & then we shall be out of the scrape," and so I became an authoress. Very modest at first, I so assure you, & remonstrating very seriously with the friends who had thought it best to put my name to the pieces, by way of getting up a reputation.

HARRIET BEECHER STOWE to Eliza Cabot Follen,
a Boston abolitionist, December 16, 1852

Born in Litchfield, Connecticut, the daughter of Lyman Beecher, a pragmatically inclined Congregational minister, and sister to Henry Ward Beecher, eloquent and pugnacious abolitionist. In 1832 she moved with her family to Cincinnati, where her father became head of the Lane Theological Seminary. In Cincinnati, Harriet could observe escaped slaves, and across the river in Kentucky, she could observe actual slave conditions.

In 1836 she married Calvin Stowe, a professor at Lane, and they had six children. In 1849 the family moved to Maine, where Calvin joined the Bowdoin College faculty. Harriet began writing articles and sketches about New England. In 1852 she brought out *Uncle Tom's Cabin.* The sales were staggering at home and abroad (in England, forty different publishers brought out a million and a half copies). The novel expanded and hardened northern abolitionism.

A second antislavery work, *Dred,* appeared in 1856. It was followed by a series of novels, among the best known being *The Minister's Wooing* (1859) and *Oldtown Folks* (1869). Her treatise *Lady Byron Vindicated,* in 1870, created a sensation and caused widespread resentment at her charge that Byron had committed incest with his sister Augusta. Stowe's last years were spent mostly in Florida and in increasing senility.

Portrait by Francis Holl (1815–84), stipple engraving, c. 1853,
after George Richmond (1809–96)

Unknown artist, oil on canvas, possibly based on painting by
Elisha L. Hammond (1779–1882), 1844

Frederick Douglass 1817–1895 Abolitionist, Writer, Statesman

He stood there like an African prince, conscious of his dignity and power, grand in his proportions, majestic in his wrath, as with wit, satire, and indignation he graphically described the bitterness of slavery and the humiliation of subjection to those who . . . were inferior to himself. Thus it was that I first saw Frederick Douglass.

ELIZABETH CADY STANTON, letter read at Douglass's funeral,

February 25, 1895

His photographs show him in his old age with a full mane of white hair, moustache, and full beard. He had almost a cupid's bow mouth; especially in profile his sharp nose was one of the most impressive features of a handsome man. . . . Those photographs reveal a man who has suffered much; but also a man who has conquered suffering and achieved repose through the conquest of suffering.

RAYFORD W. LOGAN, Introduction to *Life and Times of Frederick Douglass* (1962)

Born into slavery in Talbot County, Maryland. In 1826 he was sent to Baltimore, where his master's wife, Sophia Auld, began to teach him to read. After experiencing several other masters, one of whom whipped him mercilessly, Douglass made his escape in 1838 with the help of Anna Murray, a free black woman whom he shortly married.

In New Bedford, Massachusetts, Douglass made his first antislavery public talk, and soon he became the most impressive black spokesman for abolition in New England and beyond. In 1845 there appeared his autobiographical *Narrative of the Life of Frederick Douglass* (there would be two later versions). In 1847, Douglass brought out the first of his newspapers, *North Star,* and moved the family to Rochester, New York. During the Civil War he strongly supported the recruitment of black soldiers for the Union forces.

From the 1870s, Douglass was in public service, in various posts in Washington, D.C., and as U.S. minister to Haiti.

Portrait by Robert Savon Pious (1908–83), oil on canvas, 1951

Harriet Tubman c. 1821–1913 Fugitive Slave and Abolitionist

The difference between us is very marked. Most that I have done and suffered in the service of our cause has been done in public, and I have received much encouragement at every step of the way. You, on the other hand, have labored in a private way. I have wrought in the day—you in the night. I have had the applause of the crowd and the satisfaction that comes of being approved by the multitude, while the most that you have done has been witnessed by a few trembling, scarred, and footsore men and women, and whose heartfelt "*God bless you*" has been your only reward.

FREDERICK DOUGLASS, letter to Harriet Tubman,

Rochester, New York, August 29, 1868

Born a slave in Dorchester County, Maryland. Beginning in her early teens, she worked as a field hand on the plantation. In 1849 she escaped slavery by following the North Star. Soon after she began working on the Underground Railroad, sneaking back into the South to free other slaves. Relying on her wits and possessed of great stamina, she freed over three hundred slaves, thus earning the name "Moses." After the war, Sarah Hopkins (Sarah H. Bradford) wrote on Tubman's behalf *Scenes in the Life of Harriet Tubman* (1869), later revised and titled *Harriet Tubman: The Moses of Her People* (1886), the proceeds of which helped Tubman to buy a home in Auburn, New York, where she spent the last years of her life tending to children and old people without means.

Portrait by William Sartain (1843–1924), mezzotint, c. 1860,
after photograph by Mathew Brady, 1856

Jefferson Davis 1808–1889 President of the Confederate States of America

The new President of the Confederacy was no longer the young-old man of beautiful manners and the poetic glance. . . . He was now past fifty, erect but ever more gaunt-cheeked, blind in one eye, racked by murderous neuralgia, certainly neurotic in some undiagnosable way (perhaps suffering from an inner struggle of values), given to irritability that could break through his iron mask of will. Though he was capable of tact (sometimes tact in the face of severe provocation), and even of occasional humor, he lacked the indefinable sense for "handling" men, the intuitive understanding of others, and, ultimately, perhaps, self-confidence. He was incapable of catching the public imagination. He could sometimes inspire devotion, but his enclosed personality sometimes made him seem "cold as a lizard," as Sam Houston put it. . . .

Poor Davis!—he was not a modern man in any sense of the word but a conservative called to manage what was, in one sense, a revolution. Honor, perhaps, more than victory was, in the midst of ill fortune, ineptitudes, and even stupidities, his guiding star.

ROBERT PENN WARREN, *Jefferson Davis Gets His Citizenship Back* (1987)

Born in Kentucky. After graduating from West Point (1828) and serving a stint in the army, he settled on the Mississippi plantation where his kinfolk had become wealthy. He achieved hero's status in the Mexican War; then, successively, he served as senator from Mississippi (1847–51), secretary of war under Franklin Pierce (1855–57), and again as senator (1857–61). His energies were directed toward the extension of slavery into all territories.

With the start of the Civil War, Davis was chosen president of the new Confederate government by acclamation. As president he revealed an inability to handle men or to distinguish between competent and incompetent field commanders—along with dedication, fortitude, and a rocklike integrity. After the fall of Richmond, Davis was captured and imprisoned (for treason) in Fortress Monroe for two years. His postwar life was somber, physically and financially stricken. In 1978, almost a century after his death, Jefferson Davis's citizenship was restored by act of Congress.

Thomas J. "Stonewall" Jackson 1824–1863
Confederate General

He had this strange combination of religious fanaticism and a glory in battle. He loved battle. His eyes would light up. They called him "Old Blue Light" because of the way his eyes would light up in battle. He was totally fearless, and had no thought whatsoever of danger at any time when the battle was on. And he could define what he wanted to do. He said, "Once you get them running, you stay right on top of them, and that way a small force can defeat a large one every time." . . . He was not a strict disciplinarian. He would shoot men, but he didn't care how they were dressed, whether they saluted properly or any of that foolishness.

SHELBY FOOTE, in Geoffrey C. Ward, with Ken Burns and Ric Burns,
The Civil War (1990)

Born in West Virginia; an orphan and impoverished. He graduated from West Point in 1846. Early in the Civil War, at the first Battle of Bull Run, he earned his popular name when a fellow officer rallied his troops by pointing to Jackson with his brigade standing "like a stone wall." He performed brilliantly in the Shenandoah campaign with his "foot cavalry"; was disappointingly indecisive in the Seven Days Battle (summer 1862); but was again inspiringly aggressive at the second Bull Run, at Antietam, and at Fredericksburg. At Chancellorsville in early May 1863, Jackson was at the height of his inventiveness and daring; but while exploring the territory between the lines in the darkness, he was shot by one of his own men. His first wife died in 1856, within a year of their marriage; he married again in 1857. At home and with close friends, he relaxed somewhat the strict Calvinist severity of his public persona.

Portrait by Adalbert John Volck ("V. Blada," 1828–1912),
etching, 1898 (printed from 1862 plate)

Mathew Brady 1823–1896 Photographer

The skilled, hard-working and productive portraitist who spent his life creating distinctive images of others is hard to see, as if reluctant to come out from behind his camera. When Mathew Brady posed for his own portrait with his new bride and sister, he decorously placed them in the foreground; in the numerous images that show him on the field and in camp during the war, he stands at the side or turns away from the camera; occasionally he shows off his distinctive profile, but still eludes our gaze. In interviews from the 1850s, Brady is an ambitious, energetic artist. Forty years later, speaking to journalist George Alfred Townsend in his Washington studio, Brady spun a shroud of legend and anecdote from which he emerged as a genial relic, a friend to Civil War generals and antebellum celebrities.

MARY PANZER, *Mathew Brady and the Image of History* (1997)

Born of immigrant Irish parents in Warren County, New York. In the late 1830s he came to New York City as the student of the painter William Page. In 1844 he opened his own daguerreotype studio at Broadway and Fulton Street, and for twenty years was the most successful daguerreotypist in the city, with a mass of portraits of distinguished New Yorkers and visiting notables. Out of this he carved his "Gallery of Illustrious Americans." In 1853, Brady opened a second New York studio, at Broadway and Tenth Street. With the outbreak of the Civil War, Brady set himself to recording the drama photographically, working from the Washington office he had opened in 1849, and with major assistance from the exceptionally gifted Alexander Gardner. Brady employed as many as twenty teams of photographers and was personally present at Bull Run (1861), Antietam, and Fredericksburg. After the war his activities diminished, his eyesight failed, and his income vanished. Congress bought his collection in 1875 for $25,000. Brady worked for other photographers for some years and died in a New York charity ward. A standard encyclopedia calls him "perhaps the most important figure in American photographic history."

Portrait by Mathew Brady Studios (active c. 1844–83),
photograph, albumen silver print, 1861

Ulysses S. Grant 1822–1885 Civil War Leader, Eighteenth President of the United States

Ulysses Simpson Grant was the general in the civil war in the United States.

He was not as stout or as heavy or as dark or as broad a man as one might think.

He was paler and smaller and lighter and shorter and narrower than might have been thought. . . .

Grant he never said war was hell or anything new. No he just said I will fight it out on this line if it takes all summer, and he knew before he had begun that he was through of course he knew.

GERTRUDE STEIN, *Four in America* (1946)

> A quiet Man, and plain in garb—
>   Briefly he looks his fill,
> Then drops his gray eye to the ground,
>   Like a loaded mortar he is still;
> Meekness and grimness meet in him—
>   The silent general.

HERMAN MELVILLE, "The Armies of the Wilderness," in *Battle-Pieces* (1866)

Born Hiram Ulysses Grant, in Ohio; in 1839, he went to West Point, where he was renamed Ulysses Simpson Grant by clerical error. Served with an infantry regiment, in Mexico and elsewhere, until 1854. In 1848 he married Julia Dent of Missouri. In 1854–59 he worked unsuccessfully at farming, selling firewood, clerking in a leather goods store. In 1861–63 he commanded volunteer forces, with notable victories at Fort Donelson, Fort Henry, Chattanooga, and, climactically, Vicksburg, Mississippi. In early 1864 he was given command of all the Union armies. He commanded the Battle of the Wilderness, and his campaign in Virginia in 1865 led to Lee's surrender at Appomattox.

In 1868, Grant was elected president of the United States; despite a seriously marred administration, he was reelected in 1872. He completed his *Personal Memoirs* (for Mark Twain's company) shortly before his death.

Portrait by Mathew Brady (1823–96), photograph, albumen silver print, 1864

Standing, from left: O. O. Howard, W. B. Hazen (conspicuous at Stone's River, Tennessee, December 1863), Jefferson C. Davis (no relation to the Confederate statesman, a pro-slavery and pro-Union Indianian), J. A. Mowery

Seated: J. A. Logan (hero of the battle at Kenesaw Mountain, near Atlanta, in June 1864), Sherman, H. W. Slocum

Portrait by Mathew Brady Studios (active 1844–83), photograph, albumen silver print, 1865

William Tecumseh Sherman (1820–91) and His Generals

Sherman was nervous, rumpled, irritable. He wore shoes rather than military boots, slept little and talked a lot, "boiling over with ideas," a friend said, "while discussing every subject and pronouncing on all." "[He was always] too busy to eat," an aide added.

He ate hardtack, sweet potatoes, bacon, black coffee off a rough table, sitting on a crackerbox, wearing a gray flannel suit, a faded old blue blouse and trousers he had worn since long before Chattanooga. He talked and smoked cigars incessantly, giving orders, dictating telegrams, bright and chipper.

GEOFFREY C. WARD, with Ric Burns and Ken Burns, *The Civil War* (1990)

Born in Lancaster, Ohio, orphaned at age nine and raised in the home of a neighbor. Sherman graduated from West Point in 1840 and served in the Mexican War. In 1853 he left the army to pursue a banking career (unsuccessful) in San Francisco. With the outbreak of the war, he rejoined the army as a colonel. For a year he suffered from what seems to have been manic depression, and he was even pronounced "crazy" by his associates. He emerged as a major military leader at Shiloh in April 1862. Thereafter he scored key victories at Vicksburg and Chattanooga. His Atlanta campaign—May to September 1864—won Lincoln's reelection, and introduced the concept of "total war"—war on civilians and economic resources as well as enemy troops. His "march to the sea" ended at Savannah in December 1864; the following April, General Johnson surrendered to Sherman in Durham, North Carolina. After the war, Sherman served as commander-in-chief of the U.S. Army until his retirement in 1883; and in 1884 he famously refused to be nominated for president by the Republican Party.

Robert E. Lee 1807–1870 Confederate General

[Lee] was a large, austere man, and I judge difficult of approach to his subordinates. To be extolled by the entire press of the South, after every engagement, and by a portion of the press North with equal vehemence, was calculated to give him the entire confidence of his troops and to make him feared by his antagonists. It was not an uncommon thing for my staff officers to hear from Eastern officers, "Well, Grant has never met Bobby Lee yet."

ULYSSES S. GRANT, *Personal Memoirs* (1885–86)

Lee belongs, as does no other public figure of his generation, to the Roman phase of the Republic. . . . It was an instinctive emulation of his ancestors, the manifestation of a regional patriotism more deeply rooted than loyalty to the United States. Virginia regarded Virginia as itself an autonomous country, which, with the help of certain New Englanders and certain Philadelphians, had expelled the monarchical forces and established in America a republican society. . . . The same sense of honor and independence which stimulated Virginia to stand up to the Crown later spurred them to stand up to the Yankees. With Lee this was almost automatic; he had no understanding of politics, no interest in economics. He had only the ancient value and the tradition of a certain sort of role which the Lees had been appointed to play.

EDMUND WILSON, *Patriotic Gore* (1962)

Born in Virginia, the son of "Light-Horse Harry" Lee, cavalry hero in the Revolution, Lee graduated from West Point in 1829, and two years later married the plantation heiress Mary Custis. He served with distinction under Winfield Scott in the Mexican War; from 1852 to 1855 he was superintendent of West Point. But when the Civil War began, Lee, though revering the Union and said not to favor slavery, followed his Virginia homeland into the Confederacy.

As commander of the army of Northern Virginia, though suffering a grave setback at Antietam (September 1862), Lee won impressive victories—especially at Fredericksburg and (in May 1863) at Chancellorsville. There followed the disaster of Pickett's Charge at Gettysburg, several confrontations with Grant in the Wilderness campaign, and finally, with the collapse of his troops, the surrender to Grant at the Appomattox Court House, Virginia, in April 1865.

For several years afterward, Lee served as president of Washington College (later Washington and Lee) in Lexington, Virginia.

Portrait by Mathew Brady Studios (active 1844–83),
photograph, albumen silver print, 1865

Abraham Lincoln 1809–1865 Sixteenth President of the United States

He was dressed in a rusty black frock coat and pantaloons, unbrushed, and worn so faithfully that the suit had adapted itself to the curves and angularities of his figure, and had grown to be an outer skin of the man. He had shabby slippers on his feet. His hair was black, still unmixed with gray, stiff, somewhat bushy. . . .

The whole physiognomy is as coarse a one as you would meet anywhere in the length and breadth of the States; but, withal, it is redeemed, illuminated, softened, and brightened by a kindly though serious look out of his eyes, and an expression of homely sagacity that seems weighted with the results of village experience.

NATHANIEL HAWTHORNE, "Chiefly About War Matters" (1862)

I think of Lincoln, shambling, homely, with his strong, sad, deeply furrowed face all the time. I see him in the different rooms and halls. For some reason or other he is to me infinitely the most real of the dead presidents.

THEODORE ROOSEVELT to Henry S. Pritchett, December 14, 1904

And then our Lincoln. . . . He does not seem to belong in a list at all; he seems to stand unique and singular and complete in himself.

WOODROW WILSON, *Early Papers* (1960)

Born in a Kentucky log cabin, he grew up on the frontier, with virtually no schooling. In 1836 he moved to Springfield, the capital of Illinois, to practice law. Lincoln served a term in Congress; then, in 1856, as senatorial candidate for the new Republican party (his acceptance speech warned against a "house divided"), he won national attention in his debates with Stephen A. Douglas.

In 1860, helped by a Democratic split, Lincoln was elected president. During the Civil War he enormously extended the presidential powers, even while being attacked from all sides. His emphasized priority was to preserve the Union, but his Emancipation Proclamation of January 1, 1863, though assailed for referring only to the Confederate states, in fact marked the end of slavery in America. His address at Gettysburg (1863) is one of the greatest moments of American oratory. Thanks in part to Sherman's capture of Atlanta in September 1864, Lincoln easily won reelection. In his second inaugural address he spoke of "malice towards none." A month later, he was assassinated at Ford's Theatre in Washington, D.C.

Portrait by Alexander Gardner (1821–82), photograph, albumen silver print, 1865

John Wilkes Booth 1838–1865 Actor, Assassin

Through the general hum following the stage pause, with the change of positions, came the muffled sound of a pistol-shot, which not one-hundredth part of the audience heard at the time—and yet a moment's hush—somehow, surely, a vague startled thrill—and then, through the ornamented, draperied, starr'd and striped space-way of the President's box, a sudden figure, a man, raises himself with hands and feet, stands a moment on the railing, leaps below to the stage, (a distance of perhaps fourteen or fifteen feet,) falls out of position, catching his boot-heel in the copious drapery, (the American flag,) falls on one knee, quickly recovers himself, rises as if nothing had happen'd, (he really sprains his ankle, but unfelt then)—and so the figure, Booth, the murderer, dress'd in plain black broadcloth, bare-headed, with full, glossy, raven hair, and his eyes like some mad animal's flashing with light and resolution, yet with a certain strange calmness, holds aloft in one hand a large knife—walks along not much back from the footlights—turns fully toward the audience his face of statuesque beauty, lit by those basilisk eyes, flashing with desperation, perhaps insanity—launches out in a firm and steady voice the words *Sic semper tyrannis*—and then walks with neither slow nor very rapid pace diagonally across to the back of the stage, and disappears.

WALT WHITMAN, "Death of Abraham Lincoln,"
lecture delivered in New York,
April 14, 1879, and on later occasions,
in *The Collected Writings of Walt Whitman* (1964)

Born on the farm where he grew up, near Bel Air, Maryland. At seventeen he launched his stage career in Baltimore, working constantly and with great success until temporary retirement due to sickness in 1863. Acting only sporadically after that, his last performance was at Ford's Theatre on March 18, 1865. By fall 1864 he was conspiring to capture and ransom Lincoln, but some time after the war ended he revised his goal to assassination. On April 14, 1865, he snuck into the presidential box at Ford's Theatre and shot Lincoln. Jumping from the box to the stage, he caught his spur in the flag hanging from the balcony, landed off balance, and broke his leg. Nevertheless, he rose, shouted "Sic semper tyrannis!" and fled the theater. On April 26 he was trapped by a group of soldiers and detectives in a barn just south of the Rappahannock River, and refusing to surrender was killed.

J. H. Bufford and Company, (active 1835–90), lithograph, 1865,
after the photograph by Charles DeForest Fredricks

American Indian Leaders

THESE FIGURES, AS THEY PASS BEFORE US, REPRESENT KEY SUCCESSIVE MOMENTS in the history of the American Indian in North America, from the time of the Revolution to late in the nineteenth century. They represent as well a series of the geographical areas where that history was concentrated, often heroically, sometimes tragically: from western New York to the Ohio Valley, to the territories west and northwest of the Mississippi, and from Tennessee to Arizona and Texas.

The earliest of them, Joseph Brant, a Mohawk warrior from New York, actively supported the British cause during the Revolution, in the eventually blasted hope that the tribe he headed might thereby preserve their lands from colonial encroachment. Some thirty-five years later, the Shawnee leader known as the Shawnee Prophet (brother of the more famous and shorter-lived Tecumseh) similarly sought to protect his followers against American dominion, drawing on religious inspiration as well as military skill; only to have his entire force routed in 1811 by William Henry Harrison, at Tippecanoe in the Indiana territory.

Sequoyah, the great Cherokee who invented a native alphabet for tribal communications, served as a mediator between the western branch of his nation and the remnants of the eastern Cherokee tribes, which were driven from their Georgia homeland in the 1830s and harried westward along the Trail of Tears to the new settlements. Peter Pitchlynn, the diplomatically agile Choctaw chief, helped acquire new lands for his people after they were driven west of the Mississippi, and later was an effective liaison with the government in Washington.

There follow four leaders of varyingly special gifts and personalities from the post–Civil War period, a time of often bitterly intense and fast-riding and shooting conflict between Indians and whites (and the epoch most frequently and least accurately depicted by American moviemakers). Starting off is Red Cloud, probably the best-known and most powerful leader in the history of his tribe, itself the largest band of the Sioux nation. Red Cloud gained prominence in late 1866 when, in an effort to halt the building of a road from Fort Laramie, Wisconsin, to Bozeman, Montana, and the nearby gold regions, he led the way in a massacre of Colonel Fetterman and about ninety men. The action was in part a reprisal for the slaughter of six hundred Indians, the majority of them women and children, at Sandy Creek near the Arkansas River the year before; this action being commanded by one Colonel Chivington, who had been heard saying that he had come west "to kill Indians . . . it is right and honorable to use any means under God's heaven to kill Indians." Later, however, Red Cloud became a strong advocate for peace between his people and the white people, however much he distrusted the government's Indian agents. Meanwhile, the Apache chieftain Geronimo was earning a reputation as the most fearsome warrior in the southwest, spreading terror through the territories and down into Mexico. In fact, Geronimo did his periodic best to cooperate with the white military authorities, but he was invariably deceived and misled.

Sitting Bull, the renowned Sioux chief and medicine man, was forcibly opposed to any compromise with the white powers, especially as the inexorable white westward migration expanded in the 1860s and 1870s. His efforts reached a climax in June 1876 when the Sioux warriors, under Sitting Bull and Crazy Horse, destroyed General George Armstrong Custer and the Seventh American Cavalry (264 men) at the battle of Little Big Horn. Sitting Bull's enduring attitude, as our literary portrait reminds us, was that he and his people would avoid the Long Knives, the American armed troops, if they could, but "if we cannot, we will fight." It is not inappropriate that the last of the American Indian leaders whom we look at, Chief Joseph of the Nez Perce, is heard promising with sad finality: "From where the sun now stands, I will fight no more forever." The words were spoken on October 15, 1877, at the moment of Chief Joseph's surrender to Generals Miles and Howard, thirty miles from the Canadian border, and after the chief had led his band of 250 warriors, with 450 women, children, and old folk (and 2,000 horses), on a thousand-mile escape run from Oregon across Montana toward Canada.

The pictorial imaging of the American Indian forms an illuminating chapter in our cultural history. It began, effectively, around 1821 in Washington, under the auspices of Thomas L. McKenney, the first and probably the best head of the Bureau for Indian Affairs. McKenney crafted a gallery of Indian portraits, many of them by Charles Bird King, a competent local artist then in his mid-thirties; others were commissioned in the field. In 1827 congressional funding came to a halt when the congressman from Kentucky, speaking for many colleagues, denounced "the pictures of these wretches, the use of which it would be impossible to tell." McKenney was forced to resign his post in 1830; but he persisted in his general efforts, and in the years following, with the collaboration of James Hall, a Cincinnati writer who supplied the text, he produced the three-volume *Indian Tribes of North America* (1837–44).

Our first three portraits come from this landmark collection: Joseph Brant, the Shawnee Prophet, and Sequoyah. All three in fact are copies of copies. The King originals were copied by Henry Inman, a popular and versatile artist (and founder of the National Academy of Design); and these in turn were lithographed by four skilled artists, chief among them Albert Newman.

Peter Pitchlynn, next to appear, is portrayed by George Catlin (1796–1872), Pennsylvania-born, who grew up on Indian legends and who, in 1830, set forth to become the "historian" of the Indian race in America, dedicated to "rescuing from oblivion the looks and customs of the vanishing race of native man in America." He painted more than six hundred portraits of Indian men and women; the pictures and his accounts of his travels in search of Indian subjects constitute an archival treasure.

Photography is the source of the portrait of Red Cloud, seen with Yale University professor O. C. Marsh in the latter's town, New Haven, Connecticut, a pipe of peace between them. Sitting Bull is likewise seen in a photograph; this one by Rudolf Cronau, a correspondent from a German magazine (and bespectacled, hence instantly renamed Iron Eyes), who came to Fort Randall in 1881 to depict Sitting Bull and others.

Geronimo is memorialized in a bronze bust of very recent years, 1986; a work intended to commemorate the Apache leader's betrayal and defeat (by General Miles). So announced its creator, Allan Houser, one of the country's leading sculptors, winner of countless awards and honors, himself of Apache descent—his father served as Geronimo's interpreter during their years of captivity together.

Chief Joseph, finally, is present in a photogravure of 1903 (the year before his death) by Edward Sheriff Curtis, a man of remarkable vitality and ambition. Between 1909 and 1930, Curtis wrote, illustrated, and published twenty volumes of Indian portraits in *The North American Indian*, the aim of which was to capture a "vision of a vanishing race." J. P. Morgan funded this immense undertaking, and Theodore Roosevelt wrote the introduction.

American Indians also have been portrayed in *moving* pictures, from the first days of the film industry. Some of these films are well made (think of *Stagecoach* and *The Searchers*), but for the most part they are woefully off the mark as reflections of history, and they suffer inevitably from being almost exclusively the white man's view of things. This is even true of the recent *Dances with Wolves*, with its earnest effort to sympathize with Indian ways; and it is true, to some extent, of the literary portraits in this section.

The radically contradictory perspectives of white commentators is illustrated in our first entry, with the virulent image of Joseph Brant in the 1830s balanced by the more admiring verdict of a modern biographer. The personalities of the Shawnee Prophet, Geronimo, and Sitting Bull are also reconsidered in well-researched biographies of our time. Sequoyah is seen (quite shrewdly) in a contemporary account, as quoted in a later biography. Peter Pitchlynn is handsomely described "from life" by Charles Dickens, from his American travel notes in 1842. Sitting Bull is heard briefly in his own words; and a century later, Robert Penn Warren, in his last completed long poem, gives us the voice of Chief Joseph in a moment of endless resonance.

Note: The National Portrait Gallery owns about a dozen portraits of Indian figures beyond those in this section. They include Tecumseh, the bold Shawnee chief (his picture is too faded for satisfactory reproduction); Black Hawk, the Sauk leader who initiated the disastrous Black Hawk war of 1832, and later wrote a much-valued autobiography; the attractive Seminole figure Osceola, who was viciously betrayed by federal forces and died in a South Carolina prison in 1838; Billy Bowlegs, who managed to hold off the removal of his Seminole tribe from Florida to Oklahoma for two decades; and the Senecan athlete Lewis Bennett, called Deerfoot because of his extraordinary ability as a long-distance runner—in England, in the early 1860's he set new records for ten and twelve-mile runs.

Joseph Brant [Thayendanegea] 1742–1807 Mohawk Leader

Brant was the war chief of [the Six Nations, in 1775], and was employed chiefly . . . in pillaging and murdering a defenceless people, with whom his own followers had been living on friendly terms, and with whom they had no quarrel. . . . He ravaged the fields and burned the dwellings of our people; he stole upon them in the defenceless hours of the night, and slaughtered men, women and children, or carried them to a captivity worse than death. . . . He carried the horrors of war to the fireside and the altar, burned churches and granaries, and practiced all the cruelties of savage warfare.

THOMAS L. MCKENNEY AND JAMES HALL,
The Indian Tribes of North America, vol. 3 (1834)

In the opinion of many historians, Joseph Brant is the only true statesman the American Indian tribes have ever produced. . . .

He was a brave warrior. Yet religious training helped him to be merciful in battle. . . .

Because he fought with the British, Brant is not generally considered one of our American heroes. But he can be judged—fairly—as a remarkable enemy and a great man.

JOHN JAKES, *Mohawk: The Life of Joseph Brant* (1969)

Born in western New York, the son of a Mohawk chief; his family name derived from his mother's second husband, Nikus Brant, also a Mohawk. Brant grew up in the home of his sister and her husband, Sir William Johnson, in charge of Indians in northern Ohio. He later attended a school in Connecticut, where he learned to read and write English. During the Revolution he was a commissioned colonel in the British forces, and he organized and led a series of lively skirmishes against colonial settlements. His belief both in the British and their protection of Indian lands was shattered by events. After the war he lived on a pension and a large gift of land in Ontario, Canada.

THAYENDANEGEA
THE GREAT CAPTAIN OF THE SIX NATIONS

PUBLISHED BY F. W. GREENOUGH, PHILAD.ª
Drawn Printed & Coloured at I.T.Bowens Lithographic Establishment N.º 94 Walnut St.
Entered according to act of Congress in the Year 1838 by F.W.Greenough, in the Clerks Office of the District Court of the Eastern District of Penn.ª

Unidentified lithographer, 1838, after Charles Bird King (1785–1862); published
in McKenney and Hall, *Indian Tribes of North America,* vol. 2

The Shawnee Prophet [Tenskwatawa]
c. 1775–1836 Shawnee Leader

On an April evening in 1805, in his Ohio Valley wigwam, the young Shawnee fell uncon-scious before his fireplace.

At first the neighboring Shawnees were skeptical that Lalawethika (the Noisemaker) was seriously ill. Most knew him as a notorious alcoholic and assumed that Lalawethika had fallen into a drunken stupor. . . . [But] slowly regaining his senses, Lalawethika told a strange tale of death, heaven and resurrection. The Shawnee claimed that the Master of Life had sent two handsome young men to carry his soul into the spirit world, where he had been shown both the past and the future. . . . He was permitted to gaze on a paradise, which he described as "a ripe, fertile country, abounding in game, fish, pleasant hunting grounds and fine corn fields. . . ." The souls of sinful tribesmen also followed the road toward paradise, but after glimpsing the promised land they were forced to turn away . . . and were subjected to fiery torture. . . .

A changed man, he no longer was the drunken braggart known as Lalawethika. Henceforward he would be called Tenskwatawa (the Open Door), a name symbolizing his new role as a holy man destined to lead his people down the narrow road toward paradise.

R. DAVID EDMUNDS, *The Shawnee Prophet* (1983)

Born near present-day Springfield, Ohio, the son of a Shawnee chief. After a Shawnee debacle in 1794, he became a drunkard and a braggart, and lost the sight of an eye. In February 1806 he under-went a remarkable mystical experience, a vision of the next world, and as a result of it began to preach a return to Shawnee rites and customs. He became a Shawnee leader as a religious prophet and, with his brother Tecumseh, an organizer of confederated Indian resistance to white encroach-ment. During his brother's absence in 1811, Tenskwatawa led an ill-advised raid on the troops of William Henry Harrison; his band was overwhelmed at Tippecanoe Creek in Indiana. Tenskwatawa fled to Canada, returning finally in 1826 to settle in Wyandotte, Kansas.

Portrait by Henry Inman (1801–46), oil on canvas, c. 1830, after Charles Bird King
(1785–1862); published in McKenney and Hall, *Indian Tribes of North America,* vol. 1

Attributed to Henry Inman (1801–46), oil on canvas, 1837, after Charles Bird King (1785–1862); published in McKenney and Hall, *Indian Tribes of North America,* vol. 1

Sequoyah 1770?–1843 Indian Statesman and Educator

In 1840, Sequoyah visited John Howard Payne, a historian of the Cherokee people, at the Arkansas home of Cherokee Chief John Ross, with an interpreter in attendance. Payne's account follows.

We were all in the cockloft of Mr. Ross's story and a half log house, where the light and wind entered through thousands of chinks. Guess [Sequoyah] sat in one corner of the fireplace and I on the opposite side at a desk; the other two between. Guess had a turban of roses and posies upon a white ground girding his venerable gray hairs; and a long dark blue robe, bordered around the lower edge and the cuffs, with black. . . . He had a long dusky white bag of sumac with him, and a long Indian pipe, and smoked incessantly, replenishing his pipe from his bag. His air was altogether what we picture to ourselves of an old Greek philosopher. He talked and gesticulated very gracefully—his voice alternately swelling—and then sinking to a whisper—and his eyes firing up and then its wild flashes subsiding into a gentle & most benignant smile.

JOHN HOWARD PAYNE, quoted in Grant Foreman, *Sequoyah* (1938)

Born in a village near the Tennessee River. His mother was the sister of seven Cherokee chiefs; his father was a white man named Nathaniel Gist (an associate of Washington's). Sequoyah was a man of many skills: hunter, farmer, mechanic, silversmith, and painter. But an injury had left him lame; and he gradually became convinced of the relation between the ability to write and the acquisition of power. After twelve years' intensive work, 1809–21, Sequoyah created a Cherokee alphabet of eighty-six symbols, each (but one) representing a syllable of spoken language. Eventually, almost all Cherokees could communicate in the language; in 1828 the *Cherokee Phoenix*, a Cherokee-English weekly paper, began printing. Sequoyah was also active in negotiating treaties about the location of the displaced eastern and the western Cherokees. A memorial was erected in Washington in his honor, and the redwood Sequoia of California is named for him.

Portrait by George Catlin (1796–1872), oil on canvas, c. 1834

Peter Perkins Pitchlynn [Ha-Tchoc-Tuck-Nee]
1806–1881 Choctaw Statesman

There chanced to be on board this boat, in addition to the usual dreary crowd of passengers, one Pitchlynn, a chief of the Choctaw tribe of Indians, who *sent in his card* to me, and with whom I had the pleasure of a long conversation.

He spoke English perfectly well, though he had not begun to learn the language, he told me, until he was a young man grown. He had read many books; and Scott's poetry appeared to have left a strong impression on his mind. . . .

He was a remarkably handsome man: some years past forty I should judge; with long black hair, an aquiline nose, broad cheek-bones, a sunburnt complexion, and a very bright, keen, dark, and piercing eye. There were but twenty thousand of the Choctaws left, he said, and their number was decreasing every day. A few of his brother chiefs had been obliged to become civilised, and to make themselves acquainted with what the whites knew, for it was their only chance of existence.

CHARLES DICKENS, *American Notes* (1842)

Born in Mississippi, the son of a Choctaw woman and a white agent for the federal government. He made his way one hundred miles to a school in Tennessee. Later, as a farmer in Mississippi, he married a white woman in a Christian ceremony. Pitchlynn's growing interest in education led him to found a school for Indian children in Kentucky. After removing, with his family, to Indian territory, he became the elected chief of the Choctaw tribes, overseeing treaties and representing his followers in Washington. After his death in Washington, he was buried in the Congressional Cemetery. He was perhaps the best-liked and most outgoing of the leading Indian chiefs of his time, among both Indians and whites—and despite his proper Indian name, Ha-Tchoc-Tuck-Nee (Snapping Turtle).

Red Cloud [Mahpina-Luta] 1822–1909 Sioux Chief

Red Cloud's father was a big chief, but the son had to fight hard and do great deeds of valor before he became the acknowledged head chief of the whole Sioux nation. This was what he had accomplished at the age of thirty years. He was a magnificent specimen of physical manhood and, when in his prime, as full of action as a tiger. As a young man he was a terror in war with other tribes. The old warriors who fought by his side have told me of his killing five Pawnees in one fight, using only his knife as a weapon after sending one arrow from his bow. . . .

His friendship for me saved not only my own life, but also the lives of several other cowboys who, with me, once took a bunch of Indian contract cattle into their country; so that I have occasion to be most grateful to him.

JAMES H. COOK, *Fifty Years on the Frontier* (1923)

Born in north-central Nebraska, the descendant of distinguished Sioux families. He ultimately became the outstanding figure in the history of the Sioux nation; his name may have come from the cloud of red blankets worn by his men as they swept across the plains. His vigorous opposition to the western expansion of the whites took active form in 1865–66, when he forcibly prevented the construction of the Powder River road from Wyoming into Montana and the gold territory. In August 1867, Red Cloud led an attack on a circuit of wagons in the Sullivan Hills; the Sioux were mowed down (1,200 lost) by the new breech-loading rifles used by Major Powell's men. Red Cloud was a peace advocate after that. He became friendly with several serious and sympathetic white persons: among them the Nebraska cattle rancher Captain James Cook, who wrote eloquently about Red Cloud in his memoirs; and Professor O. C. Marsh of Yale, who came out to search for Indian fossils. In 1878, Red Cloud retired to the reservation at Pine Ridge, South Dakota; but he traveled regularly over the next years, to Washington as Indian spokesman and conferee, to New York, and to Yale and New Haven. Many of his views and memories have been recorded.

Unidentified photographer, 1883. Red Cloud with Othniel Charles Marsh,
paleontologist, Yale professor, and Smithsonian member,
in New Haven, Connecticut.

Rommler and Jones lithography company, colored collotype, 1885,
after Rudolf Cronau (1855–?)

Sitting Bull [Tatanka Iyotanka] 1831?–1890 Sioux Warrior

In May 1879, Stanley Huntley of the Chicago Tribune *obtained an interview with the Sioux chief, at a point just south of the Canadian border.*

His black, piercing eyes especially struck Huntley, who thought the heavy lids hung down at the corners "as if the brain had escaped into them." Stocky, muscular, with "awfully dirty" hands, Sitting Bull was garbed in blue leggings, beaded moccasins, a skin shirt, and a blanket loosely drawn about his waist.

On the hunt: "I am a hunter, and will hunt as long as there is wild game on the prairie. When the buffalo is gone I will send my children on the prairie to hunt mice."

On Indian agencies in the United States: "I never wanted to go to a gift-house, and I never will. They want my people to farm. I will not farm."

And on the Long Knives [American troops] even then assembling to force the Sioux from the buffalo herds: "We will avoid them if we can. If we cannot, we will fight."

Ever since 1870, that had been Sitting Bull's creed and practice.

ROBERT M. UTLEY, The Lance and the Shield (1993)

A member of the same tribe, Hunkpapa Sioux, dominated by the somewhat older Red Cloud. In 1876 a government edict ordered all Indian hunting bands to report to reservations. In support of this order, a large gathering of U.S. forces converged on Bighorn Valley in eastern Montana. On June 25, 1876, General George Custer led an attack on the Sioux encampment along the Little Big Horn River; the force was annihilated and General Custer killed in one of the historical Indian victories. It was also one of the last. After passing a period of near starvation in Canada, Sitting Bull surrendered in the summer of 1881 and was sent to the Standing Rock Reservation between North and South Dakota. For a year, 1885–86, he traveled with Buffalo Bill's Wild West Show. In October 1890, during a dispute over Sioux Ghost Dance ceremonies, Sitting Bull and several of his tribesmen were killed by Indian policemen sent by the U.S. government agent to arrest them.

Geronimo [Goyathlay] 1829–1909 Apache Chief

In the publicity that marked his arrival at Fort Sill [Oklahoma, 1894], Geronimo appeared as the bloody stereotype of the savage Indian. . . . [Artist E. A. Burbank arrived from Chicago to paint Geronimo's portrait.] Burbank was glad that the "bloodthirsty savage" was in prison so that he could safely paint him behind bars. Arriving at the post, he learned that the captive lived in his own house and enjoyed the freedom of the reservation. . . . Geronimo was out hunting his horses. He soon came riding up, "an elderly Indian, short, but well built and muscular. His keen, shrewd face was deeply furrowed with strong lines. His small black eyes were watery, but in them there burned a fierce light. . . ."

Gambling also . . . brought out Geronimo's latent fierceness. Once he invited Burbank to accompany him to a sports meet, probably the annual Fourth of July field day at the post, with horse races and other contests between the soldiers and the Kiowas and Comanches. There he joined a game of monte, dealing the cards expertly with his small quick hands and shouting at the top of his voice as he raked in his winnings.

ANGIE DEBO, *Geronimo: The Man, His Time, His Place* (1976)

Born in Arizona of Apache descent. In the late 1850s, Geronimo's wife, their three children, and his mother were slaughtered by Mexicans. Geronimo gained his reputation as the most fearsome of the Apache leaders during the period 1866–86, when he led innumerable raids on U.S. troops and American settlements, but he also made frequent vengeful raids into Mexico. In the early 1880s he was persuaded by the well-disposed General George F. Crook to withdraw to a farm near Fort Apache; but he left there in 1885 and hid out with a small band until he was promised safe settlement on an Apache reservation. General Nelson Miles, who then took over the negotiations, betrayed Geronimo several turns thereafter, and Geronimo ended up not in Apache country but at Fort Sill, Oklahoma. Here he farmed, lived not altogether uncomfortably, joined the Dutch Reform Church, and dictated his autobiography (to S. M. Barrett).

Portrait by Allan Houser (1914–94), bronze, 1986

Chief Joseph *[Heinmot Tooyalakekt]* 1841–1904
Nez Perce Chief

> . . . Joseph, not straight, sits his mount,
> Head forward bowed, scalp-lock with otter-skin tied.
>
> Black braids now framed a face past pain.
> Hands loose before him, the death-giving rifle
> Loose-held across, he comes first.
> The bullet scar is on his brow . . .
>
>   Arrow-straight
> He suddenly sits, head now lifted. With perfect ease,
> To the right he swings a buckskinned leg over . . .
>
> Standing straight, he thrusts out his rifle,
> Muzzle-grounded, to Howard. It is
> The gesture, straight-flung, of one who casts the world away . . .
>
>   His heart gives words.
> But the words, translated, are addressed to Howard . . .
>
> *Hear me, my chiefs, I am tired. Heart is sick and sad.*
> *From where the sun now stands, I will fight no more forever.*
>
> Robert Penn Warren, *Chief Joseph of the Nez Perce* (1983),
> at the moment of Chief Joseph's surrender to General Howard
> at Bear Paws Mountain, Montana, October 1877

Born in Wallowa Valley in eastern Oregon. At age thirty he became chief of the tribe known as Nez Perce on the death of his father, Old Joseph. Chief Joseph headed a band of one thousand who refused to accept an 1863 treaty, which proposed drastically reducing the tribe's land holdings. For years Chief Joseph and his followers managed to resist the white demands; but in 1877, the chief decided to make for Canada, to join Sitting Bull and the Sioux. The chief, in a classic feat, led the tribe some 1,500 miles across Idaho and Montana, until, in October, and with many of the tribe sick or wounded, he surrendered to General Howard at Bear Paws Mountain, near Chinook. After a series of broken promises, the chief and his tribe were finally taken to the Colville Reservation in Washington, where Chief Joseph died of what was said to be a broken heart.

Portrait by Edward Sheriff Curtis (1868–1952), photogravure, 1903

The Gilded Decades

"MONEY IS THE ROMANCE, THE POETRY OF OUR AGE," SAYS THE WEALTHY Boston Brahmin Bromfield Corey in William Dean Howells's 1885 novel, *The Rise of Silas Lapham.* Money exerted the greatest appeal in America during the decades following the Civil War, and it is the primary theme of this section: money, and the varying ways of pursuing it—some of them distinctly criminal, some spectacular, innovative, and entertaining. The spirit of the time was captured, and the period given its title, by the careening novel *The Gilded Age,* written jointly by Mark Twain and Charles Dudley Warner.

We start off with three of the most accomplished moneymakers in our history, their careers covering several generations: Cornelius Vanderbilt, who made a fortune out of transportation—ferryboats and steamboats, and then railroads; John D. Rockefeller, who in effect created the oil industry; and J. P. Morgan, who went to the heart of things, to money itself, eventually founding what became the most powerful banking house in the world.

Then there were those who contributed to the romance of the age in a lawless manner. One of the most famous was Jesse James of Missouri, who, with his brother Frank and others in the James band, began to rob banks and then trains in the late 1860s. Jesse was shot and killed by a member of his gang in 1882; his visage is seen just after that event. Another legendary moneymaker of criminal practice, likewise cherished by many but on the eastern-urban scene, was Boss Tweed, whose crafty fraudulence is said to have cost New Yorkers up to $200 million.

The age bore witness as well to individuals who spoke and acted for the betterment of society, rather than for wealth and privilege. Among the most devoted of these was Elizabeth Cady Stanton, who appears here in all her solid benevolence. Stanton, with several others, moved on logically from the prewar antislavery movement to the issue of women's rights, inspired to a degree by Lucretia Mott (seen earlier) and sustained at every turn by Susan B. Anthony (who deserves her own place in these pages).

Meriwether Lewis appears in this section, out of place chronologically—the great expedition he led with William Clark through the Dakotas, Montana, Idaho, and Oregon to the Pacific Ocean occurred in 1804–6—but he can stand for, and at the head of, the enormous westward movement, the conquest of the west that continued through much of the century. An appropriate successor to Lewis is John Muir, seen here in a portrait by Orlando Rouland: after making what became known as the "1,000 mile walk" from Kentucky to Florida, Muir turned his attention westward and in 1886 arrived in California and had his first glimpse of the Sierra Nevada. Out of the event, belatedly, came the Sierra

Club, the most important element in the country's burgeoning conservationist movement; and Muir is probably our finest nature writer, after Thoreau.

But the westernizing enthusiasm could be moneymaking too, as was aptly perceived by William Frederick Cody, who—after a career as an expert buffalo hunter and taking the name Buffalo Bill—created a traveling Wild West exhibition. For a period in the 1880s, Sitting Bull was one of the show's star attractions. Cody took the exhibition to Europe, where it was also a box-office hit, as is suggested in our portrait of Buffalo Bill in the exceedingly graceful poster based on the painting by the French artist Rosa Bonheur.

Profitable showmanship on a large scale was similarly practiced by Phineas T. Barnum of Connecticut, co-originator of the Barnum & Bailey Circus, the "Greatest Show on Earth." With his midget Tom Thumb and his elephant Jumbo and other phenomena, Barnum, in the words of his biographer Neil Harris, invented the idea of "mass amusement."

A very different kind of showmanship was displayed by Edwin Booth, a supremely gifted actor, remembered especially for his Shakespearean roles and above all as Hamlet. Booth, it may be said, survived the shattering disaster of his brother John Wilkes's assassination of Lincoln, though it evidently deepened the congenital sadness of his visage.

Artists and writers, too, could be performers: the age provided no more histrionic personality than James Abbott McNeill Whistler. Mark Twain, another classic showman, joins our other two fiction writers, William Dean Howells and Henry James, in compiling the literary record of the age of money. (Howells, in his Utopian novel of 1894, *A Traveler from Altruria*, also supplied one of the chief literary antidotes to the age.)

We are introduced to "twelve well-known American authoresses," in the phrase describing the composite photograph arranged by Eugene l'Africain in Montreal in 1884. They are mostly New Englanders; women writers had not yet begun to emerge from more distant places, as men had been doing. Several could be described as activists, for women's suffrage or for the rights of American Indians (the far-seeing Helen Hunt Jackson). Harriet Beecher Stowe has her place in an earlier section; and it was an arguable decision not to include Julia Ward Howe, admirable suffragist and author of "The Battle Hymn of the Republic." Sarah Orne Jewett would probably be on our list, were a Gallery portrait available, and we similarly regret the absence of Stephen Crane and Kate Chopin.

The portraits themselves vary between "high art" and the popular culture of the day: a mix notable almost everywhere else on the cultural scene. The portrait of John D. Rockefeller, approaching eighty, was made in 1918 by John Singer Sargent and then used as the basis of a wood engraving by Timothy Cole. Another international composition is the etching of Whistler, formerly of Massachusetts, by Mortimer Menpes, formerly of Australia and later a devoted student of the American artist. Anna Elizabeth Klumpke painted her portrait of Elizabeth Cady Stanton in 1889, the same year Bonheur did her beguiling portrait of Buffalo Bill. At a later moment Klumpke wrote to ask whether she might make a portrait of Bonheur. She was invited to do so, moved in with the older woman, eventually inherited Bonheur's chateau at the edge of the Fontainebleau forest, and wrote a biography (1908) of her patroness.

The finest single work in this section is the bas-relief at once delicate and animated of Howells and his daughter Mildred, done in 1898 by Augustus Saint-Gaudens. The latter had long been acknowledged as America's leading sculptor. His memorial to Colonel Robert Shaw and the 54th (Black) Regiment had been unveiled in Boston the previous May; William James spoke at the ceremony.

At a distinct cultural remove, yet hardly less engrossing, is the picture of Jesse James; it served as the cover of *Frank Leslie's Illustrated Newspaper* two weeks after the shooting. The vivacious engraving of P. T. Barnum—"blowing with all his might, for his 'happy family,' the confiding public"—adorned the cover of the September 13, 1862, issue of *Vanity Fair,* a spirited but short-lived (1859–62) magazine that featured cartoons and pungent satire. In like manner, the head and face of the Honorable William M. Tweed occupies the title sheet for the song "Solid Men to the Front / Quickstep," composed and dedicated to Tweed by Charles S. Grafulla. This fulsome tribute—displaying among other things an Indian peace pipe and liberty cap atop a pole—was put together in 1870, the same year that Tweed came under ferocious attack by Thomas Nast and the *New York Times.*

Photography, in these years, became ever more central to the art of portraiture. The two pictures by Napoleon Sarony, both made in 1870, of Cornelius Vanderbilt and Edwin Booth, show that sense of intense alertness which was Sarony's specialty. Sarony, himself an exuberantly showmanlike character, was the first important photographic chronicler of the American stage. A generation later the young artist Alvin Langdon Coburn was coming into his own with portraits of Henry James (1906) and Mark Twain (1908).

It is with the impressively forceful image of J. P. Morgan in 1903 that one of the country's premier photographers makes his appearance here: Edward Steichen, who had only recently been a founding member of the organization called Photo-Secession, directed by Alfred Stieglitz and dedicated to the principle (still not sufficiently acknowledged) of photography as a fine art.

Among the verbal imagings, a fast-spiraling little poem by e. e. cummings on Buffalo Bill pairs off with an anonymous ballad mythologizing Jesse James. A literary reflection by Henry James on his friend Howells is matched by Edith Wharton's reflection on her friend James. Howells and Twain exchange opinions of each other, as it were. The distinguished novelist and social historian Louis Auchincloss glances back at Cornelius Vanderbilt; and one of the sweeping impressionistic biographies that give John Dos Passos's trilogy *USA* its modernist tone is the source for a profile of J. P. Morgan. In another mode, a "phrenological reading" (a once popular practice) offers hints about the character of Elizabeth Cady Stanton. And Edward Hoagland, one of the leading nature writers of our own time, provides a new and compelling portrait of his distinguished predecessor John Muir.

Portrait by Napoleon Sarony (1821–96), photograph, albumen silver print, 1870

Cornelius Vanderbilt 1794–1877 Financier

He was a tall, thin six feet one, a great height for a man born in the eighteenth century (1794) to have attained. He had a clear complexion, ruddy cheeks, a large bold head, a strong nose, square jaw, a high, confidence-inspiring brow, and thick, long gray hair, which turned magnificently white. If he gave his mornings to business, he was never a grind. In the afternoons, at least in his later years, he drove out with his trotters, racing anyone encountered along the road who would accept the challenge, and was not averse to dashing across a grade crossing before a charging locomotive. At night he drank whiskey and played whist with his cronies.

LOUIS AUCHINCLOSS, *The Vanderbilt Era* (1989)

Born on Staten Island, New York, of Dutch descent (the name was originally written van der Bilt). At age sixteen, untutored and nearly illiterate, he started a ferry service Manhattan, then acquired several schooners for the coastal trade. In 1829 he set up a line of steamboats between New York and Philadelphia. By the late 1840s he was a millionaire and was addressed as "Commodore." The gold rush to California led him to build fast steamships to Nicaragua, from which roads were constructed to the west coast. Vanderbilt then turned his attention to railroads. By 1865 he controlled two lines connecting New York and Albany, and by 1869 he had taken over the New York Central with service to Chicago. Late in life he gave a million dollars to what became Vanderbilt University in Nashville, Tennessee. At his death in 1877 he was the richest man in New York City. He left $90 million to his son William Henry, who soon doubled it.

Portrait by Timothy Cole (1852–1931), wood engraving, 1921–24,
after John Singer Sargent (1856–1925), 1918

John D. Rockefeller 1839–1937 Industrialist

I am having a very good, though intellectually a strenuous, time here. Strong is excellent, his wife sweet, and glorious old John D. still sweeter, a most loveable personality, whom you must steel yourself to hear me praise without protesting or wincing. He confided his secretest sorrows, financial and moral, to me yesterday, and I should like to borrow him for a year from Strong, as a father-in-law, to get better acquainted with so complex, subtle, oily, fierce, strongly good and strongly bad a human being.

WILLIAM JAMES to Alice Gibbens James, April 11, 1904

While his subtle, ruminative, daring mind solved large problems by an acid process of thought, he presented to the world a front of silence which was like smooth steel.

ALLAN NEVINS, *Study in Power* (1959)

Born in Richford, New York, the son of a farmer and local trader. Rockefeller had virtually no formal schooling. In 1859 he established a successful business partnership dealing in farm goods. In 1864 he married Laura Spelman; they had four children.

Rockefeller's enormous wealth came principally from oil, through the creation of oil refineries in the early 1860s and in 1870 of the Standard Oil Company of Ohio. Within a decade Standard Oil, largely through Rockefeller's extraordinary managerial skills, dominated both the American and the foreign oil markets.

In 1897, Rockefeller retired from business and gave himself to carefully arranged philanthropies. He helped found the University of Chicago with a gift of $600,000 (the family later gave $80 million); and went on to found other entities, the Rockefeller Institute for Medical Research and the Rockefeller Foundation "to promote the well-being of mankind throughout the world."

J. P. Morgan 1837–1913 Financier

J. Pierpont Morgan was a bullnecked irascible man with small black magpie's eyes and a growth on his nose; he let his partners work themselves to death over the detailed routine of banking, and sat in the back office smoking black cigars; when there was something to be decided he said Yes or No or just turned his back and went back to his solitaire.

Every Christmas his librarian read him Dickens's *A Christmas Carol* from the original manuscript.

He was fond of canary birds and pekinese dogs and liked to take pretty actresses yachting. Each *Corsair* was a finer vessel than the last.

JOHN DOS PASSOS, *1919* (1932)

Mr. Morgan was dynamic both in intelligence and in will. . . . The boldest man was likely to become timid under his piercing gaze. The most impudent or recalcitrant were ground to humility as he chewed truculently at his big black cigar. The lesser monarchs of finance, of insurance, of transportation, of individual enterprise, each in his own domain haughty as Lucifer, were glad to stand in the corridor waiting their turn . . . while he sat at his desk in his library room within, looking hastily through the pile of newly bound volumes which the binder had sent for his inspection.

EDWARD MITCHELL, newspaper editor, quoted in Andrew Sinclair,
Corsair: The Life of J. Pierpont Morgan (1981)

Born in Hartford, Connecticut, the son of Junius Spencer Morgan, himself the son of a successful man of business affairs (hotels and fire insurance). The elder Morgan became the partner of George Peabody in the latter's London bank in 1854, and young Pierpont began his career in London in 1856 (after schooling in Switzerland and Germany). He later acted as the New York agent of the London firm, founded his own firm of Morgan and Drexel in 1871, and in 1895 created the internationally powerful banking house of J. P. Morgan.

The buying and reorganization of large railroad systems contributed to Morgan's wealth and influence. During the government crisis of 1895, Morgan virtually rescued the national treasury via a loan of $65 million in gold, taking hugely profitable bonds in return. He came to the rescue again in the panic of 1907, by which time he was, in one historian's phrase, the "supreme symbol of financial power" in the public mind. A congressional investigation of 1912 into financial dealings left him unscathed.

Morgan was perhaps the leading art collector of his time. His holdings formed the Pierpont Morgan Wing at the Metropolitan Museum. The Pierpont Morgan Library is another legacy.

Portrait by Edward Steichen (1879–1973), photogravure, 1903

Unidentified artist, wood engraving, after a photograph by Alexander Lozo,
published in *Frank Leslie's Illustrated Newspaper,*
New York, April 22, 1882

Jesse Woodson James 1847–1882 Outlaw

Jesse James was a lad who killed many a man.
He robbed the Glendale train.
He stole from the rich and he gave to the poor,
He'd a hand and a heart and a brain.

Chorus:
> Jesse had a wife to mourn for his life
> Three children, they were brave.
> But that dirty little coward that shot Mr. Howard,
> Has laid Jesse James in his grave.

Jesse was a man, a friend to the poor.
He'd never see a man suffer pain.
And with his brother Frank he robbed the Chicago bank,
And stopped the Glendale train.

"Ballad of Jesse James," in Homer Croy,
Jesse James Was My Neighbor (1949)

The worst man, without exception, in America. He is utterly devoid of fear, and has no more compunction about cold-blooded murder than he has about eating his breakfast.

ALLAN PINKERTON, detective, quoted in
Croy, *Jesse James Was My Neighbor*

Born in Clay County, Missouri. Involved as a boy in the violent Missouri-Kansas border fighting; his family was partisan to the Confederate cause and as a result suffered at the hands of the Union militia. In retaliation Jesse joined his brother Frank in the guerrilla forces of William Quantrill and "Bloody" Bill Anderson. In the years after the Civil War he was declared an outlaw. He became leader of the James band (which included Frank James and the Younger brothers), robbing banks and trains in the South and West.

In July 1881 the governor of Missouri, Thomas Crittenden, stung by the state's reputation for banditry and crime, met with railroad and express company officials and offered a reward for the capture of the band. Bob Ford, a recent recruit with brother Charlie to the James gang, in April 1882 shot and killed Jesse when his back was turned. His death by a traitor contributed to his popular heroic image.

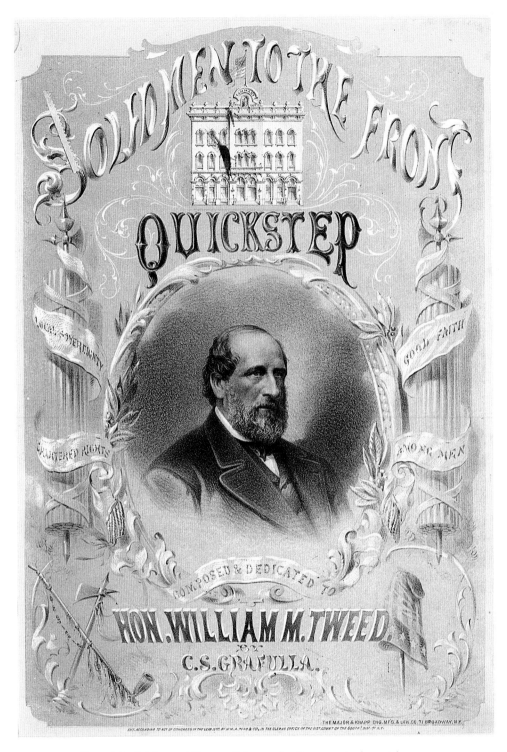

Portrait by Major and Knapp, lithograph, 1870; music sheet title page:
"Solid Men to the Front / Quickstep"

William Marcy "Boss" Tweed 1823–1878 Political Boss

He had a booming hearty personality that befitted his physique. For William Marcy Tweed looked like something that God hacked out with a dull axe. A craggy hulk of a man, he was nearly six feet tall and weighed almost 300 pounds. Everything about him was big; fists, shoulders, head (which sprouted receding reddish-brown hair, like weeds growing from a rock, carved into a moustache and closely cropped chin whiskers); eyes blue and friendly; the diamond, which "glittered like a planet on his shirt front"; and his nose, a particularly rocky pinnacle. "His nose is half-Brougham, half-Roman," said one observer, "and a man with a nose of that sort is not a man to be trifled with!"

ALEXANDER B. CALLOW, JR., *The Tweed Ring* (1966)

Tweed's impudent serenity is sublime. Were he not a supreme scoundrel, he would be a great man.

GEORGE TEMPLETON STRONG, quoted in Callow, *Tweed Ring*

Born in New York City, the grandson of an immigrant Scottish blacksmith. At age twenty-seven he was elected as one of the city's forty aldermen, a group later known as the Forty Thieves. He served in Congress briefly (1853–55) but then renewed his energetic interest in the city's politics and money. By 1860 he had gained control of Tammany Hall, the headquarters of the city's Democratic politicians, and soon he had absolute control of the party. Through a variety of large-scale fraudulent transactions, Tweed and his associates—known as the Tweed Ring—fleeced the city of an amount that has been reckoned as high as $200 million. Among other ventures, he took over the city's entire printing industry; blackmailed wealthy capitalists; and oversaw the building of a new county courthouse, himself taking $8 million of the $12 million cost.

In 1870 he came under attack for what amounted to criminal dishonesty: first by the cartoonist Thomas Nast of *Harper's Weekly* and then by the *New York Times,* whose owner, George Jones, turned down a $5 million offer by the Tweed Ring to cease its attack. In 1873 Tweed was tried and convicted on various charges, then his sentence was reduced to one year, with a fine of $250. He escaped to Spain but was brought back and again sent to prison, where he died. Tweed was married in 1854 to Mary Jane Shakden, who bore him eight children and died in 1880.

Portrait by Anna Elizabeth Klumpke (1856–1942), oil on canvas, 1889

Elizabeth Cady Stanton 1815–1902 Reformer

Mrs. Elizabeth Stanton

You have a predominance of the vital and mental temperaments with a full degree of the motive, but the last is not so sustaining in its influence, the vital having the ascendancy and not being abused.

So your life principle is ample and health perfect; few perhaps have a better organization for longevity.

You derive the tone of your mind and constitution from your mother, hence partake of the nature of the Livingston family rather than that of your father. You have a plump round form, fair complexion and animated expression.

Phrenological character reading, done at Seneca Falls on October 10, 1853,
by leading American phrenologist Lorenzo Fowler

Born in 1815 in Johnstown, New York. Raised in an atmosphere of submissive obedience to elders, in which boys were clearly favored over girls, Elizabeth was intelligent and witty, and she possessed a rebellious spirit and a will to shape her own character.

Important in her life was her cousin Gerit Smith, a liberal much involved with abolition and reform. At the Smiths' she met Henry Brewster Stanton, a well-known abolitionist speaker and an executive of the American Anti-Slavery Society. They married in 1840 and traveled to London to the First World Anti-Slavery Convention, to which he was a delegate. Here she encountered Lucretia Mott and found "in this new friend a woman emancipated from all faith in man-made creeds, from all fear of his denunciations. Nothing was too sacred for her to question as to its rightfulness in principle and practice." This meeting inspired Stanton's lifetime commitment to women's suffrage. With Mott and a few other women she conceived the first Woman's Rights Convention in Seneca Falls, New York, in 1848.

A staunch political activist throughout her long life, Elizabeth Cady Stanton and her close friend Susan B. Anthony were leading figures in the nineteenth-century women's rights movement.

Eminent Women 1884

In 1855, Nathaniel Hawthorne complained to his publisher of "that damned mob of scribbling women"—a reference to the many women novelists of the time, a number of whom were outselling Hawthorne himself. As the popular press developed commercially in the nineteenth century, women writers—novelists, essayists, political activists—began to publish their work widely and successfully. While Hawthorne spoke with distaste of the "ink-stained Amazons" who had the audacity to "stand with their minds naked" before the public, most women writers clothed themselves in decidedly feminine garb when they took pen in hand. As keepers of the home, middle- and upper-class white women were expected to be keepers of the moral compass of the family, mindful of Christian duties and the proper education of their children. Women writers parlayed this moral authority into their public works, speaking and writing on issues of temperance, abolition, education, women's suffrage, and religion. They forged a new public profile for women and a legacy for generations to come.

ELIZABETH DILLON (1998)

Standing, from left: Mary Rice Livermore (1820–1905), New England and Chicago, Sanitary Commission worker in the Civil War, then a leading activist for women's suffrage; Sarah Orne Jewett (1849–1909), New England, author of *The Country of the Pointed Firs* and other distinguished literary works; Grace Atkins Oliver (1844–99), New England, biographer and memoirist, widely active in regional women's societies; Helen Hunt Jackson (1830–85), New England, novelist, poet, essayist, crusader for Indian rights, author of *A Century of Dishonor* (1881), an angry account of governmental oppression of American Indians, and the enormously successful romance *Ramona* (1884), a fictional case history of such ill treatment; Nora Perry (1831?–96), New England, prolific poet and short story writer, newspaper correspondent; Lucy Larcum (1824–93), New England, poet, anthologist, student and teacher of literature, friend and protégé of Whittier; Frances Hodgson Burnett (1849–1924), English-born, then resident of Knoxville, Tennessee, author of *Little Lord Fauntleroy* (1886), *The Secret Garden* (1911), and other novels

Seated, from left: Elizabeth Stuart Phelps Ward (1844–1911), New England, author of immensely popular novels dealing with religious aspirations and with the hypocritical treatment of women in American society; Louise Chandler Moulton (1835–1908), New England, author of magazine articles and stories, best known as an elegantly hospitable literary hostess—in Boston, of Emerson, Longfellow, the Sargents, and others, at her second home in London, of Swinburne, Burne-Jones, Oscar Wilde, and later Yeats, Ezra Pound, and Mallarmé; Louisa May Alcott (1832–88), New England, the daughter of Bronson Alcott and protégée of father's friends Emerson, Thoreau, and others, the author of *Little Women* (1868–69), *Little Men* (1871), and a number of other novels, several of which have been recently reprinted; Julia Ward Howe (1819–1910), New England, strong abolitionist and lecturer for women's suffrage, author of "The Battle Hymn of the Republic" (1862); Harriet Beecher Stowe: see her entry

MARY·A·LIVERMORE · SARA·JEWETT · GRACE·A·OLIVER · HELEN·HUNT · NORA·PERRY · LUCY·LARCOM · FRANCES·HODGSON·BURNETT

ELIZABETH·STUART·PHELPS · LOUISE·CHANDLER·MOULTON · LOUISA·M·ALCOTT · JULIA·WARD·HOWE · HARRIET·BEECHER·STOWE

EMINENT WOMEN

Compliments of the Travelers Insurance Company

NOTMAN PHOTO © 3 PARK ST. BOSTON. MASS.   Copyrighted.   Eng. L'Africain 1884.

By Eugene l'Africain (1859–92), collotype, 1884; created in Montreal from photographs made in Boston by Notman Photographic Company

Portrait by William Strickland (1788–1854), aquatint, 1818, after an 1807
painting by Charles de Saint-Mémin (1770–1852)

Meriwether Lewis 1774–1809 Explorer

He was a man of high energy and was at times impetuous, but this was tempered by his great self-discipline. He could drive himself to the point of exhaustion, then take an hour to write about the events of the day, and another to make his celestial observations. . . .

Where he was unique, truly gifted, was as an explorer, where all his talents were necessary. The most important was his ability as a leader of men. He was born to leadership, and reared for it, studied it in his army career, then exercised it on the expedition.

. . . He knew his men. He saw to it that they had dry socks, sufficient clothing. He pushed them to but never beyond the breaking point. He got out of them more than they knew they had to give. . . .

He shared the work. He cooked for his men, and poled a canoe. He was hunter and fisherman. From crossing the Lolo Trail to running the rapids of the Columbia, he never ordered the men to do what he wouldn't do.

STEPHEN E. AMBROSE, *Undaunted Courage* (1996)

Born in Albemarle County, Virginia; his parents were neighbors of the Jeffersons and Randolphs. Lewis served in the regular army from 1795 to 1801, when newly elected President Jefferson invited Lewis to become his private secretary. Jefferson at the time was much concerned to find a land route to the Pacific Ocean, and in January 1803 he proposed to Congress a journey of discovery. He chose Lewis to head the venture (judging him, in his later words, to be "of courage undaunted" and possessing strong "perseverance of purpose"), and Lewis asked his former army friend William Clark to be co-leader. The epic expedition started from St. Louis in the spring of 1804, ascended the Mississippi to the Missouri; proceeded along the wide Missouri past what is now Bismarck, North Dakota, eventually to the Columbia River and so westward and by November 1805 to the Pacific. Along the way there were successive encounters with Indians: Sioux, Mandans, Shoshones (where Lewis's guide Sacagawea recognized the chief as her brother), and Nez Perce (who extended life-saving hospitality). Lewis was back in Washington in late December 1806. Jefferson then appointed Lewis governor of the new Louisiana Territory. He served effectively but ran into some technical troubles. En route to Washington to discuss them, he was seized by one of his recurring fits of deep depression and committed suicide at an inn in central Tennessee.

John Muir 1838–1914 Naturalist

"We too must write Bibles," Emerson had said; and John Muir, loosely a disciple, did so. Many people in Muir's day kept diaries, but he began to have the idea of speaking to the nation on behalf of wild nature, both in order to protect what he loved and to evangelize. Like the eastern Transcendentalists, he was not advocating polytheism. Nor was he secular. Muir believed that wilderness, like man, was an expression of one God; that man was part of nature, and not, as in Genesis, set over all Creation to subdue and rule. "I have never yet happened upon a trace of evidence that . . . any one animal was ever made for another as much as it was made for itself," Muir wrote in 1875, nine years before his first book, *The Mountains of California,* came out.

"I will touch naked God," he wrote once, while glacier-climbing. And on another jaunt, lunching on his customary dry crust of bread: "To dine with a glacier on a sunny day is a glorious thing and makes common feasts of meat and wine ridiculous." "Divine with the jewelry of winter" is his phrase for Mount Tissiack. Mount Shasta, a volcanic cone built way up into the blue, has been remodeled by "a down-crawling mantle of ice upon a fountain of smouldering fire." "Heaven bless you all," he wrote in his journal from the Sierras, meaning all of California's citizenry, including its lizards, grasshoppers, ants, bighorn sheep, grizzly bears, bluebottle flies (who "make all dead flesh fly"), "our horizontal brothers," as he was apt to describe the animal kingdom—"the love-work of Nature." And in "the blessed wilderness" of Strawberry Meadows, there springs "an outburst of organic life . . . the air stirred into one universal hum with rejoicing insects, a milky way of wings and petals . . . a foam of plant bloom and bees. . . . The deeps of the sky are mottled with singing wings of every color . . . enameling the light."

"All this good world," he will say. Or, "Wild with delight."

EDWARD HOAGLAND (1997)

Born in Dunbar, Scotland. His harshly Calvinist father took the family to America in 1849, settling on a farm near Portage, Wisconsin. John attended the University of Wisconsin, astonishing the authorities with his mechanical inventions. On September 2, 1867, he set off on a thousand-mile walk, from Louisville, Kentucky, down through Tennessee, a slice of North Carolina, Georgia, and Florida, reaching Cedar Key, Florida, in early 1868. A few months later he made his way to San Francisco and then to his first view of Sierra Nevada (a "Range of Light," in his phrase) and the Yosemite Valley. He explored glaciers there and in Canada.

Emerson visited with him in Yosemite in the spring of 1871, finding him "the right man in the right place." In 1890, Muir and Robert Underwood Johnson helped to get Yosemite Valley declared a national park (by Congress). Two years later Muir helped found the Sierra Club.

Portrait by Orlando Rouland (1871–1945), oil on canvas, undated

William F. Cody, "Buffalo Bill" 1846–1917 Showman

Buffalo Bill's
defunct
            who used to
            ride a watersmooth-silver
                                    stallion
and break onetwothreefourfive pigeons just like that
                                    Jesus

he was a handsome man
                        and what i want to know is
how do you like your blueeyed boy
Mister Death

              E. E. CUMMINGS, *Collected Poems* (No. 31), 1938

Born in Scott City, Iowa; very little schooling. During the Civil War and later, he served as an army scout. In 1867 he was employed by a food merchant to furnish buffalo meat; his remarkable feats with a rifle earned him his nickname. He then produced the stage show *Scouts of the Prairie,* with himself in the lead; "Wild Bill" Hickock joined the cast in 1873. In 1883 he opened his Wild West exhibition, presenting it in this country and abroad, and in his later years dividing his time between the show and his large ranch north of North Platte, Nebraska.

Unidentified artist, color lithograph poster, 1889,
after portrait by Rosa Bonheur (1822–99)

PHINEAS TAYLOR BARNUM:

BLOWING, WITH ALL HIS MIGHT, FOR HIS "HAPPY FAMILY," THE CONFIDING PUBLIC.

Portrait by Babbett and Hooper (active 1855–70), wood engraving, published in *Vanity Fair,* New York, September 13, 1862, after Henry Louis Stephens (1824–82)

Phineas Taylor Barnum 1810–1891 Showman

Barnum himself declared that there was "no picture so beautiful as ten thousand smiling, bright-eyed, happy children; no music so sweet as their clear-ringing laughter. . . ." Reporters described his diversion of a circus route to pass a house where a little boy lay sick. He even entertained at children's gatherings, doing a little juggling and telling some of his famous stories. "A happy smile on a child's face acted like a tonic on the old man," wrote the *New York Times* in its obituary. "He loved them all, black and white, homely and pretty, so long as there were smiles on their faces."

During his career, Barnum had continually surrounded himself with appeals to the childlike: Tom Thumb, Lavinia Warren, Admiral Dot, Commodore Nutt, Cordelia Howard, Jenny Lind, Jumbo, the beautiful baby contests—so many of his greatest exhibits represented either the innocence of the child and the naif, or exploited the sense of lost innocence in adults.

NEIL HARRIS, *Humbug: The Art of P. T. Barnum* (1973)

Born in Connecticut of poor Yankee ancestry. His career began with a profitable exhibition tour of Joice Heth, a former slave who said she was 160 years old and the one-time nurse of George Washington. In the 1840s and 1850s, P. T. Barnum put on widely popular shows featuring such acts as the midget Tom Thumb and the soprano Jenny Lind. Then he opened Barnum's American Museum of Curiosities, or "freaks of nature," to which many thousands flocked. It was in the early 1870s that he invented and exploited his three-ring traveling circus, with his young partner, James A. Bailey: the "Greatest Show on Earth," displaying the elephant Jumbo, imported from London, and the "White Elephant" of Siam. He can be credited, in the words of Neil Harris, with "the creation of mass amusements" in America. He was married to Charity Hallett (d. 1873) and then to Nancy Fish, but he had no children.

Edwin Booth 1833–1893 Actor

A strain of gentle melancholy ran through his nature, although at times a spirit of boyish playfulness cropped out in his conversation and his letters. He was absolutely unaffected, despised being "gold-badged and banqueted," and when called upon to speak in public to represent the dramatic profession on some state occasion, he was so shy that he deplored the fact that he had not taken his father's advice and learned a trade.

DAVID BELASCO, My Life's Story (1915)

Edwin Booth in the year 1880 was in the flower of his artistry, and at the height of his power. . . . His ambition was dauntless; his body flexible and obedient to his will; his face, beautiful and melancholy, showed nothing of his later lassitude, and the music of his voice which held to the very end, was never more harmonious. No actor of the time so completely filled the eye, the ear, and the mind with the ideal of romantic tragedy as Edwin Booth. His Hamlet, Shylock, Iago, Mercutio, Richard II and III, Ruy Blas, Macbeth, Richelieu, and Othello became the criteria by which other actors were judged.

OTIS SKINNER, Footlights and Spotlights (1924)

Born near Bel Air, Maryland, the son of the acclaimed (and eccentric) actor Junius Brutus Booth, and named for another famous actor, Edwin Forrest. He made his stage debut in 1851, in the title role of *Richard III;* after which he did a tour of California with his father and brother Junius Jr., and toured Australia, giving his first performance as Shylock. Booth came fully into his own in New York in 1857, with *Richard III* and as Iago in *Othello.* In 1864 he gave an unheard of one-hundred-night performance as Hamlet, a role fully suited to his own melancholy temperament. He survived his brother John Wilkes's assassination of Lincoln and returned to the stage early in 1866. In the 1870s and '80s he was recognized as the country's greatest actor. In 1881, in London, during a nineteen-night engagement, he alternated with Henry Irving as Iago and Othello. In 1888 he founded the Players' Club on his recently purchased property on Gramercy Park, New York.

Portrait by Napoleon Sarony (1821–96), photograph, albumen silver print, 1870

Portrait by Mortimer Menpes (1855–1938), etching and
drypoint on tinted paper, c. 1900

James Abbott McNeill Whistler 1834–1903 Artist

An alert, wiry little person of five feet four or five; using a single eyeglass and very neatly dressed, though always with something singular in his attire—the artist's self-conscious protest which gave him a certain exotic flavor and individuality. He wore his abundant curly black hair rather long, and just over the forehead a little lock of quite white hair like a plume. . . .

Whistler's eyes were grey-blue and gimlet-keen—"anything but kindly," and the moustache and carriage intensified the cocky challenge of the fighter: Whistler always reminded me of a bantam.

FRANK HARRIS, *Contemporary Portraits* (1915)

Everything in Whistler justified the curiosity and affection Mallarmé felt for him: his mysterious and ponderous art, full of subjective practices and complicated formulae. The singularity of his person, the intelligent tension in his face, the lock of white hair amid the black, the diabolical monocle restraining his frowning brows, his prompt wit in the face of scathing retorts and cruel ripostes. That ready and incisive wit which was the weapon of defense and attack.

Quoted in Ronald Anderson and Anne Koval, *James McNeill Whistler* (1994)

Born in Lowell, Massachusetts. The family lived in Russia from 1843 to 1849, where his father was chief consultant in the building of the railway connecting St. Petersburg to Moscow. They returned to the United States after the father's death.

Whistler attended the U.S. Military Academy at West Point and was dismissed after three years (for failing a course). He had an early wish to be an artist (some of his teenage drawings survive). That, and a desire to go to Europe, particularly to Paris, where avant-garde art flourished, spurred him to leave the United States. He departed in 1855 and never returned.

He established himself in Paris and London, where he met, among many colorful and influential people, Degas, Courbet, Manet, Fantin-Latour, and Baudelaire; and later, Oscar Wilde and pre-Raphaelites Swinburne and Rosetti.

An original artist who developed his own style, he was known not only as a painter but as a brilliant and controversial talker, frequently involved in contretemps, as when he sued the critic John Ruskin for libel after Ruskin had attacked a painting.

Among his best known works are *Arrangement in Grey and Black: The Artist's Mother; Symphony in White No. 1: The White Girl; Nocturne in Black and Gold: The Falling Rocket;* and *The Peacock Room.*

Portrait by Alvin Langdon Coburn (1882–1966), photogravure, 1908

Samuel Langhorne Clemens, "Mark Twain"
1835–1910 Author

[Mark Twain's] great charm is his absolute freedom in a region where most of us are fettered and shackled by immemorial convention. He saunters out into the trim world of letters, and lounges across its neatly kept paths, and walks about on the grass at will, in spite of all the signs that have been put up from the beginning of literature, warning people of the dangers and penalties for the slightest trespass. . . .

One of the most notably Southern traits of Mark Twain's humor is its power of seeing the fun of Southern seriousness, but this vision did not come to him till after his liberation from neighborhood in the vaster far West. He was the first, if not the only man of his section, to betray a consciousness of the grotesque absurdities in the Southern inversion of the civilized ideals in behalf of slavery, which must have them upside down in order to walk over them safely.

WILLIAM DEAN HOWELLS, "Mark Twain: An Inquiry" (1901)

Grew up in Hannibal, Missouri. After training as a Mississippi river pilot (1857) and prospecting in Nevada (1865), he became a reporter. "The Celebrated Jumping Frog of Calaveras County," written in San Francisco in 1865 under the pen-name of Mark Twain, made him famous. A tour of Europe and the Holy Land led to *The Innocents Abroad* in 1869. In 1870 he married Olivia Langdon and moved with her to Hartford, Connecticut. Twain's first novelistic effort was *The Gilded Age* in 1873 (with Charles Dudley Warner). *The Adventures of Tom Sawyer* in 1876 was followed by *Life on the Mississippi* in 1883 and *The Adventures of Huckleberry Finn* in 1884; *A Connecticut Yankee in King Arthur's Court* came out in 1889. A business blunder led to bankruptcy in 1894, and to endless lecturing around the world to pay off debts. His final years were crowded with honors.

William Dean Howells 1837–1920 Author

In February 1903, Howells tried to call on Mark Twain at Twain's home in New York, but was rebuVed by Twain's houseman Sam. Next day, Twain wrote Howells in apology, saying he had heard voices and had come downstairs but Howells had gone.

I encountered Sam coming up . . . & he said it was a stranger, who insisted on seeing me—"a stumpy little gray man with furtive ways & an evil face."

"What did he say his name was?"

"He didn't say. He offered me his card, but I didn't take it."

" . . . I wish you had taken his card. Why didn't you?"

"I didn't like his manners."

"Why? What did he do?"

"He called me a quadrilateral astronomical incandescent son of a bitch."

"Oh, that was Howells. Is that what annoyed you? What is the matter with it? Is that a thing to distort into an offence, when you couldn't possibly know but what he meant it was a compliment?"

MARK TWAIN to Howells, February 13, 1903

You saw your field with a rare lucidity; you saw all it had to give in the way of the romance of the real, and the interest and the thrill and the charm of the common, as one may put it; the character and the comedy, the point, the pathos, the tragedy, the particular home-grown humanity under your eye and your hand and with which the life all about you was closely interknitted. Your hand reached out for these things with a fondness that was in itself a literary gift.

HENRY JAMES, "A Letter to Mr. Howells," *North American Review,* April 1912

Born and grew up in Ohio. In 1860, his campaign biography of Abraham Lincoln was rewarded with the American consulate in Venice. In 1865, as editor of the *Atlantic Monthly,* he came to know Mark Twain, Henry James, and others. His first novel appeared in 1872; but Howells's major novelistic phase was the 1880s, with *A Modern Instance, The Rise of Silas Lapham,* and *Indian Summer.* Howells's requickened political conscience led in 1894 to the Utopian fantasy *Traveler from Altruria.* As a critic, Howells was the most astute and generous figure of his time. The death of his daughter Winifred in 1899 was a devastating blow; his younger daughter Mildred was a main support in the later years.

Portrait by Augustus Saint-Gaudens (1848–1907), bronze relief of Howells
and his daughter Mildred, 1898

Portrait by Alvin Langdon Coburn (1882–1966), photogravure, 1906

Henry James 1843–1916 Author

It was really in monologue that he was most himself. I remember in particular one summer evening, when we sat late on the terrace at The Mount, with the lake shining palely through dark trees, and one of us suddenly said to him, "And now tell us about the Emmets—tell us all about them."

The Emmet and Temple families composed, as we knew, the main element of his vast and labyrinthine cousinship . . . and for a moment he stood there brooding in the darkness, murmuring over to himself: "Ah, my dear, the Emmets—ah, the Emmets." Then he began, forgetting us, forgetting the place, forgetting everything but the vision of his lost youth that the question had evoked, the long train of ghosts flung with his enchanter's wand across the wide stage of the summer night. Ghostlike indeed at first, wavering and indistinct, they glimmered at us through a series of disconnected ejaculations, epithets, allusions, parenthetical rectifications and restatements, till not only our brains but the clear night itself seemed filled with a palpable fog; and then, suddenly, by some miracle of shifted lights and accumulated strokes, there they stood before us as they lived, drawn with a million filament-like lines.

EDITH WHARTON, *A Backward Glance* (1934)

Born in New York City, the son of Henry James, Sr., a highly charged religious philosopher, and the younger brother of William James. Henry grew up in New York, near Washington Square, with several years of schooling in Europe. In the mid-1860s he was a casual student at Harvard Law School. His literary career began in 1864 with a short story and a review of a book about fiction. In the later 1860s, encouraged especially by William Dean Howells, he produced short fiction and reviews at a steady pace. His family home was now in Cambridge, Massachusetts, though James himself was often in England, France, or Italy.

James's first notable full-length novel was *Roderick Hudson* (1876), about a failed artist, but it was the touching novella *Daisy Miller* (1879) that won international acclaim. By this time James had expatriated to Europe, settling soon in England. His masterpiece *Portrait of a Lady* (1881) was a culmination of the process. James's life from then on was that of the Master, the supreme literary artist and craftsman. Work followed work: *The Aspern Papers* (1888), *The Real Thing and Other Tales* (1893), *The Spoils of Poynton* (1897), *The Two Magics* (1898, containing "The Turn of the Screw"). There was also incessant critical and travel writing, and a fling at the stage.

James's literary peak comprised three novels between 1902 and 1904: *The Wings of the Dove, The Ambassadors,* and *The Golden Bowl.*

James's devotion to England and to his countless friends there led him to become a British citizen in 1915.

Entering the Twentieth Century

AMERICA, GERTRUDE STEIN WAS GIVEN TO SAYING, ENTERED THE TWENTIETH century ahead of the rest of the world and might thus be described as the oldest inhabitant of that epoch. America indeed, she said, "created the twentieth century." Her immediate reference was the "commercial conceptions" precipitated in America by the Civil War and eventually supplying the basic conditions of life worldwide. (Those conceptions were imaged in "The Gilded Decades.") As many another Stein text can show, she was also thinking of the extraordinary mechanical genius displayed by Americans in the later phases of the nineteenth century and afterward. Wilbur Wright and his flying machine, for example: Stein meditated on Wright in her tantalizing, almost-comprehensible prose—"I always like to think about Wright not seeing what he saw. He saw how he moved. Yes. Yes."—in *Four in America,* from which we took the sketch of Ulysses S. Grant. And she liked to compare her prose style to Henry Ford's assembly-line repetitions. The "continuous present" of the style—"a rose is a rose is a rose"—was simply, she once argued, a "beginning again and again, the way they do in making automobiles."

Wright and Ford are here, helping to beget the century, preceded by such makers-of-the-new as Alexander Graham Bell, Thomas Alva Edison, and George Washington Carver, and followed by D. W. Griffith and Albert Einstein. Gertrude Stein herself sits, all appropriately, perched among them, a "modern Buddha," in the phrase of her portraitist Jo Davidson. Surveying the group, one finds a line from a song by George and Ira Gershwin coming irresistibly to mind: "The radio and the telephone and the movies that we know." It has been claimed for Henry Ford (the words are quoted later) that he was really the one to create the twentieth century. Given the cultural dominance of film and television in our time, some may want to make the claim for D. W. Griffith.

But there were other ways that the twentieth century was entered and shaped. One of these is represented by W. E. B. Du Bois, the crucially influential black leader, spokesman, and polemicist. Two decades before the Harlem Renaissance, six decades before the uprisings of the 1960s shook and reformed American society, Du Bois, in his book *The Souls of Black Folk* (1903), prophetically defined the century in a dominant aspect: "The problem of the twentieth century is the problem of the color-line." George Washington Carver, working away peaceably in Tuskegee, Alabama, belongs in this special category as well; the child of black slave parents, whose mother had been kidnapped and murdered by white raiders, Carver became a national and biracial model of achievement by performing fabulous feats of invention with the peanut and sweet potato. Coming from a differently repressive background, Emma Goldman, the Russia-born anarchist, sounded the alarm for individual rights in the increasingly complex American society until she was jailed and deported.

Charlotte Perkins Gilman makes an oddly suitable companion figure with Emma Goldman, as a warrior in the struggle for women's economic independence—see especially her *Women and Economics* (1898)—and of total social and political equality (as she argued winningly in her Utopian novel of 1915, *Herland*). And the uniquely skillful and innovative dancer Isadora Duncan gave rhythmic bodily form to human aspirations and longings as they had been voiced by Walt Whitman. Hart Crane, after watching Isadora Duncan dance in Cleveland in December 1921, wrote a friend that he had been "stimulated beyond the power to walk straight," and reported that Duncan had come out on the stage afterward to tell a silent audience to "go home and take from the bookshelf the works of Walt Whitman."

In the philosophical arena, William James, as his keenly observant younger colleague George Santayana said of him, broke free from the country's "genteel tradition" to lead philosophy along new paths of pragmatism and the active will; no one was more at home in the twentieth century than James, at home in its urban uproar and vitality. John Dewey, who always acknowledged James as providing the groundwork of his vision, carried the pragmatic ideas into the field of education, championing what he regarded as the proper education for an individual fitting himself for life in a democratic society.

As to the artists in this section, it can be said that they led American art into the twentieth century, but not all of them led the rest of the world as well. Thomas Eakins, with Winslow Homer (whose absence is due purely to space constraints), stood "midway in the history of American art between the towering figures of John Singleton Copley in the eighteenth century and Jackson Pollock in the twentieth century." The typically cogent words are from Jules Prown, who notes that Eakins and Homer were quintessentially American as artists—as, even more so, Prown remarks, was Albert Pinkham Ryder, whose haunted images of subconscious stirrings (for example, *The Race Track* [Death on a Pale Horse]) owed no little to the poetry and fiction of Edgar Allan Poe. (Ryder's exclusion was peculiarly painful.)

Eakins and Ryder both studied in Paris, at greater or lesser length, but they found themselves on native grounds artistically. Mary Cassatt, on the contrary, though Pittsburgh born and Philadelphia bred, actually joined the French Impressionist group in Paris at the invitation of Edgar Degas, and she showed her work in Impressionist exhibitions from 1877 to 1886. Degas's portrait of Cassatt, done in the 1880s as their relationship was deepening, was purchased for a goodly sum by the National Portrait Gallery in 1984, and it is one of its crowning masterpieces. Childe Hassam, coming to Paris a trifle later, adapted the techniques of French Impressionism to his own delicately textured landscapes; with John H. Twachtman, J. Alden Weir, and a few others, Hassam formed the group of American Impressionists known as The Ten. The first exhibition of their combined work was mounted in 1895.

Frank Lloyd Wright can unquestionably be listed with the other inventive geniuses gathered in this section. He was the most influential and in every sense creative architect of his time: a time that extended from just after the Civil War, to 1959. Wright's productions punctuated that period—from the Prairie School houses of the early 1900s to the Imperial Hotel in Tokyo in 1922, with its "agitated forms," to Falling Water, the residence cantilevering over a waterfall that Wright built for Edgar J. Kaufman in Bear Run, Pennsylvania, in 1936, to the Guggenheim Museum, with its upward-spiraling interior, in 1959.

The portraitist of Frank Lloyd Wright, Berenice Abbott, might likewise be credited with helping to beget the twentieth century; with Steichen and Stieglitz she brought photography to major artistic status—especially with her documentation of New York City in the 1930s. Carl Van Vechten, the source of our Emma Goldman (and several other images later on), was a tireless and original photographic artist, with his own gallery of distinguished Americans. Jo Davidson in turn created an unmistakable sculptural style with his busts of Gandhi, Woodrow Wilson, Rudyard Kipling, James Joyce, and—our own offering—Gertrude Stein. John Sloan, who gives us Isadora Duncan, was in the vanguard of the new brand of realists in painting who were bringing the art into the city and the lives of the middle and lower classes.

Even as American culture in these years spread in all directions across the land and grew ever more various and multilayered, one notices how many in this congerie of originals interconnected with each other, almost as in the much earlier and more provincial days. Gertrude Stein and W. E. B. Du Bois were both valued students at Harvard of William James; Santayana was James's Spanish-born colleague and Dewey his follower. Stein, as was mentioned, was stimulated by the doings of Wilbur Wright and Henry Ford; and the young Ford once approached Edison to ask the inventor whether he thought that gasoline would make a good motor fuel (the answer was yes). Edison's daughter Madeleine was a friend and classmate at Bryn Mawr of William James's daughter Peggy (whose best friend at college was Marianne Moore). Alexander Graham Bell's helpful shadow fell on Edison and Wright.

Literary figures contribute an assortment of verbal portraits. Walt Whitman, that man of luminous opinion, is heard reflecting on his recent meeting with Thomas Eakins; Wallace Stevens gazes in verse at the "old philosopher" George Santayana in Rome; Katherine Anne Porter recalls a visit with Gertrude Stein and her companion Alice B. Toklas in Paris. Edison is observed listening to his assistants singing a ditty parodying a song from Gilbert and Sullivan, and is later glimpsed by Henry James. The twenty-five-year-old Sinclair Lewis sizes up Emma Goldman, and a decade or so later H. L. Mencken adds his journalistic picture. John Dos Passos, who has already given us his sketch of J. P. Morgan, here considers Henry Ford and Wilbur Wright.

William James and Charlotte Perkins Gilman engage in self-analysis—one as to present tendencies, one reminiscently. Biographers provide insights into John Dewey, Bell,

Carver, and Einstein. Oliver Wendell Holmes, Jr., appraises John Dewey's cosmic vision—ill-expressed, he thinks, but phenomenal in scope and quality. A remarkably harmonious match-up is that of John Sloan, musing in his diary about Isadora Duncan—"all womanhood . . . the mother of the race"—after seeing her dance and then painting her portrait.

William James 1842–1910 Philosopher

I have often thought that the best way to define a man's character, would be to seek out the particular mental or moral attitude in which, when it came upon him, he felt himself most deeply and intensely active and alive. At such moments, there is a voice inside which speaks & says "*This* is the real me!" . . . This characteristic attitude in me always involves an element of active tension, of holding my own as it were *trusting* outward things to perform their part so as to make it a full harmony, but without any *guarantee* that they will. Make it a guarantee—and the attitude immediately becomes to my consciousness stagnant and stingless. Take away the guarantee, and I feel . . . a sort of deep enthusiastic bliss, of utter willingness to do and suffer anything, which translates itself physically by a kind of stinging pain inside of my breastbone.

WILLIAM JAMES to Alice Gibbens, June 7, 1877

Born in New York City (in the Astor Hotel), the first child of Henry James, Sr., theologian and polemical essayist, and Mary Walsh James (brother Henry was born fifteen months later). After schooling in New York, Europe, and Newport, and an attempt at painting under John La Farge, James entered the Lawrence Scientific School at Harvard in 1861, and thence to the Harvard Medical School in 1864. These years were interrupted by participation in Louis Agassiz' expedition to Brazil, by bouts of depression and physical illness, and by further stays in Europe. In 1872, James began teaching at Harvard, at first courses in physiology and then increasingly in psychology, establishing the first psychology laboratory in the country. Out of this, in 1890, came the landmark *Principles of Psychology,* along with a great many essays and reviews.

In 1878, James married Alice Howe Gibbens, an able Boston schoolteacher; they had five children over the years, one of whom died in infancy. James's remarkably lively lecturing, with his steady stream of essays (*The Will to Believe and Other Essays* came out in 1897), made him by the turn of the century the most admired philosopher in the country. His Gifford Lectures of 1901–2 became the influential *Varieties of Religious Experience;* and his career was crowned in 1907 by *Pragmatism,* perhaps his most characteristic work. A productive rivalry with brother Henry lasted through his adult life; Emerson, Josiah Royce, John Dewey, Santayana, W. E. B. Du Bois, and Gertrude Stein were among his mentors, associates, and students.

Portrait by John La Farge (1835–1910), oil on cardboard panel, c. 1860

John Dewey 1859–1952 Philosopher

Dewey, who shared his wife's interest in woman suffrage, did what he could to advance it. . . . On 8 August 1912 Dewey addressed the summer students at Columbia on woman suffrage; according to one press report, "so many people came to hear him that many could not get inside the doors." . . . [He] occasionally took part in the parades designed to publicize and help the woman suffrage movement. According to an anecdote widely circulated at the time, just before the start of one parade Dewey had thrust into his hands without reading it a banner proclaiming: "Men can vote! Why can't I?" and was considerably puzzled by the amused smiles which greeted him as he proceeded to march down Fifth Avenue.

GEORGE DYKHUIZEN, *The Life and Mind of John Dewey* (1973)

Although John Dewey's book [*Experience and Nature*] is incredibly ill written, it seemed to me after several rereadings to have a feeling of intimacy with the inside of the cosmos that I found unqualified. So methought might God have spoken had He been inarticulate but keenly desirous to tell you how it was.

OLIVER WENDELL HOLMES, JR., to Sir Frederick Pollack,
from Washington, May 15, 1931

Born and reared in Burlington, Vermont, and a graduate (1879) of the University of Vermont; Dewey's Vermont drawl and rustic demeanor never left him. At Johns Hopkins University in Baltimore, Dewey imbibed the new reverence for empirical science. At the University of Chicago from 1894 to 1904, he began to formulate his theory of "instrumentalism," in some sense adapting William James's pragmatism and individualism to more socially oriented purposes. Dewey's primary interest became the field of education; and here, convinced that truth was a human affair, and was relative to circumstance and human intentions, he established the concept of "learning by doing"—something he promulgated in *The School and Society* (1899). He also founded the Laboratory School at the university. During and after his years at Columbia University (1904–30), Dewey published, among other texts, *Reconstruction in Philosophy* (1920), a blast at metaphysics and abstract thought as elitist, *Experience and Nature* (1925) and *Freedom and Culture* (1939). He became the best-known philosopher of his time, worldwide, and an incalculable influence on educational methods; he remained an unpretentious informal and thoughtful lecturer, with a rumpled look about him.

Portrait by Jacob Epstein (1880–1959), bronze bust, 1927

Portrait by Harry Wood, Jr. (b. 1910), oil on canvas, 1950

George Santayana 1863–1952 Philosopher

The bed, the books, the chair, the moving nuns,
The candle as it evades the sight, these are
The sources of happiness in the shape of Rome,
A shape within the ancient circles of shapes,
And these beneath the shadow of a shape

In a confusion on bed and books, a portent
On the chair, a moving transparence on the nuns,
A light on the candle tearing against the wick
To join a hovering excellence, to escape
From fire and be part of that which

Fire is the symbol: the celestial possible . . .

It is a kind of total grandeur at the end,
With every visible thing enlarged and yet
No more than a bed, a chair, and moving nuns,
The immensest theatre, the pillared porch,
The book and candle in your ambered room,
Total grandeur of a total edifice,
Chosen by an inquisitor of structures
For himself. He stops upon the threshold,
As if the design of all his words takes form
And frame from thinking and is realized.

WALLACE STEVENS, "To an Old Philosopher in Rome" (1952)
(Santayana died in the convent-clinic of the Blue Nuns in Rome)

Born in Spain of Spanish parents; came with them to the United States in 1872. Santayana took a bachelor's degree at Harvard in 1886, and a Ph.D. in 1889. He then taught at Harvard until 1912, as the younger colleague of William James and Josiah Royce, in the exceptionally distinguished philosophy department. After 1912, Santayana lived for forty years in Europe, settling finally in Italy. Most of his abundant writing came from this period.

Santayana brought a classical perspective to bear on philosophical questions, and he was also one of the most acute observers and analysts of the intellectual currents of his day. This quality is reflected in such collections as *Winds of Doctrine* (1913), which contains the landmark "Genteel Tradition in America" (in which both James brothers figure), and *Character and Opinion in the United States* (1920). His memoirs *Persons and Places* appeared between 1944 and 1953. Santayana's more purely theoretical writings include the intellectually grandiose *Life of Reason* (five volumes, 1905–6), and *Realms of Being* (1928–40). His novel *The Last Puritan* caused an immense admiring stir when it came out in 1935.

William Edward Burghardt Du Bois 1868–1963
Civil Rights Statesman

Always a controversial figure, he espoused racial and political beliefs of such variety and seeming contradiction as to bewilder and alienate as many Americans, black and white, as he inspired or converted. Beneath the shifting complexity of alliances and denunciations, nevertheless, there was a pattern, a congealing of inclinations, experiences and ideas, more and more inclining Du Bois to a vision of society that became, in contrast to the lives of most men and women, increasingly radical as he grew older, until the day came when the civil liberties maverick was supplanted by the full-blown Marxist. A proud, solitary man, awesome to most people, courtly with associates, Du Bois was on intimate terms probably with no more than a dozen men during his long life. With women, Du Bois was more accessible; he was in fact enormously attractive to many women and deeply loved by several. His monumental book, *Black Reconstruction in America,* is dedicated to one inamorata—in Latin, to be sure. One of the most vociferous male feminists of the early twentieth century . . . Du Bois fell somewhat short of his principles in his most intimate dealings with women.

DAVID LEVERING LEWIS, introduction to *W. E. B. Du Bois: A Reader* (1995)

Born in Great Barrington, Massachusetts, of richly mixed ancestry: Dutch, French, African. He grew up in an unstable household. Du Bois graduated from Fisk University in Nashville in 1888, then transferred to Harvard and earned a second bachelor's in 1890. Later at Harvard, where he was a student and an occasional house guest of William James, Du Bois completed his Ph.D. with a prizewinning essay on the African slave trade.

In 1903, while teaching history at Atlanta University, Du Bois brought out his volume of essays *The Souls of Black Folk,* the most important text in black cultural history, with its dramatic theme: "The problem of the twentieth century is the problem of the color-line." The same year, he contended in an article that the "Negro race" would be saved "by its exceptional men," the "Talented Tenth" of its population. In 1909, Du Bois helped found the National Association for the Advancement of Colored People; and the next year, he founded its organ, *The Crisis,* which he edited until 1934.

Du Bois's long career was characterized by unending activity and controversy in connection with the status and condition of American blacks, and in studies of the complex history of the black race. It featured clashes with other black leaders, notably Booker T. Washington, whom Du Bois saw as far too accommodating to whites, and Marcus Garvey, whom he regarded as merely power hungry. In 1948 he broke with the NAACP. In his very late years Du Bois began an encyclopedia of African history, joined the American Communist Party, and, in 1961, at the age of ninety-three, became a citizen of Ghana, dying there two years later.

Portrait by James E. Purdy (1859–1933), photograph, gelatin silver print, 1907

Alexander Graham Bell 1847–1922 Inventor

During more than half of his lifetime, millions throughout the world knew the name of Alexander Graham Bell, and many would have recognized him at sight. He was a world traveller as well as a world figure. He met emperors and at least one empress. He was lionized in society, cheered at exhibitions, applauded at scientific meetings, and sought out by reporters. Medals, prizes, and honorary degrees were showered upon him. And he looked his part. He bore himself with the majesty of a Moses and the benevolence of a Santa Claus. When he entered a room, he seemed to fill it. . . .

Yet his son-in-law David Fairchild said of him soon after his death: "Mr. Bell led a peculiarly isolated life; I have never known anyone who spent so much of his time alone."

Paradoxical though it may seem, Fairchild meant his observation literally, and he made a good case for it. Bell's lifelong habit of working alone through most of the night and sleeping through most of the morning; the designedly limited social activity of his Beinn Bhreagh summers, especially the quarter century and more of weekend withdrawals to the total seclusion of his houseboat, immersed in silence except for the sound of waves and forest; his nocturnal ramblings in woods or on city streets; his hours of solitary piano-playing after everyone else had gone to bed—these were the evidences Fairchild offered.

ROBERT V. BRUCE, *Alexander Graham Bell and the Conquest of Solitude* (1973)

Born in Edinburgh, Scotland, the son and grandson of notable Scottish teachers of speech. While studying in London, Bell taught at a school for the deaf. With his family, he moved to Canada in 1870, then came to Boston, where, in 1872, he founded his own school for the deaf; soon after, he became professor of vocal physiology at Boston University. His inventive genius led him in 1874 to the basic concept of the telephone: in his own words, by making a "current of electricity vary in intensity precisely as the air varies in density during the production of sound"; and on March 10, 1876, the first complete sentence was transmitted by telephone, in his laboratory: "Mr. Watson, come here, I want you."

Bell was able to patent his telephone, against six hundred other claimants, and became exceedingly rich and famous. The first Bell Telephone Company was founded by his father-in-law, Gardiner Hubbard (whose daughter, Mabel, entirely deaf from childhood, Bell married in 1877). Bell, later, in effect invented the iron lung, made Edison's phonograph commercially practical, and experimented for years with aviation. He was president of the National Geographic Society from 1896 to 1904. He died in his summer home in Nova Scotia.

Portrait by Moses Wainer Dykaar (1884–1933), marble bust, 1922

Thomas Alva Edison 1847–1931 Inventor

The mood in the laboratory that winter [1880] was light and festive. Over midnight supper of smoked herring on hard crackers washed down with cold water, the men gathered around the organ even went so far as to improvise an irreverent tribute to their boss, sung to the tune of Gilbert & Sullivan's "I am the captain of the *Pinafore*" from *H. M. S. Pinafore*:

> I am the Wizard of the electric light
> And a wide-awake Wizard, too.
> I see you're rather bright and appreciate the might
> Of what I daily do.
> Quadruplex telegraph or funny phonograph,
> It's all the same to me;
> With ideas I evolve and problems that I solve
> I'm never stumped, you see.
> What, never?
> No, never!
> What, never?
> Well, hardly ever!

NEIL BALDWIN, *Edison: Inventing the Century* (1995)

At last his wonderful blue eyes, more luminous than his own incandescent lamps, enabled me to read his mind. I knew I must win him over, and instinctively I exerted all my powers of fascination to vanquish the delightful, if bashful, savant.

SARAH BERNHARDT, quoted in Arthur Gold and Robert Fizdale,
The Divine Sarah: A Life of Sarah Bernhardt (1991)

Born in Ohio, the youngest son of seven children; found dreamy and "addled" in school (due partly, perhaps, to his early deafness), he was taught at home by his mother. At an early age he became interested in chemistry. During his adolescence he worked on the railroad, selling wares on the run between Port Huron, Ohio, and Detroit: on layover stops at Detroit his education continued during long hours at the library.

His interest moved to telegraphy, then to acoustic telegraphy (competing in that field with Alexander Graham Bell). His continuing interest in the communication media led him and two partners to create the Bureau of Electrical and Telegraphic Engineering. Thereafter he established his own research laboratory, where his was the guiding spirit behind many collective inventions.

The phonograph has been considered his "greatest single achievement from the standpoint of daring imagination." He also made the incandescent lamp commercially practical for common use.

He was competitive and had astonishing stamina, spending little time away from his work. His inventive genius led him constantly into new fields, and in 1928, Congress honored him "for development and application of inventions that have revolutionized civilization in the last century."

Portrait by Abraham Archibald Anderson (1847–1940), oil on canvas, c. 1889

George Washington Carver 1864–1943 Scientist

[As his reputation grew] offers came from commercial firms, offers noting large salaries and richly equipped laboratories. But he continued at his post. There, if you rise early enough, you can see him at seven entering his office. He is a very dark man, with no appearance of white blood. He stoops a little, and his coat is a bit frayed at the sleeve, but there is a flower in his buttonhole and he puts a bunch of flowers in a vase on his desk. Over an old secretary hangs a hornets' nest, and papers lie all about. It is an old-fashioned office with an air of homeyness, and the man who greets you is old-fashioned, too, singularly lacking in the business man's brusque "What can I do for you" attitude, as he seats himself in his swivel chair. When Professor Carver seats himself to talk to you at his old desk, you know there will be no pressing a button to call in a smart office boy to deliver impressive orders for the day.

MARY WHITE OVINGTON, *Portraits in Color* (1927)

Born in Missouri, the sickly child of black slave parents. His father died; and after his mother, with his sister (who survived the experience), was kidnapped and presumably killed by Arkansas slave raiders, George was raised by his parents' owner, Moses Carver. He secured admission to Simpson College in Iowa and began to study art there but was persuaded to transfer to Iowa State University, at Ames, and take up the study of agriculture.

He earned a master's degree in 1896 and then was invited by Booker T. Washington to become director of agricultural work at Tuskegee Institute in Alabama. Here he taught and carried out experiments for almost fifty years. His special aim was to help debt-burdened black farmers, visiting them with his wagon load of equipment (his "mobile school") and teaching them about soil conservation, plant protection, and the development of crops—especially the peanut and the sweet potato, along with cotton. In his laboratory Carver extracted 325 items from the peanut and 115 from the sweet potato. He became a national and even international cult figure, testifying before Congress (in 1921), lecturing across the country, and suffering exploitation from many special-interest groups. He was also an inspirational figure to young white as well as young black students, and he maintained his warmth of personality throughout his lifetime.

Portrait by Clifton Johnson (1865–1940), photograph of Carver, *left*, with a
student, gelatin silver print, c. 1900

Portrait by Edgar Degas (1834–1917), oil on canvas, c. 1880–84

Mary Cassatt 1844–1926 Painter

After one of her dinners, you would find her spellbinding an admiring group of guests, herself a striking personality, beautifully gowned (usually in gray, always high at the neck), her hair parted and waving on each side of a broad forehead, large eyes whose glance came frankly forward to meet yours, a wonderfully flexible mouth, and a nose like Garrick's—remarkable in its modeling, and with those sensitive flaring nostrils which I always said made her an artist in spite of herself. Miss Cassatt's tall figure, which she inherited from her father, had distinction and elegance, and there was no trace of artistic negligé or carelessness which some painters affect. Once having seen her, you could never forget her—from her remarkable small foot to the plumed hat with its inevitable tip upon her head and the Brussels lace veil without which she was never seen. She spoke with energy and you would as soon forget her remarks when she conversed as to forget the motion of her hands. Not even to a Spaniard need she yield anything in the matter of gesture or expressiveness.

LOUISINE HAVEMEYER, *Sixteen to Sixty: Memoirs of a Collector*

Born in 1844 in Pennsylvania into a prosperous family, she spent many childhood years with them living abroad. After attending the Pennsylvania Academy of the Fine Arts, she returned to Europe to continue studying and painting. Her work was noticed and admired by Degas, who brought her into the Impressionist group. Although influenced at first by Degas, Manet, and others, she developed her own distinctive style, her subjects frequently being everyday women, often with their babies. Although she seldom returned to the United States, she considered herself decidedly American and remains today one of our most important woman painters.

She helped her lifelong friend Louisine Elde Havemeyer to select the paintings for her now famous collection, most of which is at the Metropolitan Museum in New York. Thus Cassatt contributed notably in introducing the Impressionists to America in the 1870s.

Attributed to Susan Macdowell Eakins (1851–1938), photograph, c. 1890

Thomas Eakins 1844–1916 Artist

It was probably in the spring of 1887 that Talcott Williams, associate editor of the Phila-delphia *Press* and friend of both Whitman and Eakins, took the painter over to Camden to meet the poet. Later Whitman expressed his opinion of Eakins, recorded by [Horace] Traubel: "I asked: 'Does Eakins wear well? Is he a good comrade?' W.: 'He does: he is: he has seen a great deal: is not too ready to tell it: but is full, rich, when he is drawn upon: has a dry, quiet manner that is very impressive to me, knowing, as I do, its background.' I asked: 'Did you find him to lack the social gifts? he is accused of being uncouth, unchary, boorish.' 'Perhaps: I could hardly say: "lacking social gifts" is rather vague: what are social gifts?' Then after further cogitation: 'The parlor puts quite its own measure upon social gifts: I should say, Tom Eakins lacks them as, for instance, it would be said I lack them: not that they are forgotten, despised, but that they enter secondarily upon the affairs of my life. Eakins might put it this way: first there is this thing to do, then this other thing, maybe this third thing, or this fourth: these done, got out of the way, *now* the social graces. You see, he does not dismiss them; he only gives them their place.

LLOYD GOODRICH, *Thomas Eakins* (1982)

Born in Philadelphia, he attended the Pennsylvania Academy of the Fine Arts and studied anatomy at Jefferson Medical College in Philadelphia. After spending three years in Paris at the Ecole des Beaux-Arts, he traveled in Italy, Germany, and Spain, returning to Philadelphia in 1870.

His paintings combined his unusual scientific knowledge with draftsmanship and unflinching realism. Besides his famous rowing paintings (he himself enjoyed sculling and sailing), his figure paintings are among his strongest works. He painted portraits of friends, students, and people whose personal character interested him or whose profession (in medicine, music, science) struck a responsive note. They are remarkable for their evocative emotional force as well as for their paint-erly quality. His medical portraits contributed to his lifelong reputation as a controversial figure: the famous portrait of Dr. Gross (*The Gross Clinic*), now considered one of his masterpieces, was greeted by many in the art world with shock and revulsion.

Eakins was an inspired and revered teacher at the Pennsylvania Academy, becoming its director in 1882, but his insistence on using nude models, male and female, evoked criticism, and he was forced to resign in 1886.

Noted as representing a distinctly American sensibility, Eakins, along with Albert Pinkham Ryder and Winslow Homer, is considered one of America's greatest artists.

Childe Hassam 1859–1935 Artist

He has founded his art not on any recondite ideas. He has no interest in subject as subject. There are few traces of sentiment in him. But all through his paintings there is disclosed the best foundation of all—a feeling for beauty . . . the beauty of nature pure and simple, an affair of light and color, of some casual moment of sensuous charm.

ROYAL CORTISSOZ, *American Artists* (1923)

The deep affection that grew between Hassam and the older Celia Thaxter is evident in the many sonnets she composed in his honor. The earliest, dated July 25, 1890, is a play upon the crescent moon device he used at the time to sign his painting. It begins,

> A crescent with its glory just begun,
> A spark from the great central fires sublime,
> A crescent that shall orb into a sun,
> And burn resplendent through the mists of time

DONELSON F. HOOPES, *Childe Hassam* (1979)

Born in Dorchester, Massachusetts. After finishing two years of high school he went to work in Boston, his aptitude for drawing leading him into the field of art. He learned wood engraving and became known as an illustrator, meantime studying painting and drawing at the Boston Art Club, and as a private pupil of a German painter. He soon began sketching from nature, using watercolor in his early years.

In 1883 he traveled abroad, and in 1886 he returned for a three-year stay in Paris, where Impressionism was in full flower. By the time he returned to America his paintings were full of light and color. He settled in New York, where he painted Union Square and other city scenes; summer months he spent on the New England Isles of Shoals, at Appledore, where his masterpiece *The Room of Flowers* was painted.

In New York he was a lively member of the art world. Along with fellow artists John Twachtman and J. Alden Weir and others, he withdrew from the established Society of American Artists, and with them formed a group of American Impressionists who became known as The Ten. They exhibited together over the next twenty years. Hassam, Weir, and Twachtman (posthumously) were represented in the famous Armory Show of 1913.

By 1915, Hassam began spending much time in printmaking, etching in particular, but he is best known for his painting: *The Flag Series,* his airy interiors, and rich, atmospheric landscapes.

He died in East Hampton, where in 1917 he had established his permanent summer home.

Self portrait, etching and drypoint, 1915

Charlotte Perkins Gilman 1860–1935 Reformer and Writer

Mr. Howells told me I was the only optimist reformer he ever met. Perhaps because I was not a reformer, but a philosopher. I worked for various reforms, as Socrates went to war when Athens needed his services, but we do not remember him as a soldier. My business was to find out what ailed society, and how most easily and naturally to improve it.

· ·

As to looks, if I had been sex-conscious and dressed the part I think I should have been called beautiful. But one does not call a philosophic steam-engine beautiful. My dress was not designed to allure.

CHARLOTTE PERKINS GILMAN, in *The Living of Charlotte Perkins Gilman:*
An Autobiography (1935)

Born in Hartford, Connecticut, a descendant of Lyman Beecher. Her father, Frederick Perkins, left home soon after Charlotte's birth, and her childhood was dominated by a distantly severe mother.

From early years she felt a commitment both to public service and to writing, but she found paralyzing difficulty in combining a public and intellectual life with a role as wife and mother. After marriage to Charles Walter Stetson and the birth of their daughter, Katherine, in 1885, she suffered a serious breakdown. A second marriage to her cousin George Gilman was successful.

Through her many writings, Charlotte Gilman became widely known as a humanist, a social theorist, and a cultural analyst, with a central concern for the subordination of woman to man and woman's economic dependence on man, as was spelled out in *Women and Economics* (1898). She is best known today for *The Yellow Wallpaper* (1892), a powerful and personal short story about a woman's descent into madness. With Kate Chopin's *The Awakening*, it is now considered a key feminist text of the era. Mention should also be made of her lively and feminist futuristic fantasy *Herland* (1915).

Portrait by Ellen Day Hale (1855–1940), oil on canvas, c. 1890

Portrait by Berenice Abbott (1898–1991), photograph, 1950

Frank Lloyd Wright 1869–1959 Architect

. . . so I took him [Wright] to Washington and he wore a cloak over his shoulders and had a big cane and never took his hat off when he came into the Oval Room and he stopped at the door with great drama and said, so the President could hear, "You know, Carleton, I've always told you I would rather be Wright than President," and then he wheeled around and came up to the President's desk and shook hands with him and he said. . . "Franklin," or "Frank," he called him, "Frank," he said, "you ought to get up out of that chair and look around at what they're doing to your city here, miles and miles of ionic and corinthian columns!"

CARLETON SMITH, quoted in Brendan Gill, *Many Masks:*
A Life of Frank Lloyd Wright (1987)

Among Wright's tiny penciled annotations is a description of himself as he suspects the reader is bound to see him: "The man apparently was a sort of clever confidence-man, winning by sheer dexterity over those of more solid worth and greater attainments. . . . Many suffered in silence that he might glitter—I know! I know!"

BRENDAN GILL, *Many Masks*

Born in Wisconsin. While studying briefly at the University of Wisconsin he worked for a builder, then went to Chicago, where he was associated with the much admired architect Louis Sullivan. They separated after six years.

Wright claimed that the blocks he played with as a child (designed by Friedrich Froebel, the founder of the kindergarten) had a profound influence on his architecture: his earliest works had a cubistic form. Japanese architecture was another early influence (he probably saw the replica of the Japanese temple at the World's Columbian Exposition in Chicago in 1893). The two-story, horizontal house with low, overhung eaves was characteristic of Wright's design, which he named Prairie style, publicized in 1901. His own studio-house Taliesin, in Spring Green, Wisconsin, was its great example. By 1914 his style was changing, his work becoming more abstract. From 1916 to 1922 he lived in Japan, completing the famous Imperial Hotel in Tokyo in 1922.

Although always original, Wright's work reflected the movements of the times: the skyscraper and art deco in the 1920s, in the '40s and '50s the International style (Le Corbusier, Gropius, and Mies van der Rohe were the famous three responsible for its influence). Celebrated examples of his genius are Falling Water (1936), Taliesin West in Arizona, and the Guggenheim Museum in New York City (1959).

An orderly account of his personal life would be difficult to present, since even the year of his birth is not altogether certain. His autobiography contributes to the general haziness, and among several biographies Brendan Gill's title, *Many Masks,* gives us a clue to his contradictory though apparently engaging personality. His work is our reminder that this iconoclast and genius was the most influential and exciting American architect in the twentieth century.

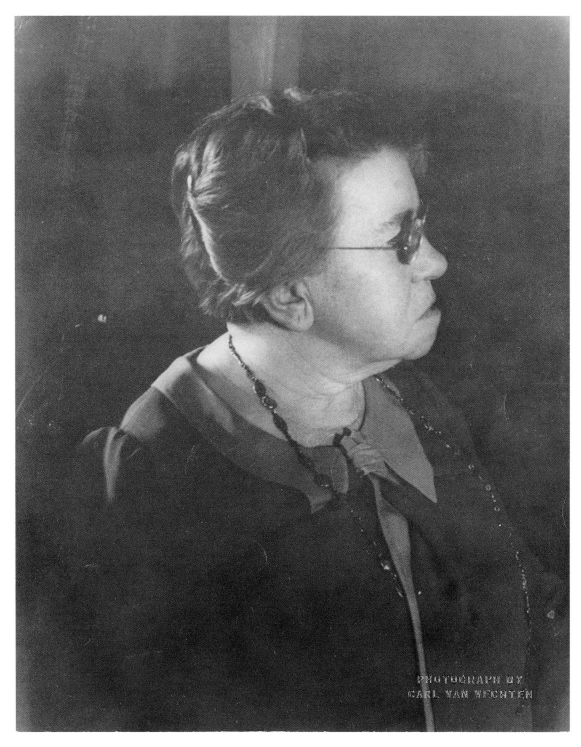

Portrait by Carl Van Vechten (1880–1964), photograph, 1934

Emma Goldman 1869–1940 Political Activist

She is so violent a radical that a U.S. soldier was given three years in the military prison at Leavenworth for merely attending one of her lectures and then shaking hands with her. . . . And this bomb-thrower proved to be a stout, plain-faced, eye-glassed woman like a Jewish haus-frau with a little education. . . . Just a comfortable, busy, immensely practical and undreamy and anti-violent housewife and engaged in—hear me now, this is literal—standing at a counter selling pies and tarts and ice cream for The Cause!

> SINCLAIR LEWIS in a letter of 1910, quoted in Mark Schorer,
> *Sinclair Lewis: An American Life* (1961)

One commonly hears of such persons as Emma Goldman and Alexander Berkman only as remote and horrendous malefactors, half human and half reptilian. . . . All this indignation, unfortunately, conceals something, and that is the somewhat disconcerting fact that both are extremely intelligent—that once their aberrant political ideals are set aside they are seen to have very sharp wits. They think clearly, unsentimentally and even a bit brilliantly. They write simple, glowing and excellent English. Their feelings, far from being those of yeggmen, cannibals, and prohibition enforcement officers, are those of highly civilized persons.

> H. L. MENCKEN, 1925, in Marion Elizabeth Rodgers, ed.,
> *The Impossible H. L. Mencken* (1991)

Born in Russia, she immigrated to the United States in 1885, and in 1886 she became a U.S. citizen. Having as a child witnessed the abuse of power in Russia and in her own home, she now found injustice in the New World. On the Lower East Side in New York, where she worked as a seamstress, she was incensed by the plight of the worker. The system that allowed the increasing exploitation of workers by their wealthy employers became intolerable, and Goldman turned to anarchism.

With her longtime lover and ally Alexander Berkman (a revolutionist who attempted to assassinate industrialist Henry Clay Frick), she published the radical monthly *Mother Earth* and spoke passionately from coast to coast, agitating for freedom of the individual, free speech, and birth control. She was censored, jailed, and deported with Berkman to Russia in 1919. There she was disillusioned by the suppression and the Bolsheviks' abandonment of the Revolution. She left Russia and continued to fight her causes for freedom in England, Spain, and Canada, where she died.

Henry Ford 1863–1947 Industrialist

. . . at last, in nineteeneight, he felt he was far enough along to risk throwing up his job with the Detroit Edison Company, where he'd worked his way up from night fireman to chief engineer, to put all his time into working on a new gasoline engine. . . .

and in driving his mechanical buggy, sitting there at the lever, jauntily dressed in a tightbuttoned jacket and a high collar and a derby hat, back and forth over the level illpaved streets of Detroit,

scaring the big brewery horses and the skinny trotting horses and the sleekrumped pacers with the motor's loud explosions,

looking for men scatterbrained enough to invest money in a factory for building automobiles.

JOHN DOS PASSOS, "Tin Lizzie," in *The Big Money* (1936)

Born on a farm near Dearborn, Michigan. At age sixteen Ford took a job in a Detroit machine shop, where he exercised his mechanical inventiveness working with the new internal combustion engine until, in 1890, he produced his first car. By 1903 he had established the Ford Motor Company, and in 1908 he brought out the Ford Model T (after Models A, B, C, and so on). Ford also perfected the assembly-line method of production, and thus in 1916 brought out more than 730,000 Model T's at the low selling price of $360 each. At the same time, Ford announced that his workers would earn $5 a day, against the average $11 per week. Ford was now internationally famous, as well as colossally rich, and seemed to have a political career in view. But his ignorance and bigotry worked against him: his scurrilous anti-Semitic magazine articles, his bumptious anti-intellectualism ("History is bunk" was one of his much-quoted aphorisms). In 1932, Ford introduced the eight-cylinder Ford V-8, which was a great success, but the day of Ford's dominance in the industry was over. He spent his last years in retirement; but it has been recently said of him that Ford "more than any other individual perhaps, invented the twentieth century."

Portrait by Hanz Wollner (c. 1899–c. 1946), bronze bust, cast after 1937 plaster

Wilbur Wright 1867–1912 Pioneer Aviator

They stayed home instead of marrying the way other boys did, and puttered all day about the house picking up a living with jobprinting,

bicyclerepair work,

sitting up late nights reading books on aerodynamics.

Still they were sincere churchmembers, their bicycle business was prosperous, a man could rely on their word. They were popular in Dayton.

In those days flyingmachines were the big laugh of all the crackerbarrel philosophers. . . . The Wrights' big problem was to find a place secluded enough to carry on their experiments without being the horselaugh of the countryside. Then they had no money to spend;

they were practical mechanics; when they needed anything they built it themselves.

They hit on Kitty Hawk,

on the great dunes and sandy banks that stretch south towards Hatteras seaward of the Albemarle Sound,

a vast stretch of seabeach

empty except for a coastguard station, a few fishermen's shacks and the swarms of mosquitoes and the ticks and chiggers in the crabgrass behind the dunes.

JOHN DOS PASSOS, "The Campers at Kitty Hawk,"
in *The Big Money* (1936)

Born in Indiana, grew up in Dayton, Ohio; his father was a bishop of the United Brethren in Christ. With his brother Orville (b. 1871), Wilbur earned pocket money by selling homemade mechanical toys. In the late 1880s the brothers built their own bicycle and formed the Wright Bicycle Company. In the mid-1890s they began experimenting with air flight, building their first glider and trying it out at Kill Devil Hill, near Kitty Hawk, North Carolina. Over several years and visits they made a thousand glider flights of six hundred feet and more.

They then turned their attention to the powered machine. On December 17, 1903, Orville Wright made the first airplane flight, with Wilbur running alongside, holding the wing in position, until the plane left the ground. It was airborne for twelve seconds and ran 120 feet; later in the day, Wilbur flew the plane 852 feet in fifty-nine seconds.

The brothers secured a patent for their invention in May 1906 and continued to make ever longer and loftier flights. In 1909, Wilbur won the huge admiration of the French with his flights, including one trip over Paris. He negotiated construction contracts in France, England, Germany, and Italy. He died of typhoid fever.

Photographer unknown (camera belonging to Léon Bollée, 1870–1913),
photograph, summer 1908, near Le Mans, France

Gertrude Stein 1874–1946 Writer

On sunny mornings, when the streets of the Right Bank were full of people, a hallucination would sometimes overtake you. From around the corner there appeared the vision of a great Buddha on wheels, erratically charging down the thoroughfare, divinely indifferent to the fate of mortal traffic, heedless of laughter or imprecation. The sudden vision was all too real; it was merely Miss Gertrude Stein single-mindedly bound upon some practical errand in her model-T Ford.

LLOYD R. MORRIS, *Not So Long Ago* (1949)

The pavilion atelier in rue de Fleurus was a catch-all of beings and created objects, and everything she looked upon was hers in more than the usual sense. Her weighty divans and armchairs covered with dark, new-looking horsehair; her dogs, Basket and Pepe, conspicuous, special, afflicted as neurotic children; her clutter of small tables each with its own clutter of perhaps valuable but certainly treasured objects; her Alice B. Toklas; her visitors; and finally, ranging the walls from floor to ceiling . . . her celebrated collection of paintings by her collection of celebrated painters. . . . Miss Stein herself sat there in full possession of herself, the scene, the spectators, wearing thick no-colored shapeless woolen clothes and honest woolen stockings knitted for her by Miss Toklas, looking extremely like a handsome old Jewish patriarch who had backslid and shaved off his beard.

KATHERINE ANNE PORTER, "The Wooden Umbrella" (1952),
in *The Days Before*

Born in Pennsylvania. Radcliffe, 1897, where she studied with William James (whose influence, with that of Bergson, she described in *Lectures in America* in 1935). She left this country in 1902 and lived thereafter mostly in France, where her Paris salon became famous for the presence and works of Matisse, Picasso, and other artists. Her work of fiction *Three Lives* appeared in 1909. In 1914 came *Tender Buttons,* a vast collection of small grammarless non-logical poems, each begetting some object. Other books included *The Making of Americans* (1925), *The Autobiography of Alice B. Toklas* (1933), and *Paris France* (1940). Her opera, *Four Saints in Three Acts,* with music by Virgil Thompson, was completed in 1934. She herself compared her writing technique with that of the sequence frames in a motion picture.

Portrait by Jo Davidson (1883–1952), terra-cotta bust, 1923

Unidentified photographer, c. 1923

D. W. Griffith 1875–1948 Motion Picture Director

He had long legs and walked fast; during rehearsals he was everywhere. Sometimes he would make drastic plot changes; at other times he would suggest to an actor an odd walk, a curious mannerism or some other bit of business to make the character interesting and individual.

. . . As rehearsals continued, Mr. Griffith would move around us like a referee in the ring, circling, bending, walking up to an actor, staring down over his great beak of a nose, then turning away. By the time that we had run through the story several times, he had viewed the action from every conceivable camera angle.

. . . He grew quiet when filming started. He usually put his head as close as possible to the lens to view the angle of each shot. Then he would sit down on his wooden chair and nervously twirl his ring or jingle a handful of coins in his pocket. He would shift the coins from one hand to the other.

LILLIAN GISH (with Ann Pinchot), *The Movies, Mr. Griffith, and Me* (1969)

Born in Kentucky of an impoverished farm family; his father had been a heroic Confederate cavalry officer, known as "Roaring Jake," in the Civil War. After several years of bit-part acting and attempted playwriting, David Wark Griffith in 1908 was hired by the new Biograph film company and soon became its principal director. Over the next dozen years Griffith made more than four hundred films of all types and lengths. In his development of various techniques—the long shot, the closeup, the fadeout, the more actorly facial expression—D. W. Griffith (as he was now known) virtually created the art of the cinema. His 1915 epic film *The Birth of a Nation* was an enormous success; it stirred resentment then and later through its favorable view of the Ku Klux Klan, but with filmmakers and historians it is generally regarded (in the careful view of one expert) as the "single most important film in the development of cinema as an art." *Intolerance* (1916), about man's inhumanity throughout the ages (and at three hours even longer than its predecessor), is likewise described as "surely one of the all time great movies." In 1919, with Mary Pickford, Douglas Fairbanks, and Charlie Chaplin, Griffith founded United Artists Corporation. In the 1920s, Griffith's prestige dwindled, and he had difficulty funding new ventures; he continued to be involved with filmmaking through the '30s, but with no notable success. In his last years he was a lonely and half-forgotten man.

Isadora Duncan 1878–1927 Dancer

[After watching Isadora Duncan dance to music from Wagner's *Tristan and Isolde* in Carnegie Hall:]

It's hard to set down how much I enjoyed this performance. Isadora as she appears on that big simple stage seems like all womanhood—she looms big as the mother of the race. A heavy solid figure, large columnar legs, a solid high belly, breasts not too full and her head seems to be no more important than it should to give the body the chief place. In one of the dances she was absolutely nude save for a thin gauze drapery hanging from her shoulders. In none was she much clothed, simple filmy coverings usually with a loincloth.

JOHN SLOAN, Diary, February 15, 1911

Born in San Francisco, youngest of four children, she was raised by her unconventional mother. As a little girl she showed talent in dancing, and by age eleven she was teaching dancing classes.

Early on she dismissed ballet's classical movements in favor of the free expression of the body, developing motion from the solar plexus and introducing the idea of dancing barefoot. She was inspired by ancient Greece, but it was nature that most moved her. Believing that the dance should be an expression of universal thought and emotion, she felt the body should follow the movements of nature and messages from the soul. Her advice in her autobiography, *My Life,* was to "listen to the music with your soul . . . feel an inner awakening. . . . This awakening is the first step in dance."

She suffered terrible personal tragedies during her life, and American audiences were unresponsive to her art, but she found success in Europe and Russia, performing and teaching, inspiring in her expression and her unordinary vision. Her own technique, since it was improvisational, could not be copied, but her incomparable contribution was in liberating the spirit.

Portrait by John Sloan (1871–1951), etching, 1915

Portrait by Antonio Frasconi (b. 1919), woodcut, 1952. © Antonio Frasconi /
Licensed by VAGA, New York, NY.

Albert Einstein 1879–1955 Scientist

> Only the stars defined his radius;
> His life, restricted to a wooden house,
> Was in his head. He saw a fledgling fall.
> Two times he tried to nest it, but it fell
> Once more and died; he wandered home again—
> We save so plain a story for great men.
> An angel in ill-fitting sweaters,
> Writing children naïve letters,
> A violin player lacking vanities
> A giant wit among the homilies—
> We have no parallel to that immense
> Intelligence.

HOWARD MOSS, *New Selected Poems* (1985)

You had to see Einstein in a small skiff to be able to judge the strength of the roots which attached him to a primitive life. Barefoot or in sandals, his white ducks baggy at the knees, sagging at the hips, his broad chest molded in an old pullover or a faded swimming suit, his powerful neck bare, reddened by sun and wind, his leonine head with its aura of long hair standing on end, he stood swaying gently to the rocking of the boat as though nailed to the deck and at one with the sail he maneuvered.

ANTONINA VALLENTIN, quoted in Hilary Cuny, *Albert Einstein: The Man and His Theories* (translated by Mervyn Savill, 1963)

Born in Ulm, Germany, and grew up in Munich; he and his family were nonpracticing Jews. As a child he seemed to be a dangerously slow learner, but in his early teens he developed a strong interest in physics and mathematics. He entered the Swiss Federal Polytechnic School in Zurich, where he flourished; and he so much appreciated the democratic ambiance of Switzerland that in 1901 he became a Swiss citizen and remained one all his life.

For six years in the early 1900s, Einstein worked as an assistant in the Swiss Patent Office in Berne, and it was during this time that he published the scientific papers that would earn him the Nobel Prize in physics in 1921. One of these, "On the Electrodynamics of Moving Bodies" (1905), established his theory of relativity: essentially, that the speed of light is constant and all motion is relative to it. In another paper the same year he offered the equation $E = mc^2$—that the energy of a body is equal to its mass multiplied by the square of the speed of light. When energy changes, the mass also changes. The theory anticipated the splitting of the atom in 1940.

In 1913, Einstein became professor of physics at Berlin and created his own Institute of Physics, where, among other discoveries, he set forth new laws of motion. But in 1933, deeply disturbed by the surge of German anti-Semitism, he left Germany to become a member of the Institute for Advanced Studies in Princeton, New Jersey. Here he remained for the rest of his life, a familiar, friendly figure in the neighborhood. During World War II, rather against his will, he advised on the Manhattan Project.

Faces on the Public Scene: Through the 1920s

"PRIVATE FACES IN PUBLIC PLACES," W. H. AUDEN SAID ON A CERTAIN POETIC occasion, "Are wiser and nicer / Than public faces in private places." Most of the individuals in this segment occupied public places of one kind or another. Two of them, Theodore Roosevelt and Woodrow Wilson, were presidents of the United States, and both had previously been governor of a state. One, Oliver Wendell Holmes, Jr., was a Supreme Court Justice. One, Booker T. Washington, was head and in effect creator of a public educational institute in Alabama, and a tireless platform speaker across the country. Another, Eugene V. Debs, was at the highly visible center of the labor union struggles for more than thirty years.

Still another, Clarence Darrow, was the object of fascinated public attention for his courtroom performances, whether defending (and saving from execution) two young Chicagoans accused of killing a third youth for the thrill of it, or representing a Tennessee schoolteacher whose alleged crime was teaching the theory of evolution. Two others, Sacco and Vanzetti, were forced into public view by the dragging ineptitude and prejudice of the Massachusetts legal system, and put to death (in August 1927) while the world watched. The journalist H. L. Mencken was not as visually familiar as those just mentioned, but from his permanent home base in Baltimore he had his nationally attended-to say on the follies, political, legal, and intellectual, of the American public scene. Al Capone, finally, managed to become far more closely watched than he ever wished.

To what extent, then, were there "private faces" among these characters? As to the actual portraits, Oliver Wendell Holmes, in a charcoal drawing of 1926 by S. J. Woolf, appears exactly as he was: as an eighty-five-year-old Supreme Court justice—but with a detectable private personality, a tough and independent spirit, glinting out at us. Woodrow Wilson, on the other hand, in a lithographic poster of 1918 by Leo Mielziner, gives us the public face par excellence; the poster in fact functions as a presidential summons to all Americans to "Answer the Red Cross Christmas Roll Call for Universal Membership" (it is so inscribed, at bottom right), a dire necessity as the Great War rumbled on.

Eugene Debs and Clarence Darrow are the subjects of that often, or in earlier times, more public mode of portrayal, the bust, respectively by Louis Mayer in 1919 and Jo Davidson in 1929; but each, differently, suggests the private man. Debs appears tight-lipped and watchful, as befitted a person on trial at that very moment for allegedly obstructing the country's recent war effort. (Justice Holmes wrote the majority opinion that sent Debs to jail; it was the action most regretted and criticized by Holmes's admirers, but one that Holmes justified on the grounds that Debs's attempt to sabotage army recruiting had constituted a "clear and present danger.") Darrow, in Davidson's rendering, shows the facial lines of profound and wrenching experience, and the humanity and humor that sustained him.

Theodore Roosevelt is caught, in a 1903 photograph by Peter A. Juley, in a moment of relaxation, sitting under a tree at his summer home in Oyster Bay, Long Island, temporarily removed from public cares and duties; but ready on the instant, one feels, to spring to his feet and plunge into some new phase of the strenuous life. The photograph of Booker T. Washington, taken in 1895 (probably), near the time of his Atlanta speech, by Elmer Chickering, is something of a surprise; and reminds us that, when Washington made that (for the moment) electrifying address to the Cotton States Exhibition and became overnight the leading figure in American black education, he was only thirty-nine years old; he looks, if anything, quite a few years younger than that—alert and expectant, to be sure, but as yet untried.

H. L. Mencken, in a 1940 photograph by Aubrey Bodine, seems decidedly his own man. It is a private face, the most so of any in this group, but the face of one who peers intently at the public scene (consider his eyes) and reflects on it and prepares to tear it apart in his writing. The pictures of Sacco and Vanzetti and of Al Capone are themselves public documents. The two Italian immigrants, sitting silent and perhaps stunned, were photographed by an unidentified official in the prison at Dedham, Massachusetts, about the time, in the summer of 1921, that they were found guilty of first-degree murder by Judge Webster Thayer's court. Al Capone was snapped by an unidentified police authority on the day after Christmas in 1925, following the murder of a gangland leader named Lonergan, and two of his henchmen, in a Brooklyn nightclub. Capone had been present in the nightclub, visiting from Chicago, and an eyewitness to the event, but he vowed to the police, as they took him off to prison, that he simply couldn't remember a thing.

In the verbal imagings, most of these individuals demonstrate the Auden maxim that the private face in the public place is not only nicer but wiser than the other way around. Woodrow Wilson is a case in point. The official Wilson, one feels, is a frozen figure, nothing but public; but in a typical letter of 1913 from the White House to his wife, Ellen, summering in New Hampshire, the private Wilson appears, expressing his sense of personal connection with the nameless citizens on farms and in cities whom it was his obligation to represent and to govern. At first glance, admittedly, Wilson's husbandly prose may bring to mind Henry James's comment about Emerson: "There was no familiarity in him. . . . Even his letters to his wife are courtesies, they are not familiarities." And yet a closer look discloses a certain personal coloration, a quiet intimacy of language. Holmes is described moving on from an elaborate public ceremony toward his new Washington home, recalling his Civil War days in the same neighborhood, and then wondering whether his wife, Fanny, will have enough heat in their house. But Holmes was the very type whose most striking quality was the personal wisdom and the personal rhetoric of his public pronouncements.

Roosevelt, too, as Edith Wharton tells us, brought a sometimes fiercely personal note both to his public dealings, as with the secretary of the navy, and to the "whirlwind welcomes" he accorded more personal visitors. The great appeal of Eugene Debs, as one "hard-bitten socialist" is heard remarking, was the wise simplicity of his personality. Something of the same can be said of Clarence Darrow, in Lincoln Steffens's report on him: the private anxieties breaking through and lending a humanizing touch to the public self-assurance. Booker T. Washington, on the contrary, may provide negative support for the Auden argument; he was insistently the public man, keeping his private self (busy and even ruthless as that self could be) out of sight; it was Washington himself who chose the newspaper account of him as a public presence to illustrate a phase of his autobiography *Up from Slavery*. There is perhaps a trace more of the personal Washington in Dudley Randall's amiably satiric poem than in *Up from Slavery:* of the Washington who continues almost wistfully to give his thoughts on racial improvement to the implacably opposed W. E. B. Du Bois.

The glimpses of Sacco and Vanzetti in 1916 and in 1927 are passages in Upton Sinclair's novel *Boston* (1928). It is a work of fiction by a writer with more than thirty years' experience. It is drawn carefully from the knowable facts and is regarded by students of the matter as the best account of it ever put together. Al Capone, after a ruminative comment on him by Damon Runyon, is allowed to speak for himself, and he comes forward in his self-proclaimed role of public benefactor.

And then there is H. L. Mencken, brought to life with a force of comic insight and expression worthy of the Baltimore prophet; a profile composed by Mencken's literary and journalistic heir and fellow Baltimorean Russell Baker. Baker too has "made a difference," very much for the better, in our contemporary cultural situation, and it does this book good to have him in it.

Oliver Wendell Holmes, Jr. 1841–1935
Justice of the United States Supreme Court

On Monday, December the eighth [1902], Holmes, dressed in his heavy long black gown, stood in the old Courtroom in the Capitol building and laid his hand on the great Bible before him. On this Bible, John Marshall had been sworn in, Taney and Storey. Around him in niches on the wall, Justices in marble looked down; overhead the red, white and blue shield gleamed. . . .

Afterward walking the streets of Washington, with his long stride, Doherty [his secretary] trotting beside him, Holmes looked eagerly about. The excitement of the ceremony had moved him, made him doubly conscious of all his surroundings. The wide avenues, the flamboyant statues of generals and statesmen, crowded suddenly by a block of tumble-down Negro shacks. . . .

Turning the corner from H Street and coming suddenly upon the historic square that was to be his home, Holmes halted. How well he remembered this square! Here, some forty years ago, tired soldiers had bivouacked; the grass of the park had been trampled into mire. But how tall and sturdy the trees were now and how orderly it looked with the painted benches, the fat pigeons pecking where the ground was wet. Only the statue of General Jackson was the same, prancing forever on its bronze rocking horse, waving its cocked hat in a gesture ridiculous and touching.

"Doherty!" Holmes said. "The last time I walked here, I was ankle deep in mud. There were signs along the street: *Undertaker. Bodies embalmed while you wait.* And now I'm an elderly judge, and it's nineteen hundred and two, and there's been a coal strike. And how the devil, Doherty, are we to get coal into 16 Lafayette Square before Mrs. Holmes arrives on Thursday?"

CATHERINE DRINKER BOWEN, *Yankee from Olympus:*
Justice Holmes and His Family (1944)

Born in Boston, the son of the writer, physician, and wit Oliver Wendell Holmes. Holmes graduated from Harvard in 1861. He enlisted in the Massachusetts Volunteers, was wounded at Antietam and Chancellorsville, and mustered out as a captain. He was admitted to the bar in 1867. In 1881, Holmes produced *The Common Law,* which turned on the principle that "the life of the law has not been logic; it has been experience." In 1882, Holmes was appointed to the Supreme Court of Massachusetts, serving there twenty years and becoming its chief justice in 1899.

In 1902, President Roosevelt appointed Holmes to the U.S. Supreme Court. Here he served for thirty years, retiring just after his ninety-first birthday. Through the pungency and resonance of his minority opinions he became known as the Great Dissenter, setting forth such concepts as a "clear and present danger" being the only reason for curtailing free speech, and advocating "free thought— not free thought for those who agree with us but freedom for the thought that we hate." But Holmes delivered many a tartly worded majority opinion as well.

Portrait by S. J. Woolf (1880–1948), charcoal on paper, 1926

Portrait by Elmer Chickering (dates uncertain), photograph, c. 1895

Booker T. Washington 1856–1915 Educator and Political Spokesman

There was a remarkable figure, tall, bony, straight as a Sioux chief, high forehead, straight nose, heavy jaws, and strong, determined mouth, with big white teeth, piercing eyes and commanding manner. The sinews stood out on his bronzed neck, and his muscular right arm swung high in the air, with a lead-pencil grasped in the clenched brown fist. His feet were planted squarely, with the heels together and the toes turned out. His voice rang out clear and true, and he paused impressively as he made each point. Within ten minutes the multitude was in an uproar of enthusiasm—handkerchiefs were waved, canes were flourished, hats were tossed in the air.

CORRESPONDENT JAMES CREELMAN, dispatch to the *New York World,* September 18, 1895, from Atlanta, following Washington's speech to the Cotton States Exposition; quoted in Booker T. Washington, *Up from Slavery* (1901)

"It seems to me," said Booker T.
"That all you folks have missed the boat
Who shout about the right to vote,
And spend vain days and sleepless nights
In uproar over civil rights.
Just keep your mouth shut, do not grouse,
But work, and save, and buy a house."
"I don't agree," said W. E. B.
"For what can property avail
If dignity and justice fail?

Unless you help to make the laws,
They'll steal your house with trumped-up clause" . . .

DUDLEY RANDALL, "Booker T. and W. E. B.," in *Cities Burning* (1969)

Born in Franklin County, Virginia; his father was probably a white man, his mother a cook in the slave-holding James Burroughs family. After emancipation Washington moved with his family to Malden, West Virginia. He taught for a few years at a public school in Malden, earning a name for speaking out about the economic betterment of poor blacks. When a black normal school was chartered in Tuskegee, Alabama, in 1881, Washington was asked to head it. When he died in 1915, Tuskegee Institute had 100 buildings, 1,537 students, 197 faculty members, 2,000 acres of land, and an endowment of $2 million.

From the mid-1880s onward, Washington was in great demand as a public speaker, most famously at the Cotton States Exposition in Atlanta, where his address—with its advice to "cast down your buckets where you are"—electrified the audience and the country. His emphasis was always on black economic self-determination, and accommodation with the white community; activists—Du Bois chief among them—attacked him as too little concerned with civil rights and higher education.

Theodore Roosevelt 1858–1919 Twenty-sixth President of the United States

"Well, I *am* glad to welcome to the White House some one to whom I can quote 'The Hunting of the Snark' without being asked what I mean!"

Such was my first greeting from Theodore Roosevelt after his accession to the Presidency. . . . "Would you believe it," he added, "no one in the Administration has ever heard of Alice, much less of the Snark, and the other day, when I said to the Secretary of the Navy, 'Mr. Secretary, *What I say three times is true,*' he did not recognize the allusion, and answered with an aggrieved air, 'Mr. President, it would never for a moment have occurred to me to impugn your veracity'!"

These whirlwind welcomes were very characteristic, for Theodore Roosevelt had in his mind so clear a vision of each interlocutor's range of subjects that when he met any one who interested him, he could never bear to waste a moment on preliminaries. . . .

With his faculty of instantly extracting the best that each person had to give, he seldom failed, when we met, to turn the talk to books. So much of his time was spent among the bookless that many people never suspected either the range of his literary culture or his learned interest in the natural sciences.

EDITH WHARTON, *A Backward Glance* (1934)

President Roosevelt takes a great amount of physical exercise. He enjoyed most, perhaps, his experience as a ranchman out West and his hunting trips after big game, in which he has bagged Rocky Mountain sheep, grizzlies and California lions whose skins now decorate his home. But in Washington he has to content himself with riding through the neighboring woods and fields of Maryland and Virginia, or, in inclement weather, with fencing or singlestick, in both of which exercises he is an expert.

Fads and Fancies (1905)

Born in New York City into a wealthy family; graduated from Harvard in 1880. After a spell in the Dakota Territory, in the wake of his first wife's death, and a second marriage, to Edith Kermit (who bore him five children), Roosevelt entered the public scene, serving as police commissioner of New York (1895–97) and assistant secretary of the Navy (1897–98). His exploits as colonel of a volunteer cavalry unit (the Rough Riders) during the Spanish-American War gained him great popularity and the governorship of New York. In 1901 he was made vice-president under William McKinley; upon McKinley's assassination later that year, Roosevelt became president and served through two terms (1901–9). His presidency featured aggressive efforts to control the big corporations ("malefactors of great wealth"), a vigorous role in foreign affairs (he helped end the Russo-Japanese war in 1905), and enormous activity in preserving public lands and creating national parks and wildlife refuges. By 1912, Roosevelt was self-appointed candidate of the Progressive, or Bull Moose, Party. The party in fact helped elect the Democrat Woodrow Wilson. Roosevelt urged American entry into the Great War long before 1917.

Portrait by Peter A. Juley (1862–1937), photograph, 1903

Portrait by Leo Mielziner (1898–1935), lithographic poster, 1918

Woodrow Wilson 1856–1924 Twenty-Eighth President of the United States

I seem in my present isolation to feel more than ever my relations of fellowship and innate sympathy with all the unnamed people about me. The little children in the streets and on the roads, the plain people at the cottage doors and in the fields and coming and going in the hot city bring the tears to my eyes. My responsibility to them somehow makes me comprehend them better. I seem to know what they are thinking and what they are looking for. And the lamp that guides my thought in it all is my love for you and for our darling daughters, the sweet incomparable little ladies who are the fruit and sanction of our love for one another.

WOODROW WILSON TO ELLEN AXSON WILSON,
from the White House, August 17, 1913

Born in Staunton, Virginia, the son of a Presbyterian minister and later professor of theology. Wilson graduated from Princeton in 1879 and earned a Ph.D. at Johns Hopkins in 1886. The year before, he married Ellen Axson, who deeply shared his social and political ideals; they had three daughters over four years. In 1890, Wilson joined the Princeton faculty (as professor of political economy), and there his effectiveness as a teacher, and his brilliance and success as a historian (*History of the American People* in five volumes, 1902), led to his appointment as the president of Princeton in 1902. During eight years in the post, Wilson transformed Princeton into one of the country's finest universities; but his emphasis on intellectual achievement and his curtailing of undergraduate life led to his unpopularity and then to his retirement in 1910. The same year, he was elected governor of New Jersey; and his energetically pursued progressive reforms gained him national attention and, in the three-way election of 1912, the presidency. As president, Wilson followed the Rooseveltian example by strengthening the executive power, seeking to limit big business, and giving aid to education and agriculture. Ellen Axson Wilson died in 1914; in 1916, Wilson married Edith Bolling Galt. A confirmed pacifist, Wilson was slow to engage the United States in the Great War in Europe; but when circumstances forced a change of attitude, Wilson organized both the army and country for all-out war. American troops substantially helped turn the tide of the conflict. Wilson was instrumental in negotiating the armistice in November 1918, the Versailles Peace Treaty, and the covenant of the League of Nations. Wilson was then incapacitated by a sudden illness in October 1919, and during his last months in office he was unable to perform his duties.

Eugene V. Debs 1855–1926 Labor Organizer and Socialist Leader

Scores of businessmen, who had no sympathy with Debs socialism, still observed: "He's a great man," or "I love him." Heywood Broun later recorded a comment on this subject by a "hard-bitten Socialist": "Gene Debs is the only one who can get away with the sentimental flummery that's been tied onto Socialism in this country. Pretty nearly always, it gives me a swift pain to go around to meetings and have people call me 'comrade.' That's a lot of bunk. But the funny part of it is that when Debs says 'comrade' it's all right. He means it. That old man with the burning eyes actually believes that there can be such a thing as the brotherhood of man. And that's not the funniest part of it. As long as he's around, I believe it myself."

RAY GINGER, *The Bending Cross: A Biography of Eugene Debs* (1949)

. . . Clearly, the White House is the only safe place for an honest man like Debs.

GEORGE BERNARD SHAW, in Ruth Le Prade, ed., *Debs and the Poets* (1920)

Born in Terre Haute, Indiana; his parents were Alsatian immigrants who ran a grocery store. He entered local politics, and by 1885 he was elected to the Indiana State Assembly. Debs at this time was resistant to large-scale labor movements, but his experience in a frustrating railroad strike in 1888–89 brought about a change of conviction. He helped organize and then headed the American Railway Union (ARU), leading it into the historically important 1894 strike against the Pullman Company of Chicago. Federal power broke the strike and sent Debs to jail. He emerged an ardent Socialist, and he was the Socialist candidate for president in 1900, 1904, 1908, 1912, and 1920. In the aftermath of World War I, Debs was tried and convicted for, in effect, opposing America's entrance into the war. He ran his 1920 candidacy from prison and received a million votes. Debs traveled endlessly, speaking and arguing in support of workers' rights. The specifics of his political programs were not greatly attended to; what swayed countless thousands across the country was his passionate insistence on the need for human beings to help one another.

Portrait by Louis Mayer (1869–1969), bronze bust, 1968, cast after his 1919 original

Clarence Darrow 1857–1938 Lawyer

When people ask me what sort of man Darrow is, I ask them the apparently irrelative question: When? And my answer is that at three o'clock he is a hero for courage, nerve, and calm judgment, but at 3:15 he may be a coward for fear, collapse, and panicky mentality. A long, lean, loose body, with a heavy face that is molded like an athlete's body, he is more of a poet than a fighting attorney. He does fight; he is a great fighter as he is a good lawyer, learned and resourceful, but his power and his weakness is in the highly sensitive, emotional nature which sets his seeing mind in motion in that loafing body. His power is expression. He can say anything he wants to say, but he cannot conceal much; his face is too expressive. One day when we were walking from court along the street to his office he was expressing a winning sureness of his case. A passer-by halted, and drawing him aside, whispered a few words and went on. When Darrow rejoined us his face was ashen, and he could hardly walk; he was scared weak, and he did not recover for an hour. "I can't stand it to have a man I am defending hanged. I can't stand it." And then, an hour later, he was cock-sure, humorous, almost gay with self-possession and the call to encourage his associates in the case.

LINCOLN STEFFENS, *Autobiography* (1931)

Has he always won? Superficially, yes; actually, no. Did Darrow beat Bryan at Dayton? There, I think, he came closest to an actual victory. The thing was inconceivably dramatic: two ancient warlocks brought jaw to jaw at last. It was superb to see Darrow throw out his webs and prepare his baits. His virtuosity never failed. In the end Bryan staggered to the block and took that last appalling clout. It was delivered calmly, deliberately, beautifully. Bryan was killed as plainly as if he had been felled with an axe.

H. L. MENCKEN, quoted in *Vanity Fair: A Cavalcade of the 1920s and 1930s,*
edited by Cleveland Amory and Frederic Bradlee (1960)

Born in rural northeastern Ohio; studied briefly at Allegheny College and the University of Michigan Law School before being admitted to the Ohio bar in 1878. Darrow moved in 1888 to Chicago, which was his home for the rest of his life. In the pre–World War I years he was effective in making juries understand the causes of labor unrest. He then entered criminal law and was featured in a series of spectacular trials, where his eloquence and energy won national attention. Among these was the 1924 trial of the teen-agers Richard Loeb and Nathan Leopold, accused of killing a boy for thrills. They were convicted, but Darrow's innovative use of psychiatric evidence led to their receiving life imprisonment rather than being executed. Darrow was next triumphant in the 1925 "monkey trial" of the schoolteacher John T. Scopes, accused of illegally teaching evolution. Darrow's badgering of his opponent, William Jennings Bryan, a biblical literalist, was epochal. Darrow later wrote fiction, literary essays, and criminological studies, and he performed brilliantly on the lecture platform, attacking Prohibition and capital punishment and endorsing prison reform and scientific knowledge.

Portrait by Jo Davidson (1883–1952), bronze bust, 1929

H. L. Mencken 1880–1956 Critic and Editor

Like his fellow Baltimorean Babe Ruth, he was a natural. Fresh out of high school, too full of sass and beans to dawdle in college or the family cigar business, he walked into a newsroom and asked for work.

In the next thirty years he became the rude and raucous voice of a generation shaking free of nineteenth century fustian and jeering at boobs too dim to understand that God was dead, democracy ridiculous, and Puritanism a fraud.

Blessed with the most gorgeous vocabulary ever wasted on newsprint, he could make scorn hilarious or fashion a memoir of gossamer delicacy. He edited the two most brilliant magazines of his time, published a formidable scholarly work on "the American language," and was the shrewdest literary critic of his day.

He was also the funniest American writer to appear between Mark Twain and James Thurber. The humor was sometimes cruelly mean; he could speak viciously of people who thought him a close friend.

An uncle of mine lived two doors from his Hollins Street home in 1937, and though his own literary tastes favored "Doc Savage" and "The Shadow," he was surprised once when I, an illiterate 11-year-old, had to ask, "Who is Mencken?"

"He writes things in the newspaper that make people mad," my uncle explained. So he did. Many are still mad today. That would have pleased Mencken.

RUSSELL BAKER (1998)

Born in Baltimore, where he spent his entire life. Mencken joined the Baltimore *Morning Herald* in 1893 as a reporter; seven years later he moved on to the Baltimore *Sun,* and remained there as reporter, columnist, and reviewer. In 1908, Mencken became book editor of the magazine *Smart Set,* which published James Joyce, Aldous Huxley, and Willa Cather, among many others. With George Jean Nathan, in 1924, Mencken founded the magazine *American Mercury*. Mencken's masterwork was *The American Language* (1919, with several later editions). Some of his best columns were collected in *Prejudices* (1919–27), and he wrote three very readable autobiographical volumes in the 1940s.

Portrait by A. Aubrey Bodine (1906–70), photograph, 1940

Nicola Sacco 1891–1927
and Bartolomeo Vanzetti 1888–1927
Philosophical Anarchists

1916, autumn: Vanzetti and several friends, en route to an Italian-language play in Stoughton, Massachusetts, stop for a visit.

They drove to the home of a comrade whom Vanzetti had recently met at one of the East Boston gatherings. Nicola Sacco was his name, and he lived in a fine cottage, which had formerly belonged to his boss. "Great feller, Nick," explained Bart. "He work shoe-factory, is edge-trimmer, mooch skill work, he make so mooch fifty, sixty dollar week, that boy—smart feller, got lovely wife, you see."

Their host ran out to the gate to meet them, a chap of twenty-five, with even, regular features and black hair and eyes; very active, like a cat, a figure all of steel springs.

1927, summer, while the two are awaiting sentence.

For five years Bart had been tried in the fire, and he had withstood the test; it would be hard to say how any man could have stood it better. Outside, in times of excitement, he had been fanatical and violent; but now those faults were remedied by prison bars; now he was of necessity the student and thinker. He met persons of the cultivated class, and learned that they, too, were concerned about "joostice." . . .

He was gentle, he was wise, and he was dignified. The humiliations of prison life had failed to affect him. A few days after his arrest, Mike Stewart, bluff and burly, had patted him on the back and called him "Bertie"; but now the guards understood that he was a superior man, and before his death the life of the prison had come to revolve about him.

UPTON SINCLAIR, *Boston* (1928)

Sacco was born near Foggia, in southern Italy; Vanzetti in the Italian Piedmont. Both immigrated to America in 1908. Sacco became a skilled "edger" in a Massachusetts shoe factory, and Vanzetti a fish peddler. The two came to embrace the ideals of "philosophical anarchism," in the Tolstoy manner. In May 1920, Sacco and Vanzetti were arrested and charged with the murder, a month before, of a paymaster and guard at a shoe factory in South Braintree, Massachusetts, and the theft of $16,000. Their trial began in May 1921 in Dedham, before Judge Webster Thayer, a man of outspoken anti-radical prejudice. The evidence against them was flimsy, and in 1923 a condemned criminal named Madeiros confessed to the slaying and the theft. The two were nonetheless convicted and condemned to death, and all efforts to secure a retrial failed. The governor of Massachusetts was prodded into appointing a committee, consisting of the presidents of Harvard and the Massachusetts Institute of Technology and a former judge, to investigate the claims of prejudice, but the committee found no basis for a retrial. Intense national and international support for Sacco and Vanzetti increased; at one time 150 persons were arrested for picketing the Boston State House. On August 23, 1927, Sacco and Vanzetti were electrocuted.

Unidentified photographer, photograph, c. 1921;
Bartolomeo Vanzetti, *left,* and Nicola Sacco

Al Capone 1899–1947 Bootlegger

It is impossible to talk to Capone without conceding that he has that intangible attribute known as personality, or, as we say in the world of sport, "color."

DAMON RUNYON, quoted in John Kobler, *Capone: The Life and World of Al Capone* (1971)

I've been spending the best years of my life as a public benefactor. I've given people the light pleasures, shown them a good time. And all I get is abuse—the existence of a hunted man. I'm called a killer. Ninety percent of the people of Cook County drink and gamble and my offense has been to furnish them with those amusements. Whatever else they may say, my booze has been good and my games have been on the square. Public service is my motto. I've always regarded it as a public benefaction if people were given decent liquor and square games.

AL CAPONE, quoted in a press conference, in Kobler, *Capone*

Born in Brooklyn, New York. After dropping out of school at fourteen, he worked at a succession of odd jobs, including that of a barroom bouncer. It was in this occupation that he received the knife wound that earned him the nickname, popularized by the press, "Scarface." In about 1920, and coinciding with the start of Prohibition, he moved to Chicago with his new wife and joined John Torrio, a former New Yorker, in a burgeoning bootlegging operation. Capone rose rapidly within the organization and soon began capturing headlines linking him not only to bootlegging but also to illegal gambling, prostitution, and even murder. The city's highly publicized beer wars of the mid-1920s were a result of the intense rivalry of underworld gangs. The famous St. Valentine's Day Massacre of 1929 was perpetrated by Capone's men against seven members of a rival organization. Capone himself stayed above the bloody fray. Sporting fashionable suits, smoking expensive cigars, and riding about in a custom-built Cadillac, surrounded by bodyguards, Capone became a tourist attraction and the subject of books and popular movies. An arrest in 1929 for carrying a concealed weapon, followed shortly thereafter by a conviction for income tax evasion, brought Capone's criminal career to an end at the age of thirty-two.

Biography composed by Fred Voss, historian, National Portrait Gallery

Unidentified police photographer, photograph, December 26, 1925

The Harlem Renaissance

THE THICKLY POPULATED, INTERNALLY COMBUSTIBLE CULTURAL MOVEMENT known as the Harlem Renaissance (it was so dubbed at an early stage) began more or less officially in the spring of 1925 with an elaborate dinner ceremony in a New York restaurant, where literary awards were handed out to young black writers. Among the characters who make up our section, Langston Hughes won the first prize in poetry for "The Weary Blues," his recent evocation of a musical moment in Harlem—

> Droning a drowsy syncopated tune,
> Rocking back and forth to a mellow moon,
> I heard a Negro play
> Down Lexington Avenue the other night.

—and Zora Neale Hurston won second prize for her short story "Spunk" (about gigantic Spunk, who gets his comeuppance from a ghost). Among the two dozen judges on the panel were James Weldon Johnson (poetry), and Alain Locke (short story).

To name the other two in our group: Jessie Fauset was undoubtedly present at the dinner; it was she more than any one who, as literary editor of *The Crisis,* the powerful black monthly magazine, had gained recognition for Hughes and others of comparable talent. Richard Wright in 1925 was still in Memphis, and he would not move, even to Chicago, for two more years.

The six just mentioned were writers of distinction; Johnson, Fauset, and Locke are here primarily because of their roles as begetters and synchronizers of the Renaissance. James Weldon Johnson was among the remarkable figures of his century. Enormously gifted and amazingly versatile, he was a hymn writer ("Lift Ev'ry Voice and Sing," 1900, now a so-called black national anthem), a songwriter ("Under the Bamboo Tree," early 1900s), an influential novelist (*Autobiography of an Ex-Coloured Man,* 1912), an accomplished poet (*God's Trombones,* 1927), a collector and editor of black poetry and spirituals, an effective organizer for the NAACP, and an inspiring presence in American and black cultural life for almost forty years. Jessie Fauset was the author of four novels, between 1924 and 1933, dealing variously with life in middle-class black communities; but as implied, she had a remarkably keen literary eye, providing the Renaissance with much of its cultural momentum. Alain Locke was the professor-editor-sponsor of the movement, as it were its master-of-ceremonies; the one who not only encouraged new talent but often saw to crucially needed financial aid, via his wealthy, eccentric, and generous friend Mrs. Charlotte Mason.

It was the anthology *The New Negro,* edited by Locke with strikingly original illustrations (racial types and African motifs) by Winold Reiss, and by the young black artist of exceptional promise Aaron Douglas (b. 1899), that helped establish the Renaissance by offering contributions from thirty-four black writers. The 1925 volume was an expansion of sorts on two essays by Locke the previous March, in a special edition of the *Sunday Graphic* called "Harlem: Mecca of the New Negro," in which Locke predicted that Harlem would be as important for the "New Negro" as Dublin had been for the "New Ireland."

Langston Hughes's first book, *The Weary Blues,* named for its key entry, was published in 1926. Hughes was the major poet of the Renaissance—perhaps, all things considered, its major literary figure. He brought out some ten books of poetry, along with several volumes of fiction; and his engaging satirical anecdotes about Jesse B. Simple, the black Harlemite who time and again outwits his seeming superiors, ran for years in daily newspapers and made up five collections (1960–63). Most of all, it was Hughes who, following the example of Paul Laurence Dunbar, brought black literary expression into energizing play with the black idiom and jazz rhythms.

Zora Neale Hurston, though a prizewinner in 1925, did not have a book in print until *Mules and Men* in 1935, a magical assembly of folk tales (for example, "Why Negroes Are Black"—because they were all asleep the day God gave out color to recently created mankind) that we watch Hurston listen to and record during a return visit to her Florida community. Hurston's literary career, like her private life, was both impressive and checkered; she rather disappeared from view before her death in 1960. But within less than three decades, with impetus from Afro-American studies and women's studies, and particular help from writers like Alice Walker, she became recognized as the leading literary performer she clearly was.

Richard Wright, born in 1908, belongs properly to the generation after the Harlem Renaissance. His apprentice days began in Chicago in 1927, and it was not until 1937 that he came to New York and began to associate with Hughes, Locke, and the others. The works that made Wright acclaimed as the country's greatest black writer—*Uncle Tom's Children* in 1938, the sensationally successful *Native Son* in 1940, and the autobiographical (and beautifully effective) *Black Boy* in 1945—were all composed in New York. Much of the rest of his life was spent in Paris, where, in 1953 he completed *The Outsider.*

It was a rich and diverse panorama, the Harlem Renaissance, and its extent can only be hinted at in these few pages. Two people who figured in it have already appeared: Booker T. Washington, who died in 1915 but continued to cast a long if thinning shadow; and W. E. B. Du Bois, still occupying a sizable cultural space. On the directorial side, beyond our three were Charles Spurgeon Johnson, who schemed, manipulated, and edited for the greater cultural good of Harlem; and Walter White, vibrant and ego-driven, blue-eyed and blond but with what he called an "invisible pigmentation" (his grandfather was an octoroon), who was cheerfully and endlessly active in helping writers get published and artists get shown.

On the literary side, again beyond our three, there were, minimally, Claude McKay, Jean Toomer, and Countee Cullen. McKay was a poet of whom much was expected; with his book *Harlem Shadows* (1922) he became for the time the best known of American black poets; but he was an uneasy spirit, given to misjudgments and fallings-out, and with his long visit to Russia in 1923 he began to disassociate from the Harlem scene. Toomer brought out a hypnotic masterpiece titled *Cane,* a novel of interweaving short stories, in 1923; but after that he wrote virtually nothing and more or less vanished into the mystical circles of Georgi Gurdjieff. Cullen was something of a prodigy: a prize-winning poet by age twenty, a Harvard Phi Beta Kappa with a roving imagination, as displayed in his first book of poems, *Color* (1925). Further collections of verse, a novel, a translation of Euripides, and a musical play ensure Cullen a small but conspicuous place in the canon.

Other participants thronged across the landscape, as David Levering Lewis reminds us in his inestimable study *When Harlem Was in Vogue.* Music played a large part in the Renaissance; to mention two artists who show up in our own later section, there was Duke Ellington at the Cotton Club (in these early days, seeking to rival Fletcher Henderson at the Savoy), and Bessie Smith, the blues singer. And then there were those whom Zora Neale Hurston nicknamed the "Negrotarians," white individuals who showed an active interest in black culture and its support: Heywood Broun, Joel Spingarn, Sinclair Lewis, Carl Van Doren, Clarence Darrow, Fannie Hurst, Dorothy Parker, and many others. One who should be singled out is Carl Van Vechten: Iowa-born in 1880, drama and music critic, novelist (*Nigger Heaven* in 1926, despite its title, is a sympathetic and informed look at Harlem life), and in the 1930s the admirable historian-photographer of black writers and leaders (white writers, too: his portrait of Willa Cather will be seen later). Van Vechten, busy life-enjoyer, lavish party-giver, unfailing party-attender, ready to hold forth on any phase of the movement: the Harlem scene cannot be described without him.

Of the portraits here, two in fact are by Van Vechten: Zora Neale Hurston in 1935, with her stylish hat and jaunty air of not missing a trick; Richard Wright in 1939, smoldering and barely contained. One is by Winold Reiss, the artist and portrayer of countless American Indian subjects as well as blacks: the image of Alain Locke in 1925, the year of *The New Negro,* the man in charge. The expert image of James Weldon Johnson, immersed in the day's work, by the New York photographer Doris Ulmann, is from the very year the Renaissance got under way, 1925. The portrait of Langston Hughes, one that nicely captures his smiling personality, is by Edward Weston, much better known (in his own wording) for an "epic series of photographs of the West . . . from satire on advertising to ranch life, from beach kelp to mountains." (Reiss himself did an image of Hughes, and a brilliant one; but in its makeup—head bent slightly, chin in hand, eyes gazing afar—it derives all too plainly from Joseph Severn's 1819 painting of John Keats; which is aesthetically pleasing but thematically misleading, since Hughes worked to detach black poetry from the English Romantic traditions and connect it with native styles.) Jessie Fauset is portrayed masterfully, knowingly—in pose, bearing, and physical contour—by her friend Laura Wheeler Waring (they traveled to Europe together in 1924), an artist who warrants fuller attention than she has received.

The literary images display almost inevitably what might best be called the dialectics of the cultural movement. Claude McKay, while admiring Fauset, finds her too prim and peaceable; Margaret Walker, Richard Wright's biographer (and a one-time Chicago associate), sees Wright's fiction as driven by fury. (James Baldwin, in a 1951 article, would say that Wright's fiction had gotten itself "fixed in an ever more unrewarding rage.") Zora Neale Hurston is presented in what Alice Walker calls a "partisan view," a favorable look at her, knowing that Hurston's sheer pleasure in being black brought her into conflict with some of her literary contemporaries. Locke indeed criticized *Their Eyes Were Watching God* in his bluebook-marking way, for not being "social document fiction," and Wright attacked it as lacking in socio-political ideas. Such talk led Hurston to coin the term "Niggerati" for black writers and intellectuals who put the cause of civil rights ahead of the cause of literary excellence.

It was an issue that bedeviled many of the Harlem Renaissance figures, not least James Weldon Johnson, who, in 1929, left the NAACP for a year in order to (he said) get on with "work more in accord with my heart's desire"—writing. When it is said that the Harlem Renaissance ended in about 1932, what is meant is that this was the time when the withering effects of the Depression became apparent in all aspects of black American life. Black cultural activity continued apace, as may be suggested by the resonantly symbolic moment in 1937 when Ralph Ellison, freshly arrived in Harlem from Oklahoma, met by accident Langston Hughes and Alain Locke, and through Hughes's intervention was put in touch with Richard Wright and so began his literary career. But support, economic and political, for black civil rights and the betterment of black life faded away in the early 1930s. The Negrotarians had other things on their minds.

James Weldon Johnson 1871–1938 Writer, Songwriter, Civil Rights Leader

The outstanding trait in this man of many talents is his charm. Charm is a hard thing to define. Friendliness must surely be there and a kindly spirit. But many feel friendliness and are unable to express it. An unconscious self-respect must also be present. Then the personality escapes in a gesture, an expression, a word, and meets its friend. So it is with this colored man.

MARY WHITE OVINGTON, *Portraits in Color* (1927)

In a Kansas City church in 1919, Johnson listens to the preacher "intoning the old folk-sermon that begins with the creation of the world and ends with Judgment Day."
He was wonderful in the way he employed his conscious and unconscious art. He strode the pulpit up and down in what was actually a very rhythmic dance, and he brought into play the full gamut of his wonderful voice, a voice—what shall I say?—not of an organ or a trumpet, but rather of a trombone, the instrument possessing above all others the power to express the wide and varied range of emotions encompassed by the human voice—and with greater amplitude. He intoned, he moaned, he pleaded—he blared, he crashed, he thundered. I sat fascinated; and more, I was, perhaps against my will, deeply moved; the emotional effect upon me was irresistible. Before he had finished I took a slip of paper and somewhat surreptitiously jotted down some ideas for the first poem, "The Creation."

JAMES WELDON JOHNSON, preface to *God's Trombones:*
Seven Negro Sermons in Verse (1927)

Born in Jacksonville, Florida; his father, a freeborn Virginian, was headwaiter in a local deluxe hotel. Johnson was the first black to be admitted (in 1897) to the Florida bar. Soon afterward he moved to New York; and here, to honor Abraham Lincoln's birthday in February 1900, Johnson and his brother John Rosamond Johnson composed the stirring "Lift Ev'ry Voice and Sing." In the early 1900s the two also composed a number of songs for Broadway musicals, including "Under the Bamboo Tree" and "The Congo Love Song." After writing a campaign song for Theodore Roosevelt in 1904, Johnson was appointed by Roosevelt as consul to Venezuela and then Nicaragua. In 1916, Johnson became field secretary of the NAACP, enormously enlarging its membership; he served as its chief administrative officer until 1930.

Johnson's literary career began auspiciously with *The Autobiography of an Ex-Colored Man* (1912), a fictional story of a black man who passes as white. *Along This Way*, Johnson's actual autobiography, appeared in 1933. Meanwhile, he was producing verse, including *God's Trombones*. He also edited *The Book of American Negro Poetry* (1922) and bestselling collections of black spirituals. There were contradictions in the man: a civil rights leader who opposed labor unions; an advocate of assimilation who deplored the loss of racial identity. But Johnson was unequivocal in his belief that modern civilization, and especially modern music, had its origins in Africa. Johnson was killed when his car, driven by his wife (who survived), was hit by a train in Wascasset, Maine.

Portrait by Doris Ulmann (1882–1934), photograph, 1925

Jessie Fauset 1882–1961 Author

Jessie Fauset was assistant editor of *The Crisis* when I met her. She very generously assisted at the Harlem evening of our *Liberator* prayer meetings and was the one fine feature of a bad show. She was prim, pretty and well-dressed, and talked fluently and intelligently. All the radicals liked her, although in her social viewpoint she was away over on the other side of the fence. She belonged to that closed decorous circle of Negro society, which consists of persons who live proudly like the better class of conventional whites, except that they do so on much less money.

But Miss Fauset is prim and pretty as a primrose, and her novels are quite as fastidious and precious. Primroses are pretty. I remember the primroses where I lived in Morocco, that lovely melancholy land of autumn and summer and mysterious veiled brown women. When the primroses spread themselves across the barren hillsides before the sudden summer blazed over the hot land, I often thought of Jessie Fauset and her novels.

CLAUDE MCKAY, *A Long Way from Home* (1937)

Born in New Jersey of a long-established Philadelphia black family. Fauset graduated from Cornell in 1905, the first black woman to earn a Phi Beta Kappa (it was in classics). For fourteen years she taught French and Latin in a Washington high school; then, in 1919, she moved to New York to become an editor of *The Crisis,* the NAACP's monthly magazine, working closely with W. E. B. Du Bois, to whom she had felt a strong emotional attachment from her college days. Supremely knowledgeable in literature ancient and modern, European and American, Fauset did more, practically, than anyone to promote the literary fortunes of new black writers, in particular detecting at once the talents of Jean Toomer and Langston Hughes. She herself published four novels—*There Is Confusion* (1924), *Plum Bun* (1928), *The Chinaberry Tree* (1931), and *Comedy: American Style* (1933)—all dealing with the theme of a black woman wrestling with her identity while seeking to get ahead with a career or a private life. They have something of the Jane Austenish quality ascribed to them by Claude McKay, but they are authentic renderings of one segment of the east coast American black community.

Portrait by Laura Wheeler Waring (1887–1948), oil on canvas, 1945

Alain Locke 1886–1954 Author and Editor

Invariably, his summers were spent in Europe—in Paris and Berlin and the bathing spas. Yet he always seemed to be in Harlem, walking with his quick step and furled umbrella from Hotel Olga along Lenox and Seventh Avenues, riding the subway to downtown meetings and luncheons. He was, as Charles Johnson said, a natural "press agent" for the Harlem Renaissance, on the *qui vive* for talent, a superb disciplinarian, and an elegant and eloquent booster. Young artists and writers suffered fussy imperiousness far more readily from Locke than they would have from others, anecdotally relishing it as part of the professor's nervous but caring hauteur. With him, they were always undergraduates who were made to feel that they must do better than their best.

DAVID LEVERING LEWIS, *When Harlem Was in Vogue*
(1981; Penguin edition, 1997)

Born, like Jessie Fauset, into a family of "O.P.'s" (Old Philadelphians); his first name was pronounced Al-*lane*. His father, Pliny Locke, was the first black graduate (1874) of the Howard University Law School. Young Locke, in turn, after graduating from Harvard in 1907 with a Phi Beta Kappa, became the first (and for sixty years the only) black American Rhodes Scholar. At Oxford, however, he was either shunned or ignored; two years in Berlin and Paris were better. Back in the United States, Locke was appointed to the faculty of Howard University in 1912; by 1915 he began to teach philosophy there. He devised courses on race relations and history that had to be given as extra-curricular offerings. By 1925, Locke was one of the most admired and influential teachers at Howard, but that same year, during an ill-conceived reorganization, he was fired, along with several others.

At the same moment, in the esteemed New York journal *Survey Graphic,* Locke published an article called "Enter the New Negro," in which he argued that a "deep feeling of race" had replaced "social disillusionment" as the "mainspring of Negro life," and that the "pulse of the Negro has begun to beat in Harlem." Also in 1925 he brought out his landmark anthology, *The New Negro,* with abundant graphics by German-born Winold Reiss and the black artist Aaron Douglas. Jessie Fauset, Jean Toomer, Claude McKay, Langston Hughes, and Countee Cullen were among the new Negro writers introduced, and the Harlem Renaissance was under way.

Also at this time Locke became associated with Mrs. Charlotte Mason, who became the patroness and "godmother" of many "new Negro" writers and artists. In 1927, Locke was reappointed at Howard, where he served until his highly celebrated moment of retirement in 1953. His intellectual interests in the late years focused in part on his developing (and ahead of its time) theory of "cultural pluralism." He also gave himself to the collection of African art and to an effort to start an African studies program at Howard, as well as to books, articles, and important academic services.

Portrait by Winold Reiss (1886–1953), pastel on artist board, 1925

Langston Hughes 1902–1967 Poet

This is a song for the genius child.
Sing it softly, for the song is wild.
Sing it softly as ever you can—
Lest the song get out of hand.
Nobody loves a genius child.

Can you love an eagle,
Tame or wild?

Wild or tame,
Can you love a monster
Of frightening name?

Nobody loves a genius child.

Kill him—and let his soul run wild!

LANGSTON HUGHES, "Genius Child," *Fields of Wonder* (1947)

"My chief literary influences have been Paul Laurence Dunbar, Carl Sandburg, and Walt Whitman. My favorite public figures include Jimmy Durante, Marlene Dietrich, Mary McLeod Bethune, Mrs. Franklin D. Roosevelt, Marian Anderson, and Henry Armstrong. I live in Harlem, New York City. I am unmarried. I like: *Tristan,* goat's milk, short novels, lyric poems, heat, simple folk, boats, and bullfights; I dislike *Aida,* parsnips, long novels, narrative poems, cold pretentious folk, busses, and bridges."

LANGSTON HUGHES, quoted in *Twentieth Century Authors:*
A Biographical Dictionary of Modern Literature (1942), edited by Stanley J. Kunitz and
Howard Haycraft, from September 21, 1940, article in *Saturday Review of Literature*

Born in Joplin, Missouri, the son of a shopkeeper and a schoolteacher; his mother's uncle had been the first dean of the Howard Law School, as well as a U.S. congressman from Virginia. Hughes led a nomadic life, especially after his parents' divorce in 1913. His poem "The Negro Speaks of Rivers" ("I've known rivers; / I've known rivers ancient as the world") appeared in 1921. With his volume *The Weary Blues* (1926), Hughes was fully established. Ten volumes of verse appeared over thirty-five years, along with novels and short stories, the long diverting series on Jesse Simple, a collection of poems, and a one-act play about the Scottsboro case. Hughes's autobiographical volume *The Big Sea,* a treasure for cultural historians, came out in 1940.

In 1930–31, Hughes and Zora Neale Hurston collaborated on a stage comedy called *Mule Bone,* taken from one of the folk tales Hurston had collected. Hughes then learned that it was about to be produced as written solely by Hurston. A bitter dispute followed; the play was not staged; and the estrangement between Hughes and Hurston was final. "That spring for me (and I guess all of us)," Hughes wrote afterward, "was the end of the Harlem Renaissance."

Portrait by Edward Weston (1886–1958), photograph, 1932

Zora Neale Hurston 1891–1960 Author

Zora was funny, irreverent (she was the first to call the Harlem Renaissance literati the "niggerati"), good-looking, sexy, and once sold hot dogs in a Washington park just to record accurately how the black people who bought the hot dogs talked. She would go anywhere she had to go: Harlem, Jamaica, Haiti, Bermuda, to find out anything she simply had to know. She loved to give parties. Loved to dance. Would wrap her head in scarves as black women in Africa, Haiti, and everywhere else have done for centuries. On the other hand, she loved to wear hats, tilted over one eye and pants and boots.

In addition, she talked too much, got things from white folks (Guggenheims, Rosenwalds and footstools) much too easily, was slovenly in her dress, and appeared maddeningly indifferent to other people's opinions of her. With her easy laughter and her Southern drawl, her belief in doing "culled" dancing authentically Zora seemed—among these genteel "New Negroes" of the Harlem Renaissance—*black*. No wonder her presence was always a shock.

ALICE WALKER, "Zora Neale Hurston: A Cautionary Tale and a Partisan View"
(1979), in *In Search of Our Mothers' Gardens* (1984)

Born in 1891 (not 1901, as often said) in Macon County, Alabama. In 1894 her family moved to the tiny, all-black village, incorporated in 1886, of Eatonville, Florida, near Orlando. Hurston would recall her enjoyment in hearing adults "tell lies" on their front porches. In 1918 she moved to Washington, D.C., where she worked as a waitress and came to know Alain Locke. In 1925 she went to New York, met Hughes and other young black writers, wrote prizewinning stories herself, and enrolled in Barnard College. She studied anthropology with Franz Boas, which led to *Mules and Men* (1935), a classic collection of southern folklore and voodoo tales. Before that there had been a novel, *Jonah's Gourd Vine,* and in 1937 came her fictional masterpiece *Their Eyes Were Watching God,* a re-creation in the present of a black woman's experience in Eatonville.

From the late 1920s into the 1940s, Zora Hurston was a prolific writer of articles and reviews, engaged in many other literary ventures, and was a lively, familiar figure in Harlem gatherings. But in 1931 she had a bitter falling-out with Langston Hughes over the rights to the play *Mule Bone* (misunderstandings on all sides). In 1939 there appeared Hurston's agile black biblical tale *Moses, Man of the Mountain.* Her autobiography, *Dust Tracks on a Road,* came out in 1942. She continued to write, but her life became troubled. A false suit for sexual harassment of a young boy was brought in 1948 (and dismissed in 1949). In 1959 she suffered a stroke. She died a year later and was buried in an unmarked grave in a segregated Florida cemetery. In 1973 Alice Walker discovered and marked the grave with a new stone. In 1995 the Library of America published a two-volume edition of her work.

Portrait by Richard M. A. Benson, photogravure, 1983,
from a 1935 negative by Carl Van Vechten (1880–1964)

Richard Wright 1908–1960 Author

To see him in light and shadow is damnably difficult. To do this is to remember both the open loquaciousness and visibly charming gaiety of the man over against the somber figure in solitude whom we only know because he wrote such intense and grisly, violent and morbidly criminal stories. He was not guilty of these crimes. He was on the surface a very gentle man. But this kindest, most vulnerable and tender-eyed fellow was also a brooding, frightened, angry and ambivalent man. His fiction reveals a sublimation of the "dark and haunted tower" and a psychological transformation of rage and suffering, the artistic results of the sexual dynamics of anger. To understand him demands more than simplistic answers; more than taking only the word of friends, or, for that matter, of enemies.

MARGARET WALKER, *Richard Wright: Daemonic Genius* (1988)

Born near Natchez, Mississippi, grew up in Memphis. The family was deserted by the father when Richard was three; the boy passed a troubled childhood, shuttling between one aunt's house and another. Later, via H. L. Mencken's columns, Wright was led to the work of Theodore Dreiser, Sinclair Lewis, and Sherwood Anderson. In 1927 he moved with his sickly mother to Chicago, where he earned a small living as a postal worker and occasionally as a ditch digger. In 1934 he joined the Communist Party; he pulled back from it after a few years over the issue of the writer's freedom, and he left it formally in 1940 (see his essay in *The God That Failed*, 1950). After attempts at poetry and magazine writing, Wright in 1938 brought out *Uncle Tom's Children*, a collection of four stories; it won a short-story prize. Wright had moved to New York the year before; and in 1939 he married Dhima Rose Meadman, with his twenty-five-year-old protégé Ralph Ellison as best man. In 1940 came *Native Son*, the story of Chicago slum-born Bigger Thomas and his ravaged, crime-infested life. It was a Book-of-the-Month Club selection, and it sold 215,000 copies in three weeks and half a million copies altogether. *Black Boy*, his account of his own early years, came out in 1945. Wright was now acclaimed as the leading black American writer; but resentment over racial prejudice, and restiveness with the literary scene, induced Wright to leave the country and settle in Paris. Here his reading of Camus's *The Stranger* helped spark his own existentialist novel *The Outsider* (1953). Journalistic accounts of the African Gold coast and of Asia and Spain followed in the later 1950s. Wright's first and hitherto unpublished novel *Lawd Today!* from the 1930s and dealing with his postal service days, was included in the two-volume *Richard Wright* of the Library of America in 1991.

Photogravure, 1983, from a 1939 negative by Carl Van Vechten (1880–1964)

The Champions

SPORTS IN AMERICA, WHETHER AMATEUR OR PROFESSIONAL, TOOK LASTING hold on the national imagination in about 1920. Admittedly, the figure most observers would name the greatest and most versatile American athlete of all time, the Indian-territory-born Jim Thorpe, came into his own as early as 1912: first as an extraordinary football player at Carlisle Indian School (25 touchdowns that year, and 198 points), and then at the Olympic games in Stockholm, where he won both the pentathlon and the decathlon. But the period now generally regarded as the first golden age in sports began at the onset of the 1920s. It has been so called in good part because of the sudden appearance of an entire cluster of dazzling performers. Among them, and representing boxing, base-ball, and tennis, were Jack Dempsey, Babe Ruth, and Bill Tilden. All three have their places in this section, and all three exude across the years an aura, a shadow-casting per-sona, beyond and above the statistics that record their exploits—as Red Smith suggests in his model portrait of Babe Ruth.

Most commentators would add the name of Red Grange as football's golden age repre-sentative: No. 77, the Galloping Ghost of Illinois, who in 1924 (for example), against an undefeated Michigan team, scored four touchdowns in twelve minutes, with runs of 95, 67, 56, and 45 yards. But those who retain a dim personal memory of Grange's football feats in that far-off epoch may be surprised to learn that No. 77 is not eligible for this book: he died only in 1991, at age eighty-eight.

Longevity is one reason for the absence from these pages of various sports champions. As Casey Stengel persistently put it, "You could look it up"—one excellent source being Ralph Hickok's nearly 900-page encyclopedia *A Who's Who of Sports Champions* (1995). As a further instance: Helen Wills, who won national women's singles championships all through the 1920s and Wimbledon tennis titles all through the 1930s, certainly belongs to the golden age; but Wills, born in 1905, lived to be ninety. And if there are no basket-ball players at all among our champions, it is because as a national resource basketball is still very young—Bill Russell, for one, was not even born until 1934, and Willis Reed not until 1942.

Another reason for regrettable exclusions is lack of portrayal in the National Portrait Gal-lery. This accounts for the nonappearance of Bobby Jones, the golfing hero of the golden age, the choreographer of the approach shot (and founder of the Masters Tournament). It accounts as well, to list a few obvious names, for the absence of Ty Cobb and Lou Gehrig in baseball; of Knute Rockne, the fabled coach of the Notre Dame football team; and Branch Rickey, the influential owner of the Brooklyn Dodgers.

The ones we do have are mostly pictured in action, or ready for action. Bill Tilden is seen, in a 1930 photograph by Underwood and Underwood, poised at center court, after (presumably) delivering a smashing backhand. Jackie Robinson, in a 1947 print by Harry Warnecke, stands at the plate, bat in hand, displaying his tense readiness to Brooklyn fans as his first major-league season moves ahead. Babe Didrikson, in another print by Warnecke (also of 1947), is no doubt on her way to another golf championship. Joe Louis, in a second Underwood and Underwood image, is being helped into his plaid robe by Jack Blackburn, the fighter's testy and all-knowing trainer, in 1935, the year Louis won knockout victories over Primo Carnera and three others. Babe Ruth, in a picture by Nickolas Muray probably taken during the Sultan of Swat's glory year, 1927, sits quietly on the bench awaiting his turn at bat. And Casey Stengel, in what is, aesthetically speaking, the champion portrait in this section, is depicted by the highly endowed and innovative sculptor Rhoda Sherbell, with his well-remembered stance and his lined, appealing seventy-five-year-old face, in the 1965 season, when he hustled the New York Mets into some sort of decent baseball behavior.

The gripping panoramic spread by James Montgomery Flagg, the graphic artist and illustrator, gives us not only Jack Dempsey, crouching with loaded fists beneath the towering Jess Willard in the July 1919 championship bout (which Dempsey won by a clobbering knockout in the third round). It also assembles a number of then familiar faces pressing around the ringside: Damon Runyon, tale spinner and author of a special vernacular (glasses and hat, to the right of Dempsey's right knee); Rube Goldberg, the comical inventor of hopeless devices (hatless, between Dempsey's knees); Bugs Baer, the general columnist (far right corner). Made in 1944 from newspaper pictures of the event (one guesses), the canvas re-creates both a major moment in sports history and the opening phase of the golden age itself.

Sportswriters with less familiar names are among those at ringside. And in fact, canny journalistic students of the sporting scene have provided us with nicely animated verbal images of these great athletes, again in postures of characteristic action. H. L. Mencken, in an article of 1921, dispatches one of the most telling descriptions of its kind ever contrived: that of Dempsey's left hand having a "wallop . . . like the bump of a ferryboat into its slip"; one can fairly feel the jarring impact of the blow. Red Smith, the finest sheer writer among sports commentators, carries Babe Ruth's baseball image into the realm of poetry, helping us recognize the Babe circling the bases with "pigeon-toed mincing majesty." Franklin Pierce Adams, the pungent analyst of the native scene, who published his column "The Conning Tower" over the name F. P. A., reflects on Bill Tilden's histrionics, as Tilden made an easy match look dramatically threatening.

Other cultural genres are drawn upon. Joe Louis is celebrated in the 1941 recording of Paul Robeson singing "King Joe (Joe Louis Blues)," a blues folk-poem composed by Richard Wright (himself fresh from following the seven-city tour of the stage version of

Native Son), with musical accompaniment by Count Basie and his orchestra. Babe Didrikson is the recipient of a versified effusion from Grantland Rice in his syndicated column "The Sportlight." Rice was a mediocre writer with a lurking strain of bigotry, but his athletic opinions were much respected, and his admiration for the female champion was well founded and unstinted, as he heralds her shift in 1935 from triumphs on the track to triumphs on the golf course.

Arnold Rampersad, the honored biographer and editor of Langston Hughes, offers a moving portrait of Jackie Robinson, huddled in loneliness in his Boston hotel room, the first black player in his first days as a major-leaguer. Jim Thorpe, in the pages of another biographer, is seen, inspired by alcohol, racing around the decks of the *Finland* (the ship that brought the contestants to Stockholm), yelling, "I'm a horse," in echo of the title bestowed on him by idolatrous fans at the Olympic games.

Casey Stengel is allowed to speak for himself, and he does so in the diverting idiom known as Stengelese. This mode of discourse was perhaps best described in the acquisition sheet for the Rhoda Sherbell figure at the National Portrait Gallery, in 1981. "[Stengel] was the joy of baseball incarnate, a screwy monologist, with the habit of tripping over his own syntax, who somehow managed to express all the seriousness and all the craziness of the national game."

Jim Thorpe 1888–1953 Athlete

Thorpe managed to get into magnificent condition for the Olympic pentathlon held on July 7 [1912], the second day of competition. He was, by calculation of physicians at Carlisle, at the peak of his physical development that summer. He stood just over 5-11 and weighed 161. His reach was 72.5 inches. He was 15.9 in the neck, 39.7 around the chest, and 32.3 at the waist. Thorpe's shoulders were narrow, about 18 inches, but he was deep-chested, 11.8 inches. Thorpe's physical mannerisms just before he was to go into action were slightly lumbering, similar in a way to the indifferent gait of professional football's Jimmy Brown as he returned to the huddle of the Cleveland Browns after one of his matchless runs. He was slightly bowlegged, which may have accentuated the attitude of casualness. . . . Olympic spectators watching him dominate the pentathlon and decathlon competition used the exclamation "Isn't he a horse?" to show their admiration for his versatility. After a little celebrating of his Olympic position one evening in the spas of Stockholm, Thorpe took to galloping around the decks of the *Finland,* yelling, "I'm a horse! I'm a horse!"

JACK NEWCOMBE, *The Best of the Athletic Boys* (1975)

Born in Indian territory, near Prague (now Oklahoma), primarily of Sac and Fox descent, but also Potawatomie and Kickapoo (with a mix of Irish and French). His Indian name was Wa-tho-Huck, meaning "bright path." At Carlisle Indian School, under Coach "Pop" Warner, Thorpe was named an All-American football player in 1911 and 1912, scoring 25 touchdowns and 198 points in 1912 alone. At the Olympics that same year (the scene of the description above), Thorpe easily won both the pentathlon and decathlon. Presenting him with his medals, King Gustav of Sweden declared, "Sir, you are the greatest athlete in the world"; to which Thorpe answered, "Thanks, King."

In 1960 the Associated Press confirmed the king's judgment by voting Thorpe the greatest American athlete in the half century. Arthur Daley in the *New York Times* proclaimed Thorpe the "best football player in history and the greatest athlete the world has ever known—excelling not only in track and field and football, but also in swimming, marksmanship, wrestling and boxing." After the Olympics, Thorpe was a big league baseball player, 1913–19, and then more effectively a professional football player from 1919–26, the first of the sport's genuine stars. Meanwhile, however, the Amateur Athletic Union, discovering that Thorpe had been paid a few dollars in 1910 and 1911 for playing minor league baseball, stripped him of his Olympic medals. They were restored to his family in 1983, thirty years after his death.

Thorpe continued to perform occasionally for some time, but alcoholism and poverty plagued his later years. In 1950 there was a fair-to-middling film, *Jim Thorpe—All American,* directed by Michael Curtiz and starring Burt Lancaster.

Underwood and Underwood (active 1882–c. 1950), photograph, 1913

Jack Dempsey 1895–1983 Heavyweight Boxing Champion

Toughness is certainly a handy thing to have when one hoofs the fatal rosin. It gets one around bad situations. It saves the day when vultures begin to circle overhead. To reinforce it, Dempsey has a wallop in his right hand like the collision of a meteorite with the Alps and a wallop in his left hand like the bump of a ferryboat into its slip.

The two work constantly and with lively synchronization.

H. L. MENCKEN, *Baltimore Sun,* July 2, 1921

Jack Dempsey was a great fighter—possibly the greatest that ever entered a ring. Looking back objectively, one has to conclude that he was more valuable to the sport or "The Game" than any prizefighter of his time. Whether you consider it from his worth as a gladiator or from the point of view of the box office, he was tops. His name in his most glorious days was magic among his people, and today, twenty years after, the name Jack Dempsey is still magic. This tells a volume in itself.

GENE TUNNEY, "My Fights with Jack Dempsey," in
The Aspirin Age, 1919–1941, edited by Isabel Leighton (1949)

Born William Harrison Dempsey in Manassa, Colorado: hence later called the Manassa Mauler. Dempsey entered professional boxing in 1914; and in July 1919, in Toledo, Ohio, he met the heavy-

weight champion Jess Willard (sixty pounds heavier). Dempsey knocked him down seven times in the first round, and knocked him out in the third. Tex Rickard, the promoter, took over Dempsey's career, and in 1921 matched him with the French war hero Georges Carpentier in what was boxing's first $1 million gate. Carpentier was a stylish boxer, but Dempsey won in a fourth-round knockout. In September 1923, Dempsey fought Luis Firpo of Argentina in another $1 million attraction. In the first round Firpo knocked Dempsey through the ropes onto a sportswriter's typewriter. Dempsey managed to climb back, survived the round, and knocked Firpo out in the next round.

After a few exhibition matches and letting himself get out of shape, Dempsey met Gene Tunney in September 1926 and lost on points. In the rematch in September 1927 (a $2 million gate), Dempsey knocked Tunney down in the seventh round but wasted precious seconds before (as the rules required) returning to his corner. Tunney got up at count nine, having been down in fact fifteen seconds: the famous "long count." He then went on to defeat Dempsey a second time on points.

Dempsey fought exhibition matches through the 1930s but retired in 1940. Sports historians record that Dempsey fought eighty-four bouts between 1914 and 1949, winning sixty-two of them, fifty-one by knockouts. In World War II he served as a lieutenant commander in the Coast Guard. In after years, Dempsey ran one of the most popular restaurants in New York City, often greeting the arriving guests himself.

Painting by James Montgomery Flagg (1877–1960), oil on canvas, 1944; depicts the 1919 Dempsey-Willard fight, with Damon Runyon, Bugs Baer, and others at ringside

Joe Louis 1914–1981 Heavyweight Boxing Champion

After Louis' victory over Carnera, his stock in the black community soared. He was as popular as Satchel Paige at a time when, as one black newspaper noted, "It takes twice as much effort to turn ordinary colored citizens into fight fans . . . when they hear of hard striving boys of their race being robbed of decisions by crooked referees, or forced to lay down to inferior white opponents. . . ." The primary obstacle was the powerful black church which was generally not in favor of boxing as a profession. Intellectuals like W. E. B. Du Bois were strongly against boxing.

Louis seemed befuddled by all this attention at first. After church services with his mother following the Carnera win, he said, "When I walked in the church, you'd have thought I was the second coming of Christ. . . . Rev. J. H. Maston . . . talked about how God gave certain people gifts . . . and through my fighting I was to uplift the sprit of my race. I thought to myself, 'Jesus Christ, am I all that?'"

ARTHUR R. ASHE, JR., *A Hard Road to Glory: A History of the African-American Athlete, 1919–1945* (1988)

Black eyed peas ask corn bread
What makes you so strong?
Corn bread say I come from
Where Joe Louis was born.
Rabbit say to the bee
What make you sting so deep?
He say I sting like Joe
An' rock 'em all to sleep.

"King Joe (Joe Louis Blues)," lyrics by Richard Wright,
music by Count Basie (1941)

Born Joseph Louis Barrow in Lafayette, Alabama. The family moved to Detroit in 1924. In his late teens Louis became an amateur boxer, winning fifty fights in rapid succession. He then turned professional, and in the single year 1935 he defeated, by knockouts, Primo Carnera, Kingfish Levinsky, and Paulino Uzcudun. The following year, however, Louis suffered a humiliating defeat by Max Schmeling, a hero of Nazi Germany. Louis won the heavyweight championship in 1937 by knocking out Jim Braddock in the eighth round; and in June 1938, before a crowd of seventy thousand at Yankee Stadium, Louis, in a return match with Schmeling, knocked out the German fighter in the first round. Louis defended his title frequently, but the available competition was so poor that each victim was dubbed "bum of the month." Louis retired in 1949; a desperate need for money (to pay overdue taxes) brought him back in 1950, but he was roundly defeated in 1951 by the new champion Rocky Marciano. Years later, after a spell in a psychiatric hospital, Louis became the official greeter in a Las Vegas gaming center.

Underwood and Underwood (1882–c. 1950), photograph, c. 1935

Bill Tilden 1893–1953 Tennis Champion

It seems as though Tilden often says to himself: "This is going to be a hard match." Coming to play, he finds it easy. So he makes it hard. He loses a set or two, usually electrifying the gallery in the winning of the match. "Playing to the stands," say his legion of sneering commentators. I am certain that he would play exactly the same game, saying the same "Oh, rotten" when he misses an easy one, if the court were in a back yard somewhere, with nobody to see it at all. His "Oh, Gerald!" and "Peach, Bill!" are sincere expressions of admiration, though sometimes the gallery thinks his meaning is "Any shot I can't get is a daisy." He doesn't mean that, but it is true. Anybody who aces Tilden has to do it with a perfect shot.

F. P. A. (FRANKLIN PIERCE ADAMS), quoted in
This Fabulous Century, vol. 3, 1920–30 (1969)

Born William Tatem Tilden II into a wealthy family in the Philadelphia suburb of Germantown. Tilden won an occasional tennis title in his early twenties, but it was not until age twenty-seven, in 1920, that he became a serious contender. That year he won the singles title at Wimbledon, becoming the first American to do so, and then the U.S. singles championship. Tilden repeated twice at Wimbledon, and five more times in a row in the United States; he also led the U.S. Davis Cup team to seven consecutive titles (his arch foreign rival in these years was France's René Lacoste). With his extraordinarily graceful style and his classy showmanship, the socially impeccable "Big Bill" Tilden did more than anyone to transform tennis from an elitist country club ritual, practiced principally at Newport, into a national pastime and an immensely popular sport, to watch or to listen to accounts of on the radio.

After losing most of his money backing bad stage plays and on the crashing stock market, Tilden turned professional in 1931, giving that dimension of the game its authenticity too. He won several hundred professional matches over twenty years. He was packing his bags in a Hollywood hotel room in 1953, preparing to leave for a Chicago tournament, when he suffered a fatal heart attack at age sixty. In 1969 an international panel of tennis writers named Tilden the greatest tennis player of all time. His aim as a player, he said in his memoirs, was to give tennis "something more vital and fundamental" than the "peculiar courtly grace" that had characterized it before his time.

Underwood and Underwood (1882–c. 1950), photograph, c. 1930

Babe Didrikson 1914–1956 Athlete

She is an incredible human being. She is beyond all belief until you see her perform. Then you finally understand that you are looking at the most flawless section of muscle harmony, of complete mental and physical coordination the world of sport has ever known. This may seem to be a wild statement, yet it happens to be 100 per cent true. There is only one Babe Didrikson and there has never been another in her class—even close to her class.
GRANTLAND RICE, 1932 sports column, quoted in William Oscar Johnson and Nancy P. Williamson, *"Whatta-Gal": The Babe Didrikson Story* (1977)

> From the high jump of Olympic fame,
> The hurdles and the rest
> The javelin that flashed its flame
> On by the record test—
> The Texas Babe now shifts the scene
> Where slashing drives are far
> Where spoon shots find the distant green
> To break the back of par.
GRANTLAND RICE, 1944, quoted in *"Whatta-Gal"*

Born Mildred E. Didrikson in Port Arthur, Texas, the daughter of Norwegian immigrants; from infancy, named "Babe" for "baby," and not (as she told the press) after Babe Ruth, for hitting home runs in teenage softball games with boys. In 1930 she became associated with a women's athletic program in Dallas, and she led a local basketball team to a national championship. The year 1932 was a banner year. Turning to track and field contests, she won American championships in hurdles and high jump; and at the Olympics in Los Angeles she won two gold medals. She was now internationally famous and had developed a brassy and wittily boastful manner, conveyed in a Texas drawl, that delighted many people but offended some. It was a manner designed to combat the current sentiment about women athletes—which was, in the words of the sportswriter Paul Gallico, that they were "at best second-rate imitations of the gentlemen."

In that same year Didrikson turned to golf, encouraged by her admirer, the sports commentator Grantland Rice. In 1936 she won her first tournament, after which she did barnstorming tours with the top male golfer, Gene Sarazen. In 1938 she met and married George Zaharias, a professional wrestler, who took expert charge of her career. In the immediate postwar years Babe Didrikson won fourteen consecutive amateur titles, including the British Women's Amateur Championship in 1947, becoming the first American to have that distinction. She turned professional the same year, with five others founding the Ladies Professional Golf Association. She was the leading money winner in 1949, 1950, 1951, accumulating a million dollars in prize money.

In 1952 she had a hernia operation; this was followed by rectal cancer. She came back in 1954 to win her third U.S. Women's Open by a dozen strokes. But she was again stricken, and she died at age forty-two.

Portrait by Harry Warnecke (1901–84), color carbo print, 1947

Babe Ruth 1895–1948 Baseball Champion

To paraphrase Abraham Lincoln's remark about another deity, Ruth must have admired records because he created so many of them. Yet he was sublimely aware that he transcended records and his place in the American scene was no mere matter of statistics. It wasn't just that he hit more home runs than anyone else, he hit them better, higher, farther, with more theatrical timing and a more flamboyant flourish. Nobody could strike out like Babe Ruth. Nobody circled the bases with the same pigeon-toed mincing majesty.

"He was one of a kind," says Waite Hoyt, a Yankee pitcher in the years of Ruthian splendor. "If he had never played ball, if you had never heard of him and passed him on Broadway, you'd turn around and look."

Looking, you would have seen a barrel swaddled in a wrap-around camel-hair topcoat with a flat camel-hair cap on the round head. Thus arrayed he was instantly recognizable not only on Broadway in New York but also on the Ginza in Tokyo. "Baby Roos! Baby Roos!" cried excited crowds, following through the streets when he visited Japan with an all-star team in the early 1930s.

RED SMITH, in *The Red Smith Reader,* edited by Dave Anderson (1982)

Born George Herman Ruth into a poverty-stricken environment in Baltimore. At age nineteen, Ruth, then playing with a minor league team, was purchased by the Boston Red Sox. In Boston, Ruth became a star pitcher, among other things setting a long-standing record by pitching 29 2/3 scoreless innings in World Series play. He also showed signs of being a hitter of prowess, and he was sold to the New York Yankees for $125,000 plus a huge loan. In New York the left-hand hitting outfielder set record after record over fifteen years: 50 home runs in four separate seasons, 60 home runs in 1927 (the most legendary of his years), 714 home runs overall (a record finally broken by Hank Aaron in 1974), 15 home runs in World Series games, and, along with that, 2,056 bases on balls and 2,211 runs batted in. Ruth's lifetime batting average was the almost unthinkable .342.

But as Red Smith says, it was not less the style of the man, at bat or rounding the bases, that created the legend. There was in addition the private life—the boozing and womanizing and occasional irresponsibility—only hinted at by sports reporters but adding much fascination to the Babe Ruth figure. In 1930 and 1931, Ruth earned $80,000, a vast sum indeed in the Depression years. He played briefly with the Boston Braves, and portrayed himself in *The Pride of the Yankees,* the first-class 1942 film biography of his old batting-mate Lou Gehrig, who had died the year before.

Portrait by Nickolas Muray (1882–1963), photograph, 1978, from a c. 1927 negative

Casey Stengel 1890–1975 Baseball Manager

When Stengel retired from professional baseball in 1967 after nearly 60 years in the sport, he said, "I want to thank all my players for giving me the honor of what I was." It was a typical Casey Stengel line, an appropriate way for him to bow out.

RALPH HICKOK, *Who's Who of Sports Champions* (1995)

In July 1958, Stengel testified before the Senate Subcommittee on Antitrust and Monopoly, Senator Estes Kefauver presiding. At a certain point—

Kefauver: Mr. Stengel, are you prepared to answer particularly why baseball wants this bill passed?

Stengel: Well, I would have to say at the present time, I think that baseball has advanced in this respect for player help. That is an amazing statement for me to make, because you can retire with an annuity at fifty and what organization in America allows you to retire at fifty and receive money.

Now, the second thing about baseball that I think is very interesting to the public or all of us is that it is the owner's fault if he does not improve his club, along with the officials in the ball club and the players.

Stengel continues for some minutes, with references to team travel, ball park attendance, and receipts.

Kefauver: Mr. Stengel, I am not sure that I made my question clear.

Stengel: Yes, sir. Well, that is all right. I'm not sure I'm going to answer yours perfectly, either.

Transcription in *The Red Smith Reader,* edited by Dave Anderson (1982)

Born Charles Dillon Stengel in Kansas City, Missouri. He entered professional baseball in 1910. Over twenty-one years he played on six minor league teams and five major league teams, with occasional fine performances (for example, with the New York Giants in the World Series of 1923). He then underwent a number of frustrating years as a manager with both major and minor league teams. But in 1949 he took over the New York Yankees, with Joe DiMaggio, Yogi Berra, Phil Rizzuto, and other players, and won five world championships in five years. After an interval, Stengel led the Yankees to five more pennants and two world championships. He was named American League manager of the year in 1949, 1953, and 1958.

In 1960, after a bitter dispute with the Yankee brass, Stengel was fired. Two years later he signed on to manage the lowly New York Mets. The team was athletically hopeless (it lost 120 games one year), but the players and their manager were the beloved of New York. In 1965, close to 1.8 million people paid to watch the Mets at the new Shea Stadium. Stengel retired that year, and in 1966 he was inducted into the Hall of Fame at Cooperstown, New York, alongside Ted Williams. In 1924, Stengel had married Edna Lawson, a silent screen actress who had become a skilled accountant. They had no children.

Portrait by Rhoda Sherbell (b. 1933), polychromed bronze, 1981,
cast after 1965 plaster

Portrait by Harry Warnecke (1901–84), color carbo print, 1947

Jackie Robinson 1919–1972 Baseball Star

In April 1947, in the early days of his rookie year with the Brooklyn Dodgers—
A two-game series in Boston, against the Braves, was lost to falling snow. The maddening weather and enforced idleness darkened his mood. Visiting him in his room at the Kenmore Hotel, a white writer found a somber scene, or described one: "Jackie is sitting on the bed. The room is dark, the shades are halfway, and here is a lonely guy. His head sunk in his hands. He feels friendless." The two men talk about baseball but not at all about race. "Jackie smiles and seems to brighten. It's nice to talk to somebody even if it is only a baseball writer he never had met before." . . . About this time in an often-echoed line, Jimmy Cannon of the *New York Post* called Jackie Robinson "the loneliest man I have ever seen in sports."

In mid-May, a month later—
Against the Pirates, Brooklyn dropped two out of three to continue its slide. . . . But for Robinson the series was a personal triumph, with six hits in thirteen at-bats for his best performance in a series thus far. He was also well received by some Pirate players and fans. In one play, hustling to beat out a hit, he collided with the massive first baseman, Hank Greenberg, in his first season with Pittsburgh and his last as a player, after a league-leading forty-four home runs for Detroit in 1946, but the two players dusted themselves off and chatted amiably. Years before, Greenberg had endured nasty baiting from various players and fans as a Jew. "Stick in there," Jack remembered Greenberg telling him. "You're doing fine. Keep your chin up." "Class tells," Jack commented to a reporter. "It sticks out all over Mr. Greenberg."

ARNOLD RAMPERSAD, *Jackie Robinson* (1997)

Born near Cairo, Georgia; before his first birthday, his mother (deserted by his father) took him to California. Robinson grew up in a poverty-stricken, crime-ridden neighborhood, but in 1937 he won a scholarship to UCLA. He was a star in baseball, football, basketball, and track as an undergraduate. He served in World War II, discharged in 1944 as a lieutenant. He joined the Kansas City Monarchs of the Negro American League in 1945. That same summer, Branch Rickey, the president of the Brooklyn Dodgers, searching for ways to integrate major league baseball, interviewed Robinson at length. Rickey told Robinson that, as a major league player, he would be subjected to vicious racist insults and possibly even physical abuse; but that, if he wanted to make it, he would have to do his best to refrain from hitting back.

Robinson agreed reluctantly to do so. After a year with the Dodgers' Montreal farm team Robinson went to Brooklyn: the first black player in major league history, as far as anyone could remember (there in fact had been two back in 1888). In his first year Robinson hit .297 and led the league with 29 stolen bases; he was voted rookie of the year. Two years later Robinson led the league in batting (.342) and stolen bases (37) and was voted the most valuable player. Over ten years, Robinson's batting average was .311, with 197 bases stolen and 1,518 hits.

After his retirement from baseball, Robinson worked for the civil rights movement, wrote articles, and did TV commentary.

Writers and Artists: The Second Flowering

MALCOLM COWLEY GAVE THE TITLE "A SECOND FLOWERING" TO AN ENGAGING and instructive collection of essays in 1973. What Cowley, the preeminent chronicler of the successive waves of American literary history, had in mind was a generation of writers whose "first" lives came joltingly to an end with World War I, and who, in the postwar period, found themselves leading a second life in a very different world. Their second flowering took the form of a dissociation from the cultural mores and manners of the prewar age; a "revolt" led by Hemingway, "against big words and noble sentiments."

Our own reference is to the more largely conceived generation of writers and artists who, in the 1920s and for a decade or two afterward, produced an amazing number of works of the highest order. These writers and artists constitute the second major epoch of cultural achievement in this country after the Renaissance of the mid-nineteenth century. The section ranges chronologically from Edith Wharton, who was born in 1862, to Robert Lowell, who was born in 1917. But it centers on that complex set of ingredients called "modernism"; and we begin with three novelists—Edith Wharton, Theodore Dreiser, and Willa Cather—who in their individual ways can be called "premodernist," with their fictional recordings of actual places and times: New York, from Park Avenue to the Bowery, Chicago, the Great Plains. Not long after, they are joined by three novelists who helped establish the mode of fictional modernism in America, each in turn with his well-imagined stage of poetically arranged events: F. Scott Fitzgerald, casting his Minnesota-trained eye on the eastern seaboard and the French Riviera; Ernest Hemingway, trailing through France, Italy, and Spain; William Faulkner, encased in his historical and mythical South.

Poetry was in fact the dominant genre in literary modernism, and poets are the most numerous here. Five of them appear in sequence: Robert Frost, Ezra Pound, T. S. Eliot, Marianne Moore, and e. e. cummings. The first four, as it happened, were western-born, with each, following a different itinerary, becoming an easterner or a European. Only twenty years separate the birthdates of Frost (1874) and cummings (1894). Pound led the way in publication, with two books of verse in 1909; the others came to fruition between 1913 and 1923, highlights being Frost's volume *A Boy's Will* in 1913 (published in London with the help of Ezra Pound) and Eliot's *Prufrock and Other Observations* in 1917.

Wallace Stevens, born in 1879, is a coeval with Frost and the others, but we hold him back a little. For one thing, though he brought out his first volume, *Harmonium* (with its cherishable lyric forays), in 1923, his poetic career did not truly begin until 1935, when he

271

produced *Ideas of Order,* followed by six more books in a dozen years. For another thing, Stevens explored imaginative vistas in the spirit and wake of Emerson and Whitman, of the American Romanticism that Eliot had seemed to declare nonoperative. Hart Crane, too, was a modernist Romantic, invoking Walt Whitman in techniques borrowed from Eliot. The much younger Robert Lowell speaks for a later generation. *His* war was World War II, during part of which he was imprisoned as a conscientious objector; and his work enacted a wrenching away from the tightly constructed, studiously nonpersonal manner endorsed by Eliot.

Two playwrights take part in the flowering. Eugene O'Neill, the supreme figure thus far in American stage history, made his mark in 1916 with *Bound East for Cardiff* and with *The Long Voyage Home* in the year following; but his greatest dramatic triumphs came several decades later, with *The Iceman Cometh* in 1946 and *A Long Day's Journey into Night* (posthumously) in 1956. Lillian Hellman, the strenuously innovative dramatist and author of *The Children's Hour* (1934) and *The Little Foxes* (1939), is, like Robert Lowell, essentially of a subsequent generation; her play *Toys in the Attic* was produced in 1960, and her memoirs date from the 1970s. She may even be thought of as the youngest figure in this book, since she lived until 1984 and is thus only barely eligible.

Surveying most of these writers, personally acquainted with many of them, commenting on them and assigning them places in the country's moveable cultural feast is Edmund Wilson, generally regarded as the finest and most cultivated literary critic (as against the theoretical variety) that we have yet had. Wilson was a novelist and short story writer and playwright, too, and the author of such classics of scholarly journalism as *Axel's Castle* and *The Scrolls from the Dead Sea;* but it was finally as a critic of American and European literature that he made a measurable difference. It may well be that Wilson's single most reprehensible misjudgment was his caustic dismissal of the genre of mystery writing, as in his (in)famous essay "Who Cares Who Killed Roger Ackroyd?" In any case, mystery writing has made its own difference in our culture, enjoyably so, beginning with the work of the writer Dashiell Hammett, who, for all intents and purposes, created the American form of it.

The names of writers who are not present here throng in the mind, more so than with any previous section. Of William Carlos Williams, the beneficent doctor and long-lasting poetic personality—his unforgettable salute to the red wheelbarrow in the rain comes from 1923, and his *Pictures from Breughel* won a Pulitzer Prize in 1963—the Gallery has as yet no portrait. Of Edwin Arlington Robinson there is only an unbecoming sketch (a drypoint of 1933) of him folded into a chair; Robinson is probably the poet whose absence we regret most. Any overview of American poetry since 1920 would have to consider John Crowe Ransom and Allen Tate, as well as Carl Sandburg and several more; space is lacking for any one of them. And beyond these factors, the particular tastes of readers and critics may well diverge from our own. With regard to novelists, a larger or a different book would find a place for the Nobelists Sinclair Lewis and John Steinbeck, for Thomas Wolfe, and decidedly for John Dos Passos (whose voice is heard more than once in these pages).

The artists in this section are relatively few. There are two very differently accomplished photographers, Alfred Stieglitz (b. 1864) and Walker Evans (b. 1903). There is the matchless painter of southwestern desert light, Georgia O'Keeffe. There are two composers: Charles Ives (b. 1874), who, in the words of Aaron Copland, became the long-awaited American "figure in the world of symphonic literature" comparable to Emerson and Whitman in their own literary world; and George Gershwin (b. 1898), who expanded the thematics of jazz into a new world of symphonic literature.

The Gallery has no images, among the pictorial artists one might expect to see, of Jackson Pollock, Mark Rothko, or Hans Hofmann; Willem de Kooning and Robert Motherwell are ruled out on chronological grounds. There are four portraits of Alexander Calder (1898–1976), the inventive genius of the mobile; it was a painful matter trying and failing to decide which of the other artists or writers we might dislodge to make a spot for him.

But in a general way, we take comfort from the array of top-flight artists who are distinctively present in the section as the sources of the visual portraits. They are mostly photographers, and as a group they demonstrate the remarkable aesthetic reach of photography in this century. Walker Evans (also here as a subject) gives us a Hart Crane lit by the passion of thought. Henri Cartier-Bresson, the legendary Parisian, the man of a thousand anecdotes, displays his uncanny ability to be in the right place at the right moment for the significant image, in his picture of the shirt-sleeved William Faulkner, somewhere in the open, with his two dogs. With his friend, Robert Capa, Cartier-Bresson founded the cooperative picture agency Magnum in Paris in 1947; and Capa is on hand with his image of Ernest Hemingway. Capa, Hungarian-born, was the supreme war photographer—in Spain, in World War II, and in Vietnam, where he was killed by an exploding mine in 1954. He is exactly the right photographer of Ernest Hemingway, whom, as John Updike points out, he catches in a pose that combines rifle-carrying alertness with scholarly concentration.

We have spoken earlier of Edward Steichen, the great pioneer of artistic photography and here the author of the portrait of Eugene O'Neill: settled comfortably in meditation, as it seems, on some challenging dramatic venture, possibly *Ah, Wilderness!* (both picture and play are from 1933). Clara Sipprell, who opened a studio in Greenwich Village in 1915 and became known for the originality and psychological accuracy of her portraits, displays just those gifts in images of Charles Ives and Robert Frost. Irving Penn had a notable interest in characters who relish novelty in experience: like Lillian Hellman, seen as relaxed but somehow ready to make a spring at life. Arnold Newman offers an early (1944) example of his knack for locating subjects in actually or symbolically appropriate contexts—by juxtaposing the partners Alfred Stieglitz and Georgia O'Keeffe. Something of that same imaginative ability is reflected by Rollie McKenna, in her posing of Wallace Stevens in a business suit, outside of (perhaps) a Hartford office building, and Robert Lowell, near a bridge in Florence.

George Gershwin and e. e. cummings contribute self-portraits, each stylishly distorted to fit the artist's self-appraisal. Theodore Dreiser is delineated in a questioning mood, by Henry Varnum Poor, otherwise known as a craftsmanlike house designer and muralist. Edmund Wilson wears an interested but slightly disapproving air in the drawing by George Biddle, painter and lithographer and keen activist in federal arts projects. And Edith Wharton, whose fixed image for her friends and readers alike is that of the thoroughly adult woman, appears at age eight (if not younger) in a painting by Edward May: it is the Gallery's only likeness of her.

Four of the verbal portraits were composed especially for this volume, the author in each case drawing on his professional experience: the playwright John Guare, talking sagely about Eugene O'Neill; the novelist John Updike, reliving his first readings of Hemingway and responding to the Capa portrait; the poet John Hollander, making his way with all felicity through the verbal refinements and syntactical intricacies of Wallace Stevens; the mystery writer Robert B. Parker detecting the creative essence of Dashiell Hammett. These portraits, taken together, form a unique plateau of commentary.

Elsewhere, we hear two distinguished composers, Aaron Copland and Virgil Thomson, welcoming the phenomenon that was Charles Ives. Subsequently, the composer Leonard Bernstein salutes his predecessor George Gershwin, while the elegant English writer and art historian Harold Acton thinks back to Oxford evenings in the 1920s when the "Gothic twilight" was permeated by "Rhapsody in Blue." The critic Alfred Kazin braves the cosmic "homelessness" of Theodore Dreiser, and Richard Poirier looks at the disconcerting contradictions in Robert Frost. Edith Wharton, lecturing two young English friends about the tangled knots of marriage, gives a rare self-revelation. T. S. Eliot puts forward a jaunty poetical view of himself as he might be seen by hostile observers.

The cultural age, for all its ranging multiplicity (of geography and genre, of style and vision), displays, like most of its predecessors, recurring intimacies, connections, likenesses. To draw only on these entries: we notice Ezra Pound helping Frost and Eliot on their poetic careers; T. S. Eliot writing a crucial word of praise for the poetry of Marianne Moore; Fitzgerald and Hemingway eyeing each other warily. There are the couples—Stieglitz and O'Keeffe, Hammett and Hellman. And there are the two New England insurance executives, Charles Ives and Wallace Stevens, born only five years apart, developing in their leisure time into titans of music and poetry.

Similar connections are represented in the verbal pictures. John Peale Bishop, in a sad and glowing epitaph, recalls the Scott Fitzgerald of the Princeton days. Elizabeth Bishop, in one of her most graciously animated poems, summons into view the Marianne Moore she had known from her own Vassar days in the 1930s, and with whom she visited (in

Brooklyn) and exchanged views ("Elizabeth, don't speak to me about that man!" Miss Moore once said to her about Walt Whitman) for more than thirty-five years. Helen Vendler, the leading poetry critic, remembers Robert Lowell in the classroom at Harvard; and Lowell in turn tells of encountering the battered but still pugnacious Ezra Pound in Rapallo in 1965. John Hersey, in a dazzling single-sentence etching, brings to palpable life his old friend and Martha's Vineyard neighbor Lillian Hellman. And Stieglitz and O'Keeffe, husband and wife for twenty-odd years, express themselves each on the other, as spouse and as artist.

Portrait by Edward Harrison May (1824–87), oil on canvas, 1870

Edith Wharton 1862–1937 Author

Two English friends, John Hugh Smith, a banker, and Percy Lubbock, Wharton's literary protégé, had expressed disapproval with the play Oliver Latimer *(by Rudolf Besier) because it gave favorable treatment to a discontented married woman.*

Dear me! What *jeunes féroces* you & Percy are!—I shuddered at your reasons for repudiating "Oliver Latimer" so scornfully. If what you said had been addressed to Mrs. Campbell's acting, I shd have understood; but no, it's the subject you scorn. My first impulse, *of course,* was to truckle but, as I cast my eye backward over literature, I seemed to remember a few other neurotic women who were discontented with their husbands and relations—one Clytemnestra, e.g., & Phaedra, & Iseult, & Anna Karenina, & Pia Tolomei, too Francesca da Rimini. And I wonder, among all the tangles of this mortal coil, which one contains tighter knots to undo, & consequently suggests more tugging and pain, & diversified elements of misery, than the marriage tie—& which, consequently, is more "made to the hand" of the psychologist & the dramatist?

EDITH WHARTON to John Hugh Smith, from Paris, February 12, 1909

Born Edith Newbold Jones into an upper-middle-class New York family; educated at home and in Europe. In 1885 she married Edward Wharton, an amiable Bostonian of no particular vocation. Marital restiveness spurred her first literary efforts, in the early 1890s: short stories, reviews, the tasteful *Decoration of Houses*. She had purchased twin houses on Park Avenue in 1891; they gave way in 1893 to Land's End, a handsome home in Newport that was succeeded in 1902 by The Mount, a mansion near Lenox, Massachusetts, built to her specifications.

Wharton's first major literary and commercial success was *The House of Mirth* (1905), a novel exploring contemporary New York. After several more volumes there appeared *Ethan Frome* (1911), the well-knit drama of New England rural life that was long the most widely read of her books. In that same year she sold The Mount and in effect separated from her husband and moved to Paris. She was in the late stages of an intense but unfulfilling love affair with Morton Fullerton, a Paris-based American journalist, attractive but feckless.

Her friendship with Henry James, begun in 1903, became a main source of comfort. *The Custom of the Country,* Wharton's most powerful novel of social conflict, came out in 1913. During World War I, Wharton worked for refugee relief, winning praise and honors. Soon after the war she produced *The Age of Innocence,* her craftiest study in social contrasts; it won the Pulitzer Prize (and has been filmed twice). During the 1920s and into the 1930s Wharton remained prolific, producing novels and short stories. She divided her time between a chateau on the French Riviera and a villa outside Paris. Her hospitality was immense, and her creative energy of composition amazed her friends.

Forty years after her death her reputation was revived. All her books returned to print, and she was considered perhaps the leading American exemplar of the "woman novelist."

Theodore Dreiser 1871–1945 Author

The great realists have always been those for whom the "real" world is always strange, who are fascinated by the commercial and industrial world because they know that this world is not *theirs*. For Dreiser the emotion of the provincial Carrie in the big city has become a powerful ingathering symbol of the interest and fascination of a society that, by reducing everyone in it to a feeling of complicity and powerlessness, makes *everyone* feel provincial. Only a writer like Theodore Dreiser, to whom success in the external world and some understanding of man's destiny were equal passions, could have created such unforgettable images of man's homelessness in both society and the universe at large as Dreiser did when he described Carrie rocking in her chair, or Cowperwood in prison looking up at the stars with a sense that he was no more to the world of infinite space than he felt himself to be to the conventional world of marriage and business.

ALFRED KAZIN, introduction to Laurel paperback series of Dreiser novels (1959)

Born in Terre Haute, Indiana, of a perennially poor family; his brother (with name respelled) was Paul Dresser, the popular songwriter ("On the Banks of the Wabash"). With his family, Dreiser drifted to Chicago at a young age, like his fictional character Carrie Meeber. Here he found work as a newspaper reporter; by 1894 he was in New York, free-lancing for newspapers and magazines. In 1898 he married Sara White; his infidelities brought about a divorce in 1912.

Dreiser's first novel, which some think his best, was *Sister Carrie:* a work that established the Dreiserian view, sometimes called "naturalism," of the individual confronting the unknowable and probably hostile universe (conveyed by the first chapter's subtitle, "A Waif Amid Forces"). It appeared in 1900, but the publisher, Doubleday, suddenly frightened by its "immorality" (nonmarital relations), virtually suppressed the book. There followed some years of magazine editing, followed by Dreiser's second novel, the appealing *Jennie Gerhardt* (1911), and Dreiser's literary career was in full bloom. *The Financier,* the first and most powerful volume in the early trilogy about the businessman Frank Cowperwood, and based on the story of the Chicago tycoon Charles T. Yerkes, came out in 1912. A decade of prolific nonfiction writing led, in 1925, to *An American Tragedy,* Dreiser's most successful work, dealing with an impoverished youth maneuvered by fate into committing a murder. Dreiser's genuine if muddled social concerns induced him to flirt with communism and finally, in 1945, to join the American Communist Party. In 1944 he married Helen Richardson, his mistress of many years.

Dreiser is a perennial challenge to literary historians and critics; one of the latter called *An American Tragedy* the "worst-written great novel in the world." His lapses of diction and taste are regularly condemned; but no less regularly he is celebrated for his extraordinary fictional vision of *power* in human experience.

Portrait by Henry Varnum Poor (1888–1970), oil on canvas, 1933.
© Henry Varnum Poor / Licensed by VAGA, New York, NY.

Willa Cather 1873–1947 Author

One can see at a glance that she herself has always been that rare accident of Nature, a perfectly natural person. She speaks, without the shadow of a doubt, in the accent she acquired as a child. Her voice is deep and resonant. Her dresses are bright in color; she likes brilliant embroidery, boldly designed materials, and exotic strings of beads. She is of medium height and of the build best described as stocky. She stands and moves solidly. She sits with an air of permanence, as though the chair were, and had always been, her home. She smokes a cigarette as though she really liked the taste of ignited tobacco and rice paper. Her eyes are fine—gray-blue—and set well apart. She has a thorough smile.

LOUISE BOGAN, Profile of Willa Cather, *The New Yorker,* August 8, 1931

The first nine years of her life were on a Virginia farm. She spent an idyllic childhood, educated at home by her grandmother, with much time spent outdoors. Her father moved the family to Nebraska in 1883. Here on the Great Plains she found friends among others who had been uprooted from their familiar surroundings, including settlers from such far-off lands as Sweden, Poland, and Russia.

After graduating from the University of Nebraska she worked on a newspaper in Lincoln, then continued her journalistic career in Pittsburgh. The publication of a volume of poetry in 1903 and short stories in 1905 led to a job at *McClure's* magazine in New York. Here she was managing editor from 1908 until her resignation in 1912, after which she devoted herself full time to writing.

In her early novels she drew on the landscape and people of her Nebraska youth—*O Pioneers!* (1913), *My Ántonia* (1918); their courage, strong will, their drive for survival and achievement. With the decline of the pioneering era, the arrival of the machine, and the onset of a less heroic time there is an added poignancy to her tales: *One of Ours* (1922) and *A Lost Lady* (1923). In her later work she turned from remembered characters to pioneers further back in history. *Death Comes for the Archbishop* (1927) and *Shadows on the Rock* (1931) tell of the French missionaries in the early Southwest and French Canadians in Quebec.

Her writing is distinguished by its unaffectedness, her voice clear and natural. Howard Mumford Jones calls her style "grave, flexible, a little austere, wonderfully transparent, everywhere economical." In the *New Yorker* profile quoted above, Louise Bogan says "she is a writer who can conjure up from the look of a place and the actions of people a narrative as solid as a house, written in prose as surely counterpointed as music."

Portrait by Carl Van Vechten, photograph, 1936

Georgia O'Keeffe 1887–1986 Artist
Alfred Stieglitz 1864–1946 Artist

Sometimes I've been talking with O'Keeffe. Some men express what they feel by holding a woman's hand. But I have wanted to express the more, to express the thing that would bring us still closer. I would look at the sky, for the sky is the freest thing in the world, and I would make a photograph from the clouds and the sky and say to O'Keeffe, "Here is what we were talking about."

ALFRED STIEGLITZ, quoted in *Portraits of American Women: From Settlement to the Present,* G. J. Barker-Benfield and Catherine Clinton (1991)

His power to destroy was as destructive as his power to build—the extremes went together.

There was a constant grinding like the ocean. It was as if something hot, dark and destructive was hitched to the highest brightest star.

For me he was much more wonderful in his work than as a human being. I believe it was the work that kept me with him—though I loved him as a human being. I put up with what seemed to me a good deal of contradictory nonsense because of what seemed clear and bright and wonderful.

GEORGIA O'KEEFFE, introduction to *Georgia O'Keeffe: A Portrait,* by Alfred Stieglitz (1978)

Georgia O'Keeffe. Born in Wisconsin, she showed early artistic talent and studied at the Art Institute of Chicago, the Art Students League in New York, and Teacher's College, Columbia University. Several winters of teaching art in the Texas panhandle left an enduring impression of the open spaces.

In New York, Stieglitz took an interest in her early works and in 1917 arranged her first show in his gallery, "291." He continued to exhibit her work until his death in 1946.

They were married in 1924. In 1929, O'Keeffe went to Taos, New Mexico; she spent half her time there, returning to Stieglitz in New York for the other half.

Many of her paintings reflect the southwestern desert's light and terrain, which fascinated her. Her subjects range from luminous flowers to clouds, religious symbols, and animal bones. Variously labeled erotic, abstract, spiritual, realistic, her works can safely be called enigmatic.

Alfred Stieglitz. Born in Hoboken, New Jersey, he attended the University of Berlin, where he made his first photographs. By 1900 he was considered the world's leading amateur photographer. As editor of *Camera Notes* and *American Amateur Photographer,* he encouraged such artists as Alvin Langdon Coburn and Edward Steichen and championed American artists by showing their works in the galleries he directed. In founding the organization called Photo-Secession (around 1902) he, with other innovators, attempted to establish photography as a fine art. Their efforts resulted in the publication of *Camera Work,* a quarterly magazine of arts and letters, and the creation in 1905 of "291," a gallery in New York which became a forum for photography where Stieglitz also introduced "modern art" to America, showing works by Matisse, Manet, and other European artists.

Portrait by Arnold Newman (b. 1918), photograph, 1944

Portrait by Clara E. Sipprell (1885–1975), photograph, c. 1947

Charles Ives 1874–1954 Composer

It is gratifying to realize that only America could have produced a Charles Ives. Or, to be more specific, only New England in the last quarter of the nineteenth century. In mid-nineteenth century, when our literature could boast such writers as Whitman and Thoreau, Emerson and Emily Dickinson, we had no comparable figure in the field of serious music. As everyone knows, in its more cultivated forms, music is the last of the arts to develop. Not until the advent of this greatly gifted New Englander were we able to point to a comparable figure in the world of symphonic literature.

Ives, when he composed, was incredibly daring: no one before him had ever ventured so close to setting down on paper sheer musical chaos. The marvel is that he got away with it.

AARON COPLAND in *Charles Ives Remembered: An Oral History,*
edited by Vivian Perlis (1974)

His open life was that of a businessman, conventional, respected, impregnable to scrutiny. His secret life was that of a romantic artist—wildly experimental, ambitious, unchanneled, undisciplined, and unafraid.

VIRGIL THOMSON, *American Music Since 1910* (1971)

Born and raised in Danbury, Connecticut. The two early and lasting influences on his work were his father, a choir director and band master who experimented in dissonant harmonies and encouraged originality in his son, and the hymns, popular dance and folk tunes, and patriotic marches heard in his youth.

At Yale, he was not a notable academic student, but he shone in musical composition classes: he studied the organ, played in two churches, and composed his first two symphonies, the First String Quartet, and other musical pieces.

After college he moved to New York, married, and went into the insurance business. While leading a conventional and busy life as business and family man, he worked on his astonishing musical compositions, the years 1905 to 1915 being the most productive (chronic illness, beginning in 1918, curtailed his career).

America, New England, and the Transcendentalists were frequent themes in his work ("Three Places in New England," "The Concord Sonata," with movements named Emerson, Hawthorne, the Alcotts, and Thoreau), but his techniques were original and modern. Polyharmony, complex polyphony, and the simultaneous use of different meters made his music difficult, and for years, though recognized by some as gifted and remarkable, his work was found challenging and often too difficult to perform. Even Koussevitsky, a conductor open-minded and welcoming of innovative work, found his music too confused to attempt. It wasn't until years later that he was recognized and honored. Copland notes, "It is this very 'confusion' that now makes for the special excitement in Ives's music."

Portrait by Clara E. Sipprell (1885–1975), photograph, c. 1955

Robert Frost 1874–1963 Poet

Engaging yourself critically with Frost is like taking a trip with an old neighborhood friend and discovering under the stress of travel that he can on occasion be altogether more mysterious than you'd bargained for; he can be more exalted and exalting, yet show all the while flashes of a pettiness you had managed before to overlook; he can be full of wonderful excesses of imagination and generosities of spirit and yet more satisfied, it seems, by his self-control; a man ennobling in his centralities of feeling, which he will nonetheless betray by sudden reversions to formula and platitude. After the trip, you go home again among old friends. And there he sits, the same man to all appearances, whom the others know as well as you do. The difference is that now the persona has itself become, for you, an achievement altogether more powerful, impressive and interesting in what it includes, the tensions it resolves, the passions it shapes. The others who have never known him to be any different are not so much wrong about him as simply not right enough. They have not, as it were, made the journey out and back, and such a journey is perhaps the central figure for Frost's own poetic enterprise of voice and vision—off into the sublime, back to the domesticated.

RICHARD POIRIER, *Robert Frost: The Work of Knowing* (1977)

Born in San Francisco. Both his parents were New England schoolteachers, but his father had grown disaffected with the region. In 1885, after the father's death, the mother moved the family back east, to Lawrence, Massachusetts. Thereafter New England was Frost's literal, spiritual, and cultural home. His closest literary affinities were with Emily Dickinson, Thoreau, and most especially Emerson. In 1900, following a year at Harvard, Frost settled as a chicken farmer in New Hampshire with his wife (since 1895), Elinor White, his high school sweetheart. But Frost had no luck getting his poems published, and in 1912, nearing forty, he took the family to England to try his chances. He was immediately befriended and sponsored by Ezra Pound, who saw to the publication of two Frost volumes in 1913–14, *A Boy's Will* and *North of Boston*.

Frost's life over the next forty years consisted of volume after volume of poetry, awards, and prizes (four Pulitzers between 1924 and 1943), teaching (Amherst, Michigan, Harvard), and reading—or rather, in his own more precise word, "saying"—his poetry before audiences large and small from coast to coast. His most conspicuous moment was when he read his poem "The Gift Outright" ("The land was ours before we were the land's.") at the inauguration of John F. Kennedy in 1961, at age eighty-eight.

Frost is the most easily memorizable and quotable of the great American poets of the century; "Stopping By Woods on a Snowy Evening" is only one example. Readers and critics have gradually recognized, as against the image of the homespun sage, a deep strain of darkness in Frost, a non-Emersonian distrust of natural facts, and an artful deceptiveness of posture: "My kind of fooling," he called it.

Ezra Pound 1885–1972 Poet

In *Return to Yesterday,* Ford Madox Ford recalls Pound's appearance in the streets of London. He would see Pound coming toward him "with the step of a dancer, making passes with a cane at an imaginary opponent. He would wear trousers made of green billiard cloth, a pink coat, a blue shirt, a hand-painted tie by a Japanese friend, an immense sombrero, a flaming beard cut to a point, and a single, large blue earring.

LOUIS SIMPSON, *Three on the Tower: The Lives and Works of Ezra Pound, T. S. Eliot, and William Carlos Williams* (1975)

At a Pound memorial gathering in New York in January 1975, Robert Lowell recalled his last meeting with Pound, in Rapallo in March 1965.

[Pound was] emaciated, neat in blacks and whites, silver beard, he looked like the cover of one of his own books, or like an El Greco, some old mural, aristocratic and flaking. He held up his blotched, thinned away hands, and said, as if he were joking at them: "The worms are getting to me." Later, I must have said something about Hamilton or Pennsylvania College, where he had studied. He said, "Yes, I started with a swelled head and end with swelled feet." He was thinking of Oedipus. I said, "You are one of the few living men who has walked through Purgatory."

IAN HAMILTON, *Robert Lowell, a Biography* (1982)

Born in Hailey, Idaho, but grew up in Pennsylvania and attended the University of Pennsylvania and Hamilton College (degree earned in 1905). He traveled to Europe in 1907, then settled in London, where he lived until 1920. In 1914 he married Dorothy Shakespear. In England he worked as a literary editor, did a number of extraordinarily adept translations. He was the literary sponsor of aspiring American poets like Robert Frost and T. S. Eliot (about whose *The Waste Land* he gave invaluable advice). The English years were reenacted in Pound's suite of poems *Hugh Selwyn Mauberley* (1920), and his inquiry—amid a wealth of personal and learned allusions—into what "the age demanded," poetically and culturally.

In 1920, Pound went to Paris and then to Italy, settling in Rapallo until 1939. There he worked on *The Cantos,* a sort of cultural history of the western world. After America entered World War II, Pound was invited to make two broadcasts daily over Rome Radio. On January 29, 1942, he began, "The United States has been for months, and illegally, at war through what I consider to be the criminal acts of President Roosevelt." At the end of the war Pound was arrested by American military authorities in Italy and imprisoned in Pisa. During his imprisonment he wrote *The Pisan Cantos.* He was brought home and indicted for treason; a medical board, however, found him "of unsound mind," and he was committed to St. Elizabeth's Hospital in Washington. Here he stayed until 1958, with regular visits from friends and poets. After he was released he went to Merano, Italy, where he lived with his daughter until his death.

In 1949 the prestigious Bollingen Award was given to *The Pisan Cantos,* causing an enormous furor. The petition for Pound's release in 1958 was written by Robert Frost, with statements by Eliot, Marianne Moore, Hemingway, Dos Passos, Auden, Robert Fitzgerald, and Archibald MacLeish.

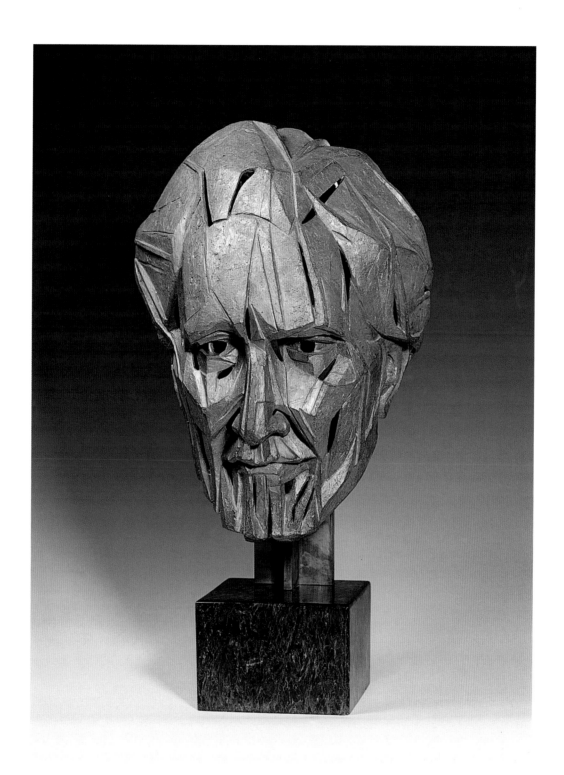

Portrait by Joan Fitzgerald (b. 1930), bronze, 1969

T. S. Eliot 1888–1965 Poet

Lines for Cuscuscaraway and Mirza Murad Ali Beg
How unpleasant to meet Mr. Eliot!
With his features of clerical cut,
And his brow so grim
And his mouth so prim
And his conversation, so nicely
Restricted to What Precisely
And If and Perhaps and But.
How unpleasant to meet Mr. Eliot!
With a bobtail cut
In a coat of fur
And a porpentine cat
And a wopsical hat
How unpleasant to meet Mr. Eliot!
(Whether his mouth be open or shut).

T. S. ELIOT, *Collected Poems, 1909–1962*

When he is writing for clerical papers or addressing a Conservative dinner, he allows himself reactionary audacities which he rarely hazards with his larger audience. I was talking about this just now with Arthur Schlesinger, usually an up-in-arms liberal, and—rather to my surprise—he anticipated my opinions by saying that all this side of Eliot didn't matter. In his poetry and in his personal relations, he is sensitive, gentle and rather touching.

EDMUND WILSON to Van Wyck Brooks, October 6, 1957, *Letters on Literature and Politics,* edited by Elena Wilson (1977)

Born Thomas Stearns Eliot in St. Louis of a New England family, variously distinguished from the eighteenth century. Eliot went to Harvard and pursued graduate study, but in 1914 he began study at Oxford, and England became his home.

His first major achievement was "The Love Song of J. Alfred Prufrock," published with the aid of Ezra Pound. It led to the slim 1917 volume *Prufrock and Other Observations*. Poetic modernism is usually dated from this moment: poetry drawing on both French symbolism and the English metaphysical, dealing in startling contrasts and conjunctions, fragmented yet aesthetically whole. In Eliot's case the mode reached its climax in *The Waste Land* (1922), the most influential poem of the century. Eliot was also establishing himself as a crucial critical voice, at once seductive and pontifical, with successive volumes of essays on traditions in poetry and the true nature of poetry.

His masterpiece *Ash Wednesday* (1930), about his religious conversion, and *Four Quartets* (1943), spurred his winning of the Nobel Prize in literature. Eliot's career as a dramatist began with *Murder in the Cathedral* (1935) and continued through the hugely successful *Cocktail Party* (1949). He became a British citizen in 1927.

Portrait by Sir Gerald Kelly (1879–1972), oil on canvas, 1962

Portrait by Michael Alexander Werboff (1896–1996), oil on canvas, 1968

Marianne Moore 1887–1972 Poet

From Brooklyn, over the Brooklyn Bridge, on this fine morning,
      please come flying.
In a cloud of fiery pale chemicals,
      please come flying,
to the rapid rolling of thousands of small blue drums
descending out of the mackerel sky
over the glittering grandstand of harbor-water
      please come flying . . .

Come with the pointed toe of each black shoe
trailing a sapphire highlight,
with a black capeful of butterfly wings and bon-mots,
with heaven knows how many angels all riding
on the broad black brim of your hat,
      please come flying.

Bearing a musical inaudible abacus,
a slight censorious frown, and blue ribbons,
      please come flying.
Facts and skyscrapers glint in the tide; Manhattan
is all awash with morals this fine morning,
      so please come flying.

ELIZABETH BISHOP, "Invitation to Miss Marianne Moore" (1948)

Born in St. Louis. After graduating from Bryn Mawr in 1909, she moved to New York City and then, in 1929, to Brooklyn, where she became an ardent fan of the Dodgers. She worked at the New York Public Library from 1921 to 1925, then until 1929 was acting director of the important literary magazine *Dial.*

She published poems in the English magazine *Egoist,* where the work of the Imagist group appeared. *Poems,* her first collection of poetry, was put together without her knowledge by writer friends H. D. (Hilda Doolittle) and Bryher (Winifred Ellerman) and published in 1921. It was followed by *Observations* (1924). Other volumes include *What Are Years?* (1941), and *Collected Poems* (1951), for which she won the Pulitzer Prize.

Her poems are compact, exquisite, and sometimes, as Louis Untermeyer said, "frankly puzzling." Her use of metaphor and symbolism has been found "exhilarating." Too individual to be linked to any school (though she has been called an Imagist), her poems are in a class by themselves. T. S. Eliot places her work among the "small body of durable poetry written in our time."

e. e. cummings 1894–1962 Poet

After a couple of brandies on top of the wine Cummings would deliver himself of geysers of talk. I've never heard anything that remotely approached it. It was comical ironical learned brilliantlycolored intricatelycadenced damnably poetic and sometimes just naughty. It was as if he were spouting pages of prose and verse from an unwritten volume.

His mind was essentially extemporaneous. His fits of poetic fury were like the maenadic seizures described in Greek lyrics. Those New York nights none of us wanted to waste time at the theater when there was a chance that Cummings might go off like a stack of Roman candles after dinner.

> JOHN DOS PASSOS, quoted in Richard S. Kennedy, *Dreams in the Mirror:*
> *A Biography of E. E. Cummings* (1980)

Born in Cambridge, Massachusetts, son of a Protestant minister and educated at Harvard. He was an ambulance driver in France before America entered the First World War. Questionable activities led to his imprisonment for some months in an internment camp, this experience providing inspiration for his successful prose work *The Enormous Room* (1922). After the war he lived and wrote in New York and in Paris, where he studied art.

Aside from being a painter of some talent (with several one-man exhibitions of his work), a novelist, and a playwright, he was an avant-garde poet, an early experimenter with language, dedicated from childhood to writing poetry.

Though his themes were often traditional, he was decidedly an innovator in the handling of them. Committed to individuality, he played with syntax, punctuation, and grammar, often combining words, sometimes inventing them to meet his poetic needs. His grammatical idiosyncrasies, even his placement of words on the page, were devices used to affect pace and rhythm and the ultimate effect of the poem on the reader.

Cummings has been criticized for not developing more significantly after his poems of the 1920s, but his work has been praised by a range of critics and fellow poets, among them Theodore Spencer, Horace Gregory, and James Dickey, who found him daringly original. His major works include *Tulips and Chimneys* (1923), *Collected Poems* (1938), and *100 Selected Poems* (1959).

Self-portrait, oil on canvas, 1958

Eugene O'Neill 1888–1953 Playwright

Eugene O'Neill set the standard for American drama that continues to this very day. He gave American theater size, ambition, daring, and, at the time of our country's great prosperity in the 1920s, put on stage what no one had heard before—race relations, capitalism, the machine, the split between dreamer and realist in the soul of modern man—everything that waits in the dark side of this dream, this idea called America that was so vast, it could easily be described as horizonless. Here in this limitless world, how does man live with the desolate boundaries within? O'Neill did not offer any solutions. Like Nietzche, he sought the "crisis that did not ask weak consolation." He absorbed into America Ibsen's theater of moral issues, Strindberg's ferocious theater of symbolism. He transmuted Nietzche's Dionysiac ecstasy into the longed-for Beautiful Isles of *Mourning Becomes Electra*. He took the themes of the ancient Greeks and found their American equivalent. He used those ancient techniques, their very masks, to find a new way to arrive at the theatrical truth. What's most American about O'Neill is this: He was the melting pot of world theater. He saw theater as a temple where the audience goes to be told the truth and, hearing that, perhaps even be healed. He demanded courage from the audience. The scope of his daring produced failures like *Lazarus Laughed*. Those failures only purified his vision to make the successes all the more blinding.

Every American playwright owes his or her career to O'Neill. Any time he or she is less than honest with the truth of his or her own dark heart and less than daring in the theatrical techniques used to get to that place of truth, that playwright betrays the stunning moral obligation this man has left us. O'Neill's affirmation of what theater can, no, *must* be is his triumph, his legacy, and our joyous and still unmatched benchmark.

JOHN GUARE (1998)

Born in New York City, the son of a popular romantic actor. O'Neill's troubled family life—his mother a morphine addict, his brother brilliant but unstable—is rehearsed in his late plays, especially in *A Long Day's Journey into Night*. O'Neill went briefly to Princeton before following a seafaring life for half a dozen years, sailing to South America, South Africa, and Europe. He suffered a breakdown in 1912 (the key year in his dramatic reminiscences) and after recovering found himself seized with an ambition to write plays.

His maritime experiences led to *Bound East for Cardiff,* produced in 1916, and *The Long Voyage Home* in 1917. *Beyond the Horizon* opened in New York to thunderous applause in 1920, won a Pulitzer Prize, and established O'Neill as the foremost and really the *first* genuine American playwright. *The Emperor Jones,* about the black Pullman porter Brutus Jones was also produced in 1920. There followed *Desire Under the Elms* (1924), *Strange Interlude* (1928), *Mourning Becomes Electra* (1931), and *Ah, Wilderness!* (1933), *The Iceman Cometh* (1946), and, posthumously, *A Long Day's Journey into Night* (1956), *A Moon for the Misbegotten* (1957), and *A Touch of the Poet* (1957).

O'Neill won the Nobel Prize in literature in 1936.

Portrait by Edward Steichen (1879–1973), photograph, 1933

F. Scott Fitzgerald 1896–1940 Author

Fitzgerald is partly Irish and . . . brings to life and to fiction certain qualities that are not Anglo-Saxon. For, like the Irish, Fitzgerald is romantic, but also cynical about romance; his is bitter as well as ecstatic; astringent as well as lyrical. He casts himself in the role of playboy, yet at the playboy he incessantly mocks. He is vain, a little malicious, of quick intelligence and wit, and has an Irish gift for turning language into something iridescent and surprising.

EDMUND WILSON, "F. Scott Fitzgerald," in *The Shores of Light: A Literary Chronicle of the Twenties and Thirties* (1952), reprinted from *The Bookman* (1922)

No promise such as yours when like the spring
You came, colors of jonquil in your hair,
Inspired as the wind, when the woods are bare
And every silence is about to sing.

None had such promise then, and none
Your scapegrace wit or your disarming grace . . .

Was it a fault in your disastrous blood
That beat from no fortunate god,
The failure of all passion in mid-course?
You shrank from nothing as from solitude,
Lacking the still assurance, and pursued
Beyond the sad excitement by remorse.

JOHN PEALE BISHOP, "The Hours" (1941), a requiem for Bishop's close friend from Princeton college days, who had died the previous December

Born in St. Paul, Minnesota, of Irish descent; named for his ancestor Francis Scott Key. At Princeton he became friends with Edmund Wilson and John Peale Bishop. After serving as an infantry lieutenant in the war, Fitzgerald went to New York and by 1920 had finished and published his first novel, *This Side of Paradise,* an early expression of postwar 1920s romantic exuberance. The same year he married Zelda Sayre, a writer from a well-known family in Montgomery, Alabama; they had a daughter, Scottie.

Two collections of Fitzgerald's stories came out in 1920 and 1922, the second giving a lasting title to the whole epoch: *Tales of the Jazz Age,* In 1925 came *The Great Gatsby,* a brilliant evocation of the vanishing American dream. Scott and Zelda now divided their time between Long Island and the French Riviera.

But times became troubled for the Fitzgeralds. Zelda suffered a nervous breakdown and was mostly incapacitated until her death in 1948, though she did write a novelistic version of their life in *Save Me the Waltz* (1932). Fitzgerald's own *Tender Is the Night* (1934) is his account of the experience.

Fitzgerald was in Hollywood for his later years, writing scenarios and working on *The Last Tycoon,* the compelling but unfinished novel about the producer Irving Thalberg.

Portrait by Harrison Fisher (1875–1934), sanguine
conté crayon on paper, 1927

Portrait by Henry Cartier-Bresson (b. 1908), photograph, 1947

William Faulkner 1897–1962 Author

Faulkner is a small man (5 ft. 5, I should judge), very neatly put together, slim and muscular. Small, beautifully shaped hands. His face has an expression like Poe's in photographs, crooked and melancholy. But his forehead is low, his nose Roman, and his gray hair forms a low wreath around his forehead, so that he looks like a Roman Emperor. Bushy eyebrows; eyes deeply set and with a drop at the outer corners; a bristly moustache. He stands or walks with an air of great dignity and talks—tells stories—in a Mississippi accent.

He got out of his chair and began pacing up and down the living room. With his short steps and small features, he gave an impression of delicacy, fastidiousness, but also of humility combined with something close to Napoleonic pride. "My ambition," he said, "is to put everything into one sentence—not only the present but the whole past on which it depends and which keeps overtaking the present, second by second." He went on to explain that in writing his prodigious sentences he is trying to convey a sense of simultaneity, not only giving what happened in the shifting moment but suggesting everything that went before and made the quality of that moment.

MALCOLM COWLEY, from his notebook entries for October 23 and 26, 1948,
during and after Faulkner's visit to the Cowleys' home in Sherman, Connecticut:
The Faulkner-Cowley File: Letters and Memoirs, 1944–1962 (1966)

There was a man and a dog too this time.
Opening sentence of Faulkner's *The Bear* (1942)

Born in New Albany, Mississippi, into a somewhat decaying Deep South clan; his great-grandfather, William C. Falkner (as it was then spelled), was an infantry commander in the Civil War, a railroad builder, and the author of *The White Rose of Memphis*, a popular melodrama. In 1902, Faulkner's father moved the family to nearby Oxford, seat of the state university, where the elder Faulkner became treasurer. Oxford was Faulkner's home for the rest of his life; it is re-created as the town of Jefferson and the human center in the novels that make up the Yoknapatawpha County saga.

That saga began with the novel *Sartoris* (1929). Before that Faulkner had tried various ventures and had made his way to New Orleans, where he became a protégé of Sherwood Anderson. It was Anderson who helped Faulkner publish his first novel, *Soldier's Pay* (1926). But *Sartoris* inaugurated the long series of interlocking stories about the families—the Sartorises, Compsons, Sutpens, McCaslins—and their gradual decline. The series moved from *The Sound and the Fury* (1929) to *As I Lay Dying* (1930), through *Light in August* (1932) to *Absalom, Absalom!* (1936). The last-named is a work so stupendously conceived but so intricately structured that it baffled many critics and even elicited charges of hoax.

The story of the rise of the Snopes clan began with *The Hamlet* (1940). Faulkner received the Nobel Prize in 1950; at the ceremony he declared his belief that "man will not merely endure: he will prevail." Faulkner wrote many other novels and collections of stories, including *Sanctuary* (1931), with its celebrated rape episode; and *The Bear* (1942), one of the best American novellas ever written. There was a stint in Hollywood in the 1930s (Faulkner coscripted the Humphrey Bogart movie *The Big Sleep*), and from 1957 he was writer-in-residence at the University of Virginia.

Portrait by Robert Capa (1913–54), photograph, 1941

Ernest Hemingway 1899–1961 Author

He projected not just a literary style but a style of life. For several generations, American men carried themselves with a laconic stoicism and consoled themselves with an elemental hedonism of sensation and beverage and place because Hemingway had done so. He brought word of the remaining good places the overused world still held—Spain and Upper Michigan and Africa and Cuba and the Paris of young and impoverished bohemians. His style needed a certain luxuriously austere diet of landscape and adventure to be so blunt and luminous. In 1924 he wrote to Gertrude Stein of his Michigan story, "Big Two-Hearted River," "I'm trying to do the country like Cézanne and having a hell of a time and sometimes getting it a little bit."

I came to him when still a boy by way of his lesser works—*Death in the Afternoon,* an intent study, with grimly antic interludes, of his era's bullfighters, and *To Have and Have Not,* a muddled and squalid novel of Depression Florida with the ringing repeated phrase "Some Chinaman." Strong stuff, it told me that the world was a brutal, burnt-out place with a shimmer of beauty. He had nearly died at age eighteen of an exploding shell in Italy, and hunting and killing was one way of keeping alive the authenticity of that experience. Here he crouches with a gun, but his glasses make him look scholarly, which in his fashion he was. As celebrity and alcohol got to him he became easy to mock, as his style was easy to parody, but up to and including his ending his own life with a shotgun he kept an epic dignity, the stark Greek dignity of those who challenge the gods.

JOHN UPDIKE (1998)

Born in the Chicago suburb of Oak Park, the son of a prosperous physician—who, many years later, in poor health and financial troubles, shot himself. At age eighteen Hemingway became a cub reporter for the *Kansas City Star:* but a year later he was in Italy, working as an ambulance driver with the Italian army. He was badly wounded by an exploding shell but managed to save another man's life before he collapsed. The whole experience resonated through Hemingway's fiction, and his way of sizing things up.

Immediately after the war Hemingway worked for the *Toronto Star.* He made the first of his four marriages and went to Paris, where he entered Gertrude Stein's literary circle. Hemingway's volume of stories *In Our Time* (1925) signaled the appearance of a major new talent. His novel *The Sun Also Rises* (1926) carried his vision of postwar malaise and of what Stein called a "lost generation." *A Farewell to Arms* (1929), contains some of the most deftly drawn scenes in the modern American novel. No later novel by Hemingway equaled it, but he continued to produce short stories of the highest order. At the same time, Hemingway was demonstrating his skills in nonfiction, with *Death in the Afternoon* and *The Green Hills of Africa* (autobiographical).

For the rest, Hemingway kept busy building his personal legend—as a boxer, trout fisherman, big-game hunter, womanizer—and exhibiting traits of the bully, the genius, and the generous host. He won the Nobel Prize in 1954; and killed himself in Ketchum, Idaho, at age sixty-two.

Portrait by Rollie McKenna (b. 1918), photograph. © Rollie McKenna.

Wallace Stevens 1879–1955 Poet

Stevens was one of the very greatest of our poets in a century during which the loudest of assertions had started to ring false. His questionings, his subordinations, his ways of evading the worst conceptual evasions were in themselves quietly heroic. Inward and outward vision always interrogate one another in his poems that, like the ever-receding frontiers of the mind itself, keep summoning our attentiveness. And in a century during which American poetry parroting Whitman's great barbaric yawps sounded like the tinkle of parlor piano strings, his encyclopedic exclamations kept faith with and renewed that earlier vigor.

Now that his presence has itself become part of our national Nature—as much as a river of rivers in Connecticut or a mountain of mountains in New Hampshire—it is hard to remember how, for poets of several later generations, he was a private discovery and a personal treasure of unguided reading. But by the midcentury his central imaginative project—central to the poetry of our time and to the depth of view of our democratic vistas—had emerged. His major poetry energetically engaged the task of preserving our cardinal nobilities from decay into trivialization and into mockeries of what they had been, and in finding our very notions of centrality and representativeness in their ever-shifting hiding places in the world we apprehend. His poems make—in his own words— "the visible a little hard / To see" and "reverberating, eke out the mind / On peculiar horns, themselves eked out / By the spontaneous particulars of sound."

JOHN HOLLANDER (1998)

Born in Reading, Pennsylvania. Stevens attended Harvard College (1897–1900), where he came to admire George Santayana, and went on to New York University Law School. In 1909 he married Elsie V. Kachel. Stevens joined the legal staff of the Hartford Accident and Indemnity Company in 1916, and in 1934 he became the company's vice president.

Stevens was a serious insurance executive, and in some sense a weekend and vacation-time poet. His first volume of poetry, *Harmonium* (containing "Sunday Morning," "Anecdote of a Jar," "Thirteen Ways of Looking at a Blackbird," among other superb items), appeared in 1923; and it was not until 1935, when Stevens was fifty-six, that his second volume, *Ideas of Order,* made its appearance. Other volumes followed more rapidly: *Owl's Clover* (1936), *The Man with the Blue Guitar* (1937), *Parts of a World* (1942), *Notes Toward a Supreme Fiction* (1942), *Transport to Summer* (1947), *Auroras of Autumn* (1950).

His early poems established for Stevens a reputation for verbal elegance and wit, and, as it were, a creatively meditative spirit. Later works, especially *Notes Toward a Supreme Fiction,* enlarge the vista to explore the wondrously complex and shifting relation between reality and the poetic imagination. As to the latter, Stevens remarked in one of his influential essays, "In an age of disbelief, it is for the poet to supply the satisfactions of belief."

Hart Crane 1899–1932 Poet

"When the Pulitzer showered on some dope
or screw who flushed our dry mouths out with soap,
few people would consider why I took
to stalking sailors, and scattered Uncle Sam's
phoney gold-plated laurels to the birds.
Because I knew my Whitman like a book,
stranger in America, tell my country: I
Catullus redivivus, once the rage
of the Village and Paris, used to play my role
of homosexual, wolfing the stray lambs
who hungered by the Place de la Concorde,
My profit was a pocket with a hole,
Who asks for me, the Shelley of my age,
Must lay his heart out for my bed and board."
      ROBERT LOWELL, "Words for Hart Crane,"
            in *Life Studies* (1959)

Born in Garretsville, Ohio. From 1910 to 1923, Crane lived mostly in Cleveland, where his father ran a chain of candy shops. Crane's later perspective, on Manhattan and other places, remained in part midwestern.

Self-educated and decidedly precocious, Crane published his first poem at age eighteen. By 1921 poems as striking and original as "Chaplinesque" and "Praise for an Urn" were in print; the three-part "For the Marriage of Faustus and Helen" followed in 1923; and his collection *White Buildings* appeared in 1926. By this time Crane had moved permanently to New York and was a conspicuous and engaging figure in the Greenwich Village literary world, with Gorham Munson, Waldo Frank, and others. Alcoholic excess and indiscriminate sexual activity hindered Crane's creative process, but he thoroughly enjoyed it all, and brought both drink and sex, openly or subtly, into his poetry. He worked with intermittent fever through the 1920s on his modernist epic *The Bridge,* which was published at last in 1930: a series of dazzling but unassimilated fragments, or a grand and ultimately coherent poetic whole, according to critical view.

Crane was awarded a Guggenheim fellowship in 1931, and he took up residence in Mexico. In late April 1932, returning by ship from Mexico to New York, he disappeared over the side. He may have committed suicide, but that is far from certain; "Lost at Sea" is inscribed on a tomb for him in the Garretsville cemetery.

Crane is one of the most mind-seizing but least penetrable of American modernist poets—not least because he openly borrowed poetic techniques and literary associations from T. S. Eliot while describing Eliot's cultural pessimism and proclaiming his own Emersonian-Whitman belief in the future greatness of America. There is no doubting his persistent intention—as he put it in his last poem and one of his finest, "The Broken Tower" (1932): "And so it was I entered the broken world / To trace the visionary company of love."

Portrait by Walker Evans (1903–75), photograph, c. 1930

Walker Evans 1903–1975 Photographer

The world that Walker caught so ferociously in his lens thirty years ago was a world I had known all my life. Facing his pictures then, I found, at first, pleasure in simple recognition, but as I pored over the pictures, it began to dawn on me that I had not known that world at all. I had walked down those roads, dusty or muddy according to season. I had stopped before those log cabins or board shacks and been barked at by the hound dog. I had swapped talk with those men and women, by the rock hearth inside or squatting on my heels under a white oak or a chinaberry tree, according to latitude. But staring at the pictures, I knew that my familiar world was a world I had never known. The veil of familiarity prevented my seeing it. Then, thirty years ago, Walker tore aside the veil; he woke me from the torpor of the accustomed.

ROBERT PENN WARREN, a toast to Evans at a dinner in January 1971,
quoted in Belinda Rathbone, *Walker Evans* (1995)

Walker Evans is giving us the contemporary civilization of Eastern America and its dependencies as Atget gave us Paris before the war and as Brady gave us the War between the States.

This at first may seem an extravagant claim for a young artist in relation to a subject as vast as contemporary American civilization. But after looking at these pictures with all their clear, hideous, and beautiful detail, their open insanity and pitiful grandeur, compare this vision of a continent as it is, not as it might be or as it was, with any other coherent vision that we have had since the war. What poet has said as much? What painter has shown as much?

LINCOLN KIRSTEIN, in *Walker Evans: American Photographs* (1938)

Born in St. Louis; after childhood years in the Midwest he moved to New York in 1919 with his mother and sister. He spent one year at Williams College.

Evans worked at the New York Public Library until 1925, when his father financed one promised year in France. There he used a vest-pocket camera to take pictures. He returned to New York in 1927 to earn a living. In a job with the Resettlement Administration, one of the work relief programs of the 1930s, he did extensive documentary photography in the mining towns of West Virginia.

His friends in New York were artists, writers, intellectuals—Ben Shahn, Lincoln Kirstein, and Hart Crane, whose poem *The Bridge* he illustrated. In the early 1930s he met James Agee, a writer on the staff of *Fortune* magazine. Agee, who had been assigned to write about white tenant farmers in the South, asked that Evans be sent as photographer. This collaborative project led to the book *Let Us Now Praise Famous Men* (1941). Evans worked for *Time* and *Fortune* and taught at Yale University from 1965 to 1974.

The little written about him seems evidence of his elusive and reserved personality. But his talent as a photographer was recognized early: his straight approach to subject, his camera's unflinching eye are remarkable for truth and purity. He became a major influence on American photography.

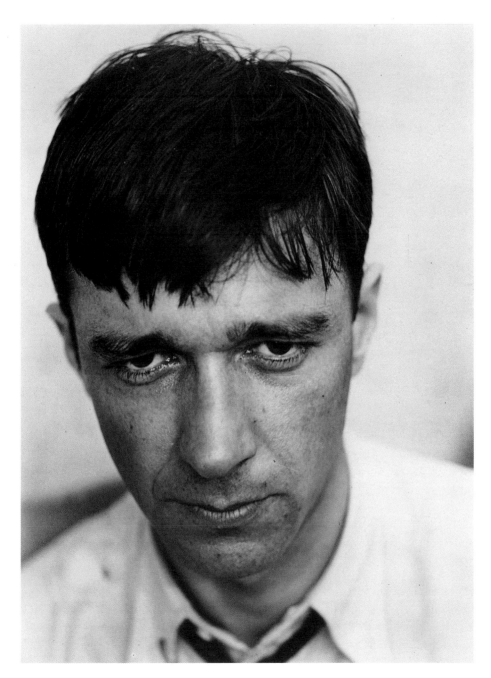

Attributed to Paul Grotz (1902–90), photograph, c. 1934

Edmund Wilson 1895–1972 Author

What was Wilson like as a man? As I briefly knew him, he was a hospitable egotist, a crisp talker but no windbag, a citizen of literature, a man with an appetite for living, eating, drinking, and loving women. There was also a streak of melancholy.

V. S. PRITCHETT, *The New Yorker,* January 5, 1987

Isaiah Berlin recalls meeting Edmund Wilson at the Princeton Club in New York in the early spring of 1946.

I was, I own, taken aback by his appearance. I do not know what I had imagined a distinguished literary critic to look like, but there stood before me a thickset, red-faced, pot-bellied figure, not unlike President Hoover in appearance; but once he began to talk, almost before we had sat down, I forgot everything except his conversation. He spoke in a curiously strangled voice, with gasps between his sentences, as if ideas jostled and thrashed about inside him, getting in each other's way, as they struggled to emerge, which made for short bursts, emitted staccato, interspersed with gentle, low-voiced, legato passages. He spoke in a moving and imaginative fashion about the American writers of his generation, about Dante, and about what the Russian poet Pushkin had meant to him.

ISAIAH BERLIN, "Edmund Wilson at Oxford," *The Yale Review,* March 1987

Born in Red Bank, New Jersey. Wilson attended Princeton University, where he formed a friendship with F. Scott Fitzgerald, and graduated in 1916. He served as an enlisted man in France during the war. His long association with New York-based magazines began with *Vanity Fair* (1920–21), went on to *The New Republic* (1926–31), and then most memorably to *The New Yorker,* where he was the potent book reviewer from 1944 to 1948 and an important contributor for many years afterward. Wilson's third marriage, from 1938 to 1946, was to the writer Mary McCarthy, who depicted him with knowing satire in her fiction. His last and enduring marriage was to Elena Thornton Mumm.

Wilson, known to many as "Bunny," was a space-filling personality in literary circles here and abroad, in places like the Algonquin Hotel, and on university campuses. He displayed his skill in all the forms of literary expression—to name only a sampling: in fiction (*I Thought of Daisy,* 1929, and *Memoirs of Hecate County,* 1946), poetry (serious and taunting), drama (*The Little Blue Light,* 1950), as a literary memoirist (*The Shores of Light,* on the '20s and '30s), an adventurous historical essayist (*To the Finland Station,* 1940, and the endlessly influential *Scrolls from the Dead Sea,* 1955), a polemicist (*The Cold War and the Income Tax,* 1963).

But he was always and especially a literary critic: "a citizen of literature," as Pritchett calls him above; broadly read and uniquely well balanced. Two of his many critical volumes may be singled out: *The Wound and the Bow* (1941), on writers (like Dickens) whose achievement was rooted in suffering or deprivation, and *Patriotic Gore* (1962), on Civil War writing.

Wilson's honors included the Presidential Medal of Freedom in 1963. With his wife, Elena, he spent his summers, in his late years, in the upstate New York village of Talcotville.

Portrait by George M. Biddle (1885–1973), silverprint drawing on paper, 1956

George Gershwin 1898–1937 Composer

Gershwin was, after all, a songwriter—in his nature, his origin, his experience, and his craft. His songs have become part of our language, or the vernacular, if you will, and they are happily hummed and whistled by people the world over. He came from the wrong side of the tracks, grew up in the ambience of Tin Pan Alley, song plugging, and musical near-illiteracy. His short life was one steady push to cross the tracks, both musically and socially—an effort guided and sustained by ambition and an enormous reserve of sensibilities.

> LEONARD BERNSTEIN, "In Appreciation," in Charles Schwartz,
> *Gershwin: The Man and His Music* (1973)

An Oxford memoir from the 1920s.

Cocktails were substituted for Amontillado, and parties motored from college to college as from night club to night club. Conversation was stifled by a gramophone, and the talkative devised a special basic English in which to shoot wisecracks at each other in the style of Noel Coward, while couples clung together forlornly, swaying to some raucous blues. George Gershwin's "Rhapsody in Blue" accompanied every rough and tumble on a sofa. Gershwin himself, whom I heard play it to perfection at the Savoy Hotel, had the sleek wax Oriental profile of some Salome-struck youth on the terrace of Wilde's one-act tragedy, and it was strange that this liquid-eyed figure from a world of spiced bazaars should have become a medium for the orchestration of the most violent transatlantic neurasthenia. That "Rhapsody in Blue" seeped through the Gothic twilight of Oxford and gave us all the fidgets. For a while it blurred the strumming of Neapolitan guitars in my blood.

> HAROLD ACTON, *Memoirs of an Aesthete* (1948)

Born in Brooklyn; died (of brain tumor) in Hollywood. Gershwin's parents emigrated from Russia to New York in the early 1880s; he grew up on the Lower East Side. Gershwin began to play and study the piano at age twelve, though he never could read music proficiently. In 1914 he left school to become a song-plugger at Remick's, the Tin Pan Alley publisher. His first published song was in 1916; his first great success was *Swanee* in 1919 (Al Jolson's recording sold in the hundreds of thousands). After 1924, George wrote songs exclusively with his brother Ira.

Paul Whiteman commissioned *Rhapsody in Blue* and performed it with Gershwin as soloist in 1924. Walter Damrosch commissioned *Concerto in F* (1925) and *An American in Paris* (1928). The musical drama *Porgy and Bess* was written in 1934–35. Among Gershwin's best-known musical comedies: *Lady Be Good* (1924), *Oh, Kay!* (1926), *Strike Up the Band* (1927), *Funny Face* (1927), *Girl Crazy* (1930), *Of Thee I Sing* (1931), *Let 'Em Eat Cake* (1933). Gershwin wrote the music for two Fred Astaire films: *Shall We Dance* (1937) and *A Damsel in Distress* (1937).

Self-portrait, oil on canvas, 1934

Portrait by Edward Biberman (1904–86), oil on canvas, 1937

Dashiell Hammett 1894–1961 Writer

Hammett has about him the look of a man who kept his integrity hard and intact. There is in the flatness of his gaze a hint of the dead-on, dead-end implacability of his take on life. There is nothing to believe in, but he perseveres. The way he was is the way he wrote. In his work, life appears to have no organizing principle. The Op and Spade maintain a kind of unyielding work ethic. Their life acquires meaning because they do their job. Hammett seems to enlarge the possibilities in *The Glass Key,* in which Ned Beaumont's loyalty to his friend might stay confusion. And in *The Thin Man* Hammett hints that love might suffice. It would be pretty to imagine such an evolution in Hammett's own life, where professionalism kept him centered before he joined Lillian Hellman and love did the job thereafter. But his portrait belies this. There is about him a chilly aloneness. It bespeaks a man whose prose style was able, in Raymond Chandler's words, to "say things he did not know how to say or feel the need of saying. In his hands it had no overtones, left no echo, evoked no image from beyond a distant hill." Looking at the thin elegant reserve of the man, we might imagine that the distant hill is all the image there was.

ROBERT B. PARKER (1998)

Born in Maryland, he attended Baltimore Polytechnic Institute for several years, then held jobs as diverse as freight clerk, yard man, and messenger; for eight years he worked for the Pinkerton Detective Agency.

After serving in the Ambulance Corps in the First World War he began his writing career. He reviewed detective fiction and in 1923 published his first stories in *Black Mask,* a magazine created by H. L. Mencken and George Jean Nathan that encouraged fast-paced stories of good quality. His first novel, *Red Harvest,* was serialized in *Black Mask* in 1927.

Credited by Raymond Chandler and Erle Stanley Gardner as being the inventor of the "hard-boiled" detective story, he earned his status in detective fiction with such works as *The Maltese Falcon* (1930) and *The Glass Key* (1931). His immortal private eye Sam Spade, hard drinking and tough but with his own brand of moral code, has been much copied, but Hammett's psychologically complex characters and distinctive and literate style created a magic that has eluded many imitators.

For a writer of such extraordinary impact and influence, his literary output was small. After *The Thin Man* (1932) he was a screenwriter in Hollywood, where he met his lifetime companion, Lillian Hellman; he also consulted on stage and radio scripts. His political activities in defense of civil liberties kept him in the public eye. A member of the Civil Rights Congress, he served a six-month jail sentence for contempt of court, and in 1953 he was staunch in his stance against Joseph McCarthy.

Lillian Hellman 1905–1984 Playwright

It is the complexity of this organism that stuns and quickens us. Energy, gifts put to work, anger, wit, potent sexuality, wild generosity, a laugh that can split your eardrums, fire in every action, drama in every anecdote, a ferocious sense of justice, personal loyalty raised to the power of passion, fantastic legs and easily turned ankles, smart clothes, a strong stomach, an affinity with the mothering sea, vanity but scorn of all conceit, love of money and gladness in parting with it, a hidden religious streak but an open hatred of piety, a yearning for compliments but a loathing for flattery, fine cookery, a smashing style in speech and manners, unflagging curiosity, fully liberated female aggressiveness when it is needed yet a whiff, now and then, of old-fashioned feminine masochism, fear however of nothing but being afraid, prankishness, flirtatious eyes, a libertine spirit, Puritanism, rebelliousness.

JOHN HERSEY, "Lillian Hellman," *Life Sketches* (1985)

Born in New Orleans, she attended New York University and Columbia, and as a young woman worked for a New York publishing house, her introduction to the literary world. After marrying Arthur Kober, a press agent, she traveled abroad; in Germany in 1929 she found the anti-Semitism that would be seen in her plays *Watch on the Rhine* (1941) and *The Searching Wind* (1944). In Hollywood with Kober, whom she later divorced, she read scripts for Metro-Goldwyn-Mayer and met the mystery writer Dashiell Hammett, with whom she had a thirty-year relationship.

Her first play, encouraged by Hammett, was *The Children's Hour,* produced in 1934. It established her as a major new figure in the American theater. Its controversial sexual subject caused a furor, but it was critically acclaimed, noted, in a review by J. W. Krutch, for its sheer power and originality. *The Little Foxes* (1939), dramatizing the saga of a rapacious southern family, remains one of her best-known works. She wrote a number of plays, the last major one being *Toys in the Attic* (1960); also play adaptations and, later, several unconventional memoirs. In *Pentimento,* the section called "Julia" was made into a popular film in 1977.

Passionate, criticized sometimes for being melodramatic, she was a vivid and outspoken woman prepared to take a strong stance. A political liberal, she was called to testify before the House Un-American Activities Committee in 1952. She wrote about this experience in one of her last memoirs, *Scoundrel Time* (1976).

Portrait by Irving Penn (b. 1917), photograph, 1947

Robert Lowell 1917–1977 Poet

Lowell at Harvard in the 1960s and 1970s.

Lowell began his classes on each successive poet with an apparently indolent, speculative, and altogether selective set of remarks on the poet's life and writing; the poet appeared as a man with a temperament, a set of difficulties, a way of responding, vocation, prejudices. The remarks were indistinguishable from those Lowell might have made about a friend or an acquaintance: the poets *were* friends or acquaintances; he knew them from their writing better than most of us know others from life. This, in the end, seems to me the best thing Lowell did for his students: he gave them the sense, so absent from textbook headnotes, of a life, a spirit, a mind, and a set of occasions from which writing issues—a real life, a real mind, fixed in historical circumstances and quotidian abrasions.

HELEN VENDLER, "Lowell in the Classroom" (*Harvard Advocate,* 1979), quoted in Ian Hamilton, *Robert Lowell: A Biography* (1982)

Born in Boston; a descendent, on his father's side of James Russell Lowell and of the poet Amy Lowell, and on his mother's side from Edward Winslow (1596–1655), *Mayflower* passenger, Puritan writer, and three-time governor of the Massachusetts Bay Colony. These ancestral elements figured importantly in Lowell's poetry and prose.

Lowell was briefly at Harvard, then went south to Tennessee, where he was taken in by Allen and Caroline Tate. He followed Tate to Kenyon College, where he graduated with honors in classics. During the war he served a prison term as a conscientious objector. Lowell's first volume, *Land of Unlikeness,* was published in 1944; it was incorporated into *Lord Weary's Castle* (1946). Poems like "A Quaker Graveyard in Nantucket" and "Mr. Edwards and the Spider" established Lowell as a major poet with a unique voice. *Life Studies* (1959) was a brilliantly executed break from modernism; deeply personal, casual in tone, informal in style. *For the Union Dead* (1964) carried Lowell's poetic reach still further.

Lowell was also a playwright: his trilogy *The Old Glory,* based on stories by Hawthorne and Melville, was produced in 1965. He was uncommonly gifted as a translator, of Montale and Baudelaire; and the author of *Imitations,* drawn from poems by Villon, Rilke, Mallarmé, and others. His prose writings reveal his learned fascination with his American literary ancestry. Lowell was badly troubled by attacks of manic-depression in the 1950s, but he overcame them. He taught at Harvard intermittently from 1963 until 1977. His marriage to Jean Stafford ended in divorce in 1949, and that to Elizabeth Hardwick in 1972. Among his many honors were two Pulitzer Prizes. Lowell's lifelong political activism grew more intense during the Vietnam War and was reflected in a long, unfinished sonnet sequence.

Portrait by Rollie McKenna (b. 1918), photograph. © Rollie McKenna.

Faces on the Public Scene: The 1930s to the 1970s

THE INDIVIDUALS ASSEMBLED HERE ARE ALMOST BY DEFINITION PERSONS OF action, and we see them, suitably, caught visually or verbally in moments of action. The list, after all, includes four presidents of the United States—Franklin D. Roosevelt, Harry S Truman, Dwight D. Eisenhower, and John F. Kennedy; one First Lady, Eleanor Roosevelt (the finest ever to occupy the White House, as many of us think); one governor and two-time presidential candidate, Adlai Stevenson; one mayor, the incandescent Fiorello La Guardia; two demagogues, stormers of the public scene Father Charles Coughlin and Senator Joseph McCarthy; and in a remarkable collage by Robert Rauschenberg, a dramatic cluster—another national political leader, Robert F. Kennedy; a magnetic civil rights spokesman, Martin Luther King, Jr.; one of the first two human beings to walk on the moon, Buzz Aldrin; and a personality whose singing voice was heard across the country, Janis Joplin.

The period covered runs more or less from 1933, when La Guardia began his first term as mayor of New York and Roosevelt became president, through the convulsive year 1968, which saw the assassinations of Robert Kennedy and Martin Luther King, and on to 1969, when the national morale was strengthened somewhat by the moonwalk of Aldrin and his companion. And among the moments of action captured for us, we have La Guardia bursting into a New York unemployment-relief station to throw the authorities into a panic; Father Coughlin in 1936 stirring his thousands of listeners into a frenzy by shouting that Roosevelt was a betrayer and a liar; FDR being surreptitiously conveyed by aircraft to Casablanca in 1943 for a meeting with Churchill, and enjoying it all like a teenager; John F. Kennedy, staring out the glass doors of the Oval Office and saying that the time had come for him to make decisions about the Cuban Missile Crisis.

These occasions are recorded both by camera and anecdote; the first recorder mentioned is George Tames, a news photographer for the *New York Times* for more than forty years, admired throughout his profession and (especially) the Washington world for the animated and revealing quality of his images—residents of the corridors of power, as it has been said, transformed into vivid human beings. Four such transformations are shown here; Roosevelt, upright behind his desk, wholly engaged in the affair of that moment; Truman jauntily waving his cane as he descends the White House steps; Stevenson listening carefully during an encounter in the 1952 campaign; John Kennedy advancing to greet exhilarated Berliners ("Ich bin ein Berliner," he had just told them).

Elsewhere, the radio priest Father Coughlin is etched in lithographic acid by the pungent and imaginative Hugo Gellert. If you look closely you will see that Coughlin is garbed in priest's clothing on his right side and civilian dress on his left; and that his right hand is raised in moral and religious thunder, while his left hand stuffs wads of money into his pocket. Altogether different in pose and import are the photographs of Eleanor Roosevelt by Trude Fleischmann, in 1944, and of J. Robert Oppenheimer by Philippe Halsman, in 1958; both disclosing the individual spirit in an interval of reflection, and both illustrating to perfection Auden's remark (see "Faces on the Public Scene" section) about the greater attractiveness and wisdom of the private face in the public place.

The most literally active figure in the entire group is Dwight D. Eisenhower, organizer and supervisor of the Allied invasions of North Africa and Italy in 1942–43, and then of France on D-Day in June 1944; and yet his is the most sedate portrait of all, a 1948 bust of the general (he was at the time president of Columbia University) by Jo Davidson, the third appearance in these pages by the gifted sculptor. Here is an army personality, yet perhaps we get a glimpse of that inner craftiness remarked on by Murray Kempton in his verbal portrait. Senator McCarthy is snapped by an unidentified news photographer during the 1954 Army-McCarthy hearings, hunched and poised for another assault on the facts. (Of all the public characters from these decades whose absence we regret, we perhaps regret most that of Edward R. Murrow, the ablest and most influential broadcast journalist of his time, and one whose courageous 1954 TV program on McCarthy helped the senator destroy himself.)

It was a time of resounding opposites: of Eleanor Roosevelt working to help the poor and the racially oppressed, and Father Coughlin fanning the flames of racial hatred; of Stevenson trying to talk sense to the American people and Joseph McCarthy telling them large-scale lies. It was a Dickensian worst of times and best of times, of epochal achievement in politics and in war and in outer space, and of great lives cut short by assassination. The extraordinary collage by Robert Rauschenberg brings much of this together on a single canvas.

The Texas-born Rauschenberg is generally credited with having devised the vocabulary of pop art. After his period of study with Josef Albers at Black Mountain College in North Carolina in the late 1940s, Rauschenberg passed through several stages; in one of them he designed what he called "combine" paintings, in which physical subjects were actually incorporated into the painting (for example, *The Bed* of 1955). In the 1960s he moved on to new combinations, vast kaleidoscopes of images drawn from newspaper and film and miraculously brought into significant harmony. The painting called *Signs,* our final entry here, is a masterpiece in this genre. It re-creates the chaos and transcending coherence of the decade just ending, the 1960s, and crowns this section.

It repays a slow study, both to make out all the elements depicted and to see how Rauschenberg has aesthetically related them. The implications are endless.

The occasion for the painting was the death, in October 1970, of Janis Joplin, at age twenty-seven, of a drug overdose. Joplin and Rauschenberg were close friends, both products of Port Arthur, Texas. For the artist, the singer's death at just that time in just that way seemed to bring the whole decade to an end. The painting was designed to reenact the sixties, and in the artist's words to "remind us of [the] love, terror and violence of the last ten years," and that "the danger lies in forgetting."

Fiorello La Guardia 1882–1947 Mayor of New York

One day [in 1934], Lowell Limpus [the mayor's friend and biographer] accompanied La Guardia to a Lower East Side relief station. Parking the car a block away, they joined a line of jobless—waiting to apply for assistance. The queue moved with infuriating slowness as one or two staffers interviewed the applicants, while others lounged around their idle typewriters. It took La Guardia but a few minutes to reach his boiling point. Then he pushed through the line to the front, knocking an unknowing attendant back into the crowd. Another came to his colleague's assistance and went the same way. Responding to the noise a natty supervisor with a derby hat and a cigar in his mouth came rushing over.

It was a mistake. Before he had a chance to understand, his cigar and his hat were on the ground. "Take your hat off, when you speak to a citizen," ordered the pint-sized disrupter. The mayor was recognized too late. La Guardia marched over to the director's office, only to learn that he was not in. He ordered a secretary to summon the welfare commissioner at once. In the meantime, he took out his watch and perched on a stool near the front of the line, rasping, "Now let me see how fast you can clear up the applicants." La Guardia had walked in at 9:15, by 9:37 many in the crowd had been interviewed and hustled on their way. When the commissioner arrived, La Guardia ordered him to "wait here . . . until your director gets here," and to fire him unless he produced a doctor's note. Others were singled out for discipline. As he strode out, the mayor paused, pointed to the man with the derby, and called back: "Oh yes. There's another SOB that has no job."

THOMAS KESSNER, *Fiorello H. La Guardia and
the Making of Modern New York* (1989)

Born in Greenwich Village, New York, of Italian and Austrian-Jewish background, La Guardia graduated from New York University Law School in 1920 and worked as an interpreter at Ellis Island, and with ethnic clientele on the Lower East Side. His second wife, Marie Fischer, was a New Yorker of German stock.

La Guardia was elected to Congress in 1916, and he served there, with an interval, until 1932. He was elected mayor of New York in 1933, and again in 1937 (the first reformer ever to win reelection), and in 1941, always on a fusion ticket with Republican endorsement. His performance as mayor combined a high visibility, a dedication to the improvement of urban life, and a stout independence from traditional politicians of both parties.

Portrait by S. J. Woolf (1880–1948), charcoal and chalk on paper, 1939

Portrait by George Tames (1919–94), photograph, 1944

Franklin Delano Roosevelt 1882–1945
Thirty-second President of the United States

In January 1943, Roosevelt, Harry Hopkins, and staff are en route to Casablanca for a conference with Churchill about where to open a second front, after the conquest of Africa.
The President was carried on to the plane this morning in the dark—it taxied out of the harbor and long before sunrise took off with few people knowing the President was on his way to Africa. I sat with him, strapped in, as the plane rose from the water—and he acted like a sixteen-year-old, for he has done no flying since he was President. The trip was smooth, and the President happy and relaxed. Dr. McIntyre was worried about the President's bad heart—nothing happened—he slept for two hours after lunch. He asked the pilot to go over the Citadel in Haiti. We saw no ships and made a perfect landing at the Naval Base in Haiti.

We had a leisurely breakfast with Admiral Oldendorf and General Pratt—the President still treats it as a first-class holiday—he told some of his old favorite stories and seemed to be in no hurry to get off tho the Secret Service was having fits.

HARRY HOPKINS, journal notes for January 11 and 12, 1943,
in Robert E. Sherwood, *Roosevelt and Hopkins* (1948)

Presidents of the caliber of Jefferson and Lincoln don't tend to reappear, but we had one in the nineteen thirties when Franklin Delano Roosevelt took over. He had the ability to make people believe he was right and go along with the things he wanted to do, and he was also very daring in action.

Where the Buck Stops: The Personal and Private Writings of Harry S Truman,
edited by Margaret Truman (1989)

Born in Hyde Park, New York, into a wealthy, patrician family; his mother was the strong-minded Sarah Delano. Roosevelt graduated from Harvard (1904) and Columbia Law School, and in 1905 he married his kinswoman Eleanor Roosevelt. In World War I he served as assistant secretary of the Navy under Woodrow Wilson. In 1921 Roosevelt was stricken with poliomyelitis; he never recovered the use of his legs, though he made a gallant show of moving about, with braces and a cane.

In 1928, encouraged by Eleanor to reenter politics, he won election as governor of New York. In 1932 he defeated Herbert Hoover in the presidential election. Forced by circumstances, he brought the powers of government to bear on unprecedented unemployment, economic disaster, and national despair. Roosevelt was reelected by a landslide in 1936, and for a third term (breaking precedent) in 1940. After 1939, against bitter opposition, Roosevelt maneuvered the nation's resources into an "arsenal for democracy" in the Allied cause. His close association with Winston Churchill was crucial to the Allies' victorious progress.

Roosevelt was elected to a fourth term in November 1944. The following April he died of a massive hemorrhage.

Eleanor Roosevelt 1884–1962 First Lady, Stateswoman

I had lost an inspiration. For she would rather light candles than curse the darkness, and her glow had warmed the world. . . . The sadness we share is enlivened by the faith in her fellow man and his future which filled the heart of this strong and gentle woman. She imparted this faith, not only to those who shared the privilege of knowing her and of working by her side, but to countless men, women and children in every part of the world who loved her even as she loved them. For she embodied the vision and the will to achieve a world in which all men can walk in peace and dignity. And to this goal of a better life she dedicated her tireless energy, the strange strength of her extraordinary personality.

ADLAI STEVENSON, eulogy before the General Assembly
of the United Nations, November 9, 1962

Member of a privileged family (the niece of President Theodore Roosevelt), she was orphaned at nine, raised by her grandmother and schooled at home until at fifteen she went to Allenswood School in England, where the headmistress Marie Souvestre was known for her radical stance on unpopular causes (defending Dreyfus, and so forth). Eleanor Roosevelt refers to those three years of "contact with a liberal mind and strong personality" as having profoundly influenced her life.

On her return to New York she involved herself with social work and taught at a settlement house. In 1905 she married her distant cousin Franklin Delano Roosevelt and raised five children under the cold and domineering presence of her mother-in-law. Her interest in social welfare never flagged, and during World War I she worked tirelessly for the Red Cross. She played an increasingly important role in her husband's rising political career in New York state politics, proving to be an effective political organizer; she joined the Women's Trade Union and was active in the state Democratic Party. Her concerns were women, children, racial discrimination, and the poor.

During the years of Franklin Roosevelt's presidency, 1933 to 1945, she expanded her role as First Lady to an unprecedented working partnership with her husband, and established herself as a politically influential figure in her own right. Travel, radio talks, and a syndicated column called "My Day" put her in the public eye, where her compassionate humanitarian views reached millions.

After FDR's death in 1945, her career continued. She stayed active in Democratic politics, and as a delegate to the United Nations, appointed by President Truman, she was a major force in the drafting of the Universal Declaration of Human Rights in 1948.

A dedicated worker for world peace, she remained a fearless advocate of social justice, far in advance in her pursuit of civil rights for black Americans, equality for women, support of the underprivileged. She was one of the most influential women of the century.

Portrait by Trude Fleischmann (b. 1895), photograph, 1944

Father Charles E. Coughlin 1891–1979 Catholic Priest, Radio Personality

Then on July 16 [1936] Coughlin addressed ten thousand Townsend Plan delegates at their convention in Cleveland. He criticized and threatened and promised. He played the audience like an organ, stroked them and lashed them and flattered and scared and comforted them, and finally rose on his toes and lifted his fists and denounced that "great betrayer and liar," Franklin Roosevelt. He ripped off his coat and his clerical collar and poured it on, while correspondents dove for the nearest telephone. Coughlin had sassed Cardinals before but he had never before called the President a liar.

When he was done, the ten thousand Townsendites, in a frenzy of devotion, paraded for an hour in Coughlin's honor. "You had all the throbbing devotion of another great moment in history," said *Social Justice* [Coughlin's newspaper], "as you watched it go on and on and heard that roaring, united voice, ten thousand, pouring up from the soul of working class America."

Maybe you had that throbbing sense, but some of the correspondents there had a crawling sense of having heard that unified voice before, in Munich or Berlin.

WALLACE STEGNER, "The Radio Priest and His Flock,"
in *The Aspirin Age, 1919–1941,* edited by Isabel Leighton (1949)

Born in Hamilton, in Ontario, Canada, of Irish descent. Brought up in strict Catholic surroundings, Coughlin was ordained priest in 1916; and in 1926 he moved to Royal Oak, Michigan, near Detroit, to become pastor of a new church, the Shrine of the Little Flower. To raise money for his tiny parish, Coughlin began to broadcast his sermons on local radio. They grew immensely popular; by 1930, according to estimates, they were drawing forty million listeners.

Coughlin then turned his radio skills to political issues, denouncing Wall Street and modern capitalism, and, after 1932, saluting Franklin D. Roosevelt as the savior of the nation. Enlarging ambition and resentment at Roosevelt's failure to honor him properly led Coughlin in 1936 to found the National Union for Social Justice, with a newspaper and a political party to go with it. Coughlin now began to launch all-out attacks on Roosevelt and the New Deal.

Coughlin's candidate in the 1936 election, William Lemke, a North Dakota congressman, polled fewer than a million votes, and Coughlin retired from broadcasting for a spell. He was soon back, however, and by 1938 was declaring the New Deal a communist conspiracy, was voicing harsh anti-Semitic statements (taken directly from a Nazi propaganda organ), and expressing strong sympathy with the regimes of Hitler and Mussolini. By 1940 his support had dwindled to the point where he could no longer afford the broadcast expenses. After Pearl Harbor he was ordered by his bishop to cease all political activities. He served at the Little Flower until 1966.

Portrait by Hugo Gellert (1892–1985), lithograph, 1936

Portrait by George Tames (1919–94), photograph

Harry S Truman 1884–1972 Thirty-third President of the United States

In the spring of 1956, Truman and his wife, Bess, during a stay in Florence, went out by invitation to Villa I Tatti, to call on the art historian and connoisseur Bernard Berenson. The luncheon-visit lasted until three.

At tea that afternoon Berenson was asked his impression of his distinguished guest. With careful deliberation he said, "I have been talking with one of the great historians of the world!" He sent a clipping of a photograph of Truman and himself to his cousin Lawrence, remarking, "I was enchanted with the almost naïve simplicity and shrewd candor of my guest. I rarely enjoyed meeting anyone as I did him." In his diary he wrote his impression of the seventy-two-year-old Truman, "as unspoiled by high office as if he had got no further than alderman of Independence, Missouri. In my long life I have never met an individual with whom I so instantly felt at home . . . ready to touch on any subject, no matter how personal. . . . If the Truman miracle can still occur, we need not fear even the [Joseph] McCarthys."

BERNARD BERENSON, quoted in Ernest Samuels, *Bernard Berenson:*
The Making of a Legend (1987)

Born in Lamar, Missouri, and grew up on a small farm in Independence. He spent five years in Kansas City, pursuing unsuccessful business ventures. In World War I he proved to be a resourceful captain of artillery in France. In 1919, Truman married Bess Wallace, a childhood sweetheart; they had one daughter, Mary Margaret. Truman returned to farming; and then, from 1923 to 1934, he acted as a county administrator.

In 1934, Truman was elected senator, with the help of the Thomas J. Prendergast machine of Missouri, which needed a candidate with Truman's record of integrity. He served until 1944, when he was given the vice-presidential nomination by the squabbling Democratic Party. And so in April 1945, after the death of Franklin D. Roosevelt, Truman became president. During his years in office Truman displayed unexpected tough-mindedness and decisiveness, as in his order to drop the atom bomb on Japan.

After the war Truman pressed forward on the Rooseveltian program, despite fading support for some New Deal measures. His varied acts aroused an uproar of opposition as well as widespread support; and in 1948 Truman won a startling victory against New York governor Thomas E. Dewey.

Truman took step after step to prevent Russian communistic control of Europe. He enunciated the Truman Doctrine, a crucial updating of the Monroe Doctrine, and stood firmly behind the Marshall Plan. The Korean War, which broke out in 1950, led to the conquest of China by communism, which had grave effects on the politics of the 1950s.

During Truman's last two decades a sort of vast national affection grew up around this man of simplicity, humor, and courage.

Dwight D. Eisenhower 1890–1969 Military Commander and Thirty-fourth President of the United States

The Eisenhower who emerges here intermittently free from his habitual veils is the President most superbly equipped for truly consequential decision we may ever have had, a mind neither rash nor hesitant, free of the slightest concern for how things might look, indifferent to any sentiment, as calm when he was demonstrating the wisdom of leaving a bad situation alone as when he was moving to meet it on those occasions when he absolutely had to.

He was the great tortoise upon whose back the world sat for eight years. We laughed at him; we talked wistfully about moving; all the while we never knew the cunning beneath the shell.

MURRAY KEMPTON, "The Underestimation of Dwight D. Eisenhower," *Esquire,* September 1967

Born in Denison, Texas, where his father was a railway worker, and raised in Abilene, Kansas. He graduated from West Point in 1915. In 1916 he met and married Mamie Doud of Denver; their first son died in childhood, but their second son, John, became a White House assistant. During World War I, Eisenhower rose to the rank of lieutenant colonel, serving entirely in the United States. Over the years following, he carried out a series of military assignments, including a stint under General Douglas MacArthur in the Philippines (1936–39).

In the summer of 1942, Eisenhower was made commander of the American and Allied forces in England, with the rank of lieutenant general, and as such he organized the invasion of North Africa in late 1942 and of Italy in 1943. Operation Overlord, the invasion of the European continent across the English Channel, beginning on D-Day, June 6, 1944, has been called Eisenhower's greatest military achievement. Other Allied commanders then and military historians later have argued about the venture, but the general verdict seems to be an admiring one.

Eisenhower was president of Columbia University (1948–50); and then, in 1952, he was nominated for the U.S. presidency by the Republican Party, winning with relative ease over Adlai Stevenson. He repeated his victory over Stevenson, with greater ease, in 1956. As Murray Kempton's verbal portrait suggests, President Eisenhower was often the butt of political liberals and politically minded intellectuals, but an overall reassessment has gradually taken place—as regards his maneuvering the Republican Party into a centrist position, as regards his staunch opposition to the use of nuclear weapons, as regards his allowing action (if with seeming reluctance) on civil rights issues, and even as regards the venomous performances of Senator Joseph McCarthy (Eisenhower is now believed to have cautiously stage-managed McCarthy's demise).

Eisenhower's farewell speech in January 1961 was a clarion warning against the dangers of the "military-industrial complex." "This conjunction of an immense military establishment and a large arms industry," declared the former five-star general, "is new in the American experience. . . . We must never let the weight of this combination endanger our liberties or democratic processes."

Portrait by Jo Davidson (1883–1952), plaster, 1948

Adlai E. Stevenson 1900–1965 Political Leader

In his almost painful honesty, he . . . has been analyzing, not asserting; he has been projecting, not an image of the big, competent father or brother, but of the moral and intellectual proctor, the gadfly called conscience. In so doing, he has revealed an integrity rare in American politics, a luminosity of intelligence unmatched on the political scene today; he has caught the imagination of intellectuals, of all those who are really informed; he has excited the passions of the *mind;* he has not excited the emotions of the great bulk of half-informed voters, nor, among these, has he created a feeling of Trust, of Authority, of Certainty that he knows where he is going and what must be done. Eisenhower does create that feeling, or that illusion, because, God knows, he is empty of ideas or certitude himself.

ERIC SEVAREID, letter to Carl McGowan of the Stevenson staff, midway
through the 1952 campaign; quoted in Porter McKeever,
Adlai Stevenson: His Life and Legacy (1989)

Born in Los Angeles, but an all-around product of Illinois. Stevenson's great-grandfather, Jesse Fell, was a close friend of Lincoln, and the one to advise Lincoln to run for the presidency; his grand-father, Adlai Stevenson, was vice-president during Grover Cleveland's second term. His father, Lewis Stevenson, was a newspaper executive, the manager of numerous family farms in Illinois, and a figure in state politics.

Stevenson went to Choate School, in Connecticut, then to Princeton, where he edited the *Princetonian* and graduated in 1922. He earned a law degree from Northwestern in 1926. In 1928 he married Ellen Borden; they were divorced in 1949. During World War II, Stevenson worked for Secretary of the Navy Frank Knox. In the later 1940s he played a central role in the formation of the United Nations and was a senior adviser to the American delegation.

Stevenson ran for the governorship of Illinois in 1948, winning by the largest majority then on record. At the Democratic National Convention in Chicago in 1952, Governor Stevenson gave a speech of welcome that electrified the delegates, who drafted him for the nomination on the third ballot. His acceptance speech included the memorable passage, "Let's talk sense to the American people." Against Dwight D. Eisenhower he campaigned valiantly, with stirring and uplifting addresses to the electorate, like the one that ended, "You, the American people, are the rulers and the ruled, the law-givers and the law-abiders, the beginning and the end." Newspaper correspondents were drawn to him, the intelligentsia flocked to him, and in November he polled more than 27 million votes; but he lost by a considerable margin. In 1956, after a less stirring campaign, he was defeated more handily.

In 1961, John F. Kennedy appointed him U.S. ambassador to the United Nations, where for several years he performed with exceptional skill.

Portrait by George Tames (1919–94), photograph, 1952

J. Robert Oppenheimer 1904–1967 Physicist

Could there, I wonder, be anyone harder to describe than he? In some ways very young, in others very old; part scientist, part poet; sometimes proud, sometimes humble; in some ways formidably competent in practical matters, in other ways woefully helpless; he was a bundle of contradictions. Of his greatness, there can, in my opinion, be no question. His mind was one of wholly exceptional power, subtlety, and speed of reaction. . . .

I recall, again, the scene at his house one rainy Sunday morning when I asked him (it was during the ordeal of the public hearings on his fitness to continue as chairman of the Scientific Advisory Committee) why he remained in this country at all in the face of such harassment. He was at home, I pointed out, in other parts of the world; he had taken his doctorate in Holland; he had many friends in the European academic world; there was not a university anywhere across the globe that would not welcome him with open arms.

He stood there a moment, tears streaming down his face. Then he stammered, with a corniness of which he was as well aware as I was but the very helplessness of which increased the force of the statement: "Dammit, I happen to love this country."

GEORGE F. KENNAN, *Memoirs,* vol. 2 (1972)

Born in New York City into a well-to-do Jewish family; his father, Julius, emigrated from Germany in 1888. Oppenheimer graduated from Harvard with highest honors in 1926, and there followed two years of study in Europe. In 1929 he joined the faculties of the University of California and the California Institute of Technology, retaining his associations with both places until 1947.

In the late 1930s, Oppenheimer became friendly with members of the left-wing circles of California. He never joined the Communist Party, but he contributed energy and money to left-wing causes. In 1942 he was asked to supervise the investigation into atomic bomb production. Thousands of scientists became involved in the project; but Oppenheimer became known publicly as the father of the atom bomb after the first explosion in Alamogordo, New Mexico, in July 1945.

In 1947, Oppenheimer was appointed director of the Institute for Advanced Study in Princeton; and at the same time, he became chief adviser to the newly formed civilian Atomic Energy Committee. He was a leading opponent of the hydrogen bomb, on both moral and practical grounds. The head of the FBI, J. Edgar Hoover, exploiting McCarthyism for his own ends, accused Oppenheimer of being a Soviet spy. Various investigatory units found him a loyal citizen but still a sort of security risk; his clearance was revoked. The restoration of his official standing began with an invitation to dinner at the White House, by President Kennedy, in April 1962. He received the Enrico Fermi award in 1963.

Portrait by Philippe Halsman (1906–79), photograph, 1958

Unidentified photographer, the Senate hearing room, with McCarthy front left, Roy
Cohn next to him, Senator Ralph Flanders of Vermont standing, 1954

Joseph R. McCarthy 1908–1957 U.S. Senator

This sovereign of the assemblies was "foul-mouthed," all right, and "a low mean fellow," and he wanted no one to think otherwise of him. He was a master of the scabrous and the scatological; his talk was laced with obscenity. He was a vulgarian by method as well as, probably, by instinct. He belched and burped in public. If he did not dissemble much, if he did little to hide from the world the sort of human being he was, it was because he had the shrewdness to see that this was not in his case necessary. He seemed to understand, as no other politician of his stature ever has, the perverse appeal of the bum, the mucker, the Dead End kid . . . to a nation uneasy in its growing order and stability.

Certainly no one who tried to see McCarthy whole could doubt that he was in some meaningful sense aberrant, even if he seemed in no meaningful way disabled or out of touch with the realities he needed (as a demagogue leading a flight from reality) to be in touch with. . . . Yet to many of us who watched him in Washington over the years, the extraordinary thing about his behavior was his composure.

RICHARD ROVERE, abridged from *Senator Joe McCarthy* (1959)

Born in Grand Chute, Wisconsin. McCarthy received an L.L.B. from Marquette University in 1935, and a few years later was appointed a circuit court judge. He later lied about his World War II service, and by this and other maneuvering secured the senatorial nomination in Wisconsin in 1946. In that Republican year (McCarthy had switched from being a Democrat), he defeated incumbent Senator Robert M. La Follette, Jr.

After a period of undistinguished and even questionable service, McCarthy, on February 9, 1950, rose in the Senate and declared that he held in his hand, there and then, a list of members of the State Department who were all communists. The numbers varied in the days following, but the staggering claims continued, though no evidence was offered. McCarthy, who quickly gained a fanatical following, began to name names: the China expert Owen Latimore, for example, was identified as the "top Russian spy" in the country. A special committee debunked the charge, but the uproar grew louder. Secretary of Defense George C. Marshall was declared a potential traitor.

In 1952, after the Republican victories, McCarthy launched his own investigation into alleged governmental treason; and in 1954 he accused the U.S. Army itself of having communist sympathies. There followed the televised Army-McCarthy hearings, at the end of which McCarthy and his two young zealots, Roy Cohn and G. David Schine, were pretty well discredited.

McCarthy was censured by the Senate. His power was gone, and within three years he was dead. "McCarthyism" remains an epithet for fanatical hate-inspired, power-seeking behavior.

Portrait by George Tames (1919–94), *Hitting the Wall* (in Berlin), photograph, 1963

John F. Kennedy 1917–1963 Thirty-fifth President of the United States

It is the classic story of the liberal man in politics. . . . And perhaps it is symbolized in a compelling picture of Kennedy that comes to us from one of Washington's most imposing men.

It is a glimpse from the Cuban missile crisis of October, 1962, a period of great tension at the White House as throughout the world. The personage and the President were alone in Kennedy's oval office, discussing what in New Frontier jargon were known as "the Options"; that month, the options were pretty grim.

Kennedy rose from his rocking chair, leaving his visitor seated on the sofa. The President went across his office to the French doors that opened on the terrace of the West Executive Wing. Beyond the terrace lay the famous Rose Garden, redesigned like almost everything else about the White House by the elegant stylists who had come to live there. But at its end still towered the famous magnolia planted by Andrew Jackson.

Kennedy stood for a long time, silent, gazing at the garden and the magnolia, his hands behind his back, the burden of decision almost visible on his shoulders. "Well," he said at last, "I guess this is the week I earn my salary."

TOM WICKER, *Esquire,* June 1964

Born in Brookline, Massachusetts; his father, Joseph P. Kennedy, was a prominent Wall Street figure. Kennedy suffered a series of illnesses, as well as serious back injury, during his youth; but he managed, after a couple of false starts, to graduate from Harvard in 1940. In 1945 he was elected to Congress, and in 1952 he was elected senator from Massachusetts. A year later he married Jacqueline Lee Bouvier. As a senator, Kennedy held back from the growing opposition to Joseph McCarthy's tactics; he spoke out most audibly against increased American involvement overseas.

In 1956, Kennedy was vice-presidential candidate on the unsuccessful Stevenson ticket. In 1960, however—and despite expressed anxieties over his youth, his Roman Catholic religion, and his independence of spirit—he was elected president by a narrow margin over Richard M. Nixon. An important novelty in the campaign was the series of televised debates between the candidates, with Kennedy exerting much the greater appeal.

Kennedy proved strong-willed during the Cuban Missile Crisis (which included a Soviet threat to invade Cuba), but he allowed the American presence in Vietnam to become larger and more active. With the shrewd help of his brother, Attorney General Robert Kennedy, the president used his executive powers most effectively in support of civil rights for black citizens.

The Kennedys together honored writers and artists, setting in motion later endowments for the arts and humanities. On November 22, 1963, while riding in an open car with Jacqueline Kennedy through Dallas, Kennedy was shot and killed at long range by Lee Harvey Oswald.

Figures of the 1960s

In this print, artist Robert Rauschenberg summarizes the promise, turbulence, and tragedy of the 1960s. Central to the piece are the images of John F. Kennedy, his brother, Senator Robert Kennedy, and civil rights leader Martin Luther King, Jr.—all charismatic leaders who seemed to promise a better world, and all three victims of assassins' bullets. Directly above Robert Kennedy is the explosive rock singer Janis Joplin, idol of the counterculture; and recalling racial violence of the late 1960s is an African American youth bleeding from a gunshot wound. The montage also contains vignettes evocative of the Vietnam War and the bitter civilian protest against it. By far the most optimistic note struck in the print is the inclusion of astronaut Buzz Aldrin, with Neil Armstrong, one of the first two men to walk on the moon and a symbol of the greatness that humankind can achieve.

A devoted friend of Janis Joplin, artist Rauschenberg was prompted to do this print by Joplin's death in late 1970 from a heroin overdose. But the picture is clearly not a tribute to only one person. For Rauschenberg, it was meant to "remind us of [the] love, terror, violence of the last ten years," and that "the danger lies in forgetting."

From acquisition page for the National Portrait Gallery (1994)

By Robert Rauschenberg (b. 1925), *Signs,* screenprint on paper, 1970. © Robert
Rauschenberg / Licensed by VAGA, New York, NY

Artists of Entertainment

"PERFORMANCE" IS THE KEY WORD IN THE PRESENTATIONS THAT FOLLOW. These artists are more or less divided into two clusters: those from the world of music, composing, singing, dancing, handling an instrument, leading an orchestra; and those related to stage or screen—a monologuist, a silent-screen comedian, a classic Shakespearean actor, a director, an animator-cartoonist, two movie stars. The range is notable, both chronologically (from about 1900 to the 1980s) and geographically (characters are observed or remembered in Mississippi, Hollywood, Albany, New York City, Paris, London, and Venice). But in most cases they are seen in performance, in the performances that identified them.

Among the visual portraits we have Josephine Baker, in the very midst of her smoothly, sensually acrobatic dance, and Woody Guthrie, strumming his guitar and singing; Buster Keaton, perched at some dangerous height and cranking his camera, and Paul Robeson, in a hushed moment of *Othello.* Cole Porter looks over at us from his piano seat, about to play some music from *Kiss Me, Kate;* Walt Disney is flanked—through the imaginative additions of Edward Steichen—by Mickey Mouse and Minnie, and looking exactly as Richard Schickel describes him (at that stage in Disney's life), with his widow's peak and thin moustache. Ruth Draper, as posed by Nickolas Muray, seems about to begin one of her spellbinding monologues; and George Cukor, in Henry Major's drawing, appears to be on the set. Louis Armstrong and Bessie Smith, one supposes, are between numbers.

Another kind of performance, no less stageworthy, is given by Tallulah Bankhead, in the 1930 painting by the recently elected member of the Royal Academy, Augustus John. "At that time," Bankhead would recall, "I was the toast of London, and that was some toast, darling." The hard-drinking, incessantly smoking, freely speaking actress transformed herself magically into a singularly gracious, quietly brooding female. The portrait too is a performance of high art. Carolyn Carr remarks that "the nearly weightless, soulful attitude of the sitter, and the evanescent pink of the negligee . . . caused one critic to compare it to the manner of the seventeenth-century Spanish painter Goya: 'wispy, a little gaunt, and eerie.'" Tallulah Bankhead in fact enters our volume in part because of the histrionic beauty of Augustus John's portrait; it is not the first time in the book that aesthetic achievement is what has finally determined a character's eligibility.

Literary sources provide matching images of performing artists. The novelist William Kennedy, a knowledgeable follower of American popular music (he has written astutely about Frank Sinatra), thinks back to a 1952 occasion in Albany, when he watched and heard Louis Armstrong, dressed in a plaid shirt and boxer shorts, playing the last bars of "Nevada" on his trumpet. In a memoir generously written for this section, Irene Worth, often referred to as the greatest actress of our time, remembers her friend Ruth Draper

347

creating—on an otherwise empty stage—an old New England country woman and a wealthy scatterbrained urban hostess. James Agee, a distinguished film commentator (as well as the author of *Let Us Now Praise Famous Men*), describes Buster Keaton running a mad treadmill inside the turning wheel of a ferryboat; and Noel Coward records in his diary how taken he was by Tallulah Bankhead's performance in his play *Private Lives*.

Experts and appreciative fellow artists have their say. Zutty Singleton, the jazz drummer, tells of Bessie Smith looking like a beautiful bronze queen as she sang "Baby Won't You Please Come Home." Pete Seeger, a renowned figure in the field of folk music, conjures up a memory of Woody Guthrie hitching his guitar around front and starting to sing an epic-long outlaw ballad. Richard Rodgers shows us Cole Porter in Venice, playing "Let's Do It" before he or that song became famous. Ivor Brown, the English drama critic, reviews the performance of Paul Robeson as Othello in 1930: "sturdy as an oak . . . a superb giant of the woods." Alistair Cooke, himself a writer and television host, sizes up Humphrey Bogart (with the help of Katharine Hepburn); and George Cukor speaks to the director Peter Bogdanovich about the primary importance, for him, of acting, of the dramatic interaction of his players, rather than cinematic experimentation.

This whole field of endeavor and achievement—sometimes called popular culture—is obviously one in which the choice of representatives is most susceptible to personal taste and individual preference. We considered the alternatives at great (and enjoyable) length; and can say only that of the famous figures who are not here, some are not in the Gallery (for example, John Ford and Preston Sturges), some died too recently (Irving Berlin, Orson Welles), and in some cases the portraits are unsatisfactory.

A ranging discourse on the blues is embedded in the first half of this section. It begins with W. C. Handy, known as the father of the blues, portrayed by Prentis Polk (the official photographer of the Tuskegee Institute for fifty years) in a picture that displays that "tension between precise formality and x-ray vision" for which Polk has been praised. Attached to Handy—and taken (by kindly local help) from the Blues Mural in the railroad station at Tutwiler, Mississippi—is an anecdote about Handy, in that same station in 1903, first hearing the music that he would perform as the blues. Handy's best-known composition is "St. Louis Blues," and a supreme moment in American musical history is the recorded rendition of that ballad by Louis Armstrong and his orchestra and sung by Bessie Smith.

But Armstrong was forging a different chapter in the story of the blues. It was Duke Ellington, in the enlightened view of Albert Murray, who brought the form to its richest expression, with his "locomotive onomatopoeia" (the instrumental copying of train sounds), that carried within it echoes of the old underground railroad and the gospel train. Here the blues fulfills its deepest impulse: in Murray's formula, providing affirmation and improvisation in the face of adversity and disruption. Murray's piece on Ellington, here, is a major statement about our culture and repays careful attention.

Louis Armstrong, however, took a crucial step further. As Murray sees it (in the same book, *The Blue Devils of Nada*), Armstrong did what William Kennedy actually saw him doing in Albany, when the trumpeter held a high note "for about a week" and then "blew it out the window." Thus Albert Murray: "What Louis Armstrong did was to mug *back* at the blues, saying 'Yeeeeah' as in Oh, yeah??? or Oh, Yeah!!!" It was that latter exultant sound that Kennedy heard in the Albany hotel.

W. C. Handy 1873–1958 Composer and Performer

In 1903 while touring the Delta and playing musical engagements, W. C. Handy was waiting for a train in Tutwiler. At the train depot an unknown musician was singing while sliding a knife blade down the strings of his guitar. The sound and effect were unforgettable to Handy and became the music known worldwide as "The Blues."

From the Blues Mural at the railroad station in Tutwiler, Mississippi

Born in Alabama eight years after the Civil War. His early interest in music was not encouraged by his father, a Methodist minister, but music was to be the center of his life. He began playing in a minstrel band and then became a cornet player and bandleader in Memphis, where Beale Street was a center for black music and night life. While playing there in 1909, Handy composed a campaign tune for E. H. Crump, a candidate in the ongoing mayoral race, a song he later called "Memphis Blues." Crump was elected, and more important for history, "Memphis Blues" was a hit, the first of his famous works. In his autobiography, *Father of the Blues,* Handy says the song "set a new fashion in American popular music."

Though proud of being called father of the blues, Handy made little pretense as to his claims to the title, stating that his themes were based on tunes, rhythms, and words he had heard at different times—that he got his inspiration from "contact with people who say and sing what they feel at the moment." Thus he credits an all-night piano player in a saloon with inspiring "Beale Street Blues" (1917). "St. Louis Blues" was inspired in 1914 by a lament he heard muttered by a jilted woman walking along the street, and "Joe Turner Blues" (1915) came from a song originally sung on a chain gang. By putting the songs on paper he earned the recognition he received as a musician, for this is how they were introduced to the public and why we know them.

The blues became a lasting part of American culture. Stanley Crouch in *The All-American Skin Game, or the Decoy of Race* (1995) notes that the "panoramic lyrics of W. C. Handy's 'Beale Street Blues' refer to a class-mixing world of secret lives . . . [and] formed the basis of the themes F. Scott Fitzgerald rendered in *The Great Gatsby.*" In his book *Black Manhattan* (1930) James Weldon Johnson says, "It is from the blues that all that may be called American Music derives its most distinctive characteristic." Ralph Ellison and Albert Murray have written eloquently on their importance.

Portrait by Prentis Polk (1898–1984), photograph, 1942

Bessie Smith 1894–1937 Blues Singer

Bessie Smith was the greatest of them all. There never was one like her and there'll never be one like her again. Even though she was raucous and loud, she had a sort of a tear, no not a tear, but there was a misery in what she did. It was as though there was something she had to get out, something she just had to bring to the fore.

ALBERTA HUNTER, blues singer, quoted in *Hear Me Talkin' to Ya,*
edited by Nat Shapiro and Nat Hentoff (1955)

Bessie Smith was a kind of roughish sort of woman. She was good-hearted and big-hearted, and she like to juice, and she like to sing her blues slow. She didn't want no fast stuff. She had a style of phrasing, what they used to call swing—she had a certain way she used to sing.

BUSTER BAILEY, clarinet, *Hear Me Talkin' to Ya*

Bessie was a real woman, all woman, all the femaleness the world ever saw in one sweet package. She was tall and brown-skinned, with great big dimples creasing her cheeks, dripping good looks—just this side of voluptuous, buxom and massive, but stately too, shapely as a hourglass, with a high-voltage magnet for a personality.

MEZZ MEZZROW, clarinet, *Hear Me Talkin' to Ya*

She'd sing things like "Gulf Coast Blues" and "Baby Won't You Please Come Home" in that big wonderful voice of hers, and, believe me, she looked like a queen up there. She was a big woman, with that beautiful bronze color and stately features. Stately, just like a queen.

ZUTTY SINGLETON, drums, *Hear Me Talkin' to Ya*

One of seven children in a poor family, she was born in Chattanooga, Tennessee. Her parents had died by the time she was nine, and she started earning small money singing in the streets, accompanied by a brother playing guitar. In 1912 she became a member of a traveling troupe that included "Ma" Rainey, and after leaving it she continued her singing career, her wonderful contralto and magnetic presence gaining her an enthusiastic following.

By the 1920s she was the highest paid black performer in the country. Advertised as "Empress of the Blues," she recorded with Columbia Records, accompanied by some of the best musicians of the time.

She was known as having a rough nature, a volatile temper, and for her tempestuous love affairs and hard drinking, but she could be generous, and always she was recognized as a vital, dynamic figure possessing a magnificent voice. Her singing of Alberta Hunter's "Downhearted Blues," "Empty Bed Blues" and "Yellow Dog Blues" is breathtaking, and W. C. Handy's "St. Louis Blues," which she recorded with Louis Armstrong, is a classic unmatched to this day. Ardently admired by Armstrong and Sidney Bechet, she was a major influence and inspiration for Billie Holiday, Mahalia Jackson, and Janis Joplin. Her death in a car accident was the basis years later for Edward Albee's play *The Death of Bessie Smith.*

Portrait by Carl Van Vechten (1880–1964), photograph, 1936

Portrait by David Lee Iwerks (b. 1933), photograph, 1962

Louis Armstrong 1901–1971 Jazz Trumpeter and Singer

A 1952 interview with Armstrong in his fifth-floor room in the deteriorating Kenmore Hotel in Albany is recalled in 1992:

When I emerged into the hallway I heard the lone wail of a horn. I didn't know the tune, but Louis would tell me later it was "Nevada," a tune he played often to warm up his chops. It was a magical sound, plaintive, out-of-place in this deserted hallway, a prelude to a meeting with the maestro. . . .

I knocked at Louis's door and announced myself and he said, "Wait a minute till I get some clothes on," and in a while he opened the door, wearing a handkerchief on his head, a plaid shirt, a pair of boxer shorts, and white socks.

I went in and sat down and he picked up his horn, feeling unfinished, and he said, "Wait till I hit the high note," and he then played a little, while I listened—the end of "Nevada." He blew some low notes, then a few higher ones, and finally he hit the high one and held it for about a week and turned it like a corkscrew and flattened it out two or three ways and sharpened it up and blew it out the window.

Then he put down the horn and smiled.

"Solid," he said.

Oh yeaaaaahhh.

WILLIAM KENNEDY, "All My Days Are the Same: Remembering Satchmo" (1992)

Born in the Storyville section of New Orleans on (so he would claim) July 4th. He quit school after fifth grade to get a job to help his mother with living expenses. "We were poor," he later told an interviewer, "but music was all around us. Music kept you rolling." Besides, he added, "I didn't need school. I had the Horn" (a cornet).

Armstrong moved to Chicago in 1922 and joined King Oliver's band. There was a year in New York with Fletcher Henderson's Harlem orchestra, then Armstrong returned to Chicago, where, between 1925 and 1928, he made a series of recordings with a group known as the Hot Five that brought Chicago jazz into prominence, created a new vocabulary of jazz, and exerted an influence that extends at least to Wynton Marsalis. Armstrong formed his own band in 1931 and with it toured America and then England and France—discovering in Europe the extraordinary popularity of American jazz.

Armstrong had replaced his cornet with a trumpet and was now regularly billed as the world's greatest trumpeter. His first wife, Lil Hardin (Oliver's piano player), was both an invaluable helper and a goad. His fourth wife, Lucille Wilson, a dancer whom he married in 1942, remained with him for the rest of his life. Armstrong, meanwhile, was touring Africa (in 1951), Europe, and the United States, and appearing in screen and stage musicals, most notably *Hello, Dolly!* He was known to all as Satchmo (short for Satchelmouth). Jazz, swing (which he helped restructure), popular songs, the blues—all were revised by Louis Armstrong. Two of his most admired numbers were "Potato Head Blues" and "Weary Blues," but Armstrong's relation to that musical mode has been expressed by Albert Murray: "What Louis Armstrong did was mug *back* at the blues, saying 'Yeeeeah' as in Oh, yeah??? or Oh, yeah!!! And then go on and riff all of that flashy-fingered elegance out into the atmosphere as if there were no such thing as the blues!"

Portrait by Soss Melik (b. 1914), charcoal on paper, 1953

Cole Porter 1891–1964 Composer

As soon as we arrived at the Lido [in the summer of 1926], Larry [Hart] went in search of the nearest bar and I went for a stroll on the beach. Suddenly I heard a friendly English voice calling my name. To my joy it was Noel Coward, whom I had not seen since our first accidental meeting in . . . New York. We quickly filled each other in on the reasons why we were there. Noel was in Venice, he told me, visiting an American friend he was sure would love to meet me. We strolled over to his friend's cabana, and I was introduced to a slight, delicate-featured man with soft saucer eyes and a wide, friendly grin. His name was Cole Porter, but at that time neither the name nor the face was in the least familiar to me. . . .

[That evening, after dinner at Porter's rented Palazzo Rezzonico] we went into the music room, where at my host's request I played some of my songs. Then Noel played. And then Cole sat down at the piano. As soon as he touched the keyboards to play "a few of my little tunes," I became aware that here was not merely a talented dilettante, but a genuinely gifted theatre composer and lyricist. Songs like "Let's Do It," "Let's Misbehave," and "Two Little Babes in the Wood," which I heard that night for the first time, fairly cried out to be heard from a stage.

RICHARD RODGERS, *Musical Stages* (1975)

Born in Peru, Indiana; his influential mother was Kate Cole Porter (Porter associated her name with the title of his musical *Kiss Me, Kate*), who used to play comical versions of popular songs on the piano. Porter traveled regularly to Chicago for music lessons during his early years. During his undergraduate years at Yale (class of 1913), Porter wrote some three hundred songs, among them the one that is chanted regularly at sporting events: "Bulldog, Bulldog, bow-wow-wow, Eli Yale!"

Soon after college he settled in Paris, married the internationally famous beauty Linda Thomas, and made the first of several unsuccessful forays on Broadway. Success finally came with the 1928 production of *Paris* (among its songs: "Let's Do It"). *Gay Divorcée* (1932) introduced the immediately and endlessly popular "Night and Day," sung and danced by Fred Astaire ("Goddamn 'Night and Day!'" Porter would say years later. "Every time I write another tune, someone is bound to say it isn't as good as 'Night and Day'"). An even greater triumph was *Anything Goes* (1934), with Ethel Merman and Victor Moore; a peak moment in the history of musical comedy, and containing "You're the Top" and "I Get a Kick Out of You," as well as the title song.

In 1937 a riding accident cost Porter the use of his legs (one was amputated in 1958). But the show went bravely on, and in 1948 there came *Kiss Me, Kate,* based on *The Taming of the Shrew* and offering some of the best of Porter's fifteen hundred lifetime songs: "Wunderbar," "So in Love," "Too Darn Hot." It ran for 1,077 performances on Broadway. There followed *Can-Can* in 1953 (with "It's All Right with Me" and "I Love Paris"), which ran for almost 900 performances.

Duke Ellington 1899–1974 Composer and Performer

Everybody knows that even now there are people all over the world dreaming of the United States in the ever-so-materialistic image and patterns of Horatio Alger. Others, however, see definitive American characteristics in terms that are no less pragmatic but are more comprehensively existential. In their view, the anecdotes most fundamentally representative are those that symbolize: (1) affirmation in the face of adversity, and (2) improvisation in situations of disruption and discontinuity.

To this end, nobody other than Ellington as yet has made more deliberate or effective use of basic devices of blues idiom statement, beginning with the very beat of the ongoing, upbeat locomotive onomatopoeia (the very chugging and driving pistons, the sometimes signifying, sometimes shouting steam whistles, the always somewhat ambivalent arrival and departure bells) that may be as downright programmatic as an old guitar and harmonica folk blues, but that also function as the dead metaphoric basis of the denotative language of common everyday discourse. . . . Incidentally, Ellington's use of locomotive onomatopoeia is resonant not only of the metaphorical underground railroad but also the metaphysical gospel train.

ALBERT MURRAY, "The Ellington Synthesis," in *The Blue Devils of Nada* (1996)

Born in Washington, D. C., as Edward Kennedy Ellington, into a reasonably comfortable middle-class black family, with a home about ten blocks from the White House. Both his parents were musical, and Duke was playing the piano from an early age. His attempt to make a living as a musician was unsuccessful, and in 1922 he moved to New York. There, with Bubber Miley (trumpet), Sam Nanton (trombone), and several others he formed the group known as the Washingtonians; they were the house band at the Kentucky Club and cut their first records in November 1924. The group specialized in pieces composed or arranged by Ellington, all exploiting the individual talents and personalities of the players. Their best-known songs today are probably "Black and Tan Fantasy" and "Creole Love Call."

In December 1927, Ellington and his band opened at the Cotton Club in Harlem, and here they remained until 1932, enthralling the hordes of affluent, black-culture-seeking white customers, and offering astonishing new musical creations, like "Echoes of the Jungle." Typical of this time was an instrumental piece by Ellington recorded in 1931 as "Dreamy Blues," rerecorded as "Mood Indigo," and then released as a song carrying the latter title, equipped with lyrics. Ellington also wrote the music for *Sophisticated Lady* (1933).

Ellington and his orchestra went from triumph to triumph. In January 1943 they performed at Carnegie Hall; in 1950, Ellington was commissioned by Arturo Toscanini to compose *Harlem,* a "concerto grosso" for the NBC Symphony. The group toured the United States, and then England and the continent. In performance, the Ellingtonian mix of orchestration and improvisation proved unique, irresistible, and inimitable. Jazz, swing, Tin Pan Alley songs, and especially the blues all figured in the compositions and arrangements.

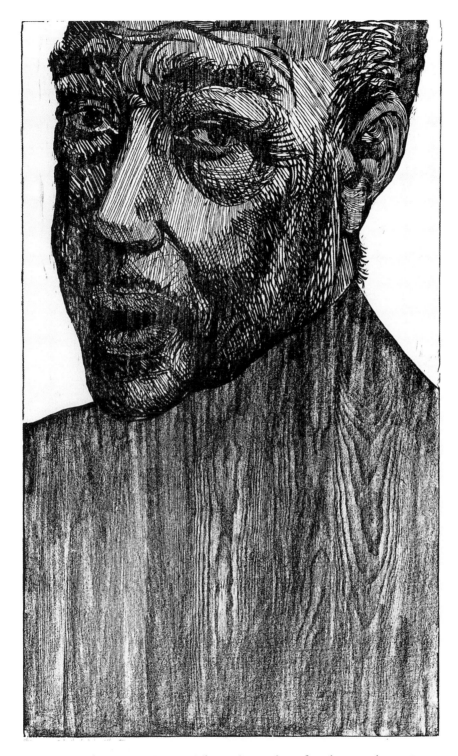

Portrait by Antonio Frasconi (b. 1919), woodcut after photograph, 1976

Woody Guthrie 1912–1967 Singer and Composer

He's gone into the world and he's looked at the faces of hungry men and women. He's been in hobo jungles. He's performed on picket lines. He's sung his way through every bar and saloon between Oklahoma and California.

ALAN LOMAX, "Woody Guthrie" (1940), in
Robert Cantwell, *When We Were Good* (1996)

Woodrow Wilson Guthrie was a short, wiry guy with a mop of curly hair under a cowboy hat, as I first saw him. He'd stand with his guitar slung on his back, spinning out stories like Will Rogers, with a faint, wry grin. Then he'd hitch his guitar around and sing the longest long outlaw ballad you ever heard, or some Rabelaisian fantasy he'd concocted the day before and might never sing again.

His songs are deceptively simple. Only after they have become part of your life do you realize how great they are.

PETE SEEGER, "So Long Woody, It's Been Good to Know Ya,"
Life Magazine (November 10, 1967)

Named for the newly elected American president, Woodrow Wilson Guthrie was born in a small town in Oklahoma. One of the happier memories of his youth was learning old songs and ballads from his mother, but his family was beset by tragedy. In his scattered childhood, living in different places, finding odd jobs, he always took note of his life and found ways of expressing his observations. For a while he put his energies into painting, but when he found he could earn money playing the guitar and singing he started putting his own words to old tunes. As he tells us in his autobiography, *Bound for Glory* (1943), "You can sing out what you think."

He hit the highway at sixteen, "struck with the travelling fever." He crossed the continent on foot and riding freight trains, chronicling the people and places he encountered. He sang about the diverse beauty of the America he discovered, about common folk, the poor and homeless, the suffering and deprivations of the Depression and the Dust Bowl, and the migrant workers.

In New York in the early 1940s he found other folk singers using their songs to seek social justice, political activists who supported labor unions, farmers, poor workers. He joined Pete Seeger and the Almanac Singers and became an increasingly popular figure, legendary by the time of his death from the cruelly destructive nerve disease that put an early end to his career.

In the *New York Times* (April 1998), Peter Applebome wrote of the opening of an archive of Guthrie's work. He referred to Guthrie as one of the most influential figures of the century, the man who "virtually created the modern folk tradition and singer-songwriter genre." Songs like "So Long (It's Been Good to Know Yuh)" and "This Land Is Your Land" are American classics, and Guthrie the inspiration for Bob Dylan, Joan Baez, Judy Collins, and other great folk singers.

Portrait by Antonio Frasconi (b. 1919), woodcut, 1972

Josephine Baker 1906–1975 Dancer

She made her entry entirely nude except for a pink flamingo feather between her limbs: she was being carried upside down and doing the split on the shoulder of a black giant. Midstage, he paused, and with his long fingers holding her basket-wise around the waist, swung her in a slow cartwheel to the stage floor, where she stood like his magnificent discarded burden, in an instant of complete silence. She was an unforgettable female ebony statue. A scream of salutation spread through the theater.

JANET FLANNER, *Paris Was Yesterday: 1925–1939* (1972)

In the end she lost about everything—but she never lost her spirit. In June 1973, when she walked out on that stage at Carnegie Hall, she was as glamorous and exciting as she'd ever been. . . . I introduced her that opening night. I said, "She was a simple little girl—she's still a simple little girl," and it was true. I don't think I've ever known anyone with a less complicated view of life, or whose life was more complicated than Josephine's.

BRICKTOP in *Bricktop,* as told to James Haskins (1983)

Born in St. Louis. As a child she earned her keep doing hard domestic labor. At thirteen she joined a dance troupe from Philadelphia, and in 1923 was in the chorus of a road company performing *Shuffle Along.* On Broadway she played in Sissel and Blake's *Chocolate Dandies.*

She had obvious talent, frenetic energy, and an unswerving determination to make herself known. Even in the chorus line she stole scenes, clowning, crossing her eyes. She was in the floor show at the Plantation Club in New York, and in 1925 she went to Paris as a member of the company of *La Revue Nègre,* a group of twenty-five black musicians, singers, and dancers brought to perform at the Théâtre des Champs-Elysées. Thanks to postwar Europe's desire for entertainment and its growing interest in African art, this was an auspicious moment for the arrival of *La Revue Nègre.* It was an immediate hit with Parisian viewers, and Josephine Baker became a star. Her "Danse Sauvage" was famous, and at the Folies-Bergère she introduced the Charleston. Flamboyant, exotic, funny, sexy, but with a childlike quality that added to her appeal, she did seemingly impossible things with her body, dancing nude but for an outlandish semi-covering of sequins, feathers, and, most famously, bananas.

Having escaped the racism that plagued black artists in the United Staes and finding acceptance in France (she became a French citizen in 1937), she then witnessed the hatred that beset Europe in World War II. She entertained troops in Africa and the Middle East, and she received the Croix de Guerre and the Legion of Honour for her work in the Resistance.

She did things on an outsize scale—having affairs, marrying three times, buying houses when she had money, and, between 1954 and 1962, adopting twelve children of different ethnic and cultural backgrounds. She retired from the stage in 1956, but to earn money to maintain her large family and home, she performed occasionally until her death.

Portrait by Stanislaus Julian Walery (active 1880s–1920s), photograph, 1926

Ruth Draper 1884–1956 Monologuist

Ruth Draper's good nature was open and irresistible. Her step was light and young from a straight spine. She had all the graces of her rich talent, but it was not until she was thirty that she took a deep breath, as it were, and flew with it. Her eye was alert and her beautiful voice was low, without the rasp of nervous hysteria. The action of her body was strong with vigor for a peasant, or as Henry James put it, "the acute case of queenship of some American women," rich and aggressive. Then she could melt into the posture of the vulnerable; the weak, poor and devastated.

Her genius exchanged the flow of energy with her audience, where no more than words and gestures and imagination conveyed the humor and transactions of the human condition. Truths were burnished by the audience. They created New Worlds together.

She stood alone on a drafty stage—stages all over the world—without scenery and with only a few shawls and hats, a chair, a chaise, a table. She was the old woman, rocking on a Maine porch, gossiping with a passerby; she was a little overeager to see her friends, she was lonely. She held her hand cupped up; and told her neighbor how she stirred the sweet oil with the two middle fingers of her right hand and "rubbed him—awful hard man to rub."

She rested on a chaise longue while she tried to cram in a lesson on Dante with a manicure, orders to the cook (something amusing, perhaps in pots), talking to her husband on the telephone, murmuring to her lover also on the telephone, and allowing a moment to see the children before rushing off, late, for lunch.

IRENE WORTH (1997)

Born in New York, she was raised in a cultivated milieu where music and the arts were central to family life. An observant child with an eager interest in the people she encountered and the world around her, she had an acute ear for nuances of speech. Even as a child she entertained and astonished her family and friends with her impersonations.

Her gift was recognized and she widened her scope, doing monologues for parties, performing around New York from 1910 to 1913; in London she was a success in some of the great private homes. Friends and admirers, who included Paderewski, Henry Adams, and Henry James, encouraged her to perform professionally. She made her professional debut in New York in 1917 and in London in 1920, and she continued her career until her death.

Performing on a bare stage with a few props, with gestures, expressions, and her remarkable voice, she created a stable of characters who became familiar to her audiences worldwide. She could portray five characters in a sketch and evoke twenty-five. In a letter to her friend Bernard Berenson she quoted young Kenneth Tynan writing in a review: "as I watched her thronging monologues . . . I could only conclude that this was the most modern group acting I had ever seen. It seems, in passing, absurd to use a singular verb in connection with so plural a player. Let me put it that Ruth Draper are now at the height of their career."

Portrait by Nickolas Muray (1892–1965), photograph, c. 1920

Buster Keaton 1895–1966 Comedian, Filmmaker

Very early in his movie career friends asked [Keaton] why he never smiled on the screen. He didn't realize he didn't. He had got the deadpan habit in variety; on the screen he had merely been so hard at work it had never occurred to him there was anything to smile about. Now he tried it just once and never again. He was by his whole style and nature so much the most deeply "silent" of the silent comedians that even a smile was as deafeningly out of key as a yell. In a way his pieces are like a transcendent juggling act in which it seems that the whole universe is in exquisite flying motion and the one point of repose is the juggler's effortless, uninterested face. . . .

Much of the charm and edge of Keaton's comedy, however, lay in the subtle leverages of expression he could work against his normal deadpan. Trapped in the side-wheel of a ferryboat, saving himself from drowning only by walking, then desperately running, inside the accelerating wheel like a squirrel in a cage, his only concern was, obviously, to keep his hat on. Confronted by Love, he was not as deadpan as he was cracked up to be, either; there was an odd abrupt motion of his head which suggested a horse nipping after a sugar lump.

JAMES AGEE, *Agee on Film II* (1960)

Born Joseph Edward Keaton in Piqua, Kansas. His parents Joseph and Myra Keaton took the boy into their knockabout vaudeville act at age three; by age six he was given top billing. The act finally broke up in 1917, at which time, through a chance encounter, Keaton entered the movies. Between 1917 and 1920 he made fifteen short comic films with the well-established movie comedian Roscoe "Fatty" Arbuckle.

In 1920, Keaton went to work for the producer Joseph M. Schenk. The years 1920–28 were the great period in Buster Keaton's career as a film comic. During this time he was featured in nineteen short and eight full-length films, among the latter being his greatest achievements, the ones in which he created the Keaton character: the slender, slight figure with the mostly expressionless face and on his head (in James Agee's words) a "deadly horizontal hat as flat and thin as a phonograph record"; the former acrobat and tumbler who passed through incredible hazards to survive and win the girl.

In 1924 there was *Sherlock, Jr.,* in which a dreamy projectionist walks into the film he is showing and takes a part (a stunt followed by Woody Allen in *The Purple Rose of Cairo,* sixty-plus years later). The same year saw the arrival of Keaton's greatest commercial success, *The Navigator.* Keaton was making $200,000 a year by this time; and in *The Navigator* he plays a millionaire who has his chauffeur drive him from one side of the street to another. In 1927 there came *The General,* a superb comedy-drama of Civil War days; and in 1928 there were both *Steamboat Bill, Jr.,* and *The Cameraman.* The latter, in which Keaton gets himself into hopelessly precarious positions, was his last major effort. His career foundered with the talkies; his first marriage, to Eleanor Norris, in 1940, was enduring and salvational. In the 1940s and into the 1960s, Keaton flourished again: touring Europe, making unforgettable cameo appearances in films, appearing often on TV. He performed to the year of his death, being last seen as one of the redeeming elements in the screen version of *A Funny Thing Happened on the Way to the Forum.*

Portrait by Jean Albert Mercier (b. 1899), color lithographic poster for
The Camerman in Paris (c. 1928)

Paul Robeson 1898–1976 Actor, Singer, Civil Rights Leader

Mr. Robeson's Ebon Othello is as sturdy as an oak, deep-rooted in its elemental passion and many branched in the early tenderness, a superb giant of the woods for the great hurricane of tragedy to whisper through, then rage upon, then break. One thinks of a tree because the greatness is of nature, not of art.

IVOR BROWN in *The Observer* (1930), quoted by Maud Cuney-Hare
in *Negro Musicians and Their Music* (1936)

Paul Robeson has come my way a dozen times. Often a year or two will go by without my seeing him or having a word from him, and then, unannounced, his great, dusky bulk will fill my doorway and my heart rejoices, for of the countless people I have known in my wanderings over the world, he is one of the few of whom I would say that they have greatness. I do not mean greatness as a football player or as an actor or as a singer . . . I mean greatness as a person.

In his case I despair of ever putting into convincing words my notion of this quality in him. I can only say that by what he does, thinks, and is, by his unassailable dignity, and his serene, incorruptible simplicity, Paul Robeson strikes me as having been made out of the original stuff of the world.

ALEXANDER WOOLLCOTT, "Colossal Bronze," in *While Rome Burns* (1934)

Born in Princeton, New Jersey. Robeson was an All-American football player at Rutgers, and in 1919 the class valedictorian. By the early 1920s he had abandoned the law for the stage; he made his first notable impression in 1924 with the lead role in a revival of Eugene O'Neill's *The Emperor Jones* (critics called him "a natural"). In 1932 he played the part of Joe in a revival of *Show Boat,* in which his rendition of "Ol' Man River" was a peak moment in musical drama history.

His greatest stage achievement was in the role of Othello: in England in 1930, with Peggy Ashcroft as Desdemona, and in New York in 1943, with José Ferrer as Iago. Meanwhile, Robeson appeared in nearly a dozen films, among them "Sanders of the River" (1935) and "King Solomon's Mines" (1937), both British made. He gave strong performances, but he gradually realized that the filmmakers had lied to him about the stereotyping of black characters; he quit the industry in 1952. Robeson's deepening resentment over racism in America drew him more and more into civil rights causes and affiliation with left-wing groups. By 1950 he was being denounced as a communist. When an exhibition of Betsy Graves Reyneau's portraits of black Americans opened in Boston in 1950, the mayor ordered the stunning image of Robeson as Othello barred from the show.

Robeson's reputation has recently been restored, and his enormous stature was celebrated in a series of shows and documentaries marking the 1998 centennial of his birth.

Portrait by Betsy Graves Reyneau (1888–1964), oil on canvas, 1943–44

George Cukor 1899–1983 Film Director

From an interview with George Cukor by Peter Bogdanovich in late April 1969:

BOGDANOVICH: Would you say the single most important thing in your work is, in fact, the selecting and then the molding of performances? Because, unlike some directors, you seem to say almost everything in your pictures through your people.

CUKOR: Yes, through the text and the players. I think human behaviour, the human heart, is to me what is very dramatic and rather complicated; and, I think, interests and moves the audience. One can do very dazzling tricks . . . but unless the human heart is there I don't think it goes very deep. I can't imagine a picture that has made a great impression without that.

. . . .

BOGDANOVICH: How do you work with actors on the set? Does it vary from actor to actor?

CUKOR: Yes, it does. I didn't work this out, but also you have to know with whom you're working: you've got to know when the actor is at his best—and stop there. You've got to know what an actor's likely to do when they're not at their best—where they go off the beam—and guard against that. . . . You've got to know just how much pressure to put on or how often: how much you've got to talk and when you've got to shut up. And then they've got to get used to you, and you've got to get used to them. It's like a marriage, you know.

PETER BOGDANOVICH, *Who the Devil Made It* (1997)

Born in New York City, raised on the Upper East Side, he was stagestruck as a child: he spent eleven years in professional theater before going to Hollywood in 1929 for the newly developed talkies. He made a name for himself with *Dinner at Eight, A Bill of Divorcement,* and *Little Women,* the latter two introducing his most remarkable find, Katharine Hepburn, with whom he made many films.

Besides Hepburn he directed many of Hollywood's most celebrated actresses in some of their best performances—Greta Garbo, Joan Crawford, Judy Holliday, Audrey Hepburn, Judy Garland. But he also coached such fine actors as James Stewart, Ronald Coleman, Charles Boyer, Spencer Tracy, Rex Harrison, and Cary Grant.

Cukor had extraordinary rapport with performers, seeming to intuit when to coax, bully, or give a free rein. He also had a gift for creating a credible milieu: in *Camille,* Cukor's Paris is convincingly Parisian, in *David Copperfield* he evokes Dickens's England, in *Holiday* and *The Philadelphia Story* his perception of the social scene is brilliant.

Called by *New York Times* critic Vincent Canby "one of the most elegant directors Hollywood has ever produced," his films cover a striking range from comedy to drama. They include *A Star Is Born, Gaslight, My Fair Lady,* and *Born Yesterday,* as well as *Pat and Mike* and *Adam's Rib,* pairing Tracy and Hepburn.

GEORGE CUKOR

Portrait by Henry Major (1889–1948), pencil on paper, c. 1933–38

Humphrey Bogart 1899–1957 Actor

Although he privately described himself as "Democrat in politics, Episcopalian by up-bringing, dissenter by disposition," he looked on acting as a trade like any other, though one calling for some craft and considerable discipline. He was always touchy about his pride, not in his artistry but in his competence, and competence was something he greatly admired in any field, from writing to seamanship, drinking to statesmanship. He measured all his fellow workers by the test of professionalism, and a professional is a man who can do his best work when he doesn't feel like it. Being also a clear-minded man of deep and quite stubborn convictions, he was something of a freak in the Hollywood factory in knowing where his craft ended and where his private life or politics should take over without let or hindrance. His admiration of Roosevelt, his steady contempt for Senator Joseph McCarthy, his mulish determination to stay in a restaurant till dawn if a drinking fit was on him, had no more to do with his acceptance or rejection of a part than a trucking company's contract with a newspaper publisher depends on the political stripe of the editorials.

ALISTAIR COOKE, *Six Men* (1977)

Bogie was funny. A generous actor. And a no-bunk person. He was an actor who enjoyed acting. Knew he was good. Always knew his lines. Always was on time. Hated anything false. . . . He was an extraordinarily decent fellow. Fair—forthright—uncomplicated. Fun too—a good sense of humor. Devilish if he thought you were a phony.

KATHARINE HEPBURN, *The Making of "The African Queen"* (1987)

Born in New York City, his father a well-known physician, his mother an artist.

After serving in the Navy in World War I (his lisp and famous scarred lip are said to be the result of a shelling incident) he won his first job in theater. In 1930 he went to Hollywood, where he played secondary film roles, returning sporadically to New York to act on the stage. In 1935 he played the gangster Duke Mantee in Robert E. Sherwood's play *The Petrified Forest,* Leslie Howard in the lead role. In 1936 they re-created those characters in the very successful film version.

He played in several gangster movies: then in 1941 John Huston was instrumental in broadening his image. The script of *High Sierra,* written by Huston with W. R. Burnett, cast Bogart again as a gangster, but with a much more complex psychological character. That same year Huston directed his first film, *The Maltese Falcon.* Bogart played Dashiell Hammett's unforgettable creation Sam Spade. That character and Philip Marlowe, in Raymond Chandler's *The Big Sleep,* ensured Bogart's lasting reputation as the quintessential tough private detective.

The range of his acting grew. In *To Have and Have Not* (where he met Lauren Bacall, who became his wife) he played an American expatriate in the center of a tense political situation—a role which he had perfected in *Casablanca* (1942), and a figure that has been revered and copied in films to this day. As hero and antihero he played in *The Treasure of Sierra Madre, Key Largo,* the funny and offbeat *Beat the Devil, The Caine Mutiny,* and *The African Queen* of 1951, for which he won the Academy Award.

Portrait by Philippe Halsman (1900–79), photograph, 1944

Tallulah Bankhead 1902–1968 Actress

Tallulah was extraordinarily good [in *Private Lives*]; she is a bit coarse in texture, but her personality is formidable and she played some of it quite beautifully and all of it effectively. . . . . [She] was touchingly thrilled that I liked her performance and ecstatic when I said she could play it in New York. She insisted on offering me an Augustus John picture that she has in the country. She is a curious character; wildly generous, a very big heart and can be both boring and amusing.

NOEL COWARD, August 23, 1947, in *The Noel Coward Diaries,*
edited by Graham Payn and Sheridan Morley (1982)

What was she to do with the thing she had become? She was different, and not alone in respect to her talent and vitality. She flailed about in paroxisms of disguised bewilderment, drinking and clowning and cursing and showing off. She was valiant and silly, and she knew it. But she was not rubbishy, and she knew that too. Out of exceptional qualities, she invented by trial and error an exceptional self, which with a child's impudent pretense of not caring she flung straight into the face of the world. Caught off guard, the world flinched and applauded, and it went on applauding to the end.

BRENDAN GILL, profile of Tallulah Bankhead, *New Yorker,* October 7, 1972

Born in Alabama, member of a prominent and respected family, her grandfather was a senator, her father Speaker of the House from 1936–40. She was proud of her southern heritage and was herself an active Democrat.

At the age of fifteen she went to New York to become an actress. Though she found no immediate professional success, her beauty, extravagant behavior, and low, throaty voice attracted attention. She was a success in London, where she lived from 1923 to 1931. There, enjoying a cultish following, she established herself as an outrageous and vivacious personality.

During her career she was in a number of mediocre plays and movies, in which she was noted for her remarkable presence rather than her acting, but two roles won her praise as a serious actress: as Regina, in Lillian Hellman's *The Little Foxes,* and Sabina, in Thornton Wilder's *The Skin of Our Teeth.* She made a lasting impression, as she did in Alfred Hitchcock's film *Lifeboat.*

Known for her disconcertingly unpredictable behavior, hard drinking, and scatological language, as well as her stunning looks, she became a legendary figure.

Portrait by Augustus John (1878–1961), oil on canvas, 1930

Walt Disney 1901–1966 Animator and Film Producer

Even his closest associates found Disney more enigmatic, more difficult to describe or to communicate with in the 1960s. No one spoke of him any more as a father figure. Instead, he was known almost universally to those who worked for him—but always behind his back—as "Uncle Walt." There is a considerable difference between a father and an uncle; one of the prime characteristics of the latter is that he tends to be a rather distant and emotionally neutral figure. As late as the mid-fifties, associates reported that Disney sat on the lawn near his office after lunch, chatting amiably with employees; he was not observed in public in so relaxed a posture afterward, though strenuous efforts were made to maintain the old down-to-earth image that had served him so well for so long. . . . The slender, smooth-faced young man of the 1930s with the thin, retail-clerk's moustache and the slick hair that formed a widow's peak had become a portly, somewhat rumpled figure in later life. His face was pouchy, the moustache, like the waistline, had thickened; the smile, when it was offered, flashed too briefly and often seemed to involve only a baring of the teeth; the eyes remained almost hidden beneath the heavy-hooded lids.

RICHARD SCHICKEL, *The Disney Version* (1968)

Born in Chicago as Walter Elias Disney; his father, Elias, was a construction worker who had moved to the United States from Ontario in 1870. At age sixteen Disney served briefly as a volunteer ambulance driver in France. In 1921 he began work with a commercial art studio in Kansas City; and here, with UB Iwerks, an artist and a lifelong friend, he made a series of animated commercials and satirical cartoons. Iwerks was in fact the more skillful and innovative craftsman and animator of the two. By 1923, Disney was in Hollywood, in partnership with Iwerks and his older brother Roy Disney, making animated shorts.

Mickey Mouse was born in 1928, to be joined by Minnie Mouse, Donald Duck, Pluto, and the others in cartoons that delighted the nation. The "Silly Symphonies"—with cartoon characters acting to the prerecorded music—soon followed. The Disney staff was now an organization, with several hundred employees working on animated films. In the mid-1930s the Disney enterprise moved on to full-length features; the first was *Snow White and the Seven Dwarfs* (1937), an artistic as well as a commercial triumph. Among the best of the many features that followed were *Pinocchio* (1940) and *Dumbo* (1941).

Disney also oversaw the production of many "live" movies, perhaps the most watchable being *20,000 Leagues Under the Sea* (with James Mason and Kirk Douglas). But the Disney empire went far beyond movies—to weekly TV shows and a TV channel, varieties of merchandise, and entertainment centers. In his 1968 study Richard Schickel reports that at the time of Disney's death, 240 million people around the world saw a Disney movie and 100 million watched a Disney television show every week, that 800 million read a Disney book or magazine and 80 million bought Disney-licensed merchandise. Untold millions visit Disney World in Florida and Disneyland in California.

Portrait by Edward Steichen (1879–1973), photograph, 1933

Commentary

Puritans and Colonials

POCAHONTAS Engraving based on an engraving by Simon van de Passe, a Dutch artist who was in England from 1615 to 1622. Among his many engravings is one of Captain John Smith, which may be the only likeness of that figure. The van de Passe print appeared in *Braziliologia: A Book of Kings* (1616), an important and valuable collection of engravings of British kings and queens, clergymen, lawyers, poets, warriors, and other outstanding persons.

Inscription around the oval: Matoaka Als Rebecca Filia Potentiss. Princ: Powhatani Imp: Virginiae. This is translated and expanded below the portrait: Matoaka als Rebecka daughter to the mighty Prince Powhatan Emperour of Attanoughkomouek als Virginia converted and baptized in the Christian faith, and wife to the Wor(thy) Mr. John Rolff. Puld. Aug. 10, 1793, by W. Richardson Castel St., Leicester Square.

Immediately below the portrait: Aetatis suae 21 (her age: 21). Anno 1616.

COTTON MATHER Mezzotint, by Peter Pelham. Pelham came to Boston from England, with his wife and two sons, in 1726. He himself had to paint the portrait of Mather, from which he then made a dozen or more impressions. These set a new standard for printmaking in America and helped establish Pelham as the finest engraver in the colonies. In 1748, Pelham married the widowed mother of ten-year-old John Singleton Copley, and through his encouragement and instruction of the boy Pelham exercised a notable influence on the development of New World art.

Cotton Mather appears here surprisingly jovial and heavily bewigged. As early as the 1690s, Mather had preached in defense of wigs, declaring them not to be emblems of wicked pride as hitherto thought.

Pelham painted Mather from life, as the Latin inscription says. It also tells us that Mather was a doctor of sacred theology and fellow of the Royal Society in London, that he lately had been head of a church in Boston, and that he was sixty-five years old.

Grandfather's Chair, published in 1841, was a child's history of New England, one of Hawthorne's several exercises in that mode. Grandfather may well be "Hawthorne's least wickedly ironical narrator" (as Michael J. Colacuccio has observed), but Hawthorne's ruminative fascination with the history and dark lore of his native region was never more evident.

JONATHAN EDWARDS Stipple engraving by Amos Doolittle, after a painting by Joseph Badger, a modestly successful Boston-based artist. Doolittle was known especially for his vivid and accurate depictions of historical scenes (for example, the battles of Lexington and Concord). This engraving—which identifies Edwards as the president of the College of New Jersey—served as the frontispiece for the 1794 volume *The Millennium,* by David Austin.

Robert Lowell (1917–77), perhaps the finest American poet of his generation, also wrote about Hawthorne, Melville, Thoreau, Col. Shaw, and other New Englanders of a former day. He wrote "Mr. Edwards and the Spider" (*Lord Weary's Castle,* 1946), a poetical rendering in Edwards's voice of parts of the Enfield sermon, with the most terrifying lines included: "It's well / If God who holds you to the pit of hell / Much as one holds a spider."

BENJAMIN FRANKLIN Oil on canvas, probably 1785, by Joseph Siffrede Duplessis (the middle name is spelled variously). Duplessis had been the chief court painter in France for some time, and was at his peak when he made this painting (he would paint rather less in his last years). His earlier portrait of Franklin, in a red fur coat and a fur collar (now in the Metropolitan Museum in New York) is the most famous picture of Franklin ever done. The present one seems to have been commissioned in 1785, at the time of Franklin's departure for America, by Mme. Brillon de Jouy, Franklin's dearest and most valued friend among the Parisian women he came to know, the one who addressed him as "Mon cher Papa" (see the delightful Claude-Anne Lopez, *Mon Cher Papa* (2nd ed., 1990).

Franklin was in his eightieth year; and, especially in the wake of the Treaty of Paris, he was probably the best known and most popular man in the world. Here we offer a judiciously appreciative view of Franklin by one of his closest French associates, the distinguished physician Pierre-Georges Cabanis (quoted by Claude-Anne Lopez). It is balanced by an impatient and skeptical American view of Franklin in the same years (see also the John Adams entry in the next section). Adams provides an early instance of the oddly persistent disparaging of Franklin by American writers to the present day.

BENEDICT ARNOLD Engraving by Benoit Louis Prevost, from a drawing by Pierre Eugene Du Simitiere. The latter, Swiss-born and French-educated, came to Philadelphia in 1762 and remained there. In 1778–79, Du Simitiere did drawings of fourteen heads of then well-known figures, most of them engaged in the Revolutionary War. Among these were Generals Washington, Gates, and Morris—and Benedict Arnold. The set was dispatched to Paris, where engravings were made by the famous Prevost. The set resulting was issued in France, pirated in Great Britain, and then returned to America, where it proved extremely popular.

The exception was the Arnold portrait, which Du Simitiere said "does not sell well in America." It is inscribed (in French): "General Arnold, deserter from the Army of the United States 3 October 1780."

The Man in the Mirror, by Clare Brandt, is the most recent (1994) and overall the most satisfactory biography of Benedict Arnold.

CHARLES WILLSON PEALE Self-portrait, oil on canvas. It was most likely painted in 1791, when Peale was fifty. A somewhat finer self-image was done in 1812, when the artist was seventy-one (this is in the Historical Society of Pennsylvania in Philadelphia).

The two verbal self-portraits are equally distant in time from each other. The letter of November 1771 was one of many to John Beale Bordley (1726–1804), a one-time student in Peale's father's school and a lifelong friend and patron of Charles Willson. Bordley was a lawyer and planter, a learned man; Peale painted his portrait in 1770,

artfully deriving it from his symbolically rich portrayal of William Pitt.

The letter of 1813 is to Peale's daughter Angelica Kauffmann (named for the gifted and acclaimed Swiss-born artist, 1741–1807), perhaps Peale's favorite among his family correspondents.

PHILLIS WHEATLEY Engraving (1773) by an unknown artist, after a painting believed to be by Scipio Moorhead. The engraving served as the frontispiece for the volume *Poems on Various Subjects . . .* by Phillis Wheatley. As the inscription below the portrait indicates, the book was published in London in 1773 by Archibald Bell.

Scipio Moorhead was also a slave, the property of the Reverend John Moorhead of Boston (who with others signed a declaration that Phillis Wheatley did indeed write the poems ascribed to her). No original work by Scipio has survived, but he may be the person referred to in a *Boston News-Letter* advertisement on January 7, 1773, which spoke of a "NEGRO ARTIST. . . A Negro [of] extraordinary genius." He is certainly the object of Phillis Wheatley's affectionate and appreciative poem "To S. M. a Young African on Seeing His Works," where she expresses her wonder at his achievement:

> How did those prospects give my soul delight,
> A new creation rushing on my sight!

The lines quoted by Alice Walker in her anguished and insightful tribute come from Phillis Wheatley's poem of October 1775, addressed to "His Excellency General Washington." The "goddess" in question is the spirit of liberty whose presence in the New World Washington is entreated to make certain. (The human goddess the poet has in mind is, as Walker says, her mistress, Mrs. Wheatley.) Washington was very pleased with the poem (which is not as hapless as Walker suggests) and invited the author to call on him at his Cambridge headquarters—"I shall be happy to see a person so favoured by the Muses." Wheatley apparently did visit Washington in March 1776, and was hospitably received.

The Early Republic: Citizens and Interpreters

GEORGE WASHINGTON The oil portrait was painted by Gilbert Stuart on April 12, 1796, in the artist's home in Germantown, Pennsylvania, outside of Philadelphia (where the president's home was located). At the same time Stuart did a portrait of Martha Washington; the two likenesses are known as the "Athenaeum" portraits, because they were purchased by the Boston Athenaeum soon after Stuart's death in 1828. Stuart left both canvases unfinished so that they might be used for important moneymaking derivatives.

Stuart had made a portrait of Washington the year before (the so-called Vaughan portrait, which became the property of the American merchant Samuel Vaughan).

The passage from Thomas Jefferson occurs in a long letter to the scholar Dr. Walter Jones in Philadelphia: a thoughtful retrospect on Washington's personality and his career.

Laura E. Richards and Maud Howe Elliott, in their biography of Julia Ward Howe (1916), quote this description of the Gilbert Stuart portrait of Washington, and of Lincoln sitting nearby, from a memoir of their mother. The passage occurs in the daughters' account of how Julia Ward Howe wrote "The Battle-Hymn of the Republic" while lying in bed at a pre-dawn hour one day, with the tune of "John Brown's Body" running through her head.

JOHN ADAMS   Gilbert Stuart apparently began this oil painting in 1798, but he left it unfinished. It was completed, some time after 1828, by Stuart's youngest daughter, Jane. It was Jane who supported the family—the widowed mother and three other daughters, all living in Newport—for a good many years. She continued to paint until her death in 1888.

The letters quoted both bear on John Adams's performance in 1783, when he helped to secure the Treaty of Paris, with Alexander Hamilton and John Jay.

Charles Francis Adams (1807–86) was the son of John Quincy Adams and the father of Henry Adams. A sometime congressman, he served most effectively as minister to England during the Civil War. He later edited his grandfather's *Works* and his grandmother Abigail's *Letters*.

THOMAS JEFFERSON   The inscription above the head reads "President Th: Jefferson 1804," but in fact the portrait is an engraving, made in the winter of 1805, based on a likeness done the previous spring. Jefferson's daugh-

ters, Martha and Maria, had been particularly eager for their father to sit for Charles de Saint-Mémin. Writing the president on February 10, 1804, Maria had said that she and her sister "both thought you had promised us your picture if ever St.-Mémin went to Washington. . . . It is what we have always most wanted all our lives."

The Journal of William Maclay has been published several times. Maclay, one of the twenty-six senators who (in those days) met behind closed doors, was a Scotsman from a farm near the then frontier area of Harrisburg. By temperament, and even more after witnessing the modes of financial corruption practiced within the Senate, he held a sharply expressed bitterness of outlook.

JOHN MARSHALL   Another portrait by Charles de Saint-Mémin. This one identifies its subject as "Marshal, Juge" and gives the date 1808. At the time, John Marshall, as chief justice of the Supreme Court, was in Richmond, Virginia, presiding over the trial for treason of Aaron Burr.

Gustavus Schmidt's recorded impressions of Marshall were quoted and paraphrased by Leonard Baker in his illuminating and full-bodied (850 pp.) study *John Marshall: A Life in Law* (1974).

JOHN QUINCY ADAMS   The lithographed silhouette of John Quincy Adams was made from life by William Henry Brown and published later in Brown's *Portrait Gallery of Distinguished American Citizens*. This volume of twenty-seven plates contained expertly lifelike silhouettes of Daniel Webster (who disliked the one of him, though others acclaimed it) and John Marshall (in his habitual disheveled dress). (The book was reproduced some years ago by G. A. Baker and Company.)

Brown (1808–83) was born in South Carolina. He made his home in Philadelphia from 1824 until the early 1840s. His artistic career, successful as it was, came to an end in about 1860, when the photograph made his "shadow pictures" less popular.

Henry Adams's comments to his brother Brooks bespeak his usual energetic ambivalence toward his grandfather—a mixture of cultivated scorn and hyperbolic praise. But in the letter of March 13, 1909, Henry is properly infuriated, in retrospect, by the gag-ruling supporters of slavery in Congress, in the 1830s and 1840s.

ANDREW JACKSON The portrait is a stipple engraving by James Barton Longacre, after a painting by Thomas Sully. In February 1819, Jackson came to Philadelphia on what was turning out to be a triumphal tour of the eastern American states; and on February 17 he sat for the first of two portraits by Sully. Sully was born in England in 1783 and had studied there under Benjamin West and in America had been influenced by Gilbert Stuart. By 1817 he had arrived at a distinctive style of his own and was becoming widely recognized. The first painting of Jackson no longer exists; but between March 22 and April 15, 1819, Sully completed a second portrait (now in a New York state office).

Sully's oil on canvas was then engraved by Longacre, twenty-four years old and just making a name for himself. He sent the impression to Sully, who returned it with some scribbled suggestions in the bottom margin (James G. Barber, *Andrew Jackson: A Portrait Study,* 1991).

The closest connection Herman Melville ever had to Andrew Jackson was the moment in 1828 when President Jackson removed Herman's grandfather, Major Thomas Melville, from the latter's post as surveyor and inspector of the port of Boston. Herman was nine years old at the time. The Melville family seems not to have borne a grudge against Jackson, or so it may be surmised from this eloquent outburst at the close of chapter 26 ("Knights and Squires") in *Moby-Dick*.

JOHN JACOB ASTOR The portrait was done in about 1825, when Astor was sixty-two years old, by John Wesley Jarvis, by this time one of the leading portraitists in the country. He was born in England and brought to Philadelphia at age five. In the early 1800s he set up a studio in New York City, and by 1814 he was gaining considerable fame. Henry Inman and John Quidor were among his pupils and assistants. Among his other sitters were Washington Irving (1809) and Andrew Jackson (1819).

Walt Whitman's verbal portrait of Astor, written in 1882, goes back more than fifty years to the time when, as a lad of eleven, Walt worked as an office boy for the Brooklyn law firm of James B. Clarke and Son. Running errands for the firm, Walt sometimes came into Manhattan from Brooklyn by steam ferry; and one January day he paused in the street to observe the spectacle of an extremely wealthy old man who turned out to be John Jacob Astor.

GILBERT STUART Anson Dickinson, author of the portrait of which the present one is a copy, was born in Connecticut, the oldest of the ten children of Oliver Dickinson (a master carpenter) and Ana Landon Dickinson. In time he became perhaps the leading American portrait miniaturist, extraordinarily prolific (at least fifteen hundred miniatures) and energetic. In Albany, in 1810, he was befriended and encouraged by Washington Irving. In 1822, after doing a portrait of Sarah Morton at Gilbert Stuart's request, the aging master offered to sit for Dickinson himself.

Benjamin Waterhouse is quoted by Richard B. K. McLanathan in his very fine study *Gilbert Stuart* (1980). The author signed his preface as of "The Stone School House, Phippsburg, Maine."

JOHN JAMES AUDUBON The portrait, an oil on canvas, follows an original by John Woodhouse Audubon, the naturalist's younger son and frequent companion in the field. On February, 11, 1841, Audubon wrote his older son Victor that "John has painted his 'old Dad' sitting in the Wilds of America admiring Nature around him, with a *Dog Companion* lying at his feet."

The background seems to be a view of the Hudson River and the New Jersey palisades, not far from where Audubon would shortly buy property.

WASHINGTON IRVING The original portrait was done in 1825, in London, by Charles Robert Leslie. Leslie was born in England of American parents. He studied with West and Allston; but after 1817 he settled down to composing humorous genre subjects from well-known literary texts (*The Merry Wives of Windsor, Don Quixote*), and on these his fame chiefly rests. Irving and Leslie became good friends in London and wrote to each other in later years.

Leslie taught for a year, 1833, at West Point; and from 1847 to 1852 he was professor of painting at the Royal Academy.

The engraving of Leslie's portrait was done by the team of Hatch and Smillie.

Irving was something of a family favorite with the

Jameses, though Henry Sr. regarded him as rather too worldly. Henry Jr. was introduced to Irving, by his father, on the ferry from Manhattan to Long Island in August 1850.

JAMES FENIMORE COOPER The lithograph portrait was made in the summer of 1827, in Paris, by Amélie Lacépede, née Kautz. With a Madame Trigant de la Tour, she ran a school in the Faubourg St. Germain, near the hotel (on rue St. Maur) where Cooper was staying with his wife and five children (ages two to thirteen) and nephew William (sixteen). Then and on a visit in 1830, Madame Kautz was able to give instruction to several of the Cooper children each day.

The treatment of Cooper in Lawrence's *Studies in Classical American Literature* displays Lawrence's peculiar brand of poetical satirizing. Here, as elsewhere, Lawrence combines remarkable sharpness and originality of insight with an old-world patronizing tone.

Warren's judgment of Cooper arises from the author's (then) recent discovery of Cooper as a powerful predecessor he had not hitherto confronted.

THOMAS COLE The daguerreotype was "attributed to Mathew Brady" by Brady himself, in a late-in-life interview, and the evidence seems to support him. By 1845, the time of this portrait, Brady was at most twenty-three years old. He was already making a name for himself as a daguerreotypist, in his studio on Broadway, with a particular interest in making portraits of well-known artists—including Rembrandt Peale, Henry Inman, G. P. A. Healy, and Frederic Church, along with Thomas Cole.

Cole's evocation of the horizon he viewed on his walks around Volterra, in his August 1831 journal entry, follows the same rhythm as several of his pictorial sequences—"sun, clouds, and storms . . . ever succeeding each other"—to the point where that grand movement seems to reflect Cole's interior psychic rhythms. Here, typically, the villages which earlier "were glittering in the sun-light" become wrapped in the gloom of the "blue shadows . . . moving from mountain to mountain"; and then "thunderstorms sweep with their tumultuous clouds," and the villages are "enveloped in their troubled darkness." Such was Cole's vision of the basic and recurring human experience.

HENRY CLAY John Neagle, who composed the portrait of Clay, was by 1842 well established as a leader in the Philadelphia art world. He began to paint in about 1818, and he was much encouraged by Gilbert Stuart, whose portrait he also painted. Neagle's masterpiece was *Pat Lyon at the Forge* in 1829: a startlingly unconventional picture of the successful Philadelphia manufacturer Patrick Lyon, not as a wealthy entrepreneur, but as a smith at his forge in a leather apron.

Charles Dickens encountered Henry Clay in Washington, during the novelist's visit to America with his wife in 1842. In the same letter Dickens spoke admiringly of John Quincy Adams. The book resulting from this tour, *American Notes,* contained adverse judgments that caused offense in many American quarters.

JOHN C. CALHOUN George Peter Alexander Healy, the portraitist whose life spanned the century, was born in Boston, the son of an Irish sea captain. His career began in 1832 with a portrait of the socially elegant Mrs. Harrison Gray Otis, caught in the act of laughing. After this he went to France for a number of years, gaining wide recognition and powerful and wealthy patrons. He alternated portraiture with genre and historical paintings: among the latter, *Franklin Urging the Claims of the American Colonies Before Louis XVI,* which won a gold medal at the Paris Exposition of 1855.

Oliver Dwyer, in late 1848, was a young newspaper reporter of fervent and unquestioned abolitionist sentiments. He sat in the Senate Chamber looking at the whole scene—the setting for the big debate—with disfavor. Calhoun in particular was his bête noir, a figure he positively hated. Then came the experience recorded—as Dwyer remembered it forty years later and set it down in his book *Great Senators in the United States Forty Years Ago* (1889). The mix or sequence of attitudes expressed represents the continuing and profound ambivalence toward Calhoun.

DANIEL WEBSTER The 1835 portrait by the Boston painter Francis Alexander has—unlike most others, as noted by Fred Voss (*The Godlike Black Dan,* 1982)—turned its subject into a "sort of Byronesque statesman-hero." It also reflects Alexander's recent encounter with

European romanticism during a two-year sojourn in Italy, France, and Britain. This unusual portrait, a gift from Mrs. John Hay Whitney, is one of the most recent (1998) acquisitions by the Gallery.

Emerson's view of Webster underwent several changes. He said as much in his "Address to the Citizens of Concord on the Fugitive Slave Law," on May 5, 1851. Webster, he observed there, "was the one eminent American of our time, whom we could produce as a finished work of nature. . . . But as the activity and growth of slavery began to be offensively felt by his constituents, the senator became less sensitive to these evils. . . . At last . . . and, very unexpectedly to the whole Union, on the 7th of March, 1850, in opposition to his education, association, and to all his most explicit language for thirty years, he crossed the line, and became the head of the slavery party in this country."

The following year, after Webster's death, Emerson reverted somewhat in the long overview to his former judgment.

LUCRETIA MOTT The portrait was apparently commissioned by a New York publisher who hoped to use the prints for publicity purposes. The artist, Joseph Kyle, was a portraitist of some standing at the time, though he is relatively little remembered today. One sign of his socio-artistic interests is that Kyle also did several portraits of black ministers.

JOSEPH SMITH The painting, by Adrian Lamb in 1971, was based on a portrait by an unidentified artist, presumed to be contemporary with Joseph Smith. Lamb studied in New York and at the Julien Academy in Paris before beginning his career. His portraits now hang in the White House, the Senate Hall of Fame, the Harvard Law School, the American embassies in Moscow and Paris, the University of North Carolina, and many other distinguished sites and institutions. His American home was in New Canaan, Connecticut.

Harold Bloom, who composed his richly evocative, indeed exemplary verbal portrait of Joseph Smith for this volume, discussed and analyzed the history of the Mormons and the character of its founder in *The American*

Religion (1992). He is also the author of many other reverberant studies, including *The Anxiety of Influence* and *Shakespeare: The Invention of the Human* (1998).

American Renaissance: Science and Letters

RALPH WALDO EMERSON Daniel Chester French, author of the Emerson bust, grew up in Concord, Massachusetts, where Emerson was the resident sage. He settled in New York in the 1880s; for the Columbian Exposition in 1893 he constructed the huge female figure *The Republic*. The bronze standing statue of Abraham Lincoln in Lincoln, Nebraska, was done in 1912, and the Lincoln Memorial (eighteen feet high and carved out of 200 tons of Georgia marble) in 1922.

Emerson visited the James family home at 58 West Fourteenth Street in New York City several times, staying for several days on each occasion, occupying what became known in the household as "Mr. Emerson's room."

William James's address was given at the Emerson Centenary, held at the old meetinghouse in Concord on May 25, 1903.

NATHANIEL HAWTHORNE The portrait of Hawthorne was painted by Emmanuel Gottlieb Leutze during the first week of April 1862, at the end of Hawthorne's visit to Washington, D.C. Hawthorne had come to Washington partly for reasons of health, and partly to get some sense of the ongoing war at first hand. He visited the White House and, as he told his daughter, had "shaken hands with Uncle Abe."

On April 1, Hawthorne began his sittings for Emmanuel Leutze. The German-born painter had returned two years earlier from twenty years in Düsseldorf. He had come to the United States as a boy and had earned some success as an itinerant portraitist. But in 1840 he went back to his native country and established his own studio in Düsseldorf. Here he gained international acclaim as a painter of historical scenes, the best known in America being that of Washington crossing the Delaware. At the time of Hawthorne's visits with him, Leutze was at work on a vast allegorical-historical mural for the House of Representatives called *Westward the Course of Empire*.

At each sitting, Hawthorne wrote a friend, Leutze "gives

me a first-rate cigar, and when he sees me getting tired, he brings out a bottle of splendid champagne." As a result, Hawthorne thought that Leutze's portrait would be the best ever painted of the same unworthy subject.

Melville's review of Hawthorne's *Mosses from an Old Manse* was written for the *Literary World* only days before Melville and Hawthorne actually met in Stockbridge, Massachusetts, in August 1850, and went together on the Monument Mountain expedition described by James Fields.

Fields (1817–81) was the partner of W. D. Ticknor in a distinguished Boston publishing house (the names still head a publishing firm). He was editor of the *Atlantic Monthly* from 1861 to 1871 and the author of several volumes of poetry and essays, including the reminiscences collected in *Yesterdays with Authors*.

His wife, Annie Adams Fields (1834–1915), conducted a notable literary salon in their Boston home and was the patroness, among others, of Sarah Orne Jewett. Her own memoir of early literary days is *Authors and Friends* (1896).

AUTHORS GROUP This composite picture consists of ten photographs made by the Notman Photographic Company. The firm was founded by William Notman (1826–91), who was born in Scotland and eventually settled in Montreal. He became Canada's most famous photographer, with scores of portraits of Canadians from all walks of life. He also had studios in New York, Albany, and Boston—and in the last-named city he made the portraits collected here. They were then sent to Montreal.

The photos were pasted to a board, and someone (a painter on the Notman staff) created a background—seemingly, the spacious library of a luxurious Boston home. A photograph was next made of the ensemble.

The artist in charge of this phase of the operation was Eugene L'Africain. He was a Montrealer (presumably a French Canadian) who also did work for the Canadian Pacific Railway. He was, in addition, a portrait painter. L'Africain was associated with the Notman Photographic Company from 1878 to 1880. (See his composite picture *Eminent Women* in the Gilded Decades section.)

Lowell's verse sketches formed part of his satirical narra-

tive, *A Fable for Critics,* published anonymously in 1848. Here we offer the critic's observations on Bronson Alcott, Whittier, Longfellow, Holmes, and Lowell himself. Of the writers in our collection, the critic said of Emerson, in a long tribute, that he was:

A Plotinus-Montaigne, where the Egyptian's gold mist
And the Gascon's shrewd wit cheek-by-jowl coexist.

And about Poe, in lines often quoted:

There comes Poe, with his raven, like Barnaby Rudge,
Three-fifths of him genius and two-fifths sheer fudge.

JOSEPH HENRY The carte de visite print of Joseph Henry was made in Mathew Brady's Washington studio, probably in 1862.

A Memorial of Joseph Henry was published for the Smithsonian in 1880, by Order of Congress and by the Government Printing Office. A number of Henry's former colleagues and associates took part.

As to Henry's status and achievement, J. G. Crowther, in *Famous American Men of Science* (1937), makes the following well-reasoned claim: "In total achievement Henry was the equal of Faraday, Helmholtz, Kelvin, Maxwell and the other great scientists of the nineteenth century." As G. B. Good has explained, Henry "did much toward establishing the profession of scientific Administration—a profession which in the complexity of modern civilization is becoming more and more essential to scientific progress. . . . Society is being disrupted by the scientific forces which have been released into it."

LOUIS AGASSIZ The photograph of Agassiz was taken, probably in late 1871, by Carleton E. Watkins in his Yosemite Art Gallery on Montgomery Street in San Francisco. Agassiz had come from Harvard on one of his long trips to study glaciers and evidence of previous glaciation.

Watkins, by this time, was widely known for his photography of Yosemite Valley, begun in 1861. By 1867 he had renamed his studio the Yosemite Art Gallery. It was Watkins's superb pictorial vistas that led to Congress ordering the preservation of Yosemite and, ultimately, of establishing it as a national park.

In March 1865, William James, then twenty-two years

old and on leave from the Harvard Medical School, was taken on as one of several assistants on an expedition to Brazil conducted by Louis Agassiz (whose lectures on zoology at Harvard James had listened to, enthralled).

HENRY DAVID THOREAU In the spring of 1856, an admirer of Thoreau, Calvin H. Greene, a divinity student in Michigan, sent Thoreau five dollars, begging him to have his picture taken and to send his books to Greene's brother. On a visit to Worcester, Massachusetts, in June, Thoreau stopped by the studio of the daguerreotypist Benjamin D. Maxham. Maxham made three almost identical prints, charging Thoreau fifty cents for the transaction. Thoreau sent one to Greene, remarking that "my friends think it is pretty good—though better looking than I," and returned $1.70 in change; the other two he gave to Worcester friends.

Franklin Sanborn (1831–1917) was a Harvard graduate who became a schoolteacher in Concord; his students included the children of Emerson, Hawthorne, and the elder Henry James. Sanborn was a leading abolitionist who was jailed for aiding John Brown.

Thoreau died on May 6, 1862. Emerson arranged for the funeral to be held in the Unitarian Church in Boston, though neither he nor Thoreau had been members of it for some years. The choir sang an ode composed by Ellery Channing; friends read selections from Thoreau's writings; and Emerson gave the address.

EDGAR ALLAN POE Edouard Manet etched this portrait of Poe (he also did two other drawings of the American writer) in 1860, seemingly for a proposed edition of articles on Poe edited by Baudelaire. The latter let it be known that he wanted a likeness of Poe for this volume; and Gaspard-Félix Nadar, a fashionable photographer, recommended his friend Manet. Manet was on the verge of artistic recognition; his professional debut in the Paris salon occurred in 1861, and the paintings that first made him prominent date from the early 1860s (*Le Déjeuner sur l'herbe,* for example, was done in 1863).

Manet came upon a suitable picture of Poe in a recent book about him by one Redfield. This was the so-called Whitman daguerreotype, made in Providence in November 1848 by the recently opened local studio of Masury and Hartshorn. Poe gave it to his friend Sarah Helen Whitman, a widowed poet six years older than he, about whom Poe had some thought of marrying.

Manet greatly revised the original and, among other things, framed the image in an oval band topped by a bow—perhaps suggestive of a Victorian picture frame or of the "feminine" quality of Poe's features that Baudelaire was known to have commented upon.

Whitman recorded his dream about Poe in an entry in *Specimen Days,* made on January 1, 1880, in a meditation, over several pages, on Poe's writing and his life. In the course of it, Whitman transcribed a report from the *Washington Star* on November 16, 1875, noting that "there occur'd about that date in Baltimore a public reburial of Poe's remains, and dedication of a monument over the grave." Whitman was the only American literary figure of any eminence to attend that ceremony.

Kenneth Silverman's life of Poe, the source of the other verbal picture, appeared in the fall of 1991 (Silverman's biography of Cotton Mather won the Pulitzer Prize in 1984).

WALT WHITMAN The engraving by Samuel Hollyer, which served as the frontispiece for the 1855 edition of *Leaves of Grass,* was based on a daguerreotype by Gabriel Harrison. Harrison was born in Philadelphia and had lived in New York City; but from 1848 on he lived and worked in Brooklyn, where he became well known in dramatic, literary, and artistic circles. He had been an early experimenter in the daguerreotype. Whitman, writing in the *Brooklyn Daily Eagle,* said in 1850 that "some pictures taken by Gabriel Harrison are perfect works of truth and art." The picture of Whitman was taken on a summer day in 1850.

Samuel Hollyer was born in London and came to the United States in 1851. He was much admired as an engraver (a picture of Charles Dickens in his study was among his other plates).

The article about Whitman in *The New Yorker*—it was titled "Walt" and appeared in "Talk of the Town" for the issue of April 13, 1992—began: "A New Yorker we know writes: A hundred years ago last week, at the age of seventy-three, happy and in unspeakable pain from spreading tubercular infection that had dissolved his organs and bones, Walt Whitman died." (Whitman died on March 26, 1892.) The author then offers a description of Whitman, from which we draw our passage, and continues: "That's Walt around the summer of 1855, when he published the first edition of *Leaves of Grass.*"

FRANCIS PARKMAN   Parkman's portrait is a daguerreotype made in about 1852. It was made by the firm of Al-bert Sands Southworth and Josiah Johnson Hawes, perhaps the most widely (even internationally) known American daguerreotypists in the period 1840–60.

The historians mentioned at the start of the first quotation are often referred to as the "literary historians." They made up a historico-literary generation in America, and they included the eminent William Prescott, author of *The History of the Conquest of Mexico* and *The History of the Conquest of Peru* in the 1840s; John Lothrop Motley, author of *The Rise of the Dutch Republic* in 1856 (Motley appears in our Authors Group portrait); and George Bancroft, ambassador and founder of the U.S. Naval Academy as well as historian, author of the ten-volume *History of the United States* (1834–76).

STEPHEN COLLINS FOSTER   The lithograph of Foster was based on a photograph by an unknown artist, made perhaps around 1860. The lithograph company of Major (Henry and Richard) and Knapp (Joseph) was active from c. 1854–1871. The picture was used, in this case, on the sheet music of "Old Black Joe," by the music publishers Wm. A. Pond & Company, of Union Square, New York.

The Civil War Years

SOJOURNER TRUTH   Harriet Beecher Stowe's article "Sojourner Truth, the Libyan Sibyl," was published in the *Atlantic Monthly* of April 1863. After the mid-1850s encounter, Stowe, for the entertainment of her friends, enjoyed mimicking her visitor's manner of speaking. Key dates in the life of Sojourner Truth, including her birthdate, are recorded variously, both by her biographers and by Sojourner Truth herself.

JOHN BROWN   The portrait of Brown by Augustus Washington, only recently rediscovered, was purchased in October 1996, via Sotheby's auction house in New York, for $115,000 by the National Portrait Gallery. In this volume it replaced the one we had originally planned to use, made at the end of Brown's career and life in 1859 by Ole Peter Hansen Balling. The Balling picture shows a heavily bearded Brown wrapped in army blankets, with manacles faintly discernible binding his wrists. It was based on sketches made by Balling during Brown's incarceration and trial.

As to Washington, in 1853 he emigrated with his family to Monrovia, Liberia, to a settlement organized by the American Colonization Society. For a while he sent back daguerreotypes and articles. The date of his death is unknown.

HARRIET BEECHER STOWE   The visit to the White House has been most fully treated in the article "Mrs. Stowe, Mr. Lincoln, and the British in the Civil War," by Wendy F. Hamand, in *New England Quarterly* 61, no. 1 (March 1988). The article was kindly put in our hands by Glenn Wallach, former dean of Morse College at Yale.

FREDERICK DOUGLASS   This picture of Douglass was long thought to be by Elisha L. Hammond. In an 1895 essay Douglass spoke of meeting Hammond fifty years earlier, presumably in April 1844, when Douglass was addressing an antislavery meeting in Northampton, Massachusetts; and in his will, Douglass spoke of "a certain portrait of myself painted more than 40 years ago by Mr. Hammond of Florence, Massachusetts." That portrait has apparently been lost; the one here presented is possibly based on the one used as the frontispiece for *Narrative of the Life of Frederick Douglass* in 1845, by an unidentified artist.

HARRIET TUBMAN   The letter from Frederick Douglass is contained in the appendix to the 1961 edition of Sarah H. Bradford's *Harriet Tubman: The Moses of Her People,* edited with an introduction by Butler A. Jones.

JEFFERSON DAVIS William Sartain, who did the mezzotint of Davis from the Mathew Brady photograph, was the son of John Sartain (1808–97), an acclaimed and prolific portraitist (Andrew Jackson, Washington Irving, and Jenny Lind, among many others) who did lithographs and etchings as well as photography. Son William, based in New York, also did portraits of Robert E. Lee, Stonewall Jackson and his family, and U. S. Grant.

The book-length essay on Davis by Robert Penn Warren was Warren's last publication (1987).

THOMAS J. "STONEWALL" JACKSON Adalbert John Volck's *Sketches* were published under the name of V. Blada, which, as he later explained, comprised the first five letters of his first name written backward, plus the initial of his surname.

MATHEW BRADY In November 1862, Brady put out a collection called *Brady's Photographic Views of the War*. Saluting this work, the *New York Times* remarked that "Mr. Brady deserves honourable recognition as having been the first to make Photography the Clio of the war"—i.e., the muse of history. In the same month, the *New York World* observed that in the battle areas, Brady's photographic team "has been a feature as distinct and omnipresent as the corps of balloon, telegraph and signal operators."

Brady spent a fortune ($100,000) on his war photography, and eventually, in 1873, went bankrupt. In his last years, he enjoyed a certain renaissance of interest in his Civil War achievements.

ULYSSES S. GRANT In *The Civil War,* Geoffrey C. Ward, Ken Burns, and Ric Burns quote a Union soldier, Elisha Rhodes, after his 6th Corps had been reviewed by Grant in April 1864: "a short, thick-set man and rode his horse like a bag of meal. I was a little disappointed in the appearance, but I like the look of his eye."

WILLIAM TECUMSEH SHERMAN Shelby Foote remarks that earlier in the war, Sherman had been "temporarily retired under suspicion of insanity" for publicly declaring that a very hard war lay ahead. By this time he had also shown signs of manic depression. In the years

after the war Sherman had an astonishing following in the South, partly because he declared that the stories about the Ku Klux Klan were exaggerated, and that the South could handle its own problems.

ROBERT E. LEE Among the twenty-odd portraits of Lee in the National Portrait Gallery are other images by Brady, two Currier and Ives lithographs, a lithograph by a French artist (F. F. Dubois-Tesselin) of Lee on horseback, and an 1870 bust by Edward Virginius Valentine.

ABRAHAM LINCOLN In his outstanding biography *Lincoln* (1995), David Herbert Donald tells of Lincoln being escorted to Brady's studio on Monday February 27, 1860, by several members of the Young Men's Central Republican Union, which was sponsoring an upcoming speech. Donald calls Brady's portrait a "work of art" and notes that Brady "retouched the negative in order to correct Lincoln's left eye that seemed to be roving upward and eliminated harsh lines from his face to show an almost handsome, statesmanlike image."

In his speech at the Cooper Union later that day, Lincoln vigorously and well-informedly supported the power of the federal government to exclude slavery from the "federal territories." At the end, the audience, which had been taken aback at first by Lincoln's ungainly figure, improperly brushed hair, and high piercing voice, stood up and cheered and waved handkerchiefs and hats.

Henry S. Pritchett, in 1904, was president of the Massachusetts Institute of Technology.

JOHN WILKES BOOTH Whitman was a great admirer of Junius Brutus Booth, especially as Shakespeare's Richard III. In May 1862, Whitman saw Junius's son John Wilkes in the same role and said his performance was "about as much like his father's, as the wax bust of Henry Clay, in the window down near Howard Street, a few blocks from the theatre, is like the genuine orator in the Capital."

Whitman had seen Abraham Lincoln on a number of occasions, and several times when the president was attending the theater. Whitman was in Washington during the Civil War, in 1862 and later. But he was not at Ford's

Theater on the night of April 14, 1865, and his seemingly eyewitness account of the assassination comes from newspaper reports and a powerfully dedicated imagination.

Note: In this section, we are especially indebted to *The Civil War,* by Geoffrey C. Ward with Ric Burns and Ken Burns (1990). This companion volume to the matchless television series is the source for the verbal portraits of Stonewall Jackson and Sherman, and for other quotations and information. *Note also:* In all matters relating to Mathew Brady, we are most grateful to Mary Panzer, curator of photographs at the National Portrait Gallery and the author of the definitive study *Mathew Brady and the Image of History* (1997).

American Indian Leaders

JOSEPH BRANT The inscription reads: "Thayendanegea / The Great Captain of the Six Nations"—that is, the Iroquois confederacy. This print was published by F. W. Greenough of Philadelphia, printers of volume 2 of the McKenney-Hall opus.

In 1785, Brant made a second trip to England, where he was celebrated, had an audience with King George III, and saw to the printing of his translation into the Iroquois language of the Gospel according to St. Mark—English one side, Iroquois the other.

THE SHAWNEE PROPHET In his 1830s portrait, Charles Bird King chose to depict Tenskwatawa in his warrior's garb and personality, rather than in his holy garb.

SEQUOYAH The fine lithograph of the Inman copy of the King original was made by the J. Y. Bowen company of Philadelphia, which employed twenty-five colorists, mostly women, for the whole work. The publisher was Edward C. Biddle of Philadelphia.

PETER PERKINS PITCHLYNN Charles Dickens encountered Peter Pitchlynn while traveling from Cincinnati to Louisville aboard the steamboat *Pike.* Among other things, the two spoke of George Catlin's London gallery of Indian portraits, which contained a likeness of Pitchlynn. Pitchlynn also expressed admiration for James Fenimore Cooper's portrayal of Indians.

RED CLOUD Red Cloud's appearance in this 1883 photograph is similar to that remembered by General Howard in his reminiscences of the same era: "He was considerably wrinkled with age, but had still a great abundance of black hair, parted in the middle and hanging down over his shoulders. He was dressed completely in citizens' clothing, including a shirt-front collar and necktie."

James H. Cook's engrossing, entirely straightforward memoir carries an introduction by General Charles King (U.S. Cavalry) which notes that Cook, an ardent pursuer of Geronimo, "was nevertheless a champion and faithful friend, from first to last, of one of the most implacable enemies of the white man, the most daring and brilliant chieftain the Sioux nation has ever claimed—Mahpina-Luta, Red Cloud."

SITTING BULL The lithograph of Rudolf Cronau's painting was done by the Rommler and Jones company, presumably a German commercial printing outfit.

Robert M. Utley, the author of *The Lance and the Shield,* has produced many distinguished historical studies on the Sioux Nation, George Armstrong Custer, and the Western Frontier; and he is the coauthor, with Wilcomb E. Washburn, of *The American Heritage History of the Indian Wars* (1977).

GERONIMO Allan Houser, the creator of this powerfully expressive bronze bust, was the great-great-grandson of Mangus Colorado, a heroic Apache leader whose contrived murder in 1863 ("while trying to escape") was characterized by Geronimo as "perhaps the greatest wrong ever done to the Indians." Houser's father, Sam Haozous (as he spelled the name), an associate of Geronimo's, spent many years in prison with him after 1886. Houser, who died in 1994, was one of the most accomplished sculptors of his time, and the leading Native American sculptor. He was the legendary director of the Institute of American Indian Arts in Santa Fe from 1962 to 1975.

Angie Debo, the author of *Geronimo,* has written several other important volumes on Indian history.

CHIEF JOSEPH The Nez Perce were so named by French trappers (hence the word "Perce" is sometimes given an accent) because of the shells the Indians were observed wearing in their pierced noses. The Nez Perce took friendly care of Lewis and Clark and their expedition when the Americans came down over the Rockies in 1805.

Chief Joseph's Indian name, Heinmot Tooyalakekt, means "Thunder cloud travelling over the mountain." He has been described as six feet three inches tall with piercing black eyes; and his face in later years showed the profound melancholy of this portrait of 1903.

There is a certain historians' disagreement as to the exact date of Chief Joseph's surrender, and as to the American officer to whom he handed his sword.

The Gilded Decades

CORNELIUS VANDERBILT Napoleon Sarony, the artist, was no taller than the French emperor for whom he was named.

JOHN D. ROCKEFELLER Timothy Cole (no relation to Thomas Cole) was brought from England to Hoboken, New Jersey, at the age of five. He later spent twenty-seven years abroad, mostly on the European continent, making engravings from paintings by such artists as Botticelli and El Greco. He was back in America by 1910.

The remarks of William James were made in a letter to his wife, Alice Gibbens James, after a visit to the Lakewood, New Jersey, home of Charles Augustus Strong, an able younger philosopher and the husband of Bessie Rockefeller, the oldest child of John D.

J. P. MORGAN Edward Steichen, in his effectively long life, exercised a major influence on the course of modern art in America. In the 1920s and '30s, Steichen, in his studio on West 40th Street in New York, made a series of fashion photographs and portraits of celebrities— including John Barrymore, Martha Graham, Maurice Chevalier, Charlie Chaplin, and, most famously, Greta Garbo. From 1947 to 1962 he was director of the department of photography at the Museum of Modern Art, where in 1966 he organized an exhibition called "The Family of Man." It has been called the greatest photography exhibition ever staged.

The Chaplin and the J. P. Morgan portraits are among

the sixteen works by Steichen in the National Portrait Gallery.

Among the other biographical sketches that pepper *1919*—the second section of *USA,* between *The 42nd Parallel* and *The Big Money*—are those of John Reed, Theodore Roosevelt, Woodrow Wilson ("Meester Veelson," as he was called at the 1919 Paris Peace Conference), and Joe Hill, the songwriting, martyred labor organizer.

JESSE JAMES The picture of Jesse James was taken in an undertaker's morgue in St. Joseph, Missouri, very soon after James was shot dead by Bob Ford. According to a report, "The corpse was strapped to a board and stood upright, so that it could be photographed."

WILLIAM MARCY "BOSS" TWEED Charles S. Grafulla had been long known as a writer of popular march tunes when he composed the "quickstep" titled "Solid Men to the Front." He had been leader of the much admired New York Seventh Regiment Band during the Civil War, and today he is regarded as one of America's best composers of marches, and a decided influence on John Philip Sousa.

On the lithograph company of Major and Knapp, see the entry on Stephen Foster.

ELIZABETH CADY STANTON Anna Elizabeth Klumpke was of Dutch and German descent. She grew up in San Francisco, where, at an early age, she suffered an injury to her right knee that caused her to walk with a cane and a brace for all her long life.

Phrenology, as a method of determining an individual's mental powers by a careful feeling of the person's cranium at certain places, had its origins in England in about 1800. It became extremely popular in the American 1850s, when (as is evident in the Stanton reading) the analysis extended to character, temperament, and physical condition. It was also associated with the cause of women's rights and other issues, which was one reason both Stanton and Susan B. Anthony admired it. Lorenzo Fowler, the reader of Stanton's character, was a leading phrenologist of his time, and was the husband of Lydia Folger Fowler, a strong women's rights advocate and a pioneering woman physician.

Susan B. Anthony (1820–1906), although not represented visually, needs to be further identified. Elizabeth Cady Stanton's longtime associate, she was born in the Berkshires, in Massachusetts, of a Quaker family. She joined the struggle for women's rights relatively late, after coming to know Mrs. Stanton in 1851. In her indispensable study *Century of Struggle: The Woman's Rights Movement in the United States* (1959), Eleanor Flexner appraised the key figures in the first major stage of the crusade: "If Lucretia Mott typified the moral force of the movement, if Lucy Stone was its most gifted orator and Mrs. Stanton its outstanding philosopher, Susan Anthony was its incomparable organizer, who gave it force and direction for half a century."

The Gallery possesses a bronze bust of Susan B. Anthony, c. 1892, by an unidentified artist, and an 1898 photograph by Theodore C. Marceau.

EMINENT WOMEN The Notman Photographic Company, which produced the composite photograph, was the creation of William Notman, who opened a studio in Montreal in 1856, and another in Boston (run by his younger brother James Notman) a little later. The Notmans were famed for their skill in using photographic techniques to create illusions. Eugene l'Africain, who put together the composite in Montreal, worked for William Notman from 1878 to 1889, after which he went into business for himself.

The names of the "Eminent Women" appear around the outside of the circular print; and the women themselves, meanwhile, are arranged as though taking part in a literary reading and discussion.

Elizabeth Dillon is a member of the English department at Yale University, with a specialty in nineteenth-century American women writers. Her comment on "Eminent Women" was written for this volume.

MERIWETHER LEWIS Charles de Saint-Mémin (see also the portraits of Thomas Jefferson and John Marshall) made his watercolor of Lewis after the latter's return to Washington in late 1807. Lewis is clad in the ermine skin given him by the Shoshone chief Cameahwait, after the chief was joyously recognized by Lewis's Indian guide as

her brother. Lewis later gave the mantle and a peace pipe to Charles Willson Peale for his museum (see Ellen Gross Miles, *Saint-Mémin,* 1994).

JOHN MUIR The 1990s saw the publication of three volumes by or about John Muir: *Nature Writings,* brilliantly edited by William Cronon for the Library of America; *The Eight Wilderness Discovery Books,* a collection of his major pieces; and *A Thousand-Mile Walk to the Gulf,* by Muir and his very capable literary executor, William Frederic Badè.

Edward Hoagland (b. 1932) is the author of highly original books about travel, rural life, and animals (*Red Wolves and Black Bears,* 1976), and several novels. He teaches at Bennington College.

WILLIAM F. CODY (BUFFALO BILL) Rosa Bonheur was, among other things, an Americanophile. As a fiercely independent woman herself, she professed to admire "the respect [Americans] have for women"; and she was captivated by the romance of the American West, even though she deplored what she called the white usurpation of "that unfortunate race," the American Indians, for whom she had a "veritable passion."

e. e. cummings's unpunctuated but rhythmically emphatic tribute to Buffalo Bill, presumably written not long after Cody's death in 1917, might have been composed with the Rosa Bonheur portrait in mind. Here, anyhow, is a "handsome man," riding a "watersmoothsilver stallion," ready, one feels, to break five pigeons at a moment's notice.

PHINEAS TAYLOR BARNUM The picture of Barnum blowing his trumpet to summon visitors to his museum was based on a sketch by the cartoonist Henry Louis Stephens, who drew for several comic magazines in addition to *Vanity Fair.*

Neil Harris, currently at the University of Chicago, has written, in addition to his enjoyable and informative life of Barnum, *The Artist in American Society: The Formative Years, 1790–1860* (1966).

EDWIN BOOTH David Belasco (1853–1931) was one of the best known and most successful, as well as innovative and (hence) controversial, New York theatrical producers of his time.

Otis Skinner (1858–1942), a grand actor of the old school, played some 325 different roles in his sixty-year career, including early Shakespearean roles with Edwin Booth. *Kismet* was one of his later triumphs. He was the father of the actress and author Cornelia Otis Skinner.

JAMES ABBOTT MCNEILL WHISTLER Mortimer Menpes came to know Whistler in London in early 1881, and, as student and "Master" (so Menpes always called the older artist), they were closely associated until 1888. Then and later, Menpes made a great many portraits of Whistler, some of them in clusters of images on single sheets. Some of these appeared in an exhibition at the National Portrait Gallery in 1995, a show identified (by reporter Hank Burchard in the *Washington Post*) as "the first ever devoted to a single artist as subject rather than as the portraitist."

Frank Harris (1856–1931), from whom our first passage is taken, was an adventurous and skillful editor, particularly of literary folk (G. B. Shaw, H. G. Wells, Max Beerbohm), and the author of the erotically boastful and probably exaggerated memoir *My Life and Loves* (4 volumes). He was a strange, self-obsessed figure, but an eloquent witness of his cultural times.

MARK TWAIN Mark Twain and William Howells had known each other since the evening in the winter of 1869 when Twain arrived at Howells's *Atlantic Monthly* office to thank him for his favorable review of *The Innocents Abroad*.

Howells's essay on Mark Twain appeared in the *North American Review* in February 1901.

WILLIAM DEAN HOWELLS AND MILDRED HOWELLS Augustus Saint-Gaudens recalled that Howells, in a *Harper's* article had warmly praised his bust of General Sherman; "so in appreciation of that . . . I begged that he allow me to make his portrait and that of his daughter Miss Mildred Howells." Mildred, called "Pi" by her family, was twenty-five at the time. In the scene, Howells the father is reading aloud, presumably from his latest manuscript, while the daughter listens intently.

Howells was the only eminent man of letters in America who was on equally good and mutually admiring terms with both Mark Twain and Henry James.

HENRY JAMES The James portrait was made in connection with the collected edition of his works, then in preparation. James appointed Coburn the chief illustrator for the edition (Coburn's landscape pictures having shown definite "painterly" qualities) and sent him to London, Paris, and Venice to record settings, both exterior and interior, which provide the basis of scenes in the fiction.

The roving reminiscences offered by James, which Edith Wharton recalled in her autobiography, occurred on an evening in July 1911. Two of Edith Wharton's closest friends were also houseguests at the Wharton home in Lenox, Massachusetts, on the occasion. To the first of them, the American Gaillard Lapsley, Wharton wrote soon afterward: "Were ever such splendours poured out on mortal heads as descended on ours during that fiery week?"

Entering the Twentieth Century

WILLIAM JAMES In the fall of 1860, the probable time of the portrait, John La Farge and William James were both students in Newport of William Morris Hunt (himself allied to the French Barbizon school of painting). The somewhat older La Farge served as mediator between Hunt and James.

James's letter to Alice Gibbens was an element in his eccentric courtship of the twenty-seven-year-old Boston schoolteacher. It was also a major early statement of James's vision of the human psyche.

JOHN DEWEY Jacob Epstein was born in Manhattan of Polish Jewish parents. He became a British citizen and was eventually knighted, though his artistic style was anything but traditionally English. Dewey's son-in-law said this bust made Dewey look like a "Vermont horse-dealer"; Epstein was pleased since he had (he said) enjoyed Dewey's "Vermont drawl and seeming casualness."

Dewey's characteristically entitled text of 1925 had the cosmic range that Holmes discovered in it.

GEORGE SANTAYANA Harry Wood, Jr., former professor of art at Arizona State University, has painted some 750 portraits of such sitters as Frank Lloyd Wright, Robert Frost, and Adlai Stevenson. He did the portrait of Santayana in the latter's rooms at the convent clinic of the Blue Nuns in Rome, where the philosopher spent his last years. Santayana was much taken with the portrait, and he detected a touch of El Greco in it.

Wallace Stevens came to know Santayana at Harvard in the late 1890s. Though never a student of the philosopher, Stevens visited him, talked about poetry and religion, and exchanged poems with him.

W. E. B. DU BOIS James E. Purdy, a Boston artist, was active in the 1890s and 1900s.

David Levering Lewis is the most gifted and accomplished scholar in the field of black American cultural history. His massive first volume of the life of Du Bois, subtitled "Biography of a Race," appeared in 1993; the second volume is forthcoming. He is also the author of a life of the Rev. Martin Luther King, Jr., and of the indispensable study *When Harlem Was in Vogue* (1981).

ALEXANDER GRAHAM BELL Moses Wainer Dykaar was born in Russia and came to America in 1916. During the 1920s he earned a high reputation with portrait-busts of Presidents Harding and Coolidge, General Pershing, Alice Roosevelt Longworth, and others, as well as Alexander Graham Bell. On March 10, 1933, depressed by ill health and financial trouble, he threw himself under a Lexington Avenue express train in the Bronx.

THOMAS ALVA EDISON Abraham Archibald Anderson maintained studios both in Paris and New York, and was equally admired for his French landscape paintings and his American portraits (Elihu Root, General O. O. Howard, William Gillette, and others). According to Anderson, his portrait of Edison was done just after the inventor perfected his phonograph by successfully bringing out the difficult sounds *P* and *S*.

Neil Baldwin, author of the graceful and thoroughly informative life of Edison, is director of the National Book Award Association.

Sarah Bernhardt, enraptured from afar by the wizard figure of Edison, made a pilgrimage from New York (after a performance of *Camille*) to the Edison home in Menlo Park, New Jersey, on a snowy winter night in 1880.

GEORGE WASHINGTON CARVER Clifton Johnson was a pioneer documentary photographer, mostly of New England rural life. Here, however, he pictures George Washington Carver and an unidentified student in a woodland area near the Tuskegee campus in Alabama. Johnson's command of the "expressive power of details" (as one commentator has put it) shows here to good effect.

Mary White Ovington was a well-to-do socialist and a founding board member of the NAACP. Her *Portraits in Color* includes telling sketches of James Weldon Johnson, Marcus Garvey, Du Bois, Walter White, Carver, Langston Hughes, Paul Robeson, and fourteen others.

MARY CASSATT Cassatt thought that Degas's portrait of her had some "artistic qualities" but felt it represented her as a "repugnant" person: the posture of leaning forward, elbows on knees, holding cards in her hands (apparently photograph-cards of women dressed in white) was unacceptable to her Victorian temperament. When the portrait was acquired in 1984, director Alan Fern said, "Surely, this will be one of the central paintings of the National Portrait Gallery's collections, taking its place next to the masterpieces by Gilbert Stuart and John Singleton Copley."

Louisine Havemeyer (1855–1929) met Mary Cassatt in Paris in 1874 and became a lifelong friend and patron. Eventually one of the great art collectors of her time (and a leading suffragist), Havemeyer served as a conduit in New York for the work of Mary Cassatt and her French associates.

THOMAS EAKINS Susan Macdowell Eakins, the probable author of this portrait, was the wife of Thomas Eakins. She worked with Eakins in photography and was herself an expert photographic artist.

Whitman sat for Eakins in July 1887. The remarkable portrait that ensued was regarded by Whitman as coming "nearest being me." It suggests a certain aging majesty. Eakins also made a death mask of Whitman in 1891.

CHILDE HASSAM The self-portrait was made in Hassam's New York studio.

Royal Cortissoz (1869–1948) was the influential art critic of the *New York Herald Tribune* from 1891 onward—grave-toned, intelligent, and antimodernist. He published books on both French and American painters.

Celia Thaxter (1835–1894) was the daughter of a lighthousekeeper on the New Hampshire coast. Her collections both of poems and prose sketches dealt primarily with the shifting appearances of the sea. Thoreau and Whittier were among the many writers and artists who visited her family-run hotel.

CHARLOTTE PERKINS GILMAN Ellen Day Hale, the portraitist, was the Boston-born daughter of Edward Everett Hale, author of *The Man Without a Country*. She studied painting with William Morris Hunt (a few years after William James) and eventually became skilled both in portraits and in landscape scenes—as in her views of Rockport, Massachusetts, where she spent many summers.

Charlotte Perkins Gilman's brilliantly harrowing *The Yellow Wallpaper* (1892) has been a model for later women writing fictional accounts of personal domestic horror.

FRANK LLOYD WRIGHT Berenice Abbott, born in Ohio, began her photographic career in Paris in the 1920s, with portraits of Jean Cocteau and others. In addition to superb and inventive portraiture, Abbott also made landmark photographic studies of urban life and aspects of physical science. A major retrospective of her work was mounted at the Museum of Modern Art in 1970–71.

Brendan Gill (1914–1997), long associated with the *New Yorker* magazine, was the author of *Here at the New Yorker,* among other books.

EMMA GOLDMAN Carl Van Vechten, born in Iowa and a graduate of the University of Chicago, served as both music critic and Paris correspondent for the *New York Times* in the 1900s. By 1920 he had published seven volumes of essays, mostly on music. After two novels—*The Tatooed Countess* (1924) and the best-selling if unhappily titled *Nigger Heaven* (1926)—Van Vechten became involved with Harlem life and culture, holding "integration evenings" in his 110th Street home. By 1932

he had become a photographer, making thousands of pictures of buildings, street scenes, and individuals.

Van Vechten is represented here with his animated portrait of Emma Goldman, and later of Willa Cather, but he is best known for his portraits of black writers and artists (in this book, of Zora Neale Hurston and Richard Wright), with a number of whom he was a close friend. It has been said about him that "no other white photographer . . . devoted anything approaching Van Vechten's energy to the sympathetic portrayal of black writers and artists" (Keith F. Davis, *The Passionate Observer,* 1993).

Sinclair Lewis (1885–1951) had worked for a time in Upton Sinclair's socialist community in New Jersey, a few years before this comment on Emma Goldman. He was still a decade away from *Main Street.*

H. L. Mencken (1880–1956) was at this time, 1925, cofounder (with George Jean Nathan) and editor of the *American Mercury.* (See the Mencken entry in the next section.)

HENRY FORD Hans Wollner, born in Germany, served in the German army during World War I, then emigrated to the United States. He served as chief engineer for several companies, producing machinery, at the same time making busts of men he admired, young women, and dogs. A friend remembered him as a "great man" and a "humanitarian."

Dos Passos's sketch of Henry Ford, early in *The Big Money,* leads into the ongoing story of Charley Anderson, who will soon get into the production of airplanes.

WILBUR WRIGHT Wright came to France in May 1908, to fulfill a contract with French manufacturers. He decided to display his new machine (shipped in crates from America) at the Humaudiérs Race Course near Le Mans, 125 miles southwest of Paris. Léon Bollée, local manufacturer and balloonist, lent several kinds of assistance. In this picture, Wright stands at the left, facing his aircraft, with portly Léon Bollée beside him. On August 8, Wright made a flight of one minute 45 seconds at 55 kilometers per hour, using stick control for the first time. On August 13, Wright made a flight over the race course of 8 minutes, 13 seconds.

Dos Passos's account of the Wright brothers, just beyond midpoint in *The Big Money,* leads back to Charley Anderson's unhappy career.

GERTRUDE STEIN Jo Davidson, the eminent sculptor, flourished, mainly in New York, through the period between the two wars, with portraits of warrior leaders in World War I, and then such notables as Gandhi, Franklin D. Roosevelt, and Rudyard Kipling. While Gertrude Stein was posing for him, Davidson recalled, she sat reading her own writing. At the end, she circled the statue with pleasure, announcing, "That's Gertrude Stein, that's all of Gertrude Stein, that's all of Gertrude Stein there is.""A Gertrude is a Gertrude is a Gertrude," Davidson replied.

D. W. GRIFFITH Lillian Gish was long known as the First Lady of the Silent Screen, making her debut with her sister Dorothy in Griffith's *An Unseen Enemy* (1912). She performed frequently for Griffith, who called her "the best actress in her profession" with "the best mind of any woman I have ever met." Lillian Gish was the ideal Victorian heroine, seemingly frail but inwardly staunch. She played in a number of sound films after 1930, appearing as late as 1978 in Robert Altman's *A Wedding.* Griffith, meanwhile, also sponsored other leading ladies whose names will arouse a flicker in genuine movie buffs: Mary Pickford, Mae Marsh, Blanche Sweet.

ISADORA DUNCAN In the 1890s, John Sloan became known for his decorative posterlike drawings in color for Philadelphia newspapers. In New York later, with close friends William Glackens, George Luks, Everett Shinn, and Robert Henri, he helped foster the new urban realism, forming a group called The Eight—its first exhibition was in 1908. Sloan's *The City from Greenwich Village* (1922) is a masterwork of this phase; as, of a later phase, when he favored the "use of color as a graphic tool" and "realization rather than realism," is his *Nude with Nine Apples* (1937).

Sloan's portrait of Isadora Duncan was made two years before he sold his first painting. He continued to watch the dancer whenever he could, and to meditate on and talk about her.

ALBERT EINSTEIN Antonio Frasconi was born in Buenos Aires of Italian parents, and raised in Uruguay. He came to New York on a fellowship in 1945. At about the same time, he shifted from painting (at which he had achieved some success) to printmaking and woodcut. He has displayed great variety of form and texture with his woodcuts. In 1962 he made a series of lithographs based on the work of the Spanish poet García Lorca. (See also, below, Frasconi's portraits of Duke Ellington and Woody Guthrie.)

Howard Moss (b. 1922) was poetry editor of the *New Yorker* for many decades, and the author of more than ten volumes of poetry from 1946 on, plus volumes of essays, reviews and sketches, and plays. His *Selected Poems* of 1971 won the National Book Award. His poetry is characterized by grace, a human intimacy, and a quietly observing intelligence.

Faces on the Public Scene: Through the 1920s

The Auden lines are part of the poet's dedication to Stephen Spender in his book *The Orators: An English Study* (1932). The editors of this volume first heard the lines quoted by the drama critic Francis Fergusson, who was applying them (in 1952) to Adlai Stevenson.

OLIVER WENDELL HOLMES, JR. S. J. Woolf was a skilled craftsman who conducted and published many interviews of leading American characters in the 1920s to 1940s, all of them illuminated by his own sketches. He will reappear later in the volume.

Catherine Drinker Bowen, in the course of her exhaustive back-of-the-book annotation, assures the reader that all the statements and conversations of her main characters come from published documents or word-of-mouth testimony. James Doherty was among those she interviewed at length.

BOOKER T. WASHINGTON Elmer Chickering was a Boston-based artist who was active most notably in the 1880s to 1900s. The National Portrait Gallery also has an 1896 photograph by Chickering of the prizefighter James J. Corbett.

Dudley Randall (b. 1914) has spent most of his life in

Detroit, a city of which he eventually became poet laureate. He has also been an important figure in Detroit's library system. He founded the Broadside Press, a major outlet for contemporary black American poetry. He has brought out several collections of his own verse. His poem "Booker T. and W. E. B." runs through forty-nine lines of entertaining but unyielding disagreement.

The 1965 edition of *Up from Slavery* has an invaluable, deeply perceptive, and very well-balanced introduction by Langston Hughes.

THEODORE ROOSEVELT During a mild legal flurry in 1909 over the use of the Peter A. Juley photograph, Roosevelt testified in the county court in Oyster Bay, New York, that he liked the picture "better than any other photograph that has ever been taken of me." Juley had brought suit against the Town Topics Publishing Company for using his portrait to highlight the section on Roosevelt in its 1905 booklet *Fads and Fancies*—about the private preferences of "representative Americans"—without acknowledging its source. Juley won the suit but with virtually no damages assigned. Juley had a studio in downtown New York City, where his son Paul P. Juley (1890–1975) joined him and continued to operate it until his death.

WOODROW WILSON Leo Mielziner, based in Washington Square, New York, was much in demand during the first decades of the century for portraits of Americans distinguished in widely divergent fields. Wilson's "summons" to join the Red Cross is inscribed on the portrait next to Mielziner's initials.

Wilson's White House letter is contained in *Priceless Gift* (1962), a volume of the "love letters" written by Woodrow Wilson and Ellen Axson Wilson from their first meeting in 1883 through their courtship and 1885 marriage and their life together until Ellen's death in August 1914. It was edited by their daugher Eleanor Wilson McAdoo, whose own birth is recorded on p. 171 of the book.

EUGENE DEBS Debs sat for the noted sculptor Louis Mayer in Akron in 1919, during his trial on charges of undermining America's war effort. Mayer, years later, recalled that Debs, towering over him, stooped to kiss Mayer on the top of the head, saying, "Louis, I've known

you for aeons and aeons." Mayer supervised the bronze casting of the bust in 1968, at the age of ninety-nine.

CLARENCE DARROW On Jo Davidson, see the Gertrude Stein entry.

Lincoln Steffens, San Francisco born, entered New York journalism in 1892 and became well known as editor of *McClure's Magazine* for his muckraking exposure of corruption in business and government. His best-known work, his *Autobiography* (1931), is a socio-political history of the times, as well as a personal memoir.

Nathan F. Leopold, Jr., Richard Loeb's codefendant in the 1925 trial, talks eloquently about Darrow in his memoir *Life Plus 99 Years*. He describes his first shocked impression of Darrow in his rumpled suit, shirt wrinkled and tie askew; and then of the later impression Darrow made—"There was about his craggy face, his unruly iron-gray hair, and his loose-jointed shambling figure a certain air of timelessness." For Leopold, "Mr. Darrow's fundamental characteristic was his deep-seated, all embracing kindliness."

H. L. MENCKEN A. Aubrey Bodine was chief photographer of the *Baltimore Sun* from 1927 to 1970. He is perhaps best known for his abundant pictorial images of the Chesapeake Bay area, which won many awards and were collected in books, including *My Maryland* (1952).

Our Baltimore entry continues with Russell Baker, who, like Mencken and Bodine, began his career with the *Baltimore Sun* (in 1947). Baker went on to the *New York Times,* where he inaugurated his vastly cherished "Observer" column in 1962. He won a Pulitzer Prize for Distinguished Commentary in 1979, and another Pulitzer in 1983, for his superb, moving, spine-tingling memoir *Growing Up.*

NICOLA SACCO AND BARTOLOMEO VANZETTI *Boston,* a two-volume novel by Upton Sinclair (1878–1968), tells of the fictional sixty-year-old Cornelia Thornwall, who comes to know Bart Vanzetti in a Plymouth boardinghouse and lives through the entire Sacco-Vanzetti ordeal, doing her unsuccessful best to help the cause. *The Jungle,* Sinclair's 1906 novel exposing the Chicago meatpacking industry, was among the one hundred books of all genres that he wrote between 1901 and 1940, before he began the Lanny Budd series with *World's End.*

AL CAPONE Damon Runyon (1884–1946) was the author of highly entertaining short stories about gangster life, Broadway doings, sports champions, and the like, all couched in his own inventive slang. Many of these tales have been made into films, from *Little Miss Marker* (1934) onward.

The Harlem Renaissance

Throughout this section we have been indebted to David Levering Lewis's *When Harlem Was in Vogue* (1981; Penguin edition with a new preface, 1997). This is a model of cultural-historical narrative: swarming with characters, each given his or her identity and role; and thick with cultural themes and phases, each brought clearly into play. The first volume of Lewis's biography of W. E. B. Du Bois (1993) won the Pulitzer Prize and other awards.

JAMES WELDON JOHNSON On Mary White Ovington, see the entry on George Washington Carver.

God's Trombones, like the folk-sermon Johnson listened to, proceeds from "The Creation" through five more "sermons" to "Judgment Day."

Doris Ulmann: New York born; a Park Avenue resident. She became known for her portraits of medical faculty and editors; then, of rural life in New England and the south. The National Portrait Gallery contains a dozen pictures by Ulmann, including portraits of Hamlin Garland, Calvin Coolidge, George Jean Nathan, and Paul Robeson.

JESSIE FAUSET Laura Wheeler Waring, Connecticut born, is best known for her portraiture (the Gallery owns her image, undated, of Du Bois), and she has been widely exhibited. She enjoyed a long association with the foundation created by William E. Harmon (d. 1928), the real estate millionaire who contributed huge funds to support black artists.

ALAIN LOCKE Winold Reiss, born in Karlsruhe, Germany, in 1886, came to the United States with his wife, Henrietta Lüthy, in 1913. Over forty years, he painted countless and telling portraits of black Americans, Ameri-

can Indians, Mexicans, and others. The Gallery owns more than a dozen of his works. The catalogue by Jeffrey C. Stewart of the 1989 Gallery exhibition of Reiss's work is a major source.

LANGSTON HUGHES "Genius Child" is in part a recollective reaction by Hughes to his hostile father.

For the non-sports-follower, the Henry Armstrong mentioned by Hughes was a supremely talented prizefighter who in 1937–38 simultaneously held the featherweight, welterweight, and lightweight world championships.

On Edward Weston, see the introduction to the section. The quotation is from Weston's Guggenheim application in the early 1930s.

ZORA NEALE HURSTON Among the many books by the distinguished writer Alice Walker (b. 1944) are *The Color Purple* and *Langston Hughes, American Poet.* In addition to the "partisan view" of Hurston, the far-reaching collection of nonfiction *In Search of Our Mothers' Gardens* contains Walker's report on searching for and finding Hurston's unmarked grave in the Florida cemetery.

RICHARD WRIGHT *The God That Failed,* the volume in which Wright told of his break with Communism, was edited by R. H. S. Crossman. It contained similar recantations by Arthur Koestler and Ignazio Silone, and differently slanted essays by André Gide, Louis Fischer, and Stephen Spender.

Margaret Walker was a highly esteemed poet and a professor of literature in Jackson, Mississippi (where Alice Walker attended her classes). She came to know Richard Wright in Chicago in the 1930s, at meetings of the South Side Writers' Group that included Arna Bontemps and others.

The Champions

JIM THORPE While an active professional player, Thorpe in 1920–21 served as the first president of the American Professional Football Association (later the National Football League), appointed thereto for publicity purposes.

JACK DEMPSEY Gene Tunney (1898–1978) served with honor in the Marine Corps during World War I. He became light heavyweight champion in 1922, and three years later a heavyweight contender. He defeated Dempsey twice on points, before enormous actual and radio audiences, in 1926 and 1927. During World War I he performed distinguished service in the U.S. Marine Corps. In his later years Tunney was an affluent businessman; and once, he lectured at Yale on Shakespeare.

The National Portrait Gallery possesses an autographed reproduction of the James Montgomery Flagg canvas, provided in 1994 by Bugs Baer's son (of the same name), each signature indicating the exact place of the signer.

JOE LOUIS Arthur Ashe (1943–93) was the first black tennis champion, as well as an invaluable civil rights activist and writer and one of the most appealing human figures in the country. His three-volume history of black athletes, *A Hard Road to Glory,* appeared in 1988, the same year Ashe discovered that he was HIV positive.

The text of "King Joe (Joe Louis Blues)," with a word about it, can be found in *Champion: Joe Louis, Black Hero in White America,* by Chris Mead (1985).

Of Louis's victims, the most memorable was Primo Carnera, the hefty artless slugger from Italy.

BILL TILDEN Franklin Pierce Adams's widely enjoyed column "The Conning Tower" featured satirical poems and a diary of notes and ruminations in the manner of Pepys.

"Peach, Bill": the reference is probably to William "Little Bill" Johnson (1894–1946), "Big Bill" Tilden's regular opponent in the finals of championship matches, almost all of which Tilden won.

BABE DIDRIKSON Harry Warnecke was a photographer for the New York *Daily News* from 1921–70, winning awards for his work and specializing (from the 1930s) in captivating color portraits for the cover of the *Sunday News.*

BABE RUTH The sports columns of Red Smith (1905–82) appeared in newspapers over fifty years, most notably in the *New York Herald Tribune* and the *New York Times.* He won a Pulitzer Prize for commentary in 1976. Dave Anderson, the editor of the *Red Smith Reader,* is Smith's successor at the *Times.*

Waite Hoyt (1899–1984) was a star pitcher for the Yankees from 1921–29 (23–7 in 1928). From 1940 onward he was the radio broadcaster for the Cincinnati Reds.

Nickolas Muray, born in Hungary, was the most stylish and inventive photographer of the New York scene from the 1920s to the 1960s, with portraits of Fred Astaire, F. Scott Fitzgerald, Claude Monet, and Marilyn Monroe, among hordes of others. He perfected the color carbo print process.

CASEY STENGEL Following Stengel's testimony at the July 1958 meeting, Senator Kefauver asked Mickey Mantle if he had any observations to make on the antitrust proceedings. Mantle: "My views are just about the same as Casey's."

Rhoda Sherbell's work has been exhibited (in New York, Chicago, Florida, and elsewhere) since 1961. Her statue of Casey Stengel brought her special fame, and invitations to take part in sports exhibitions (and to a dinner at the White House).

JACKIE ROBINSON On Harry Warnecke, see Babe Didrikson entry.

Writers and Artists: The Second Flowering

EDITH WHARTON "Mrs. Campbell": the celebrated English actress known by her married name, Mrs. Pat Campbell.

Pia Tolomei, listed among the discontented wives, is a figure who appears in *Purgatorio V* and is thought to have been a Sienese lady imprisoned by her husband, and then killed on his orders.

THEODORE DREISER Alfred Kazin, the most far-reaching American literary critic after Edmund Wilson, continued to write and lecture to the very end of his long life. *On Native Grounds* appeared in 1942; *God and the American Writer* in 1997.

WILLA CATHER On Carl Van Vechten, see the Harlem Renaissance section.

Louise Bogan (1897–1970), Maine-born, was a gifted writer in several genres, but primarily a poet; her *Collected Poems* was published in 1954 to considerable acclaim.

ALFRED STIEGLITZ AND GEORGIA O'KEEFFE
Arnold Newman has exercised and expanded his great talents for more than half a century. The Gallery also has his 1948 portrait of Alice Roosevelt Longworth, pausing on her way up a flight of stairs.

CHARLES IVES Aaron Copland (1900–90) is the exceedingly influential author of *Fanfare for the Common Man*, *Appalachian Spring*, and many other works. Although Ives was twenty-five years older than Copland, his work did not become known and performed until twenty-five years after the start of Copland's career.

Virgil Thomson (1896–1989) was a premier and forward-looking composer, conductor, and music critic. Among his best-known works are two operas done in collaboration with Gertrude Stein: *Four Saints in Three Acts* (1928), and *The Mother of Us All* (1947), about Susan B. Anthony. He was music critic for the *New York Herald Tribune* from 1940 to 1954.

ROBERT FROST Richard Poirier's study of Frost is thought by many to be the best book about a single American poet yet written. Poirier, currently the director of the Library of America, is also the author of other illuminating critical ventures, among them *The Renewal of Literature: Emersonian Reflections* (1987).

EZRA POUND The American sculptor Joan Fitzgerald lives in Venice, where Pound spent winters in his later years.

Louis Simpson (b. 1923 in Jamaica) is the author of numerous books of poetry, including the Pulitzer Prize–winning *At the End of the Open Road* in 1964. The English writer Ford Madox Ford is best known for his novels *The Good Soldier* (1915) and the four-volume *Parade's End* (1924–28). As founder and editor of the *Transatlantic Review* he published the work of Pound, Joyce, Stein, and others.

T. S. ELIOT Sir Gerald Kelly was a member of the Royal Academy. There were major exhibitions of his work in 1951 and 1972.

The poem quoted is the fifth entry in a light-toned sequence called "Five-Finger Exercises" and includes "Lines to a Persian Cat" and "Lines to a Duck in the Park."

MARIANNE MOORE. The Russian-born Michael A. Werboff survived the Russian Revolution by teaching art; he came to America in 1933. He gradually became known as a portrait photographer, much in demand, of the powerful and famous (Gandhi, King Gustav V of Sweden), opera stars (Pinza, Chaliapin), and poets (Robinson Jeffers and, as here, Marianne Moore). In his last years, he also became a celebrity in his native country.

Elizabeth Bishop (1911–79) was one of the most accomplished poets of her time, but one of the slowest to be recognized, partly because she spent much of her life in Brazil. Some of her poems—"The Fish," "The Prodigal," "At the Fishhouses"—are now among the most frequently cited of modern verse. Her volume *Poems—North and South* won the Pulitzer Prize in 1956.

E. E. CUMMINGS cummings preferred to have his name printed without capital letters, another aspect, so to say, of his self-portrait. One can also find it presented with conventional capitals.

Richard S. Kennedy is a professor of English at Temple University.

EUGENE O'NEILL John Guare (b. 1938) moved to the forefront of contemporary American playwrights with *Six Degrees of Separation* in 1990, and continues to be productive and innovative.

F. SCOTT FITZGERALD Harrison Fisher first became known, between 1903 and 1913, as an illustrator of books, among them *American Beauties*.

John Peale Bishop (1892–1944), a Cape Cod resident, was an essayist of note and a fiction writer as well as a poet. Two collections of his work were published in 1948.

WILLIAM FAULKNER Malcolm Cowley put together *The Portable Faulkner* in 1946, a book that revived or even created Faulkner's reputation. In 1966 he edited *The Faulkner-Cowley File*, a collection of "letters and memories" going back to 1944.

ERNEST HEMINGWAY John Updike (b. 1932) began his distinguished career with *The Poorhouse Fair* in

1959. *Rabbit, Run* in 1960 inaugurated the widely admired tetralogy about the picaresque Rabbit Angstrom. Among Updike's more recent writings is *Memories of the Ford Administration.* He is also a poet, and a literary critic in the great tradition.

WALLACE STEVENS Rollie McKenna is an internationally honored photographer, expert in beautifully wrought scenic shots (of the South, New York, Italy) but best known for portraits of poets: Eliot, Auden, Dylan Thomas, James Merrill, and others, including Stevens and Lowell. Her handsome book *Rollie McKenna: A Life in Photography,* with a foreword by Richard Wilbur, was published in 1991.

John Hollander (b. 1929) is a poet with a mastery of sophisticated, transitional, and entertainingly original modes, the author of some fifteen volumes of verse, from *A Crackling of Thorns* (1958) and *Visions from the Ramble* (1965) through *Harp Lake* (1988) and others. He is also a musician and a scholar of music, and one of the finest elucidators of poetry in our time. Since 1959 he has been a professor of English at Yale University.

HART CRANE Robert Lowell's probing interest in his poetic predecessors and contemporaries (displayed in his Harvard classroom, as Helen Vendler recalls in our Lowell entry) is shown in his many prose writings about them. Robert Giroux's collection of Lowell's prose (1987) includes discussions of Frost, Stevens, Ransom, Williams, Eliot, Tate, Warren, Auden, Bishop, Kunitz, Jarrell, Thomas, Berryman, and Plath.

WALKER EVANS Paul Grotz, German-born, was an architect and editor of *Architectural Forum.* With Frank Lloyd Wright he designed issues of the *Forum* dedicated to Wright's work. Grotz was also a skilled photographer on the side.

Lincoln Kirstein (1907–96), the immensely influential impresario, made his comment at an exhibition of Evans's photographs in 1937.

EDMUND WILSON V. S. Pritchett (1900–97), though perhaps best known as a critic and reviewer, is regarded by many as preeminently a writer of short stories, two volumes of which appeared in the early 1980s. He was a main figure and a choice companion in Anglo-American literary circles.

Isaiah Berlin (1909–97) was a political philosopher of distinction and power, a staunch liberal, and the author famously of "The Hedgehog and the Fox" (1953), on monist versus pluralist visions of the world and history.

GEORGE GERSHWIN Harold Acton (1904–94) was a poet and essayist and a writer of history in a tradition going back to his forebear Lord Acton (who died in 1902). He spent most of his life in a villa north of Florence, where he entertained and composed stylish histories of the Medici and of the Bourbons of Naples—the latter study being also an inquiry into his own Neapolitan strain.

DASHIELL HAMMETT Edward Biberman studied in Paris for several years in his early twenties and there developed a style in which, as he put it, "linear elements" would play a "strong role in defining form." Moving to Los Angeles in 1936, he began to paint film people, including Dashiell Hammett, whom Biberman characterized as a man "who was blazing a new literary style, [and] was himself, in appearance, the 'Thin Man' of his fiction." In the Hammett portrait, typically, the vigorous vertical lines combine with the piercing gaze to make the image strikingly dramatic.

Robert Parker (b. 1932) is the creator of the literate and physically agile Boston detective Spenser (with an "S"), who first appeared in *The Godwulf Manuscript* (1974) and has displayed his investigative skills and talent for ironic repartee in twenty narratives since. Parker is a strikingly original writer, but he is also in the tradition of Dashiell Hammett, Raymond Chandler (whose barely begun *Poodle Springs* Parker in effect wrote himself in 1989), and Ross MacDonald.

LILLIAN HELLMAN John Hersey (1914–93) was one of the country's most gifted, versatile, and personally cherished men of letters. His long article *Hiroshima* (1946) and his novella *A Bell for Adano* (1944) established his literary standing. He continued to write fiction and nonfiction for four more decades: *The Wall* (1950, about

Warsaw under the Nazis) and *The Algiers Motel Incident* (1968, about Detroit race riots) might especially be mentioned. He was associated with Yale University, as teacher and residential college master, from 1950 onward.

ROBERT LOWELL Ian Hamilton, the English poet and critic, is the editor of *The Poetry of War, 1939–45.*

Helen Vendler's most recent work, as of 1998, is a close reading of Shakespeare's sonnets.

Faces on the Public Scene: The 1930s to the 1970s

FIORELLO LA GUARDIA In the 1930s and 1940s, S. J. Woolf published many informative interviews of leading Americans, accompanied by his own charcoal drawings. This one appeared in the *New York Times* on September 17, 1939.

FRANKLIN DELANO ROOSEVELT Robert Sherwood (1896–1955) is the author of *The Petrified Forest* (1935), the prize-winning *Idiot's Delight* (1936), and other literate, entertaining, and historically observant works. For a time he was a speechwriter for President Roosevelt, and as such he came to know Harry Hopkins, Roosevelt's most valued and intimate adviser.

ELEANOR ROOSEVELT Little seems known about Trude Fleischmann. We lingered long, trying to choose between the Fleischmann portrait and several others that were distinctly impressive but a trifle more formal and public.

Stevenson's reference to lighting the candles rather than cursing the darkness has become part of the national idiom.

FATHER CHARLES E. COUGHLIN Hugo Gellert came to the United States from Hungary in 1904. Various horrendous experiences during and after World War I led him to join the Communist Party. He worked for *The Masses,* with Michael Gold and others, and helped found *The New Masses* in 1926. He was also contributing to *The New Yorker* and other journals. His work was vigorously political but brilliantly satirical, like the controversial mural displayed at the opening of the Museum of Modern Art in 1932, suggesting covert alliances between the rich

and famous and the criminal and destructive. During World War II, as head of Artists for Victory, he helped produce many officially lauded posters. He lived on to lead in artistic opposition to the Vietnam War; and was regally celebrated in 1981 for his forthcoming ninetieth birthday.

Wallace Stegner (1909–93), Iowa born and bred, is the author of many novels (among them *The Big Rock Candy Mountain,* 1943) and works of nonfiction (on Mormon history and western exploration).

HARRY S TRUMAN Among his other lasting achievements, the art historian Bernard Berenson (1865–1959) virtually established the canon of Italian Renaissance painting. His Villa I Tatti, a few miles northeast of Florence, was a center of cultivated hospitality for almost sixty years.

DWIGHT D. EISENHOWER Murray Kempton (1917–97) was probably the most insightful commentator on social and political affairs in his time. His columns appeared for years in the *New York Post,* then later in *Newsday.*

ADLAI STEVENSON Eric Sevareid (1912–92), the broadcast journalist, joined CBS Radio in 1939, soon becoming a key member of Edward R. Murrow's remarkable team of correspondents. In later years he provided program-ending editorial responses to the day's news, all of them carefully listened to and greatly respected.

J. ROBERT OPPENHEIMER An exhibition of the remarkable and far-ranging achievement in portraiture of Philippe Halsman was held in November 1998 in the National Portrait Gallery, which owns more than sixty of Halsman's works.

George Kennan (b. 1904) was a diplomat and historian of uncommon distinction. He served in a series of State Department assignments and was U.S. ambassador to Russia in 1952. It was Kennan's 1957 article in *Foreign Policy,* signed "Mr. X," that established the long-lasting American policy of "containment" toward the Soviet Empire. In 1956 he became a professor at the Institute for Advanced Study in Princeton.

JOSEPH R. MCCARTHY Ralph Flanders was the Republican senator from Vermont who, after publicly denouncing McCarthy, introduced a resolution, on July 30, 1954, to censure the Wisconsin senator.

Richard Rovere (1915–79) was the canny and influential author of *The New Yorker*'s "Letter from Washington" from 1948 on. He also wrote a fine study of the Eisenhower years (1958).

JOHN F. KENNEDY Tom Wicker (b. 1926), a North Carolinian who speaks fondly of his native state, was for many years a White House correspondent for the *New York Times,* and from 1964 head of the newspaper's Washington bureau. His calm, authoritative voice and his steadily enlightened opinion made his column a national resource.

FIGURES OF THE 1960S Robert F. Kennedy (1925–68) made important civil rights progress as attorney general under his brother. In 1964 he shifted base to New York and was elected senator. Kennedy was preparing to run for president in 1968 (there are those who think he would have made an outstanding one) when he was assassinated.

Martin Luther King, Jr. (1929–68), was born in Atlanta, and in 1947 he was ordained minister in a Baptist church in that city. He led the boycott on segregated buses in Montgomery, Alabama, in 1955, and in 1957 he was made head of the Southern Christian Leadership Conference. In August 1963, King led the great march that ended with his "I have a dream" speech. He was awarded the Nobel Peace Prize in 1964. In the spring of 1968, while standing on the balcony of his hotel room in Memphis, he was shot and killed by James Earl Ray, who quickly confessed but later declared his innocence.

Janis Joplin (1943–70), the innovative blues-rock singer, made her reputation with the best-selling album *Cheap Thrills* in 1968. More best-selling albums appeared before her death.

Edwin E. "Buzz" Aldrin (b. 1930) set a world spacewalking record on a mission in 1966 and was an astronaut aboard *Apollo II* in 1969, which climaxed with the first moonwalk.

Artists of Entertainment

Carolyn Carr: from *Then and Now: American Portraits of the Past Century from the National Portrait Gallery,* by Carolyn Kinder Carr (1987).

W. C. HANDY The passage from the Tutwiler station mural was provided by Sister Maureen Delaney of the Tutwiler Community Education Center. This transaction (by long-distance telephone) was one of the nicest experiences in the making of this book.

BESSIE SMITH The four musicians whose remarks are quoted were all well-known and admired jazz performers in the 1920s.

LOUIS ARMSTRONG David Lee Iwerks, the son of the artist UB Iwerks (see the Walt Disney entry), lives and practices in the Los Angeles area.

William Kennedy, the award-winning author of the still unfolding fictional saga of the Irish-American world in Albany (*Ironweed* and others) included the piece on Armstrong in his collection *Riding the Yellow Trolley Car* (1993).

COLE PORTER Soss Melik, born in Hungary, studied art in New York and set himself to portraying the outstanding literary and stage figures of the time, greatly aided by his friend Alexander Woollcott. Melik's large collection of such portraits (O'Neill, Wolfe, Hemingway, Marianne Moore, and many others) is now in the National Portrait Gallery.

Richard Rodgers and Lorenz (Larry) Hart, at the time of this meeting, had five shows, including *The Girl Friend,* running simultaneously on Broadway.

DUKE ELLINGTON On the highly skilled woodcut artist Antonio Frasconi, see the commentary on the Albert Einstein portrait.

Albert Murray, author of *The Blue Devils of Nada,* is our most searching analyst of black cultural history, and particularly of the blues as a major creative element in American culture. He is also a gifted novelist (for example, the enticingly titled *Train Whistle Guitar*).

WOODY GUTHRIE On Antonio Frasconi, see the commentary on the Albert Einstein portrait. Alan Lomax, working with his father John Avery Lomax, has been the leading collector and recorder of American folk music in the field. Pete Seeger (b. 1919) is a composer and singer of folk music, and an activist on civil rights and environmental issues.

JOSEPHINE BAKER Stanislaus Julian Walery, Polish born, maintained a studio in Paris for many years, and was here in 1926 when he photographed Josephine Baker.

Janet Flanner was the longtime author of the "Letter from Paris" for the *New Yorker*. Her *Paris Journal I* won the National Book Award in 1965.

Ada Smith, known as Bricktop for her flaming red hair, was for years the exuberant presence in her Paris night club on rue Pigalle.

RUTH DRAPER On Nickolas Muray, see the Babe Ruth entry.

Irene Worth, though American born, achieved international recognition for her performances in the English theater, especially in a number of Shakespeare plays, and alongside such actors as Laurence Olivier and Alec Guinness. In recent years she has been chiefly busy with dramatic monologues, drawn from Edith Wharton and Henry James, and immensely entertaining.

BUSTER KEATON James Agee (1900–55) was an accomplished poet (*Permit Me Voyage,* 1934) and novelist (*A Death in the Family,* 1957) as well as the co-begetter, with Walker Evans, of the classic 1941 *Let Us Now Praise Famous Men*. His articles on film and film personalities, written for *The Nation* and other periodicals, along with his own screenplays, were collected in two volumes (1957, 1960).

PAUL ROBESON Betsy Graves Reyneau, after studying art in Boston, spent fourteen years in Italy and England perfecting her craft. Back in America in the 1950s she found her native country a "Fascist setup," and she determined to fight the racist enemy by doing a series of portraits of (in her exhibition-title phrase) "Leading American Negro Citizens." The landmark show was seen across the country.

Alexander Woollcott (1887–1943) was a witty and urbane columnist for *The New Yorker,* and a literary commentator on radio ("This is Woollcott speaking") of enormous influence; his girth and temperament provided the model for *The Man Who Came to Dinner,* by Kauffman and Hart.

GEORGE CUKOR Henry Major, born in Budapest, came to this country in 1923 and rapidly made a name for himself as a caricaturist of famous public figures. He later became fascinated with the film industry and made perceptive comical sketches of its leading members.

Peter Bogdanovich (b. 1939) established himself as director of the acclaimed nostalgic drama *The Last Picture Show* (1971). Several films since then have been more ambitious but in general less successful.

HUMPHREY BOGART On Philippe Halsman, see the J. Robert Oppenheimer entry.

British-born Alistair Cooke (b. 1908) is a distinctively literate and sophisticated commentator on radio and television and in print. He has been for years in effect the English observer of American happenings.

Katharine Hepburn (b. 1907) costarred with Bogart in John Huston's superbly dramatic, comic, and moving film *The African Queen* (1951). She has herself been a stellar screen performer from *A Bill of Divorcement* in 1932 (with John Barrymore) through *On Golden Pond* in 1981.

TALLULAH BANKHEAD *The Noel Coward Diaries* cover the actor-writer's life from 1941 to 1969. As of 1947, Coward (1899–1973) was mostly engaged in popular revivals of his earlier plays and in cabaret entertainment.

WALT DISNEY On Edward Steichen, see the J. P. Morgan entry and others.

Richard Schickel is a much respected authority on film and on popular culture generally, a nationally known film critic, and a social historian.

Index

Page numbers in *italics* refer to visual and verbal portraits

Credits